W9-ABI-678

U. S. Supreme Court

MAGILL'S CHOICE

U. S. Supreme Court

Volume 3

Scott v. Sandford — Zoning
Appendixes
Indexes

Edited by
Thomas Tandy Lewis
St. Cloud State University

SALEM PRESS, INC.
Pasadena, California Hackensack, New Jersey

Frontispiece: *Associate justices descending the steps of the Supreme Court building during Chief Justice William H. Rehnquist's funeral services on September 7, 2005. From top to bottom, Ruth Bader Ginsburg, Stephen G. Breyer, Clarence Thomas, David Souter, Anthony Kennedy, Antonin Scalia, Sandra Day O'Connor, and John Paul Stevens.* (AP/Wide World Photos)

Essays originally appeared in *Encyclopedia of the U.S. Supreme Court* (2001). New essays and other materials have been added.

∞ The paper used in these volumes conforms to the American National Standard for Permanence of Paper for Printed Library Materials, Z39.48-1992 (R1997).

Library of Congress Cataloging-in-Publication Data

The U.S. Supreme Court / edited by Thomas Tandy Lewis.

v. cm. – (Magill's choice)

Includes bibliographical references and indexes.

ISBN 978-1-58765-363-6 (set : alk. paper)

ISBN 978-1-58765-364-3 (vol. 1 : alk. paper)

ISBN 978-1-58765-365-0 (vol. 2 : alk. paper)

ISBN 978-1-58765-366-7 (vol. 3 : alk. paper)

1. United States Supreme Court–History. I. Lewis, Thomas T. (Thomas Tandy) II. Title: United States Supreme Court.

KF8742.U5 2007

347.73'2609–dc22

2006037878

PRINTED IN CANADA

Contents

U. S. Supreme Court

Scott v. Sandford

CITATION: 60 U.S. 393
DATE: March 6-7, 1857
ISSUES: Slavery; citizenship
SIGNIFICANCE: The Supreme Court endorsed a substantive due process interpretation of the Fifth Amendment that prevented Congress from excluding slavery from the territories. It also held that a person of African ancestry could not be a citizen of the United States.

In the antebellum period, one of the burning political issues was whether slavery would be allowed to expand into the territories. Because the slave states were outnumbered in the House of Representatives, they wanted to keep a balance of power in the Senate, which would require that more slave states be added to the union. The new Republican Party, established in 1854, hoped to attack slavery by preventing its expansion.

Dred Scott was a slave who had been taken from the slave state of Missouri to the free state of Illinois and then to the western part of Wisconsin territory, where slavery had been prohibited by the Missouri Compromise of 1820. Scott could have claimed his freedom while on free soil, but for some unknown reason, he did not do so. After returning to Missouri, Scott sued for his freedom. Although Missouri's supreme court had earlier accepted residence on free soil as grounds for a claim to freedom, in this instance, the court rejected Scott's claim. Because he was then under the control of John Sanford of New York, he sued Sanford (misspelled in the transcript) in federal court under a diversity jurisdiction.

By a 7-2 vote, the Supreme Court decided against Scott. If this had been the Court's only ruling, the *Dred Scott* case would have been relatively unimportant. Speaking for the majority, however, Chief Justice Roger Brooke Taney concentrated on the property rights of the slave owner, as guaranteed by the Fifth Amendment. He stated that in prohibiting a citizen from taking his property to a territory, Congress had abridged property rights without due process of law. Thus, a major part of the Missouri Compromise was unconstitutional. In addi-

FRANK LESLIE'S ILLUSTRATED NEWSPAPER

No. 82.—VOL. IV.] NEW YORK, SATURDAY, JUNE 27, 1857. [PRICE 6 CENTS.

TO TOURISTS AND TRAVELLERS.

VISIT TO DRED SCOTT—HIS FAMILY—INCIDENTS OF HIS LIFE—DECISION OF THE SUPREME COURT.

WHILE standing in the Fair grounds at St. Louis, and engaged in conversation with a prominent citizen of that enterprising city, he suddenly asked us if we would not like to be introduced to Dred Scott. Upon expressing a desire to be thus honored, the gentleman called to an old negro who was standing near by, and our wish was gratified. Dred made a rude obeisance to our recognition, and seemed to enjoy the notice we expended upon him. We found him on examination to be a pure-blooded African, perhaps fifty years of age, with a shrewd, intelligent, good-natured face, of rather light frame, being not more than five feet six inches high. After some general remarks we expressed a wish to get his portrait (we had made efforts before, through correspondents, and failed), and asked him if he would not go to Fitzgibbon's gallery and have it taken. The gentleman present explained to Dred that it was proper he should have his likeness in the "great illustrated paper of the country," overruled his many objections, which seemed to grow out of a superstitious feeling, and he promised to be at the gallery the next day. This appointment Dred did not keep. Determined not to be foiled, we sought an interview with Mr. Crane, Dred's lawyer, who promptly gave us a letter of introduction, explaining to Dred that it was to his advantage to have his picture taken to be engraved for our paper, and also directions where we could find his domicile. We found the place with difficulty, the streets in Dred's neighborhood being more clearly defined in the plan of the city than on the mother earth; we finally reached a wooden house, however, protected by a balcony that answered the description. Approaching the door, we saw a smart, tidy-looking negress, perhaps thirty years of age, who, with two female assistants, was busy ironing. To our question, "Is this where Dred Scott lives?" we received, rather hesitatingly, the answer, "Yes." Upon our asking if he was home, she said,

"What white man arter dad nigger for?—why don't white man 'tend to his own business, and let dat nigger 'lone? Some of dese days dey'll steal dat nigger—dat are a fact."

ELIZA AND LIZZIE, CHILDREN OF DRED SCOTT.

This 1857 newspaper article describes the writer's visit to Dred Scott's home and the outcome of the Supreme Court case. (Library of Congress)

tion, Taney made a distinction between national and state citizenship. He did not deny that people from Africa could be citizens of the states, but he insisted that they could never become a part of "We the People" of the U.S. Constitution. Even if Scott had been free, therefore, he would not be a citizen entitled to sue in federal court. Two justices, Benjamin R. Curtis and John McLean, wrote forceful dissenting opinions.

Although Taney had hoped that the *Dred Scott* decision would calm the political waters, it instead intensified the passionate debate between defenders and opponents of slavery. The overturning of the Missouri Compromise infuriated Abraham Lincoln and other Republicans who had advocated congressional action to prevent the expansion of slavery into the territories. By polarizing the nation, *Dred Scott* helped set the stage for southern secession. The citizenship and the equal protection clauses of the Fourteenth Amendment were written in part to overturn Taney's opinions in the case.

Thomas Tandy Lewis

FURTHER READING

Ehrlich, Walter. *They Have No Rights: Dred Scott's Struggle for Freedom.* Westport, Conn.: Greenwood Press, 1979.

Fehrenbacher, Don E. *The Dred Scott Case: Its Significance in American Law and Politics.* New York: Oxford University Press, 2001.

Finkelman, Paul. *"Dred Scott v. Sandford": A Brief History with Documents.* Boston: Bedford Books, 1997.

Horton, James Oliver, and Lois E. Horton. *Slavery and the Making of America.* New York: Oxford University Press, 2004.

SEE ALSO Campbell, John A.; Citizenship; Civil War; Curtis, Benjamin R.; Due process, substantive; McLean, John; Race and discrimination; Slavery; Taney, Roger Brooke.

Search Warrant Requirement

DESCRIPTION: The necessity of obtaining a warrant from a judge, based on meeting certain criteria, before law-enforcement personnel can conduct a search.

SIGNIFICANCE: The Supreme Court generally ruled against warrantless searches, which violate Fourth Amendment protections against unreasonable searches, but allowed some exceptions.

While under British rule, the thirteen North American colonies were subject to a system of law, one aspect of which was the writ of assistance, which allowed government officials to conduct general searches. The writ of assistance empowered local authories to search anywhere for contraband. British judges did not need to hear any facts regarding illegal activity before a writ was issued and a search conducted. A search could be conducted on mere suspicion and at any location. After the American Revolution, the citizens of the new country were interested in limiting government searches. The Bill of Rights, ratified in 1791, contained the Fourth Amendment, which protected people from unreasonable searches. The Fourth Amendment set out the requirements the government must meet before a search warrant can be issued. The amendment states a warrant cannot be issued "but upon probable cause, supported by Oath or affirmation, and particularly describing the place to be searched, and the persons or things to be seized."

Requirements of a Search Warrant

Through numerous cases, the Supreme Court has defined the exact requirement of the warrant clause. The Court has repeatedly defined the "probable cause" needed for a search warrant to be issued. To obtain a search warrant, law-enforcement officers must show they have reliable and sufficient facts that would cause a reasonable person to believe a criminal act has been committed and that items or a person subject to seizure are at the location to be searched. Probable cause for the warrant cannot be based on what the subsequent search uncovers, only on the facts known when the warrant was issued. The Court also ruled that the probable cause must have been obtained legally. If law enforcement obtains information through an illegal search, it cannot remove the unconstitutional taint on the evidence by later applying for a search warrant. The amount of time between the gathering of probable cause and the execution of the search warrant may make the warrant "stale." If an inordinate amount of time passes and doubt arises whether the object of the warrant is still at the location, then the warrant may become invalid because of outdated probable cause.

The warrant must particularly describe the place to be searched or the item or person to be seized. The place to be searched must be described in the warrant to the extent that it can be set apart from all other locations. The Court has ruled that if an officer can with reasonable effort ascertain and identify the place to be searched then the warrant will be valid. The warrant must also describe items to be seized well enough that an officer can exclude all other items. Failure of the description to be precise enough to exclude other locations or failure to adequately describe an item or person to be seized will make the warrant invalid and the search illegal.

Although the Fourth Amendment does not expressly state that a warrant will be issued by a neutral and detached magistrate, it is generally regarded to be inherent. One of the purposes of a warrant is to allow a neutral party to decide whether law enforcement has probable cause to conduct a search. It is an essential part of the search warrant process to have a detached party review the facts and issue a warrant only if probable cause is present. Failure to have a warrant issued by an impartial and unbiased party will invalidate the warrant and make the search illegal.

The final requirement of the search warrant clause requires the warrant to be supported by an oath or affirmation. The oath or affirmation must be administered by the party issuing the warrant before testimony about probable cause. The Court has held that if the person supplying the probable cause recklessly disregards the truth or knowingly gives false evidence, the search warrant is invalid.

Exceptions

The Supreme Court has found six instances in which a search is reasonable and valid without a warrant. When an officer arrests a suspect, the officer may conduct a search incident to an arrest. However, the Court ruled that only the person and the immediate area are subject to search in *Chimel v. California* (1969). The arrest must be lawful or the evidence may be deemed inadmissible under the exclusionary rule. Under the automobile exception established by *Carroll v. United States* (1925), if the police have probable cause to believe that an automobile contains evidence of a crime, fruit of a crime, or contraband, a search may be conducted without a warrant. If law enforcement observes evidence of a crime, and they have a legal right to be at the location, they may make a warrantless search under the plain view doctrine. The Court has recognized that a citizen may waive his or her Fourth Amendment rights by voluntarily and intelligently consenting to a search, allowing an officer to make a legal warrantless search. In *Terry v. Ohio* (1968), the Court concluded that officers may conduct a limited search of a person (by frisking him or her) for weapons if they have a reasonable suspicion that the person is armed and dangerous. The Court also held that when an officer is in hot pursuit, or where evidence may be destroyed or hidden away, or the evidence is a threat to public safety, an officer may make a warrantless search.

Steven J. Dunker

Further Reading

Bloom, Robert M. *Searches, Seizures, and Warrants.* Westport, Conn.: Praeger, 2003.

Del Carmen, Rolando V. *Criminal Procedure: Law and Practice.* 6th ed. Belmont, Calif.: Thomson/Wadsworth, 2004.

Ferdico, John N. *Criminal Procedure for the Criminal Justice Professional.* 9th ed. Belmont, Calif.: Thomson/Wadsworth, 2005.

Klotter, John C. *Legal Guide for Police: Constitutional Issues.* 6th ed. Cincinnati, Ohio: Anderson, 2002.

O'Brien, David M. *Constitutional Law and Politics.* 6th ed. New York: W. W. Norton, 2005.

Stephens, Otis H., and Richard A. Glenn. *Unreasonable Searches and Seizures: Rights and Liberties Under the Law.* Santa Barbara, Calif.: ABC-Clio, 2004.

See also Automobile searches; Bill of Rights; *Chimel v. California*; Exclusionary rule; Fourth Amendment; *Hudson v. Michigan*; *Mapp v. Ohio*; Privacy, right to; *Terry v. Ohio.*

Second Amendment

Date: 1791

Description: Amendment to the U.S. Constitution and part of the Bill of Rights that provided the right of people to keep and bear arms.

Significance: The Supreme Court's rare decisions on the Second Amendment have typically been narrowly drawn, leaving the broad issues of gun control and the intent of the Second Amendment unresolved.

TEXT OF THE SECOND AMENDMENT

A well regulated Militia, being necessary to the security of a free State, the right of the people to keep and bear Arms, shall not be infringed.

The Second Amendment to the U.S. Constitution states: "A well regulated militia being necessary to the security of a free state, the right of the people to keep and bear arms shall not be infringed." In comparison to other controversial constitutional guarantees, such as freedom of speech, the Supreme Court has had little to say about the Second Amendment. The Court has generally upheld criminal laws regarding firearms, but it has done so without attempting to establish a guiding interpretation of the amendment. Although the Court overturned two federal gun laws in two decisions during the 1990's, it did not rule on the laws as they pertained to the Second Amendment. Rather, in keeping with the Court's states' rights conservatism under Chief Justice William H. Rehnquist, the Court ruled on the laws as they pertained to the limits of the federal government's power to impose its laws on state and local authorities.

In *Printz v. United States* (1997), Jay Printz, the sheriff of Ravalli County, Montana, challenged a federal law that required him to perform background checks on people in his jurisdiction who sought to buy guns. The Court accepted his argument that the federal government may not compel the states to implement federal regulations, overturning the portion of the federal act that required local law-enforcement agencies to conduct background checks. Before that, *United States v. Lopez* (1995) reached the Court after a student, Alfonso Lopez, was charged with violating the Gun-Free School Zones Act of 1990 when he carried a concealed handgun into a high school. The Court upheld an appellate ruling that the federal act exceeded the authority of Congress to legislate under the interstate commerce clause. To allow the act to stand, the Court wrote, would "require this Court to pile inference upon inference in a manner that would bid fair to convert congressional commerce clause authority to a general police power of the sort held only by the States." *Printz* and *Lopez* did not address the Second Amendment or rule on how it is to be interpreted. Nor is the controversy settled by a review of Court decisions touching on the Second Amendment.

Early Decisions

In *United States v. Cruikshank* (1876), William Cruikshank, a member of the Ku Klux Klan, was tried in federal court for violating the federal civil rights laws protecting the African American victims of a murderous riot he led. The trial court found Cruikshank guilty of conspiring to deprive African Americans of their right to bear arms. The Supreme Court, however, ruled in favor of Cruikshank, arguing that the Second Amendment applied only to Congress and that people must look to local governments for protection against violations of their rights. The *Cruikshank* decision, like the *Slaughterhouse Cases* (1873), interpreted against use of the Fourteenth Amendment as a means to enforce the Bill of Rights at the state and local level. This interpretation of the Fourteenth Amendment, however, was later abandoned in other decisions not relating to the Second Amendment.

The next major Second Amendment case was *Presser v. Illinois* (1886). Herman Presser led an armed group called the Lehr und Wehr Verein (Educational and Protective Association) on a march through the streets of Chicago. Presser argued that the Illinois law under which he was convicted was superseded by various provisions of federal law, including the Second Amendment. The Court upheld his conviction, arguing that to accept Presser's interpretations would amount to denying the rights of states to disperse mobs.

Indications of Ambivalence

The Court in *United States v. Miller* (1939) upheld the federal regulation against a shotgun's having a barrel less than eighteen inches long on the basis that the Court had no indication that such a weapon "was . . . ordinary military equipment or . . . could contribute to the common defense." It may be argued, therefore, that *Miller* indirectly defends the principle that a firearm that has some reasonable relationship to the efficiency of a well-regulated militia is protected by the Constitution. However, challenges to laws limiting civilian possession of machine guns and assault rifles, which are military weapons, have not met with success. A similar ambivalence can be inferred in *Cases v. United States* (1943), in which a lower court noted, "apparently . . . under the Second Amendment, the federal government can limit the keeping and bearing of arms by a single individual as well as by a group . . . but it cannot prohibit the possession or use of any weapon which has any reasonable relationship to the preservation or efficiency of a well-regulated militia." The Court made this observation, however, when declining to review a challenge to a provision of the Federal Firearms Act.

In *Quilici v. Village of Morton Grove* (1983), the Court refused to review a Second Amendment case and let stand a decision upholding an ordinance in Morton Grove, Illinois, banning possession of handguns. This decision has been cited to bolster the argument that the individual ownership of firearms is not a constitutional right, but the fact that the Court has done nothing to change the existing laws that allow individual possession of firearms undermines such an argument.

Eric Howard

Further Reading

Bijlefeld, Marjolijn, ed. *The Gun Control Debate: A Documentary History.* Westport, Conn.: Greenwood Press, 1997.

Cottrol, Robert J., ed. *Gun Control and the Constitution: Sources and Explorations on the Second Amendment.* New York: Garland, 1993.

Henigan, Dennis A. *Guns and the Constitution: The Myth of Second Amendment Protection for Firearms in America.* Northampton, Mass.: Aletheia Press, 1996.

Kopel, David, Stephen Halbrook, and Alan Korwin. *Supreme Court Gun Cases: Two Centuries of Gun Rights Revealed.* Fairfax, Va.: Bloomfield Press, 2003.

Malcolm, Joyce Lee. *To Keep and Bear Arms: The Evolution of an Anglo-American Right.* Cambridge, Mass.: Harvard University Press, 1996.

Spitzer, Robert J. *The Right to Bear Arms: Rights and Liberties Under the Law.* Santa Barbara, Calif.: ABC-Clio, 2001.

Uviller, H. Richard, and William G. Merkel. *The Militia and the Right to*

Arms, Or, How the Second Amendment Fell Silent. Durham, N.C.: Duke University Press, 2003.

See also Bill of Rights; Commerce, regulation of; *Cruikshank, United States v.*; Fourteenth Amendment; Incorporation doctrine; *Lopez, United States v.*; *Printz v. United States*; Rehnquist, William H.; States' rights and state sovereignty.

Sedition Act of 1798

Date: 1798

Description: Statute that made interference or attempted interference with operations of the U.S. government a crime, criminalized oral and written utterances that tended to bring the government into disrepute, and liberalized the common law of seditious libel.

Significance: The Federalists intended the act to preserve control of the government and suppress the emerging Jeffersonian Republicans. Supreme Court justices, riding on circuit, upheld the act while it was in force, but twentieth century justices viewed the act as unconstitutional.

The Sedition Act of 1798 had three substantive sections. Section 1, the least controversial, provided that opposition to governmental operations or antigovernment conspiracies could be punished by fines up to five thousand dollars and confinement between six months to five years.

Section 2, the most controversial, codified the common law of seditious libel. It penalized certain kinds of political speech and permitted criminal prosecution for "knowingly and willingly" writing, publishing, or uttering statements that were "false, scandalous, and malicious" with the intent to defame the government, Congress, or president or to bring them into disrepute. Statements that turned people against the government or that promoted opposition to the nation's laws were likewise actionable. Conviction allowed imprisonment for up to two years and a maximum fine of two thousand dollars.

Section 3 liberalized seditious libel procedures. Under the common law, libel charges against the government were actionable if they tended to disturb the public peace or create animosities. Prosecutors had to prove publication and bad tendency to secure convictions. The common law allowed truth as a defense to private libel but not to libel aimed at the government or public officials. The reformed procedures provided that juries, not judges, decided issues of publication and bad tendency. Judges continued to charge juries and explain the law, but juries decided the facts and the law and judged a statement's truth or falsity. These procedural reforms shifted decision making from judges to juries.

Early Views

The Supreme Court never ruled directly on the Sedition Act, but from its enactment to its expiration in March, 1801, justices riding on circuit upheld the measure, some heartily. Chief Justice Oliver

President Thomas Jefferson opposed the Sedition Act because he believed that Congress had no right to restrict freedom of speech. (White House Historical Society)

Ellsworth believed it limited the dangers that the national government confronted. Associate Justice Samuel Chase was the Court's most ardent defender of the measure. In cases against James T. Callendar and Thomas Cooper, prominent Antifederalist writers, Chase was, in essence, more a prosecutor than a neutral justice. Chase's overzealous involvement in Sedition Act cases was reflected in several charges in the articles of impeachment brought against him in 1804 by the House of Representatives. Justices William Cushing, William Paterson, and Bushrod Washington all warmly endorsed the act. Like Chase, they informed juries that it was constitutional and encouraged convictions.

Jeffersonian Republicans (also known as Democratic-Republicans) opposed the act from the outset and fought vigorously for its repeal in 1799, but failed. They insisted that it violated the freedom of speech and press clauses of the First Amendment and secured resolutions to that effect from the legislatures of Virginia and Kentucky. After becoming president, Thomas Jefferson pardoned those who had been convicted under the act and remitted some fines, stating that the act was unconstitutional. In 1840 Congress agreed and repaid the remaining Federalist-imposed fines.

Later Views

In a well-known dissent to *Abrams v. United States* (1919), Associate Justice Oliver Wendell Holmes wrote, "I had conceived that the United States through many years had shown its repentance for the Sedition Act." Louis D. Brandeis joined his dissent. Some thirty years later, in a dissenting opinion in *Beauharnais v. Illinois* (1952), Associate Justice Robert H. Jackson, chief prosecutor in the Nuremberg war crimes trials, observed that the enactment of the Sedition Act had come to be viewed as "a breach of the First Amendment." Continuing, he wrote that "even in the absence of judicial condemnation, the political disapproval of the Sedition Act was so emphatic and sustained that federal prosecution of the press ceased for a century."

The Sedition Act met considerable condemnation in the latter half of the twentieth century. In *New York Times Co. v. Sullivan* (1964), Justice William J. Brennan, Jr., noted that "although the Sedition Act was never tested in this Court, the attack upon its validity has carried the day in the court of history." Associate Justices Hugo L. Black and William O. Douglas concurred in Brennan's judgment that the court of history condemned the act. They noted that it had "an ignominious end and by common consent has generally been treated as having been a wholly unjustifiable and much to be regretted violation of the First Amendment." In a concurring opinion in *Garrison v. Louisiana* (1964), Douglas and Black quoted Holmes's 1919 observation that the nation had repented for having passed the act. A decade later, they reiterated their contempt for the 1798 measure in *Gertz v. Robert Welch* (1974), noting that it was a congressional attempt to "muzzle" the First Amendment, "a regrettable legislative exercise plainly in violation of the First Amendment."

FREEDOM VERSUS UNITY

In *Sullivan*, Brennan summarized not only the modern view of the act but also the classic reason for conflicting views about its constitutionality. Brennan wrote, "Thus we consider this case against the background of a profound national commitment to the principle that debate on public issues should be uninhibited, robust and wide-open, and that it may well include vehement, caustic, and sometimes unpleasantly sharp attacks on government and public officials." Although Brennan severely criticized the act and praised Jefferson for pardoning those sentenced under it, his method of interpretation comports well with that of both the Federalists and Democratic-Republicans in the early national era. National commitments were central to Brennan and those who supported or opposed the act during its short life. Expressive freedoms were not ends in themselves but served broad national commitments. When those commitments changed, interpretations of the freedom of speech and press clauses changed.

The Federalists and Democratic-Republicans had different commitments and dramatically different notions about speech and press functions. Both parties had a keen pride of accomplishment in winning the American Revolution and securing the Constitution. However, each viewed itself as the true revolutionary heir, and in the 1790's, they accused each other of deliberately squandering dearly won freedoms embodied in the Constitution. Each came perilously close to thinking of the other as an illegitimate faction, animated by a party spirit that threatened to undermine the benefits that the revolution had secured. It seemed clear that if the other party threatened the nation, it should be suppressed. They agreed that limitations on expressive freedoms were instrumental to preserving the Revolution and protecting the Constitution but split decisively over which level of government was responsible for protecting the nation from illegitimate factions.

The Federalists passed the politically inspired Sedition Act in an attempt to suppress the Democratic-Republicans. Federalist prosecutors targeted only Democratic-Republican editors, newspapers, and party leaders, enforcing the act most vigorously just before the election of 1800 in order to dampen attacks by the opposition party and to maintain control of the national government. In all, twenty-four or twenty-five individuals were arrested for violating the act. At least fifteen were indicted, and of the eleven who went to trial, ten were convicted. Because Supreme Court justices accepted the Federalist position, they upheld the act's constitutionality.

In the early nineteenth century, after Jefferson became president, Democratic-Republicans—sometimes with Jefferson's approval, if not urging—prosecuted Federalist editors. Like their Federalist counterparts, Democratic-Republican prosecutors targeted political speech. Neither party tried to curb completely the other's speech. Prosecutions were intermittent, inconsistent, and unpredictable. Each party used law to create a legal environment that forced the other to be self-censoring; if self-censorship was glaringly ineffective, prosecutors might spring into action.

The Two-Party System

Americans of the early national era believed they had good but fragile institutions, worthy of careful nurturing. Federalists and Democratic-Republicans felt obligated to shield the nation from unwarranted partisan attacks and to preserve revolutionary gains by limiting the other party's expressive freedom. In essence, the two parties bitterly contested the legitimacy of competing parties. They agreed that the other's licentious speech needed curbing but split over whether the national or state governments should impose the limits. In *Dennis v. United States* (1951), Associate Justice Felix Frankfurter noted that the central issue in the case was federalism rather than free speech or press. Jefferson, he wrote, had not condemned the Sedition Act because it limited political speech but because he thought states, not Congress, had "the right to enforce restrictions on speech."

By the end of the 1820's Americans believed that competing parties were a logical analog to the Constitution; parties gave an additional method of checking power. When one party put forth a program or set of policies, the competing party sponsored an alternative and thus acted as a check on the first party. As the party system gained legitimacy, the need for restraints on speech and press, such as those in the Sedition Act, disappeared. In the twentieth century, the Court consistently condemned the Sedition Act; however, it sustained restrictions on expressive freedoms when, as the Federalists believed in the 1790's, a good society with decent institutions was under unwarranted assault.

Lester G. Lindley

Further Reading

James M. Smith's *Freedom's Fetters: The Alien and Sedition Laws and American Civil Liberties* (Ithaca, N.Y.: Cornell University Press, 1956), which has extensive bibliographic notes, remains the standard treatment of the Sedition Act. For a somewhat simpler treatment, see John C. Miller's *Crisis in Freedom: The Alien and Sedition Acts* (Boston: Little, Brown, 1951). Leonard W. Levy's *Freedom of Speech and Press in Early American History* (Cambridge, Mass.: Harvard University Press, 1960) and *Emergence of a Free Press* (New York: Oxford University Press, 1985) put the Sedition Act in its broader constitutional and legal context.

John D. Stevens's "Congressional History of the 1798 Sedition Law," *Journalism Quarterly* 13 (Summer, 1966): 247-256, provides a useful introduction to the congressional history of the act and Federalist prosecutions under it. Walter Berns's "Freedom of the Press and the Alien and Sedition Laws: A Reappraisal," *Supreme Court Review* (1970): 109-159, examines the relationship between the Sedition Act, Federalism, and slavery. Richard Hofstadter's *The Idea of a Party Sys-*

tem: The Rise of Legitimate Opposition in the United States, 1780-1840 (Berkeley: University of California Press, 1970) considers the broader political and ideological background from which the act emerged. Gregg Costa's "John Marshall, the Sedition Act, and Free Speech in the Early Republic," *Texas Law Review* 77 (1999): 1011-1047, analyzes the prominent Federalist and future chief justice who opposed the Sedition Act.

See also Bad tendency test; Chase, Samuel; Cushing, William; Espionage acts; Holmes, Oliver Wendell; Seditious libel; Smith Act; Speech and press, freedom of.

Seditious Libel

Description: Communication written with the intent to incite people to change the government by unlawful means or to advocate the overthrow of the government by force or violence.

Significance: At the heart of the free speech clause of the First Amendment is the right of people to criticize the government. Beginning in 1919 the Supreme Court devised and applied different tests to determine if, when, and how people may criticize public officials.

Although presented with opportunities to decide the question of what is legal dissent and what is seditious libel before the twentieth century, with the Alien and Sedition Acts (1798), the Supreme Court did not address the question until 1919 in *Schenck v. United States.* In a unanimous decision, Justice Oliver Wendell Holmes wrote for the Court that the Espionage Act (1917) did not violate the First Amendment. To justify the Court's decision, Holmes created the clear and present danger test and stated that Schenck had no more right to interfere with the drafting of men to serve in the army during World War I than an individual had a right to falsely shout fire in a crowded theater.

Also in 1919 the Court further expanded what Congress could

prohibit people from saying in *Abrams v. United States.* The Court, in a 7-2 decision, stated that the amendment to the Espionage Act (1918), which outlawed any speech or writing that would interfere with or curtail the production of war materials when the United States is at war, was constitutional. With this decision, as Holmes pointed out in his dissent, Americans could not suggest that too much money was being spent on one area of the military to the detriment of another, even if they believed their opinion would be beneficial.

In the 1920's the Court expanded the power to limit seditious speech to the states. In *Gitlow v. New York* (1925) and again in *Whitney v. California* (1927), the Court upheld the constitutionality of state criminal anarchy and antisyndicalism laws. Gitlow published a pamphlet urging the establishment of socialism by strikes and "class action . . . in any form," and Whitney was a member of the Communist Labor Party. Because that party advocated the overthrow of the government by "revolutionary class struggle," it was assumed that Whitney wholly accepted all beliefs of the organization and, therefore, believed that the government should be violently overthrown. These decisions affirmed the Court's view that if people believed the government should be overthrown or interfered with and then spoke or wrote of that belief, then they could be penalized.

The Smith Act

With World War II looming and the belief that Soviet socialistic subversion could undermine American society, Congress passed the Smith Act (1940), also referred to as the Alien Registration Act. Although no cases concerning this act reached the Court during World War II, in 1948 Eugene Dennis and ten other members of the Central Committee of the Communist Party were tried and convicted of violating sections 2 and 3 of the act. These sections stated that it was unlawful to advocate the "necessity, desirability, or propriety" of overthrowing the government by force or to belong to a group that advocated this. Also, the law punished anyone who conspired with others to violate the act. In *Dennis v. United States* (1951), the Court found the Smith Act to be constitutional.

The Court began to change its stand on seditious libel when it recognized, in *Yates v. United States* (1957), that there is a difference between advocating ideas and advocating actions. Yates and thirteen others had been convicted of violating the Smith Act. In the Court's decision, which overturned the convictions, Justice John M. Harlan II wrote that there is a difference "between advocacy of abstract doctrine and advocacy of action." The former is protected speech, the latter is not.

Continuing to recognize and develop this distinction between advocating abstract ideas and advocating action, the Court, in *Brandenburg v. Ohio* (1969), added the additional standard of incitement to determine what speech is not protected by the First Amendment. Brandenburg was a leader of the Ku Klux Klan in Ohio and had been filmed making a seditious speech and advocating others to engage in sedition. Brandenburg was convicted of violating Ohio's syndicalism law, which made it illegal to advocate the "duty, necessity, or propriety of crime, sabotage, violence, or unlawful methods of terrorism as a means of accomplishing industrial or political reform." In overturning the conviction, the Court stated that to convict a person for his or her speech, the government must prove that the "advocacy is directed to inciting or producing imminent lawless action and is likely to produce such action."

Criticism of the Government

In *New York Times Co. v. Sullivan* (1964), the Court dealt with criticism of the government in the civil as opposed to the criminal courts. L. B. Sullivan sued *The New York Times* for defamation because of an advertisement in the paper. Sullivan was commissioner of public affairs for the city of Montgomery, Alabama, and therefore one of his responsibilities was to supervise the city police. In 1960 members of the National Association for the Advancement of Colored People placed a full-page advertisement entitled "Heed Their Rising Voices" in *The New York Times.* In this ad, they claimed that students engaged in nonviolent, antisegregation protests in the South were being met with an "unprecedented wave of terror," some of which originated with the police, including the police in Montgomery. There were several factual errors in the advertisement concerning such things as a song sung during a protest and how many days Martin Luther King, Jr., had spent in a Montgomery jail. Sullivan sued for libel, claiming that because one of his responsibilities was supervision of the police and because there were factual errors concerning the police in the advertisement, he had been defamed. In overturning the $500,000 judgment for Sullivan, Justice William J. Brennan, Jr., writing for the Court, stated that as long as no actual malice was involved, the people have a right to criticize officials, even if some of the facts are incorrect. Justice Brennan also wrote that to allow public officers to sue for libel, when the subject was their official conduct, would greatly curtail free speech.

Mark L. Higgins

Further Reading

Chaffee, Zechariah, Jr. *Free Speech in the United States.* Cambridge, Mass.: Harvard University Press, 1941.

Kersch, Ken I. *Freedom of Speech: Rights and Liberties Under the Law.* Santa Barbara, Calif.: ABC-Clio, 2003.

Levy, Leonard, Kenneth Karst, and Dennis Mahoney. *The First Amendment.* New York: Macmillan, 1990.

Lewis, Thomas T., ed. *The Bill of Rights.* 2 vols. Pasadena, Calif.: Salem Press, 2002.

Van Alstyne, William. *First Amendment: Cases and Materials.* Westbury, N.Y.: Foundation Press, 1995.

See also *Brandenburg v. Ohio*; Espionage acts; *Gitlow v. New York*; National security; *Schenck v. United States*; Sedition Act of 1798; Smith Act.

Segregation, de facto

Description: Separation of people by race or ethnicity through custom, tradition, or socioeconomic factors rather than by law. De facto segregation differs from de jure segregation, which is the separation of people mandated by the state.

Significance: The Supreme Court distinguished between the two types of segregation and declared de facto segregation to be constitutional.

"White Only," "Colored Only," and similar signs were once common sights in the South and were not unknown in northern states during the Jim Crow era. (Library of Congress)

The Supreme Court has held, in several decisions, that de facto segregation—which results from merely private action, without the involvement, authorization, or action of the state—is not subject to constitutional remedy. The Fourteenth Amendment protects against discriminatory conduct or actions on the part of the state, not against those of private individuals. The problems with the distinction between de facto and de jure segregation include determining where state or government conduct ends and individual conduct begins and defining action and conduct. Justices William O. Douglas and Lewis F. Powell, Jr., in *Keyes v. Denver School District No. 1* (1973), urged the Court to abandon the distinction, which Douglas said was muddied by past state actions, restrictive covenants, and other public policies.

The Court varied the breadth of its interpretations of state responsibility but tended to apply a narrow state action doctrine in which all segregation that is not intentional, explicit, and officially sanctioned is defined as de facto and is, therefore, not subject to constitutional remedy. In *Washington v. Davis* (1976), the Court ruled that de facto segregation was not unconstitutional unless it resulted from the state's having a "racially discriminatory purpose."

Kelly J. Madison

See also Race and discrimination; School integration and busing; Segregation, de jure.

Segregation, de jure

Description: Separation of races required by law or other local, state, or federal official action.

Significance: From 1896 to 1954 the Supreme Court consistently held that de jure segregation did not violate the equal protection clause of the Fourteenth Amendment as long as the facilities provided were equal.

In *Plessy v. Ferguson* (1896), the Supreme Court sustained a Louisiana law requiring passenger trains to provide separate but equal accommodations for the "white and colored races." So long as the facilities provided to the races were equal, the Court concluded, mandated segregation did not violate the equal protection clause of the Fourteenth Amendment. Three years later, however, in *Cumming v. Richmond County Board of Education* (1899), the Court refused to extend the separate but equal doctrine to matters of public education, thus permitting Richmond County to educate white children through the twelfth grade, but black children only through the eighth grade.

In a series of cases decided between 1938 and 1950, the Court suggested that segregated public schools might be constitutionally suspect. In *Missouri ex rel. Gaines v. Canada* (1938), the Court ordered the all-white University of Missouri school of law to admit an African American man who had been denied admission to the state's only law school solely because of his race. In two similar cases decided in 1950—*Sweatt v. Painter* and *McLaurin v. Oklahoma State Regents for Higher Education*—the Court ordered professional schools in Texas and Oklahoma to desegregate. These cases and others crippled de jure segregation in public education.

Finally, on May 17, 1954, the Court rendered its decision in *Brown v. Board of Education* (1954). Writing for a unanimous Court, Chief Justice Earl Warren asserted that "in the field of public education, the doctrine of 'separate but equal' has no place. Separate educational facilities are inherently unequal." In this way, the Court repudiated long-standing constitutional precedent with respect to de jure segregation. The concise opinion in *Brown* did not mention *Plessy*. Nonetheless, in *Browder v. Gayle* (1956), the Court silently overturned *Plessy* by affirming a lower court opinion that held that *Brown* had "impliedly, though not explicitly, overruled" *Plessy* in striking down a statute requiring segregated public transportation in Montgomery, Alabama. In a series of cases that followed, the Court applied the principle articulated in *Brown* to de jure segregation in other public facilities.

Richard A. Glenn

Further Reading

Clotfelter, Charles. *After Brown: The Rise and Retreat of School Desegregation.* Princeton, N.J.: Princeton University Press, 2004.

Friedman, Leon, ed. *"Brown v. Board": The Landmark Oral Argument Before the Supreme Court.* New York: New Press, 2004.

Hale, Grace Elizabeth. *Making Whiteness: The Culture of Segregation in the South, 1890-1940.* New York: Pantheon Books, 1998.

Higginbotham, A. Leon. *Shades of Freedom: Racial Politics and Presumptions of the American Legal Process.* New York: Oxford University Press, 1996.

Kluger, Richard. *Simple Justice: The History of "Brown v. Board of Education" and Black America's Struggle for Equality.* New York: Alfred A. Knopf, 1976.

Kull, Andrew. *The Color-Blind Constitution.* Cambridge, Mass.: Harvard University Press, 1994.

Rasmussen, R. Kent. *Farewell to Jim Crow: The Rise and Fall of Segregation in America.* New York: Facts On File, 1997.

Tussman, Joseph, ed. *The Supreme Court on Racial Discrimination.* New York: Oxford University Press, 1967.

See also *Bolling v. Sharpe*; *Brown v. Board of Education*; Equal protection clause; Fourteenth Amendment; *Plessy v. Ferguson*; *Swann v. Charlotte-Mecklenburg Board of Education*; Warren, Earl.

Self-incrimination, Immunity Against

Description: One's right, before any compulsory forum, to resist testifying on any matter that might ensnare one in a criminal investigation or aid in one's own prosecution.

Significance: Long regarded as the foundation of an accusatory system of justice, the immunity from self-incrimination imposes on the state the burden of presenting at trial proof of guilt without the participation of the accused. The Supreme Court's extension of this right into the pretrial stages of the criminal process has been controversial.

The right of the accused to refuse to testify against himself or herself gained acceptance in English common law after the seventeenth century, a period of strife that saw frequent reliance on the compulsory oath as an instrument of political and religious persecution. So venerated was this right in North America that it was included in the Fifth Amendment to the U.S. Constitution, which provided that "No person . . . shall be compelled in any criminal case to be a witness against himself." Because of its prominence in movies and television, it remains the defendants' right most identified in the popular mind.

Although the Constitution locates the right "in any criminal case," the Supreme Court extended it to any forum in which the individual might be compelled to testify, such as grand juries or legislative investigations. It is, however, limited to subjects on which the individual might be vulnerable to prosecution and therefore does not cover testimony that is merely humiliating or that exposes the witness to civil suit. Additionally, the right is limited to testimony and does not bar the compulsory production of nontestimonial evidence, such as fingerprints, photographs, blood samples, appearance in a lineup, or even providing voice exemplars. It is only the suspect's words that may not be used in evidence for his or her own undoing. The right can be asserted only on behalf of oneself and does not bar compulsory testimony against a relative or accomplice. Properly asserted, the right is absolute, but it can be circumvented by a grant of immunity from prosecution, on the theory that such immunity offers protection coextensive with the right. The right is frequently exercised when defendants decline to take the witness stand to avoid cross-examination. Understandably, this is a risky right to assert because juries might infer guilt from silence.

Pretrial Confessions

Assertion of immunity from self-incrimination at trial would be a hollow exercise if the suspect were compelled to confess to a criminal charge before trial and the confession later read into evidence by the prosecutor at trial. The National Commission on Law Observance and Enforcement, commonly known as the Wickersham Commission, in 1931 documented widespread use of physical brutality by police departments to extract such confessions, especially from members of groups outside the mainstream of society.

In *Brown v. Mississippi* (1936), the Supreme Court overturned the capital murder convictions of three African American defendants resting solely on confessions that had been extracted after brutal whippings at the hands of police. Aside from the inherent unreliability of such confessions, the Court sought to discourage such behavior on the part of the police. In *Chambers v. Florida* (1940), the Court formulated the voluntariness rule, requiring trial judges to assess the full circumstances surrounding pretrial confessions—not only allegations of physical brutality—to ensure that the suspects had voluntarily confessed to the charges against them. Such voluntariness was undermined by any circumstances tending to overbear on the suspect's free will, including various psychological "third degree" tactics. These cases rested on the due process clause of the Fourteenth Amendment but were subsumed under the right against self-incrimination in *Malloy v. Hogan* (1964).

The most notorious of this line of decisions was *Miranda v. Arizona* (1966). Experience with the voluntariness rule had revealed reluctance on the part of trial judges to bar confessions extracted by questionable techniques. Widespread complaints, especially by minorities, about police tactics in stationhouse backrooms and a growing egalitarian ethos on the Court led to replacement of the voluntariness rule. The Court ruled that prosecutors were barred from using any incriminating statements made by a suspect before trial unless procedures were already in place to ensure that confessions were based solely on the free will of the defendant. The Court did not specify what these procedures might be, but until the states developed effective alternatives, police would be required to read suspects the Miranda rights before any custodial interrogation. Failure to warn suspects of their right to remain silent and to inform them that statements they made might be used as evidence against them and that they had a right to counsel would result in the exclusion of any incriminating statements from trial. Although more than thirty years of empirical research has found *Miranda*'s impact on confessions to be negligible, the decision quickly became a lightning rod for attacks on the Court. Critics, such as presidential candidate Richard M. Nixon, accused the Court of favoring defendants at the expense of legitimate law-enforcement techniques.

Since the 1970's the Court has tended to restrict the application of *Miranda*. In *Harris v. New York* (1971), the Court held that statements made in the absence of Miranda warnings, while barred from direct evidence, could be used for cross-examination if the accused took the witness stand. In *New York v. Quarles* (1984), the Court permitted the use of statements obtained by police if motivated by reasonable concerns for public safety. Other decisions have turned primarily on questions of when the suspect was under custody or what constituted an interrogation.

Guilty Pleas

In court, the immunity against self-incrimination is a "fighting right," meaning it does not become effective unless specifically asserted by the accused. It can be waived, however, and usually is. More than 90 percent of all felony convictions in the United States result from guilty pleas, usually pursuant to plea bargains. The effect of a guilty plea is the waiver of all trial and pretrial rights, including relief from self-incrimination. Trial judges are obliged to examine the guilty plea on record to verify that it is offered knowingly and intelligently, but this is pro forma. Usually, the guilty plea has been arranged by counsel. Nevertheless, the Court has come a long way from *Twining v. New Jersey* (1908), in which it held the right against self-incrimination not fundamental to a fair trial, as required by the Fourteenth Amendment, or *Palko v. Connecticut* (1937), in which the right against self-incrimination was pronounced not essential to justice. Whatever might be the practice of other nations, the immunity against self-incrimination is a fundamental component of U.S. law.

John C. Hughes

Further Reading

Berger, Mark. *Taking the Fifth.* Lexington, Mass.: D.C. Heath, 1980.

Bodenhamer, David J. *Fair Trial: Rights of the Accused in American History.* New York: Oxford University Press, 1992.

Fireside, Harvey. *The Fifth Amendment: The Right to Remain Silent.* Springfield, N.J.: Enslow, 1998.

Garcia, Alfredo. *The Fifth Amendment: A Comprehensive Approach.* Westport, Conn.: Greenwood Press, 2002.

Helmholtz, R. H., Charles M. Gray, John H. Langbein, Eben Moglin, Hesury M. Smith, and Albert W. Altschuler. *The Privilege Against Self-Incrimination: Its Origin and Development.* Chicago: University of Chicago Press, 1997.

Levy, Leonard W. *Origins of the Fifth Amendment.* New York: Oxford University Press, 1968.

See also *Adamson v. California*; Bill of Rights; *Brown v. Mississippi*; Counsel, right to; Double jeopardy; Due process, procedural; Exclusionary rule; Fifth Amendment; Incorporation doctrine; Miranda rights; Plea bargaining.

Senate Judiciary Committee

Date: Founded 1816

Description: Senatorial committee with primary jurisdiction over most legislative matters pertaining to the federal courts, including the Supreme Court.

Significance: The Senate Judiciary Committee has the responsibility to investigate the backgrounds of and hold confirmation hearings for presidential nominees to the Supreme Court and other federal courts. The committee also has jurisdiction over proposed amendments to the Constitution, some of which are introduced as attempts to overturn Supreme Court or other federal court decisions.

Nominations to the Court Rejected by the Senate

President	*Year*	*Nominee*
George Washington	1795	John Rutledge[1]
James Madison	1811	Alexander Wolcott
John Quincy Adams	1828	John J. Crittenden[2]
John Tyler	1844	John C. Spencer[2]
	1844	Reuben H. Walworth[2]
	1844	Edward King[2]
	1845	John M. Read[2]
James Polk	1846	George W. Woodward
Millard Fillmore	1852	Edward A. Bradford[2]
	1853	George E. Badger[2]
	1853	William C. Micou[2]
James Buchanan	1861	Jeremiah S. Black
Andrew Johnson	1866	Henry Stanbery[2]
Ulysses S. Grant	1869	Ebenezer Hoar
	1873	George H. Williams[1, 3]
	1874	Caleb Cushing[3]
Grover Cleveland	1894	Wheeler H. Peckham
	1894	William B. Hornblower
Herbert Hoover	1930	John J. Parker
Lyndon B. Johnson	1968	Abe Fortas[1]
Richard M. Nixon	1969	Clement Haynsworth, Jr.
	1970	G. Harrold Carswell
Ronald Reagan	1987	Robert H. Bork

[1]Nominated to be chief justice.
[2]No action taken by the Senate.
[3]Nomination withdrawn when confirmation appeared impossible.

Notes: The nominations of William Paterson (1793), Edward King (second nomination, 1845), William H. Thornberry (1968), Douglas H. Ginsburg (1987), and Harriet Miers (2005) were withdrawn before going to the Senate.

Source: Lawrence Baum, *The Supreme Court* (6th ed., Washington, D.C.: Congressional Quarterly, 1998).

Established in 1816, the Judiciary Committee was one of the original eleven standing committees in the Senate. It quickly became a powerful influence on national legislation and the confirmation process for federal judges, including presidential nominees to the Supreme Court.

The Constitution requires the advice and consent of the full Senate on presidential nominees to the federal courts, but starting in 1968 the Judiciary Committee performed the initial investigation of the nominees. This investigation includes holding formal committee hearings on the qualifications of the nominees. Beginning with the administration of Dwight D. Eisenhower, the committee sought advice from the American Bar Association Committee on Federal Judiciary, which rates the nominees as "well qualified," "qualified," and "not qualified."

After the investigation and hearings are complete, the Judiciary Committee reports its findings and recommendations to the full Senate before the chamber votes on the nominee. Historically, the full Senate has failed to confirm about 20 percent of presidential nominees to the Court, although during most of the early twentieth century, presidential nominees faced little opposition. In the 1970's, 1980's, and 1990's, however, there have been some difficult political struggles over various nominees, both in the Judiciary Committee and in the full Senate.

Committee Confirmation Hearings

For senators, interest groups, the media, the public, and the nominees, the committee confirmation hearings have become an important political event. Not until 1955, however, did Supreme Court nominees regularly appear at the hearings to answer questions about their nomination. During the confirmation hearings for William J. Brennan, Jr., held in 1957, the committee questioned Brennan for a total of three hours, over two days of hearings, with no interest group testimony at the hearings. In 1969 the committee questioned nominee Thurgood Marshall for about seven hours, with only one interest group testifying.

In 1987 nominee Robert H. Bork answered questions for thirty hours over four and a half days of hearings. Bork's confirmation hearings lasted for a total of twelve days, including testimony from 112 witnesses representing 86 different interest groups. Clarence Thomas testified for twenty-four and a half hours in 1991, and his hearings included 96 witnesses. Ruth Bader Ginsburg, a relatively noncontroversial nominee, testified for nearly twenty hours in 1993, and her hearings drew some 20 witnesses. These confirmation hearings are often televised to a national audience.

Because Supreme Court justices serve life terms on the highest court in the nation, interest groups have become increasingly active during the confirmation process. Interest groups direct many of their energies toward supporting or defeating nominees in the committee deliberation stage.

A strong example of the role that interest groups can play in the nomination and confirmation processes is the Senate's rejection of Bork's nomination. Because Bork was viewed as much too conservative by many centrist and liberal interests, his nomination saw an enormous amount of grass-roots mobilization both for and against him. Among the interest groups opposing Bork were the American Civil Liberties Union, the National Association for the Advancement of Colored People, the National Organization for Women, the Sierra Club, Common Cause, and the AFL-CIO. Interest groups supporting the Bork nomination included the American Conservative Union, the Fraternal Order of Police, the National Right to Life Committee, and the National Right to Work Committee. The Bork nomination was eventually rejected by the full Senate by a vote of forty-two to fifty-eight.

Interest groups also got involved in the confirmation process for Thomas in part because of allegations of sexual harassment against him. During the Senate Judiciary Committee hearings, many women's groups were upset that an all-male committee was deciding on Thomas's confirmation to the Court. Although the full Senate did eventually confirm Thomas by a very close vote of fifty-two to forty-eight, several male senators who voted for the Thomas nomination lost their seats in the Senate. Also several women won election to the Senate following the confirmation battle, stating that the Thomas nomination was one of the main reasons they decided to run for the Senate. In addition, several women gained seats on the Senate Judiciary Committee.

Although some nominations to the Court, such as those of Antonin Scalia and Sandra Day O'Connor, drew little attention from interest groups, other nominations, such as the elevation of William H. Rehnquist to chief justice and the nominations of Bork and Thomas, produced a great deal of attention from interest groups. It is clear that the Senate will reject a nominee for both professional and ideological reasons.

Constitutional Amendments and Other Duties

In addition to its role in the confirmation process for judicial nominees, the Senate Judiciary Committee also has primary jurisdiction over proposed constitutional amendments and other legislation affecting the federal courts. Because the number of justices who sit on the Court is not specified in the Constitution, the Judiciary Committee must also handle any proposals to increase the number of justices on the Court, such as President Franklin D. Roosevelt's Court-packing plan. Roosevelt wanted to almost double the size of the Court so that he could fill it with justices amenable to New Deal reforms. Some of the proposals sent to the Judiciary Committee can involve attacks on the Court, often because certain senators are unhappy with specific rulings. The Judiciary Committee can become involved with highly controversial issues that can have a direct effect on how the Court does its business.

Mark C. Miller

Further Reading

Abraham, Henry J. *Justices and Presidents: A Political History of Appointments to the Supreme Court.* 3d ed. New York: Oxford University Press, 1992.

Baum, Lawrence. *The Supreme Court.* 8th ed. Washington, D.C.: CQ Press, 2004.

Caldeira, Gregory A., and John R. Wright. "Lobbying for Justice: The Rise of Organized Conflict in the Politics of Federal Judgeships." In *Contemplating Courts,* edited by Lee Epstein. Washington, D.C.: Congressional Quarterly, 1995.

Davis, Richard. *Electing Justice: Fixing the Supreme Court Nomination Process.* New York: Oxford University Press, 2005.

Katzmann, Robert A. *Courts and Congress.* Washington, D.C.: Brookings Institution Press, 1997.
Maltese, John Anthony. *The Selling of Supreme Court Nominees.* Baltimore, Md.: Johns Hopkins University Press, 1995.
Slotnick, Elliot E., and Sheldon Goldman. "Congress and the Courts: A Case of Casting." In *Great Theatre: The American Congress in the 1990's,* edited by Herbert F. Weisberg and Samuel C. Patterson. New York: Cambridge University Press, 1998.

See also Fourteenth Amendment; Judicial activism; Judicial self-restraint; Nominations to the Court; Presidential powers; Rehnquist, William H.; Thomas, Clarence.

Separation of Powers

Description: Also called "checks and balances" or "shared powers," the system by which the legislative, executive, and judicial branches of the government perform different functions and can restrain the other branches.

Significance: The Supreme Court has maintained and strengthened the system of separation of powers, which prevents any of the branches of the government from becoming autocratic. Because each branch can restrain the others, U.S. politics tend to operate within a narrow political spectrum near the center of public opinion.

The Framers of the U.S. Constitution believed that a system of separation of powers was necessary to protect liberty. Although the idea can be traced to older schemes of mixed government, the delegates to the Constitutional Convention of 1787 were most familiar with Baron Charles de Montesquieu's *Spirit of the Laws* (1748). Although Montesquieu's interpretation of English government, on which the book was based, was later shown to be incomplete, the principle he espoused was adopted at the Constitutional Convention. Separation of powers is woven into the U.S. Constitution in subtle and brilliant ways. Many Supreme Court decisions have operated to preserve and strengthen the system of separation of powers, and the Court is itself one of the major repositories of shared power.

The broader structure of the U.S. system helps prevent governmental excess, supplementing formal constitutional separation of powers. The United States has a federal system in which the states retain and exercise significant power. The powers of the central government are listed, and at least in constitutional theory, powers not on the list may not be exercised. Elected officials serve staggered terms and have different constituencies.

Legislature

In its lawmaking functions, Congress is subject to two immediate constitutional requirements. The first of these is bicameralism. Any bill or resolution that is to have the force of law must be passed by both the Senate and the House of Representatives in identical form. This requirement alone establishes a heavy majoritarian bias, especially given that senators and representatives come from disparate constituencies. The second requirement is presentment. Every bill must be presented to the president of the United States for approval. If he or she signs the bill, it becomes law. If the president fails or refuses to act on it within ten days (Sundays excepted), it becomes a law without his or her signature unless Congress has already adjourned at the end of a session, in which case the bill is said to be "pocket vetoed" and does not become a law. The president may veto a bill by sending it back to Congress with a message giving the reasons for disapproval. In this case, the bill does not become law unless each house of Congress passes it again by a two-thirds vote. Given the usual distribution of party strength in a two-party system, it is rare for vetoes to be overturned. Although in the early 1990's President George H. W. Bush faced Democratic majorities in both the House and the Senate, the necessary votes to reverse his vetoes could be mustered only once.

One of the most subtle and important limits on the powers of Congress is found in the appointments clause of Article II of the U.S. Constitution. This clause gives the president the power to

> nominate and by and with the advice and consent of the Senate . . . appoint ambassadors, other public ministers and consuls, judges of the Supreme Court, and all other officers of the United States whose ap-

> pointments are not herein otherwise provided for, and which shall be established by law; but the Congress may by law vest the appointment of such inferior officers as they think proper in the President alone, in the courts of law, or in the heads of departments.

Congress is excluded altogether. Congress may not appoint any person who has executive powers; therefore, it may not establish agencies that compete with the executive branch, which is run by the president. The Court has firmly and consistently reaffirmed this exclusion of Congress from executive power in several cases including *Buckley v. Valeo* (1976), which struck down a mixed presidential-congressional appointment scheme for members of the Federal Election Commission. Similarly, in *Bowsher v. Synar* (1986), the court struck down a legislative scheme that gave budget-balancing powers to the comptroller-general of the United States. The comptroller-general, being a congressional officer rather than an officer of the United States, cannot exercise executive powers or functions.

Congress may not prevent the president from dismissing executive branch officers. Although Congress has made several attempts to establish this power, it was prevented from doing so by the Court in

Trial of president Andrew Johnson, whose impeachment trial was a major test of the separation of powers. (Library of Congress)

Myers v. United States (1926), in which Congress challenged the dismissal of a postmaster by President Woodrow Wilson.

The powers of Congress are also limited by the courts, for every statute must be interpreted when it is applied. Beyond normal judicial processes is the practice of judicial review, which is the process by which the judiciary, especially the Supreme Court, scrutinize laws to see if they are consistent with the Constitution. Although this power of the courts is not explicitly set out in the Constitution, they have exercised it ever since the Court's decision in *Marbury v. Madison* (1803). In *Marbury*, the Court held that a section of the Judiciary Act of 1789 was "repugnant" to the Constitution because it seemed to give the Court original jurisdiction beyond the grant of constitutional jurisdiction found in Article III. The Court reasoned that Congress could not change the Constitution by an ordinary legislative act because the Constitution expresses the will of the entire public, and the powers of Congress are given and limited by the Constitution. Moreover, the Constitution itself defines "the supreme law of the land" as "this Constitution and the laws made in pursuance thereof." A law not in accordance with the Constitution is not part of the supreme law of the land and may not be enforced by the courts. After *Marbury*, the Court held dozens of federal laws unconstitutional, thus preventing Congress from exceeding its constitutional powers.

Executive Branch

Like Congress, the president is limited by the other branches of the government. The office's official acts are subject to review for constitutionality by the courts, so that if the president or executive officers violate the Constitution or exceed their authority, their actions can be halted.

The Constitution contains a wonderful two-edged phrase to define executive authority: The president is to "take care that the laws be faithfully executed." The president is given the power to execute the laws but must do so "faithfully"—which is to say in accordance with the will of Congress. In the landmark case *Youngstown Sheet and Tube Co. v. Sawyer* (1952), the Supreme Court held that President Harry S. Truman could not seize the nation's steel mills in order to avert a national strike in the midst of the Korean War. Although President Truman had argued that the sum of the president's executive and war powers provided constitutional justification for the seizure, the court decided that without statutory authorization, the president did not have this power. Truman released the mills.

Should a president fail to execute the laws faithfully, and if the political will exists, the president can be impeached by the House of Representatives, tried before the U.S. Senate, and if convicted, removed from office. Two U.S. presidents, Andrew Johnson and Bill Clinton, have been impeached, but neither was convicted.

The ordinary legislative powers of Congress also may serve as a powerful check on presidential power. Only Congress may appropriate money for governmental functions, and all federal agencies and bureaus are created by and may be abolished by Congress. Statutory authority given the president may be modified or withdrawn whenever Congress wishes. Most presidential appointments require the consent of the Senate, as do treaties made with foreign powers. The war powers are similarly shared: Although the president is the commander in chief, it is Congress that declares war, raises and supports armies, and makes the rules for the governance of the armed forces. Although the presidency appears to be at the center of the political system, Congress actually lies at the center of the constitutional system. Simply put, Congress can get rid of the president, but not the reverse.

Judiciary

Federal judges serve for life, but they, like the president, may be removed by impeachment if they commit crimes, and Congress has removed four federal judges for such crimes as bribery and tax evasion. Judges are appointed by the president with the advice and consent of the Senate; therefore, sitting judges have no control over the ideology of newer judicial appointees. Moreover, the entire judicial structure, except for the Supreme Court itself, is established by Congress and can be reorganized whenever Congress desires. Although the Court is established by the Constitution, Congress sets the size of the Court and may decree the length and frequency of its sittings. In fact, *Marbury* was delayed for a year because Congress passed a law canceling the Court's 1802 term. Congress also has the power to make "exceptions" to the appellate jurisdiction of the Court—that is, to take away its power to hear certain cases. This power was exercised by Congress when, just after the Civil War, it took from the Court's jurisdiction certain Reconstruction cases. The Court recognized and accepted this Congressional power in *Ex parte McCardle* (1869).

The greatest limit on the power of the judiciary, however, is the cases and controversies rule. Courts may decide only issues that come before them in cases. If there is no case, there is no judicial power. Moreover, because prosecution is an executive function, it is the president and the attorney general who decide what cases to bring and what arguments to make. Consequently courts are always responding rather than initiating. For this reason, Alexander Hamilton in *The Federalist* (1788) No. 78, remarked that the judiciary was "the least dangerous branch" of the government.

Constitutional decisions of the Court can also be reversed by constitutional amendment if there is enough public concern. The Civil War Amendments collectively reverse the Court's decision in *Scott v. Sandford* (1857), and the income tax amendment (Sixteenth Amendment) reverses *Pollock v. Farmers' Loan and Trust Co.* (1895).

Robert Jacobs

Further Reading

There are a number of fine studies of the relationship of the judiciary to the other branches of the federal government. These include Kermit L. Hall's *The Least Dangerous Branch: Separation of Powers and Court-Packing* (New York: Garland, 2000), Richard L. Pacelle's *The Role of the Supreme Court in American Politics: The Least Dangerous Branch?* (Boulder, Colo.: Westview Press, 2002), Jeffrey Rosen's *The Most Democratic Branch: How the Courts Serve America* (New York: Oxford University Press, 2006), Stephen Powers's *The Least Dangerous Branch? Consequences of Judicial Activism* (Westport, Conn.: Praeger, 2002), and *Institutions of American Democracy: The Judicial Branch*, edited by Kermit L. Hall and Kevin T. McGuire (New York: Oxford University Press, 2005).

The most powerful arguments for and best general explanations of the U.S. constitutional system are found in *The Federalist* (1788), a series of essays in support of the proposed Constitution by Alexander Hamilton, James Madison, and John Jay. Nos. 10, 69, and 78 are particularly relevant to understanding the system of separation of powers. Edward S. Corwin's *The Higher Law: Background in American Constitutional Law* (Ithaca, N.Y.: Cornell University Press, 1929) explores the theoretical rationale for judicial review, while *Nine Men: A Political History of the Supreme Court from 1790 to 1955* by Fred Rodell (New York: Random House, 1955) argues the undemocratic nature of the process.

The powerful divergent opinions of Chief Justices William H. Rehnquist and Associate Justice Antonin Scalia in *Morrison v. Olson* (1988), which involves a challenge to the constitutionality of the Ethics in Government Act of 1978, illuminate the nature of executive power and the appointments clause of the Constitution. *The Supreme Court and the Powers of the American Government* by Joan Biskupic and Elder Witt (Washington, D.C.: Congressional Quarterly, 1997) shows how the Court has limited federal power. Robert A. Goldwin, an iconoclastic conservative, and Art Kaufman have edited *Separation of Powers: Does It Still Work?* (Washington, D.C.: American Enterprise Institute for Public Policy Research, 1986), which argues that the system could still work, but it has been abandoned in practice. Some of the practical consequences of separation of powers are discussed in Howard E. Shuman's *Politics and the Budget: The Struggle Between the President and the Congress* (Englewood Cliffs, N.J.: Prentice-Hall, 1984).

See also Advisory opinions; *Boerne v. Flores*; *Clinton v. City of New York*; Elastic clause; Federalism; Judicial review; Nominations to the Court; Presidential powers; Tenth Amendment.

Seriatim Opinions

Description: Announcement of a ruling of a multimember court through separate opinions provided by each of its judges.

Significance: Early in the Supreme Court's history, the justices debated whether to adopt the practice of rendering seriatim opinions, a typical practice in English courts. The justices rejected the practice fairly early in favor of producing opinions reflecting the common views of the Court's majority.

Concurring Opinions Among Justices in 1994 and 1995

Percentage of cases in which pairs of justices supported the same opinions

	Stevens	Ginsburg	Breyer	Souter	O'Connor	Kennedy	Rehnquist	Scalia	Thomas
Stevens	—	74	72	70	58	63	50	45	44
Ginsburg	74	—	79	82	67	76	66	59	55
Breyer	72	79	—	86	75	70	63	57	54
Souter	70	82	86	—	78	74	68	60	57
O'Connor	58	67	75	78	—	77	78	70	70
Kennedy	63	76	70	74	77	—	81	74	71
Rehnquist	50	66	63	68	78	81	—	81	82
Scalia	45	59	57	60	70	74	81	—	88
Thomas	44	55	54	57	70	71	82	88	—

Note: Numbers are averages, for the two terms, of the percentages of cases in each term in which a pair of justices agreed on an opinion. Both unanimous and nonunanimous cases are included.

Source: Lawrence Baum, *The Supreme Court* (6th ed. 1998), p. 156.

The practice of issuing seriatim opinions must be contrasted with the practice of issuing opinions for a court. The former involves each judge on a court providing a statement of the basis for his or her vote on the disposition of a case. The court's judgment is based on which disposition receives the support of the majority of the judges. In this process, no opinion for the court majority is produced. The British Law Lords continue to dispose of cases by rendering seriatim opinions.

The alternative method, producing a single opinion for the court, involves a majority of the judges agreeing to a single opinion and stating their joint justification for favoring a particular disposition of the case. Judges who concur with the majority can write separate opinions elaborating on their individual reasoning if it differs from that of the majority, and those who disagree with the majority opinion can produce joint or separate dissenting opinions.

Early in Supreme Court history, the justices debated whether the Court should issue seriatim opinions. English courts issued seriatim opinions, as did the courts in some of the states, such as Virginia, and Thomas Jefferson advocated the use of seriatim opinions. John Marshall, chief justice from 1801 to 1835, made a great effort to ensure that the Court produced only majority opinions and discouraged separate dissenting statements. This brought him into conflict with justices such as William Johnson and Joseph Story, who believed it their duty to express their dissenting views. Later, the Court began to issue opinions for the Court that expressed the common views of a majority of justices, supplemented by separate dissenting and concurring opinions, a practice that reflects the positions of both Marshall and his adversaries.

The question of whether to issue seriatim opinions or opinions for the Court centers on whether the Court is perceived as an institution larger than the justices who are serving at the time or as merely the sum of the sitting justices.

Bernard W. Bell

Further Reading

Blanc, D. Ellsworth. *The Supreme Court: Issues and Opinions.* Huntington, N.Y.: Nova Science Publishers, 2001.

Morgan, Donald G. *Justice William Johnson: The First Dissenter.* Columbia: University of South Carolina Press, 1954.
Van Geel, Tyll. *Understanding Supreme Court Opinions.* 4th ed. New York: Longman, 2005.

See also Conference of the justices; Dissents; Johnson, William; Judicial review; Marshall, John; Opinions, writing of.

Shelley v. Kraemer

Citation: 344 U.S. 1
Date: May 3, 1948
Issues: Race discrimination; equal protection clause
Significance: Although it allowed private individuals to make racially restrictive covenants, this ruling meant that such covenants were worthless because they could not be legally enforced.

In *Buchanan v. Warley* (1917), the Supreme Court had ruled that laws requiring residential segregation were unconstitutional. In *Corrigan v. Buckley* (1926), however, the Court upheld the right of individuals to make private contracts not to sell or rent property to African Americans and members of other racial or ethnic groups. By the end of World War II (1941-1945), such covenants were being enforced in several northern cities. After J. D. Shelley, an African American with six children, purchased a St. Louis house that was under a racial covenant, his neighbors went to court to have the covenant enforced. Charles Hamilton Houston and Thurgood Marshall, lead counsels for the National Association for the Advancement of Colored People (NAACP), argued Shelley's case before the Court.

In making its 6-0 ruling, the Court did not directly overturn *Corrigan,* but it emphasized the traditional distinction between private acts (not restricted by the Fourteenth Amendment) and state actions (limited by the Fourteenth Amendment). The judicial enforcement of the contracts was seen as an official action that violated the principles of equal protection. Justice Fred M. Vinson's opinion for the Court emphasized that one of the purposes of the amendment was to prohibit the state from engaging in racial discrimination "in the enjoyment of property rights." *Shelley v. Kraemer* was expanded in *Barrows v. Jackson* (1953), which denied the right of a party to a restrictive covenant to recover damages from a party in violation of the covenant.

Although often criticized, *Shelley v. Kraemer* destroyed one of the important instruments used to promote residential segregation. It was therefore an early victory for the Civil Rights movement. The Civil Rights Acts of 1964 and 1968 provided statutory guidance for many of the questions raised in the ruling. In subsequent cases, the Court continued to recognize *Shelley*'s distinction between state action and private conduct.

Thomas Tandy Lewis

See also Equal protection clause; Housing discrimination; *Loving v. Virginia*; Race and discrimination; Restrictive covenants; State action; Vinson, Fred M.

Sherbert v. Verner

Citation: 374 U.S. 398
Date: June 17, 1963
Issue: Freedom of religion
Significance: The Supreme Court required that government apply the "compelling state interest" standard to justify any policy that placed an indirect burden on a religious practice.

Adell Sherbert, a member of the Seventh-day Adventist Church, was fired from her job in a textile mill because she refused to work on Saturdays, her Sabbath. The unemployment office of South Carolina turned down her claims for benefits because state policy did not accept religious conviction as a sufficient justification for not working. The state court, ruling in favor of the state, referred to *Braunfeld v. Brown* (1961), which had allowed Sunday-closing laws that indirectly disadvantaged Jewish merchants.

The Supreme Court, by a 7-2 margin, found that South Carolina's unemployment policy violated the religious exercise clause of the

First Amendment. Justice William J. Brennan, Jr., wrote that when a state's policy limited a fundamental right, the state must justify that burden with a compelling rationale. In addition, the state was required to consider alternative means for achieving its objectives and to adopt the policy that was the least restrictive of fundamental rights. In the *Braunfeld* case, the state had a compelling reason to provide a uniform day of rest, but South Carolina had no similar basis for refusing to modify its policy for unemployment compensation. Sherbert established a strong presumption in favor of protecting unconventional religious practices. The scope of this protection was limited in *Employment Division, Department of Human Resources v. Smith* (1990).

Thomas Tandy Lewis

See also *Boerne v. Flores*; Brennan, William J., Jr.; *Employment Division, Department of Human Resources v. Smith*; First Amendment; Fundamental rights; Judicial scrutiny; Religion, freedom of; Sunday closing laws.

United States v. Shipp

Citation: 214 U.S. 386
Date: May 24, 1909
Issues: Federalism; Sixth Amendment
Significance: As the only criminal trial ever conducted by the Supreme Court, this trial of a local sheriff for contempt demonstrated the Court's authority and raised the question of whether the Sixth Amendment applied to the states. The trial, however, did not appear to establish any precedents.

On January 23, 1906, a violent rape occurred in the city of Chattanooga, Tennessee. Although the evidence was weak, an African American man named Ed Johnson was convicted and sentenced to death by an all-white jury on February 11. Arguing that the trial violated the principles of due process and equal protection, Johnson's lawyer failed to obtain habeas corpus relief in the lower federal courts. He then appealed directly to the U.S. Supreme Court, where he had a personal conversation with Justice John Marshall Harlan, who persuaded his colleagues on the Court to issue a stay of execution and to schedule oral arguments for the case.

The same evening that the stay was announced, an angry mob stormed the county jail and lynched Johnson on a city bridge. There was considerable evidence that the local sheriff, Joseph Shipp, and his deputies had known that the lynching would occur but did nothing to stop it. The attorney general filed charges of criminal contempt with the clerk of the Supreme Court. Following a hearing, Justice Oliver Wendell Holmes announced that the justices unanimously agreed that the Court had jurisdiction to try Shipp and his deputies.

On February 12, 1907, the Shipp trial began in Chattanooga with the taking of evidence, and in March, 1909, the final arguments of the contending attorneys were presented before the Court in Washington, D.C. On May 24, 1909, Chief Justice Melville Fuller announced that the justices had voted six to three that the defendants were guilty. Shipp and two deputies were sentenced to three months imprisonment. Three other defendants were sentenced to terms of two months. After Shipp's prison term was completed in January, 1910, he returned to Chattanooga to an enthusiastic crowd of 10,000 supporters. In 2000, however, a county judge in Chattanooga overturned Ed Johnson's conviction and death sentence.

Thomas Tandy Lewis

Further Reading

Curriden, Mark, and Leroy Phillips, Jr. *Contempt of Court.* New York: Anchor Books, 1999.

See also Federalism; Fuller, Melville W.; Harlan, John Marshall; Holmes, Oliver Wendell; Sixth Amendment.

George Shiras, Jr.

IDENTIFICATION: Associate justice (October 10, 1892-February 23, 1903)

NOMINATED BY: Benjamin Harrison

BORN: January 26, 1832, Pittsburgh, Pennsylvania

DIED: August 2, 1924, Pittsburgh, Pennsylvania

SIGNIFICANCE: Shiras is remembered as an impartial Supreme Court judge and an independent thinker. Generally, he defended civil liberties, upheld the right of states to regulate business, and voted against the Sherman Antitrust Act of 1890.

George Shiras, Jr., studied law at Yale and in a Pittsburgh law office and was admitted to the Pennsylvania bar in 1855. Representing local railroad, banking, oil, coal, and iron interests, he earned a reputation as an extremely capable corporation lawyer. In 1881 he turned down

George Shiras, Jr.
(Library of Congress)

an offer from the state legislature to represent Pennsylvania in the U.S. Senate.

Although lacking experience in public service, Shiras was appointed to the Supreme Court by President Benjamin Harrison in 1892. As a justice, Shiras typically voted to uphold government regulation against challenges from the states but supported challenges to new extensions of national power. In many cases, Shiras voted to restrict the Sherman Antitrust Act (1890). He is best remembered for his apparent change of opinion in *Pollock v. Farmers' Loan and Trust Co.* (1895). Initially, the decision was five to four in favor of the constitutionality of the 1894 income tax law, but after reargument, one justice changed his mind, making the statute unconstitutional. For many years, Shiras was credited with changing his vote, but in 1928 Justice Charles Evans Hughes suggested that it was not Shiras who provided the crucial vote.

Alvin K. Benson

See also Antitrust law; Fuller, Melville W.; Hughes, Charles Evans.

Sixth Amendment

Date: 1791

Description: Amendment to the U.S. Constitution and part of the Bill of Rights specifying the trial rights possessed by criminal defendants.

Significance: Beginning in the 1960's, the Supreme Court actively interpreted and defined the provisions of the Sixth Amendment to ensure that criminal defendants receive their protected entitlements in both federal and state courts.

The Sixth Amendment, added to the U.S. Constitution in 1791, specifies the rights of defendants in the trial stage of the criminal law process, including the rights to a speedy and public trial, an impartial jury in the locale where the alleged crime was committed, information about the nature of charges being prosecuted, an opportunity to confront accusers and adverse witnesses, a compulsory process for obtaining favorable witnesses, and the assistance of counsel.

For most of U.S. history, the Sixth Amendment and other provisions of the Bill of Rights protected individuals against actions by the federal government only. However, during the twentieth century, the Supreme Court ruled that many provisions of the Bill of Rights, including the Sixth Amendment, also applied to state and local governments. Therefore, defendants in all criminal prosecutions came to benefit from the protections afforded by the Sixth Amendment.

Right to Counsel

Before the twentieth century, the right to counsel provided by the Sixth Amendment simply meant that the government could not prevent a criminal defendant from hiring an attorney when the defendant could afford to do so. Defendants who lacked the necessary funds were required to defend themselves in court without professional assistance.

The Court first expanded the right to counsel in *Powell v. Alabama* (1932). *Powell,* also known as the Scottsboro case, involved several African American defendants who were accused of raping two white women. The young men were convicted and sentenced to death in a quick trial without being represented by any attorneys. The case was heard at a time when African Americans were subjected to significant racial discrimination in the legal system, especially in southern states. There were troubling questions about the defendants' guilt, particularly after one of the alleged victims later admitted that she lied about what happened. Given the circumstances, the Court found the legal proceedings to be fundamentally unfair and declared that defendants facing the death penalty were entitled to representation by attorneys.

The Court expanded the right to counsel in *Johnson v. Zerbst* (1938) by declaring that all defendants facing serious charges in federal court are entitled to be provided with an attorney when they are too poor to afford to hire their own. The Court expanded this rule to cover all state and local courts in *Gideon v. Wainwright* (1963), a well-known case initiated by an uneducated prisoner who sent the Court a handwritten petition complaining about a judge denying his request for an attorney. In *Douglas v. California* (1963), the Court declared

TEXT OF THE SIXTH AMENDMENT

In all criminal prosecutions, the accused shall enjoy the right to a speedy and public trial, by an impartial jury of the State and district wherein the crime shall have been committed; which district shall have been previously ascertained by law, and to be informed of the nature and cause of the accusation; to be confronted with the witnesses against him; to have compulsory process for obtaining witnesses in his favor, and to have the assistance of counsel for his defence.

that the government must supply attorneys for poor defendants for their first appeal after a criminal conviction. Subsequently, the Court ruled in *Argersinger v. Hamlin* (1972) that regardless of the seriousness of the charges, criminal defendants are entitled to be represented by an attorney if they face the possibility of serving time in jail. Because people who possess the necessary funds are expected to hire their own attorneys, the Court's Sixth Amendment decisions primarily protected poor defendants who would not receive professional representation if it were not provided by the government. Although the Court expanded opportunities for poor defendants to receive representation during criminal trials, the right to counsel does not apply to civil trials or to cases pursued by prisoners after they have presented their first postconviction appeal.

The Supreme Court gradually recognized the right of criminal defendants to "effective assistance of counsel." This means, among other things, that defendants are entitled to have attorneys whose performance is not defective, as well as adequate time for them to consult with their attorneys. In *Strickland v. Washington* (1984), the Court held that a constitutional violation would occur if, in light of all the circumstances, "there is a reasonable probability that, but for the counsel's unprofessional errors, the result of the proceeding would have been different." Using these criteria, the Court has on occasion overturned criminal convictions. In the cases of *Wiggins v. Smith* (2003) and *Rompilla v. Beard* (2005), the Court overturned convictions because defense lawyers had failed to investigate their clients' troubled backgrounds, which could have been used as mitigating circumstances in the sentencing phases of their trials.

Trial by Jury

The Court did not interpret the Sixth Amendment to apply the right to trial by jury to all serious cases in both state and federal courts until 1968. In *Duncan v. Louisiana* (1968), the Court overturned the conviction of an African American defendant whose request for a jury trial had been denied when he was convicted and sentenced to sixty days in jail for allegedly slapping a white man on the arm. After the conviction was overturned, the federal courts prevented Louisiana from prosecuting the man again because he and his attorney had been subjected to discrimination and harassment by local law-enforcement officials during the course of his arrest and trial.

The right to trial by jury does not, however, apply to all criminal cases. In *Lewis v. United States* (1996), the Court ruled that the Sixth Amendment right to a jury trial does not apply to defendants facing petty offense charges with six months or less of imprisonment as the possible punishment for each charge. Therefore, defendants may be denied the opportunity for a jury trial if they face multiple petty offenses that, upon conviction, could produce cumulative sentences in excess of six months through separate sentences for each charge. Such defendants are entitled to a trial, but the trial will be before a judge rather than a jury.

In its early decisions, the Court expected that juries would be made up of twelve members who reach unanimous verdicts. However, the Court's interpretation of the Sixth Amendment changed during the 1970's. In *Williams v. Florida* (1970), the Court determined that juries could have as few as six members in criminal cases. In *Apodaca v. Oregon* (1972), the Court declared that states could permit defendants to be convicted of crimes by less than unanimous jury verdicts. It ruled that Oregon could convict defendants with 10-2 jury votes and Louisiana with 9-3 votes. The right to trial by jury is not implemented in identical fashion in all courts throughout the country.

Other Trial Rights

The Sixth Amendment's right to a speedy trial prevents the government from holding criminal charges over a defendant's head indefinitely without ever pursuing prosecution. People are entitled to have charges against them resolved in a timely manner. Because the Sixth Amendment provides no guidance on how long the government may take in pursuing prosecution, the Court had to establish guidelines through its Sixth Amendment rulings. The Court clarified the right to a speedy trial in *Barker v. Wingo* (1972), in which a defendant was forced to wait for more than five years for a trial after he was charged with murder. The delay occurred because the prosecution sought to convict a codefendant first but the codefendant's appeals led to orders for new trials. Therefore, it took several trials to obtain an error-free conviction of the codefendant.

When the Court examined the claim that a five-year delay constituted a violation of the Sixth Amendment right to a speedy trial, the Court refused to set a firm time limit for speedy trials. Instead, the Court said the individual circumstances of each case must be examined. The Court ruled that judges must determine whether the right to a speedy trial was violated by considering four aspects of the delay: its length, the reason for it, whether the defendant complained about the delay, and whether it harmed the defendant's case, such as through the death or disappearance of a key witness. In this case, the Court found that because the defendant never complained about the delay and his case was not disadvantaged by the delay, the five-year wait for a trial did not violate the defendant's rights despite the fact that the prosecution caused the lengthy delay. Although the Court clarified the factors to be considered in evaluating a speedy-trial claim, the exact nature of the right was not clearly defined.

The defendant's right to confront adverse witnesses is intended to prevent the government from holding trials without the defendant's knowledge or declaring the defendant guilty without permitting the defendant to challenge the prosecution's evidence. The adversary system underlying the U.S. criminal law process presumes that the best way to reveal the truth at a trial is to permit both sides to present their evidence and arguments to the judge and jury during the same proceeding.

The Court struggled with its attempts to provide a clear definition of the extent of the confrontation right. For example, in *Coy v. Iowa* (1988), the justices were deeply divided when they decided that it was not permissible for the state to place a screen in the courtroom to prevent a defendant from having eye contact with child victims who were presenting testimony about an alleged sexual assault. A few years later in *Maryland v. Craig* (1990), a narrow majority of justices approved the use of closed-circuit television to permit child victims to present testimony from a courthouse room other than the courtroom in which the trial was taking place. Thus the defendant could see the witnesses on television, but the children would not risk being traumatized by coming face to face with the person accused of committing crimes against them. The significant disagreements among the justices about the right to confrontation indicate that the Court may need to clarify the circumstances in which it is permissible to use devices to separate defendants from direct contact with witnesses testifying against them. Traditionally, defendants and witnesses were expected to be face to face in the same courtroom, but growing sensitivity to the psychological trauma experienced by crime victims who must testify in court has led to experiments with screens, closed-circuit television, and other techniques that collide with traditional conceptions of the right to confrontation.

Other Sixth Amendment issues to come before the Court include whether excessive pretrial publicity prevents the selection of an unbiased jury and in what circumstances judicial proceedings can be closed to the public. When addressing these issues, Court justices tend to focus on their assessment of factors and circumstances that may interfere with a criminal defendant's opportunity to receive a fair trial.

Christopher E. Smith

Further Reading

This subject might best be approached through a general reference work on the trial system, such as Christopher E. Smith's *Courts and Trials: A Reference Handbook* (Santa Barbara, Calif.: ABC-Clio, 2003). The development of trial rights is presented in Francis Heller's *The Sixth Amendment to the Constitution of the United States* (New York:

Greenwood Press, 1951). Many landmark Sixth Amendment cases are presented in case studies examining the people and social contexts surrounding them. Of particular note are Anthony Lewis's *Gideon's Trumpet* (New York: Vintage, 1989) concerning *Gideon v. Wainwright* and James Goodman's *Stories of Scottsboro* (New York: Random House, 1994) concerning *Powell v. Alabama.*

Alfredo Garcia's *The Sixth Amendment in Modern American Jurisprudence* (New York: Greenwood Press, 1992) presents a discussion of the modern Court's decisions affecting the Sixth Amendment. A detailed presentation of the fine points of law concerning trial rights is available in Christopher Slobogin's *Criminal Procedure: Regulation of Police Investigation: Legal, Historical, Empirical, and Comparative Materials* (3d ed. Newark, N.J.: LexisNexis, 2002).

For an examination of the Court's decision making after the 1950's and the viewpoints of individual justices concerning the Sixth Amendment, see Thomas R. Hensley, Christopher E. Smith, and Joyce A. Baugh's *The Changing Supreme Court: Constitutional Rights and Liberties* (St. Paul, Minn.: West Publishing, 1997). A liberal critique of the Rehnquist Court's decisions affecting the criminal law process is presented in John Decker's *Revolution to the Right* (New York: Garland, 1992), which argues that the Supreme Court has diminished the protections of the Sixth Amendment and other rights with respect to criminal defendants.

See also Bill of Rights; Counsel, right to; *Duncan v. Louisiana*; Exclusionary rule; *Gideon v. Wainwright*; Jury, trial by; *Rompilla v. Beard*; *Shipp, United States v.*; Witnesses, confrontation of.

Slaughterhouse Cases

CITATION: 83 U.S. 36
DATE: April 14, 1873
ISSUES: Privileges or immunities clause; federalism; civil rights
SIGNIFICANCE: In these cases, the Supreme Court made a narrow interpretation of the privileges or immunities clause (P or I clause) of the Fourteenth Amendment, with the result that none of the first eight amendments have been applied to the states by way of that clause.

The *Slaughterhouse Cases* combined three suits challenging a Louisiana law that granted a single company the exclusive right to butcher animals in New Orleans. Although the legislature tried to defend the law as a rational means of promoting sanitation, it appeared to provide a monopoly to a small group of wealthy individuals with powerful political connections. Hundreds of New Orleans butchers, operating as small businesses, were put out of work as a result of the monopolistic legislation.

The butchers, represented by former Supreme Court justice John A. Campbell, took their case to the state courts. Among other arguments, Campbell maintained that the privileges or immunities clause of the Fourteenth Amendment protected the right of American citizens to labor freely in an honest profession. After losing in the state's highest court, Campbell appealed the cases to the U.S. Supreme Court. The *Slaughterhouse Cases* presented the Court with its first important opportunity to explore the meaning of the privileges or immunities clause, which, according to some of its framers, guaranteed the fundamental rights of citizenship, including those listed in the Bill of Rights.

The Court, by a 5-4 margin, rejected Campbell's arguments and interpreted the Fourteenth Amendment very narrowly. Writing the majority opinion, Justice Samuel F. Miller held that the only real purpose of the amendment was to secure the freedom and civil equality of African Americans and not to increase protections for white Americans. He drew a distinction between the rights of state citizenship and those of national citizenship, with the second category reduced to a very small number. The new amendment, Miller asserted, had not produced any basic changes in American federalism, and it did not make the Supreme Court "a perpetual censor upon all legislation of the states." In addition to holding that the Fourteenth Amendment did not protect economic rights, the *Slaughterhouse* decision meant that the privileges or immunities clause did not authorize the federal courts to apply the Bill of Rights to the state governments. Dissenting justice Stephen J. Field, joined by three additional justices, insisted that the privileges and immunities of national citizenship included the right to labor.

Years later, the Supreme Court would broadly interpret the due process clause of the Fourteenth Amendment as a means of protecting the kinds of economic liberties that the butchers asserted, and it would also use the due process clause to apply most of the Bill of Rights to the states. Although the *Slaughterhouse* ruling has never been overturned, in *Saenz v. Roe* (1999), the Court breathed new life into the privileges or immunities clause when it held that the clause protected a right to interstate travel and migration.

Thomas Tandy Lewis

Further Reading

Labb, Ronald M., and Jonathan Lurie. *The Slaughterhouse Cases: Regulation, Reconstruction, and the Fourteenth Amendment.* Lawrence: University Press of Kansas, 2003.

See also Bill of Rights; Campbell, John A.; Due process, procedural; Due process, substantive; Federalism; Fourteenth Amendment; Incorporation doctrine; Miller, Samuel F.; Privileges and immunities; Reconstruction.

Slavery

DESCRIPTION: Institution by which, in the United States, blacks were held in service as the chattels of other people.

SIGNIFICANCE: The Supreme Court, under Roger Brooke Taney, upheld fugitive slave laws and in 1857 ruled that African Americans were not citizens of the United States.

The institution of slavery came to the colonial United States in the seventeenth century. Blacks were taken from Africa, enslaved, and brought to the New World. The majority of the slaves were taken to the southern colonies, where they performed agricultural work, especially labor-intensive tobacco farming.

From the time the United States was formed, slavery was a contentious political issue. A draft of the Declaration of Independence contained a critical reference to slavery that caused tension at the Continental Congress. In order to gain agreement among the colonies, that passage was removed and the debate regarding slavery was postponed.

THE CONSTITUTION AND SLAVERY

At the Constitutional Convention (1787), the essential question regarding slavery—whether it should exist—was postponed as part of a compromise. The compromise can be seen in the three references to slavery in the U.S. Constitution (ratified 1789). The first reference, regarding the enumeration of residents, states that the apportionment of representatives be determined by adding the number of free persons, indentured servants, and "three-fifths of other persons." "Other persons" does not include free African Americans but those held in slavery. This passage was a compromise because the South wanted to count slaves as whole persons while the North opposed counting slaves for fear that such a provision would encourage slavery.

The second reference to slavery stated that "the migration of such persons as any of the states now existing think proper to admit, shall not be prohibited by the Congress prior to the year 1808." In other words, Congress would not be permitted to ban the importation of slaves for at least thirty years. This was significant because some, in-

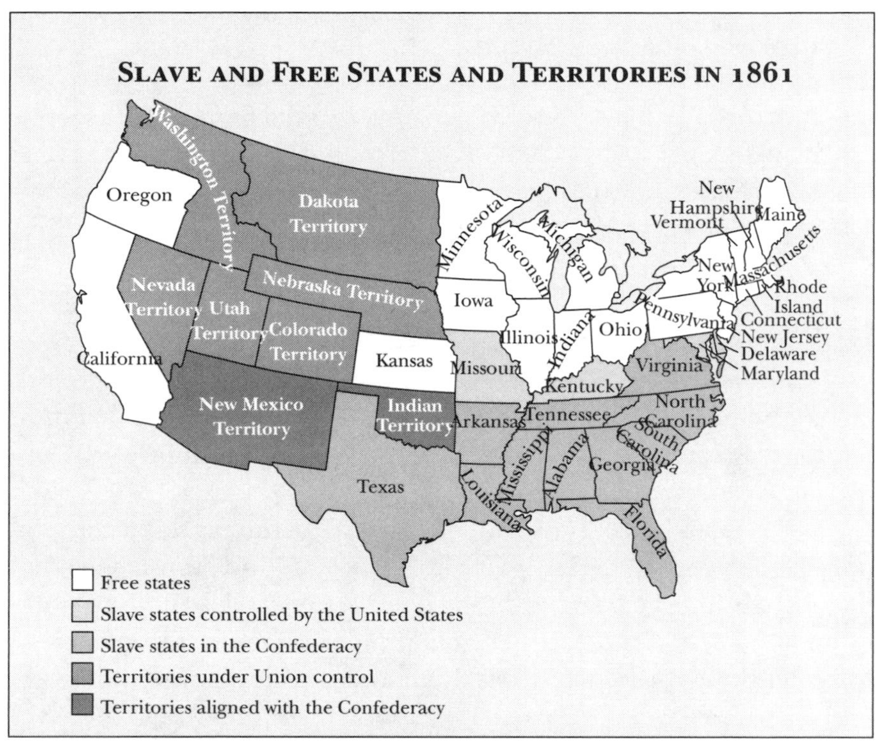

Slave and Free States and Territories in 1861

Source: Adapted from Eric Foner and John A. Garraty, eds., *The Reader's Companion to American History*. Boston: Houghton Mifflin, 1991.

cluding James Wilson, who was a prominent member of the Constitutional Convention, thought that abolishing the slave trade was the first step in ending slavery in the United States.

The final passage refers to the return of fugitive slaves, although again the word "slavery" is not used. In all these references, slavery was not explicitly mentioned because some Framers did not want the word in the document because that would give greater legitimacy to slavery. The Constitution, as it was originally written, did protect slavery, and the Supreme Court had to interpret its provisions.

The Constitution did not outlaw slavery until the adoption of the Thirteenth Amendment in December, 1865. That provision reads: "Neither slavery nor involuntary servitude, except as a punishment for crime whereof the party shall have been duly convicted, shall exist within the United States, or any place subject to their jurisdiction."

SUPREME COURT CASES AND SLAVERY

The Supreme Court addressed issues related to the slave trade in several cases. The earliest such case was *The Antelope* (1825). In this case, Chief Justice John Marshall asserted that the African slave trade was "contrary to the law of nature," but it was not piracy in itself if foreigners whose nations permitted it participated in slave trade. The case involved the capture of a pirate ship that had earlier captured a Spanish slave ship called *The Antelope.* Marshall ruled that the slaves were to be returned to the Spanish owners of *The Antelope.* This decision maintained the U.S. prohibition on slave trade while recognizing the practice elsewhere. The Court also upheld the conviction of secret owners of a vessel that was involved in African slave trade in *United States v. Gooding* (1827).

The best-known case involving the African slave trade was made famous by the 1997 film *Amistad.* The *Amistad* was a Spanish ship that had drifted into U.S. waters after the enslaved Africans on the ship mutinied. The U.S. government sought to convict the slaves for murder. Once it was prevented from doing that, the government tried extraditing the slaves to Spain. The controversy regarding this ship made it to the Supreme Court. In *United States v. The Amistad* (1841), former President John Quincy Adams served as one of the attorneys on behalf of the slaves. The Court ruled that the slaves were to be set free because slavery was illegal in Spain.

Groves v. Slaughter (1841) involved the sale of slaves in Mississippi in 1835-1836. Mississippi's 1832 constitution had banned the importation of slaves into Mississippi for sale. The state may have included this provision in its constitution to protect its white residents against a slave uprising because free residents barely outnumbered slaves at the time. In violation of the state constitution, Slaughter, a slave trader, sold slaves to Groves and others. Groves then defaulted on the promissory notes that he had put forward in order to purchase the slaves.

Two issues were involved in this case. First, the Court had to determine whether this prohibition was valid according to Mississippi law. The Court ruled that Mississippi needed to have enabling legislation to make this provision valid. However, the state had no statute regarding punishments for importing slaves until 1837. The second, more

In 1841, former president John Quincy Adams served as an attorney for the Amistad *defendants.* (Library of Congress)

important issue was whether the Mississippi prohibition on importation of slaves violated the constitutional provision that gives Congress the power to regulate interstate commerce. The Court ruled that slaves were to be treated differently from other articles of commerce such as agricultural and manufactured goods. Justice Smith Thompson in his opinion in the case said that a state "may establish or abolish slavery within her limits; she may do it immediately, or gradually and prospectively." If a state may abolish slavery within its boundaries, it is a logical extension that the same state may abolish the importation of slaves. Thompson further stated that "these state laws are not regulations of commerce, but of slavery." In his reasoning regarding the commerce clause, Thompson drew on the examination of commerce in *Gibbons v. Ogden* (1824), which also distinguished slaves from other types of commerce.

Fugitive Slaves

The Court also addressed issues related to fugitive slaves. Article IV of the U.S. Constitution contained a clause requiring the return of fugitive slaves. Congress passed the Fugitive Slave Act in 1793 indicating procedures for returning escaped slaves. At the same time, the New England states and Pennsylvania and New Jersey had either abolished slavery or were in the process of doing so. These states were concerned that southerners and bounty hunters might take advantage of the 1793 law regarding fugitive slaves and come to northern states and forcibly take free blacks. With that in mind, most of the states that had abolished slavery passed laws requiring strong evidence that an African American was in fact an escaped slave and therefore subject to being forcibly returned.

In *Prigg v. Pennsylvania* (1842), because the standards for evidence

CAUTION!!

COLORED PEOPLE

OF BOSTON, ONE & ALL,

You are hereby respectfully CAUTIONED and advised, to avoid conversing with the

Watchmen and Police Officers of Boston,

For since the recent ORDER OF THE MAYOR & ALDERMEN, they are empowered to act as

KIDNAPPERS

AND

Slave Catchers,

And they have already been actually employed in KIDNAPPING, CATCHING, AND KEEPING SLAVES. Therefore, if you value your LIBERTY, and the *Welfare of the Fugitives* among you, *Shun* them in every possible manner, as so many *HOUNDS* on the track of the most unfortunate of your race.

Keep a Sharp Look Out for KIDNAPPERS, and have TOP EYE open.

APRIL 24, 1851.

This 1851 poster cautions free blacks living in Boston against dealing with authorities, lest they be mistaken for fugitive slaves. (Library of Congress)

were greater in the state laws than in the federal laws, Justice Joseph Story struck down the state laws. At the same time, Story said that the federal structure of the government meant that the federal government could not force the states to comply with the 1793 statute. Chief Justice Roger Brooke Taney agreed with the validity of the 1793 Fugitive Slave Act but rejected Story's argument that the federal government could not force state governments to comply with the act.

Jones v. Van Zandt (1847), *Ableman v. Booth* (1859), and *Kentucky v. Dennison* (1861) also involved fugitive slaves. In *Jones*, Van Zandt contested the fine brought against him for transporting an escaped slave through Ohio. Lawyer Salmon P. Chase, who later became chief justice, argued before the Court that because Ohio banned slavery, Van Zandt could assume that all African Americans in Ohio were free and therefore was unaware that he was transporting escaped slaves. The Court was not persuaded and upheld the fine. In *Ableman*, Taney overruled the Wisconsin Supreme Court's invalidation of the federal Fugitive Slave Act. Taney stated that the federal government "must be supreme and strong enough to execute its own laws by its own tribunals." Therefore, states must enforce the federal Fugitive Slave Act. *Kentucky v. Dennison* involved the refusal of William Dennison, the governor of Ohio, to extradite from a free state to a slave state a free black who had helped a slave. Taney ruled that the federal government could not force extradition, but that states should extradite as a matter of good will.

Scott's Bid for Freedom

Although the cases dealing with the slave trade and fugitive slaves are significant, the most important case regarding slavery was *Scott v. Sandford* (1857). This case involved Dred Scott, a slave who lived with John Emerson in Illinois and in a part of the Missouri territory that later became Minnesota. Upon Emerson's death, Scott sued for his freedom, claiming that he was a free man because he had lived in free areas although he had returned to the state of Missouri. In 1850 a lower court granted Scott freedom. In 1852 the Missouri Supreme Court overruled the lower state court, making Scott a slave again. Because Scott was legally a slave again, he was the "property" of John Sanford (the name was misspelled on the suit), a resident of New

York. Scott sued again in federal court because his case was now a suit between residents of two different states.

Chief Justice Taney wrote the majority opinion. The first major argument in his decision was whether Scott had standing to sue. To sue, one had to be a citizen, and Taney ruled that no African American could be considered a citizen of the United States because the Constitution of 1787 did not include African Americans. Taney wrote that African Americans were "not included and were not intended to be included, under the word 'citizens' in the Constitution, and can therefore claim none of the privileges which that instrument provides and secures to the citizens of the United States." Without standing to sue, Scott could not obtain his freedom.

Taney could have stopped right there, but he insisted that the Court could correct mistakes made by lower courts. The mistake he sought to correct was the Court's earlier acceptance of the constitutionality of banning slavery in the territories. Taney argued that Article IV of the Constitution, which gave the federal government power over territories, applied only to territories held at the time of the adoption of the Constitution. Therefore, Scott was never free, even when he was in the Missouri territory.

Because of the Civil War and the adoption of the Thirteenth Amendment in 1865, slavery ceased being a major issue before the Court. After the Thirteenth Amendment's passage, however, the Court made some significant decisions interpreting its meaning. In the *Civil Rights Cases* (1883), which dealt with a section of the Civil Rights Act of 1875, the Court ruled that the Thirteenth Amendment prevented only slavery, not discrimination against African Americans. In *Plessy v. Ferguson* (1896), the Court made essentially the same argument, saying the Thirteenth Amendment was "intended primarily to abolish slavery as it had been previously known in this country and that it equally forbid Mexican peonage or the Chinese Coolie trade, when they amounted to slavery or involuntary servitude."

Michael L. Coulter

Further Reading

James Oliver Horton and Lois E. Horton's *Slavery and the Making of America* (New York: Oxford University Press, 2004) examines the central role that slavery played in the development of the American political system and the rise of sectional interests. Robert McCloskey's *The American Supreme Court,* revised by Sanford Levinson (3d ed. Chicago: University of Chicago Press, 2000), includes a useful discussion of the Taney court and its decisions on slavery. Timothy S. Huebner's *The Taney Court: Justices, Rulings, and Legacy* (Santa Barbara, Calif.: ABC-Clio, 2003) is a comprehensive reference work on the Court that passed down the Dred Scott decision. Don E. Fehrenbacher's *The Dred Scott Case: Its Significance in American Law and Politics* (New York: Oxford University Press, 2001) examines that ruling more closely.

Thomas West's *Vindicating the Founders: Race, Sex, Class, and Justice in the Origins of America* (Lanham: Rowman & Littlefield, 1997) has a chapter on slavery and the founding in which the author argues that the Taney court misinterpreted the Framers on slavery. *Africans in America* by Charles Johnson and Patricia Smith (New York: Harcourt Brace, 1998) is a fascinating history of slavery in the United States. Helen Kromer's *Amistad: The Slave Uprising Aboard the Spanish Schooner* (Cleveland, Ohio: Pilgrim Press, 1997) provides an excellent account of *The Amistad* and the case that went before the Court. Historian John Hope Franklin provides a detailed account of slavery in the United States and discusses the impact of Supreme Court decisions on slavery in his *From Slavery to Freedom: A History of African Americans* (New York: McGraw-Hill, 1994).

For an in-depth study of the Dred Scott case, consult *"Dred Scott v. Sandford": A Brief History with Documents,* edited by Paul Finkelman (New York: St. Martin's Press, 1997).

SEE ALSO *Civil Rights Cases*; Daniel, Peter V.; Fifteenth Amendment; Peonage; *Plessy v. Ferguson*; Reconstruction; *Scott v. Sandford*; Taney, Roger Brooke; Thirteenth Amendment.

Smith Act

DATE: 1940

DESCRIPTION: Antisedition law adopted in 1940 to deal with the perceived threats of communism and fascism.

SIGNIFICANCE: Smith Act prosecutions were the occasion for many of the Supreme Court's most important free speech decisions.

The Smith Act criminalizes advocating or teaching the overthrow of the government by force or other illegal or violent means. The crime established is similar to the old common-law crime of sedition. Because the essence of the offense is speaking or publishing alone, prosecutions under the Smith Act always involve free speech issues. The first important case under the act, brought against the top eleven leaders of the Communist Party of the United States, resulted in a conviction upheld by the Supreme Court in *Dennis v. United States* (1951).

However, the act did not fare well in subsequent decisions because of the Court's concern for freedom of speech. In *Brandenburg v. Ohio* (1968), the Court established the rule that no one may be convicted of violating the act unless the government can show that the defendant's speech or publication explicitly advocated specific illegal acts and that it created a clear and present danger that the acts would take place. This narrow test places a very heavy burden on the prosecution, so heavy that there were no successful federal sedition prosecutions under the Smith Act after *Brandenburg*.

Robert Jacobs

SEE ALSO Bad tendency test; *Brandenburg v. Ohio*; Cold War; Espionage acts; *Schenck v. United States*; Sedition Act of 1798; Seditious libel; Speech and press, freedom of.

Smith v. Allwright

Citation: 321 U.S. 649
Date: April 3, 1944
Issue: White primaries
Significance: The Supreme Court held that excluding African Americans from primaries was an unconstitutional violation of the Fourteenth and Fifteenth Amendments.

In *Grovey v. Townsend* (1935), the Supreme Court found that the federal government had no authority over primaries, which were under the direction of private political parties. In *United States v. Classic* (1941), however, the Court ruled that Congress could ensure the integrity of primaries when they were an integral part of the process for electing members of Congress. Encouraged by *Classic*, Lonnie Smith, an African American dentist of Houston, sued an election judge for refusing to allow him to vote in a Democratic primary. Thurgood Marshall, counsel for the National Association for the Advancement of Colored People, argued the case on behalf of Smith.

By an 8-1 margin, the Court reversed *Grovey*. Taking a broad view of state action, Justice Stanley F. Reed reasoned that primaries were "conducted by the party under state statutory authority," which meant that the party's discrimination constituted a form of state action. Because the state had established many rules for the primaries, the state had endorsed and participated in the abridgment of the right to vote because of race, which violated the Fifteenth Amendment. Justice Owen J. Roberts, the author of the majority opinion in *Grovey*, dissented.

The *Smith* decision is considered one of the major victories of the early Civil Rights movement. It was especially significant in the development of the public function concept, which views many activities as state actions even when performed by private actors. Texas Democrats tried to circumvent *Smith* by establishing the Jaybird Democratic Association, but the effort was invalidated in *Terry v. Adams* (1953), the last of the white primary cases.

Thomas Tandy Lewis

See also Fifteenth Amendment; Grandfather clause; Marshall, Thurgood; Poll taxes; Race and discrimination; Roberts, Owen J.; State action.

Solicitor General

Description: Person appointed by the president to represent the U.S. government before the Supreme Court.

Significance: The solicitor general decides which cases the government should ask the Court to review and determines the government's position on those cases. The office is so influential that the solicitor general is sometimes referred to as the "tenth justice."

The solicitor general, while formally a member of the executive branch, is a very important participant in Supreme Court activities. The person in this office is considered not only as an officer of the executive branch but also as an officer of the Court. The solicitor general is one of only two government officials who have responsibilities in two branches. Therefore, although the solicitor general is a member of the Justice Department, he or she also has chambers at the Court. In fact, the solicitor general is often given the informal title of "tenth justice." Several solicitors general, including William H. Taft, Stanley F. Reed, Robert H. Jackson, and Thurgood Marshall, later became members of the Court.

The Solicitor General's Role

The office of solicitor general was created by Congress in 1870, as part of its effort to provide "a staff of law officers sufficiently numerous and of sufficient ability to transact this law business of Government in all parts of the United States." Before the creation of this office, the duties fulfilled by the solicitor general were carried out by the attorney general. The solicitor general is the only officer of the federal government required by law to be "of sufficient learning, ability, and experience" in the practice of law.

The solicitor general is the chief courtroom lawyer of the executive branch. With a staff of two dozen attorneys, the solicitor general petitions for hearings, prepares briefs and supporting data, and argues the government's case before the Court. These arguments are usually presented by a member of the solicitor general's staff. Particularly important cases (maybe six or seven times a term) will be argued by the solicitor general. By tradition, when presenting oral arguments to the Court, members of the solicitor general's office wear charcoal gray morning coats.

Probably the most important function of the solicitor general is to decide which of the many cases involving the federal government and issues of importance to it are appealed to the Court. This is particularly important because 70 percent to 80 percent of the *certiorari* petitions presented by the solicitor general are granted, versus 2 percent to 3 percent of all others. Therefore, for every petition for a writ of *certiorari* presented by the solicitor general, five requests from federal agencies are rejected.

A very special relationship exists between the Court and the solicitor general. The Court will often seek out assistance from the solicitor general, even in cases in which the federal government is not involved. The solicitor general is regularly invited by the Court to submit briefs in such cases. In addition, the solicitor general is the only officer of the Court submitting *amicus curiae* briefs who is regularly given time to argue before the Court. Finally, when a member of the Court passes away, it is the solicitor general who calls for a meeting of the Court bar to honor him or her.

Success and Sources of Influence

Not only does the solicitor general enjoy a great deal of success in getting the Court to hear cases, but these cases are very often decided in the government's favor. By one count of cases in which the solicitor general was involved, either directly or through *amicus* briefs, the federal government won 70 percent of the time. The solicitor general participates in about two-thirds of all the cases fully considered by the Court and is an extremely powerful actor before it.

This influence arises largely because of the very close relationship between the solicitor general and the Court. Given the sheer volume of solicitor general involvement, it is not surprising that the solicitor general is well known and respected by members of the Court. They assume that the solicitor general argues cases before the Court only if the merits are very strong. Given the large pool of cases brought to the solicitor general's office by the various agencies, the solicitor general is free to choose only those cases that are most likely to be successful.

The solicitor general's office also brings important strengths to the relationship. The solicitor general, unlike virtually anyone else who appears before the Court, has an intimate knowledge of the members based on lengthy interaction. Furthermore, the Court will often defer to the judgment of the solicitor general, who is the official legal voice of the federal government. The Court is also likely to place the interests of the nation, as expressed by the solicitor general, above other interests.

Although the unique role of the solicitor general before the Court is widely acknowledged, there is not complete consensus on what that role should be. It has historically been assumed that the solicitor general would be above partisanship, but some presidents have attempted to use the office of solicitor general to achieve narrow partisan goals. President Ronald Reagan, for example, pushed his first solicitor general, Rex Lee, to persuade Court members to change their views on a number of major social issues, such as abortion, affirmative action, and school prayer. In general, however, solicitors general attempted to act much more as the legal conscience of the government than as partisan spokespersons for the administration. This is probably the most fundamental explanation for the success of the solicitor general before the Court.

Eduardo Magalhaes III

Further Reading

Caplan, Lincoln. *The Tenth Justice: The Solicitor General and the Rule of Law.* New York: Vintage Books, 1987.

Salokar, Rebecca Mae. *The Solicitor General: The Politics of Law.* Philadelphia: Temple University Press, 1992.

Ubertaccio, Peter N. *Learned in the Law and Politics: The Office of the Solicitor General and Executive Power.* New York: LFB Scholarly Publications, 2005.

See also Briefs; *Certiorari*, writ of; Clerks of the justices; Hughes, Charles Evans; Jackson, Robert H.; Marshall, Thurgood; Reed, Stanley F.; Taft, William H.

David H. Souter

Identification: Associate justice (October 9, 1990-)
Nominated by: George H. W. Bush
Born: September 17, 1939, Melrose, Massachusetts
Significance: As a replacement for William J. Brennan, Jr., the Supreme Court's leading liberal, Republican Souter was expected to move the Court in a more conservative direction. Although he voted with the conservative bloc during his freshman term, he later moderated his views, becoming more liberal than most Court observers had predicted.

An only child, David H. Souter moved with his parents to Weare, New Hampshire, when he was eleven years old. Except for his college years, he lived in Weare until his appointment to the Supreme Court. He graduated from Harvard University magna cum laude in 1961, then spent the next two years at Oxford University studying law and philosophy on a Rhodes scholarship. After receiving a degree from Harvard Law School in 1966, Souter practiced law for two years before becoming assistant attorney general of New Hampshire. He was named the state's attorney general in 1976 and served in that capacity until 1978. He then served as a judge on the state trial court for five years. In 1983, New Hampshire governor John Sununu appointed Souter to the state supreme court, on which he served for seven years. A frugal bachelor who followed a reclusive lifestyle in rural New Hampshire, he acquired the reputation of being rather elusive.

President George H. W. Bush appointed Souter to the U.S. Court of Appeals for the First Circuit in 1990. On July 3, 1990, before Souter had a chance to write a single appeals court opinion, Bush nominated him as associate justice to the Supreme Court. So little was known about the relatively obscure judge from New Hampshire that he was described as a "Stealth nominee." Souter had never published a book or even a law review article, and his two hundred opinions for the New Hampshire Supreme Court raised few constitutional questions. During his confirmation hearings before the Senate Judiciary Committee, however, Souter impressed the senators with his demeanor and knowledge of constitutional law. Defining his judicial temperament as moderate and undogmatic, he rejected the notion that the Court should adhere to the original intent of the Framers of the Constitution, and he defended the doctrine of *stare decisis,* or adherence to precedents, within the common law tradition. He endorsed many of the decisions of the Court under Earl Warren concerning criminal defendant rights, believing that the Court must sometimes take an active role in fashioning practical solutions to guarantee constitutional rights. The Senate confirmed his nomination by the confortable margin of ninety to nine.

Jurisprudence and Decisions

After Souter became a Supreme Court justice, his pragmatic approach to constitutional interpretation set him apart from his conservative Republican-appointed colleagues. He soon began to demonstrate a firm commitment to libertarian values of the First Amendment. Within two years, he was often joining with the more liberal members of the Court. In the highly publicized case, *Planned Parenthood of Southeastern Pennsylvania v. Casey* (1992), Souter was part of the five-member majority that reaffirmed the central holding of *Roe v. Wade* (1973), recognizing a woman's right to terminate an unwanted pregnancy. In addition to the importance of precedents, Souter explicitly located this right to privacy in a substantive due process reading of the Fourteenth Amendment. Concurring in *Washington v. Glucksberg* (1997), when the Court upheld laws banning physician-assisted suicides, Souter emphasized that all right-to-die cases should be grounded in the doctrine of substantive due process, which protects individuals from "arbitrary restraints" by government.

Souter again applied the substantive due process doctrine in *Lawrence v. Texas* (2003), joining the majority to strike down state laws that criminalized homosexual practices among consenting adults. Souter's method frequently was to balance competing constitutional interests. In 1995, he recognized that private organizers of an Irish parade in Boston had rights of expressive association that precluded the state from forcing them to allow participation by gays and lesbians. However, in *Boy Scouts of America v. Dale* (2000), he argued that this principle did not permit the Boy Scouts to ignore a state law and discriminate against gays, especially since the organization had not explicitly proclaimed its institutional opposition to homosexuality.

In the many 5-4 votes of the later years of the Rehnquist Court, Souter was almost always in agreement with the liberals. Consistently favoring a high wall between religion and government, he opposed the use of tax-supported vouchers in parochial schools in *Zelman v. Simmons-Harris* (2002), arguing that the program allowed tax money to fund religious indoctrination. He apparently never opposed any affirmative action program; thus, in *Adarand Constructors v. Peña* (1995) he opposed evaluating such programs by the strict scrutiny standard. In *Grutter v. Bollinger* (2003), he agreed with the majority's view that the goal of racial diversity in universities provides an adequate rationale to allow preferences based on race. In 2002, he joined a six-member majority to find that execution of persons with mental disabilities violated the Eighth Amendment, and in *Roper v. Simmons* (2005), he joined a five-member majority to ban executions of minors. Souter also disagreed with the emphasis that the five more conservative justices gave to states' rights in cases such as *Kelo v. City of New London* (2005).

In 2000, Justice Souter found the dispute about the election results in Florida to be quite frustrating. He dissented in *Bush v. Gore*, when the five more conservative justices ordered an end to the recount of votes, thereby ensuring George W. Bush's victory. Although he agreed with the majority's view that the process of the recount was unconstitutional, he argued that the Court had no authority to intervene and that Florida's high court should have been given more time to work out a constitutional way to supervise a recount.

John Fliter
Revised and updated by the Editor

Further Reading

Fliter, John A. "The Jurisprudential Evolution of Justice David Souter." *Southeastern Political Review* 26 (December, 1998): 725-754.

______. "Keeping the Faith: Justice David Souter and the First Amendment Religion Clauses." *Journal of Church and State* 40 (Spring, 1998): 387-409.

Hensley, Thomas R. *The Rehnquist Court: Justices, Rulings, and Legacy.* Santa Barbara, Calif.: ABC-Clio, 2006.

Tushnet, Mark. *A Court Divided: The Rehnquist Court and the Future of Constitutional Law.* New York: W. W. Norton, 2005.

Yarbrough, Tinsley E. *David Hackett Souter: Traditional Republican on the Rehnquist Court.* New York: Oxford University Press, 2005.

See also *Bush v. Gore*; Constitutional interpretation; Constitutional law; *Gratz v. Bollinger/Grutter v. Bollinger*; Nominations to the Court; *Planned Parenthood of Southeastern Pennsylvania v. Casey*; Rehnquist, William H.

Freedom of Speech and Press

Description: Constitutional rights to speak freely and to publish one's views, free of government censorship.

Significance: Viewed by most scholars and citizens alike as the very foundation of all other constitutional rights, freedom of speech and freedom of the press are American ideals, indispensable to the democracy, and the subject of many Supreme Court cases.

When most Americans consider the U.S. Constitution, the Bill of Rights, or the Supreme Court, inevitably they think about freedom of speech and freedom of the press. These twin freedoms, expressly guaranteed in the First Amendment, represent the quintessential liberties on which the United States was founded. Asked to enumerate the rights protected by the Constitution, the vast majority of Americans would readily name free speech and free press. Asked to articulate what sets the United States apart from all other nations, most Americans would identify these same freedoms.

Respect and pride for freedom of speech and freedom of the press are sincere and heartfelt—until tested in the harsh reality of the tumultuous and diverse culture, in which a wide array of political, religious, social, economic, ideological, racial, ethnic, and geographical constituencies are pitted against one another. In that crucible, pious fidelity to "free speech" and "free press" too often gives way to the inevitable qualification.

The Struggle to Protect Freedom of Speech and Press

What almost inevitably follows is an ever-increasing list of exceptions to freedom of speech and freedom of the press, including not only the small group of exceptions recognized in the law, such as obscenity, libel, fighting words, false advertising, and criminal solicitation, but also newly proposed exceptions, such as hate speech, sexual harassment, offensive or sacrilegious art, and sexually explicit yet nonobscene photographs, magazines, videos, and Internet images.

When it comes to freedom of the press, the general public and the juries on which they serve sometimes ignore the First Amendment and hold books, films, and television shows financially liable for the acts of disturbed individuals and social miscreants who commit suicide, violent crimes, or general mayhem allegedly "inspired" by what they read or saw in a film or on television.

It is in this contentious atmosphere that the Supreme Court continues to serve its historic role in interpreting the meaning, scope, and limitations of freedom of speech and freedom of the press.

The Meaning of Freedom of Speech and Press

Generally speaking, "freedom of speech" refers to the right of individuals to freely express themselves, without fear of government restrictions. "Freedom of the press" refers more to the right of the publishers of newspapers, magazines, and books; the writers and producers of motion pictures and television productions; and the creators and distributors of CDs to sell and distribute these materials, free of government censorship. Beyond this general distinction, for constitutional purposes, scholarly analysis and Supreme Court decisions often merge the two concepts under the rubric "freedom of expression," frequently applying principles developed in one area to the other. In free press cases, civil libertarians and attorneys will readily cite precedents that advance constitutional protections in free speech cases, and vice versa.

Although the First Amendment speaks in absolute and unqualified terms ("Congress shall make no law abridging . . . freedom of speech or of the press"), the question has always been what is meant by "freedom of speech" or "freedom of the press." There is a school of thought, to which only two justices, Hugo L. Black and William O. Douglas, adhered, that holds that with respect to speech and the press, the First Amendment is absolute; it means what it says: "Congress shall make *no* law . . ."—not "some laws" or "almost no laws," but "no law." First Amendment absolutists simply cite the language of the First Amendment and accept no substitutes.

The other school of thought, to which all other justices have subscribed, believes that at the time the First Amendment was ratified, there were certain limited exceptions to freedom of speech and freedom of the press, which were already part of these concepts when they were included in the First Amendment. Thus, for example, in America in 1791, there were libel laws under which people could be punished for what they wrote or said about someone else if it was false and defamatory. Likewise, there were obscenity laws under which publishers could be fined or jailed for selling books or pictures deemed obscene under prevailing standards. Given the existence of these laws at the time the First Amendment was adopted and ratified, the majority view rejects the absolutist approach in favor of an interpretation that affords the broadest sweep of constitutional protection for all subject matter and forms of communications, subject only to limited exceptions.

Consequently, the Court has held that the First Amendment protects motion pictures, radio, television, cable, recordings, and most recently the Internet, regardless of the fact that none of this technology existed when the First Amendment was written. No justice seriously argues that the First Amendment is frozen in the eighteenth century in terms of the forms of communications that existed at that time. Instead, the Court takes a functional view of freedom of speech and freedom of the press to encompass any form of communication that provides information much as books and newspapers did in 1791.

Theories of Freedom of Expression

A variety of theories have been offered for the protection of freedom of expression. One is that truth is best discovered by the free exchange of ideas. In his seminal 1644 work *Areopagitica*, John Milton confidently asked that if truth and falsehood grappled, "Who ever knew Truth put to the worse, in a free and open encounter?" In 1919 Justice Oliver Wendell Holmes wrote that "the best test of truth is the power of the thought to get itself accepted in the competition of the market." No metaphor has proved more lasting in the defense of free expression than the "marketplace of ideas."

Another important rationale upholding freedom of expression is based on the principles of human dignity and autonomy. The opportunity to freely express oneself develops inner satisfaction and individual fulfillment. In this view, freedom of expression is worthy of

Officers of the American Civil Liberties Union celebrating a favorable Supreme Court ruling in 1939. Appearing before the Court more often than any other nongovernment organization, the ACLU has often championed free speech. (Library of Congress)

constitutional protection as a step toward the realization of self-identity or what Justice Thurgood Marshall called "a spirit that demands self-expression." This rationale has nothing to do with the search for truth or the advancement of self-government. Instead, it justifies free expression based purely on its benefit to the individual.

At the other end of the spectrum is a rationale based on the common good rather than the good of the individual. Under this view, freedom of expression is indispensable to the progress of self-governance in a democratic society. For citizens to participate fully in their own government they need to exchange information and express their opinions on pending legislation, candidates, and public policy issues. Only open and unfettered communication, free of the distortions produced by government censorship, ensures the viability of democracy.

The final rationale supporting freedom of expression is closely related to the advancement of self-government but focuses on the value of dissent. Whereas the theory of self-governance looks at the role of free expression among those working *within* the system, the dissent rationale recognizes the value of those who work *outside* the system. Sometimes referred to as the "loyal opposition," dissident speech is protected because of the realization that by allowing opponents of the established order to peacefully and freely express themselves, the risk of violent opposition is reduced and perhaps eliminated. Tolerating, or even encouraging, dissent serves as a "safety valve" preventing the political system from getting "overheated."

Majority Rule and Minority Rights

Disputes over freedom of expression generally pit the rule of the majority against the rights of the minority. The question is whether the expression of ideas deemed dangerous to the purpose of ensuring order, morality, loyalty, or some other important interest valued by society at large should be suppressed. Examples of these conflicts abound through the annals of the Supreme Court.

In the early 1970's, American Nazis announced their intent to conduct a march through Skokie, Illinois, a suburb of Chicago, inhabited by a large number of Jewish families, including survivors of the Holocaust. The march seemed purposely designed to deeply offend the Jewish community in Skokie. The city officials took various steps to block the march, but the Nazis, represented by the American Civil Liberties Union (ACLU), went to court, claiming they had a right to express their views, regardless of whether they gave offense. The ACLU was attacked for representing such despicable bigots and reportedly lost thirty thousand members. Nevertheless, the ACLU stood by the principle that regardless of whether it disagreed with the Nazis, it would defend their right to speak and march. Eventually, the federal courts agreed that the First Amendment protected the Nazis' freedom of expression. Ironically, having won the right to march, the Nazis chose not to hold the event.

Another issue is whether the government can deny funding to artists because of the controversial or offensive nature of their work. This issue was squarely presented in 1991 when Congress imposed content restrictions on the grants awarded by the National Endowment for the Arts (NEA), a federal agency established in 1965 to further the progress of the arts. Congressional leaders claimed that artists could create all the controversial art they wanted, they simply had no constitutional right to demand that the government pay for it. Civil libertarians countered that once the government decided to provide funds for artists through the NEA, it could not condition those funds on whether the government agreed or disagreed with the artistic, political, religious, social, or other messages communicated by the art. Eventually, the courts agreed with the artists and struck down the congressional restrictions. The Supreme Court held that the NEA could establish goals encouraging "decency" and respect for diverse American values but could not reject specific works of art based on their controversial content.

Every advance in technology has renewed the battle over freedom of expression. Most recently, the conflict has centered on the Internet, the revolutionary worldwide web. In 1996 Congress passed the Communications Decency Act (CDA) making it a crime to communicate "indecent" material to persons under eighteen years old. The ACLU promptly challenged the CDA, first before a federal three-judge panel and later before the Supreme Court.

The Court had never ruled on a case involving freedom of expression on the Internet. The CDA case squarely presented the question of whether the Internet would enjoy the same wide-open, robust constitutional protection accorded to books, newspapers, and magazines or the more restricted, narrow protection granted to television and radio. In other words, the Court had to decide whether the print model or the broadcast model would apply to the Internet. In 1998 the Supreme Court established the Internet model. The Court found that the Internet was a vast marketplace of ideas entitled to the widest possible constitutional protection. With respect to the CDA, the Court held that the adult population could not be reduced to what is acceptable for children. In the absence of effective age verification technology, the Court found that the responsibility for protecting children from indecent material on the Internet rested with their parents, not the government.

Even before the Internet, sexually explicit speech in books, art, films, and home videos has proven to be a perplexing subject for public debate and Court review. No other area of First Amendment litigation has prompted such heated and persistent controversy, pitting libertines against moralists. By 1968 the Court had adopted a three-part test for defining obscenity: sexually explicit material could not be banned unless it appealed to a prurient, or morbid, interest in sex; exceeded contemporary community standards; and was utterly without redeeming social value.

In 1973, in the case of *Miller v. California*, the Court recast the third prong (in an apparent effort to expand the scope of unprotected obscenity). Under *Miller*, material could be banned if it lacked "serious literary, artistic, political, or scientific value." Although one leading First Amendment scholar optimistically entitled his 1969 book *The End of Obscenity*, federal and state governments continue to prosecute material deemed obscene, while at the same time, the adult video business is thriving. Given the power and mystery of sex, on one hand, and the tendency of legislators to pass laws they believe are necessary to protect people from themselves on the other, the controversy over obscenity is unlikely to end in the near future.

The Court held that generally laws that punish defamation do not violate the First Amendment, except when it comes to public officials and public figures. Defamation, which encompasses libel (the written word, as well as radio and television), is defined as a false statement of fact that holds someone up to shame and humiliation. The defamation of a private person implicates little or no First Amendment concerns. However, allowing an individual or a publisher to be punished for attacking an elected official or a celebrity or famous person tends to suppress the sort of public criticism that is at the heart of the First Amendment.

In 1964 the Court faced a historic dispute that presented these important issues in the case of *New York Times Co. v. Sullivan.* At the height of the Civil Rights movement, a group called the Committee to Defend Martin Luther King took out an ad in *The New York Times* condemning racism and the actions of the officials in Montgomery, Alabama. One of the officials, L. B. Sullivan, sued for libel and won a $500,000 judgment against the *Times.* The Court overturned the verdict and established powerful protection for freedom of the press.

In a groundbreaking opinion by Justice William J. Brennan, Jr., the Court held that the freedom to criticize the government was so important, and the possibility that journalists might make innocent mistakes was so great, that defamation suits against public officials could not go forward unless the official proved that the defamatory statement was made with what the Court called "actual malice," that is, knowledge of falsity or reckless disregard for the truth. Nothing less, according to Justice Brennan's eloquent opinion, would serve the "profound national commitment to the principle that debate on public issues should be uninhibited, robust, and wide-open."

Freedom of speech encompasses not only what is spoken and written but also actions that are intended to communicate a message, such as burning a draft card to protest a war or burning a U.S. flag to express disagreement with government policy. Symbolic speech, as these expressive activities are called, is entitled to constitutional protection when it does not involve violence or destruction of private property, because it conveys, often in a most dramatic fashion, political, social, and other ideas.

In 1989, in *Texas v. Johnson,* Justice Brennan, speaking for the majority of the Court, characterized as "a bedrock principle underlying the First Amendment" that "the Government may not prohibit the expression of an idea simply because society finds the idea itself offensive or disagreeable." Justice Brennan suggested that there was "no more appropriate response to burning a flag than waving one's own."

One of the greatest threats to freedom of expression is prior restraint. This term refers to any effort by government to suppress speech even before it is published. The history of England is stained by examples of the Crown preventing books and newspapers from being printed. Indeed, the origin of modern copyright laws was a system of royal licensing with permission bestowed only on those publishers favored by the rulers. Many scholars argue that the essential purpose of the First Amendment was to prohibit prior restraint. If so, it has fulfilled that goal admirably because the Court has never upheld a prior restraint. In the landmark case involving the Pentagon Papers, a series of secret U.S. Defense Department studies on the Vietnam War, the Court rejected the request of the administration of Richard M. Nixon to enjoin *The New York Times* and *The Washington Post* from publishing the controversial reports. What the king of England could have done with a stroke of a pen, the First Amendment prohibited the U.S. government from doing.

Speech Codes

Although American campuses in the 1960's were a hotbed of freedom and openness, by the 1990's the antithesis emerged at many colleges and universities in the form of speech codes. These campus regulations prohibited, usually in broad and ambiguous terms, speech that was offensive to women and minorities. However, from the standpoint of freedom of expression, campus speech codes posed a serious threat. With little precedent and even less guidance, neither students nor faculty members could tell what sort of statements could get them in trouble.

Self-censorship out of fear of punishment is often referred to as the "chilling effect" caused by government regulation of speech. Because most people will steer clear of punishment, they will refrain from making statements or publishing material that is constitutionally protected for fear they may run afoul of the government. When this happens, freedom of expression suffers. This is one of the primary reasons that laws or regulations affecting speech must be written with great certainty and cannot be vague or ambiguous.

Campus speech codes were generally far from clear and certain.

They usually spoke of speech that was "offensive," "degrading" or "hostile," terms that were highly subjective and lacked any objective definition. Consequently, the courts have consistently struck down campus speech codes when they were challenged on First Amendment grounds. Generally, the courts found that controversial ideas were at risk of being censored in the name of combating racism, sexism, and bigotry.

Justice Oliver Wendell Holmes wrote that the true purpose of the First Amendment was to protect the ideas Americans hate. Justice Louis D. Brandeis believed that the answer to offensive speech was *more* speech, not *less.* In other words, in a democratic society, committed to freedom of expression, the remedy to social evils is free and open debate.

Stephen F. Rohde

Further Reading

Freedom of speech and press is a broad subject that can be explored through studies of the First Amendment, such as Daniel A. Farber's *The First Amendment* (2d ed. New York: Foundation Press, 2003) and Geoffrey R. Stone's *The First Amendment* (2d ed. New York: Aspen, 2003). Ken I. Kersch's *Freedom of Speech: Rights and Liberties Under theLaw* (Santa Barbara, Calif.: ABC-Clio, 2003) extends that approach to examine free speech as a fundamental right of citizenship. Stephen F. Rohde's edition of *Webster's New World American Words of Freedom* (New York: Hungry Minds, 2001) is a concise collection of foundation documents relating to basic freedoms, with commentaries.

Louis E. Ingelhart's *Press and Speech Freedoms in the World, from Antiquity Until 1998: A Chronology* (Westport, Conn.: Greenwood Press, 1998) takes an international approach, covering the concept of freedom of speech and press from ancient times until the modern period. Margaret A. Blanchard's *Revolutionary Sparks: Freedom of Expression in Modern America* (New York: Oxford University Press, 1992) also takes a historical approach, covering the concept from the beginning to the end of the twentieth century. *The First Freedom Today: Critical Issues Relating to Censorship and to Intellectual Freedom* (Chicago: American Library Association, 1984), edited by Robert B. Downs and Ralph E. McCoy, also covers the history of the concept but provides numerous essays examining the modern issues and controversies involving the First Amendment rights.

Two books concentrating on the origin and meaning of the First Amendment are *The First Amendment: The Legacy of George Mason* (London: Associated University Presses, 1985), edited by T. Daniel Shumate, and George Anastaplo's *The Constitutionalist: Notes on the First Amendment* (Dallas: Southern Methodist University Press, 1971).

See also Brandeis, Louis D.; Brennan, William J., Jr.; Censorship; Douglas, William O.; First Amendment; Flag desecration; *Gitlow v. New York*; Hate speech; Holmes, Oliver Wendell; Sedition Act of 1798; Seditious libel; Smith Act; Symbolic speech; Vietnam War; *Virginia v. Black*.

Standing

Description: A jurisdictional requirement in federal court that a litigant have been injured or threatened with imminent injury by the governmental action of which he or she complains. Sometimes called "standing to sue."

Significance: The Court is frequently suspected of using this procedural device, designed to restrict access to the federal courts to plaintiffs who have sufficiently significant stakes in the outcome of litigation, to affect the substantive outcome of cases by allowing it to hear a particular case or to avoid deciding a difficult one.

Unlike the other federal justiciability doctrines—mootness, ripeness, political question, and the ban on advisory opinions—standing focuses primarily on the party bringing an issue before the court and only secondarily on the issues the party seeks to adjudicate. To have standing, any litigant raising an issue in federal court must meet three constitutionally mandated requirements: injury, causation, and redressability. In addition, the Supreme Court has imposed nonconstitutional, or "prudential," restrictions, prohibiting third-party claims and generalized grievances. Plaintiffs challenging agency action under a federal statute must satisfy a third prudential requirement: The rights they are attempting to vindicate must fall within the "zone of interests" protected by the statute. The so-called prudential requirements, not being constitutionally mandated, may be waived by Congress.

A variety of reasons have been articulated by the Court and by scholars for the standing requirements. By requiring that a plaintiff have a personal stake in the outcome of a case, standing was said in *Baker v. Carr* (1962) to improve judicial decision making by ensuring the "concrete adverseness which sharpens the presentation of issues upon which the court so largely depends for illumination of difficult constitutional questions"; it is also said to promote judicial efficiency by preventing a deluge of lawsuits brought by persons with nothing more than a political or ideological interest in the outcome. By ensuring that plaintiffs can litigate only their own rights, standing is said to promote fairness by excluding meddlers who may be trying to protect the interests of those who do not want or feel the need for such protection. Finally, and probably most important, standing limits the availability of judicial review of congressional and executive decisions and thus promotes the separation of powers, which the Court has called the "single basic idea" of standing in *Allen v. Wright* (1984).

As a jurisdictional requirement, standing cannot be waived by the parties; even when the defendant does not raise it, the court may do so *sua sponte*, or voluntarily, at any stage of the proceedings, even on appeal. If a decision is ultimately made against standing, the case is dismissed, even if the matter has already been decided on the merits by the trial court and has gone through one or two appeals.

INJURY

The Court ruled that a plaintiff must "show he personally has suffered some actual or threatened injury" in *Valley Forge Christian College v. Americans United for Separation of Church and State* (1982). The requirement ensures the existence of an actual dispute between litigants and is at the heart of the standing doctrine. The "personal" component was emphasized in *Sierra Club v. Morton* (1972), where the Court denied standing in an environmental case to an organization that had failed to allege that any of its members had used the land threatened by the challenged governmental policies and therefore could not show any injury to the members. The "actual or threatened" component was explained in *City of Los Angeles v. Lyons* (1983). A black man who had been injured when subjected to a choke hold by police officers was permitted to sue for damages, but he was denied standing to seek an injunction against future use of the life-threatening choke hold by police officers because he could not show that he himself was likely to be subjected to it again.

No rule or defining principle exists to determine what kind of injury will satisfy standing. However, clearly injuries to common law (personal injury, contract, property), constitutional, and statutory rights are sufficient to confer standing. In addition, the court has recognized the fact or threat of criminal prosecution (*Wisconsin v. Yoder,* 1972), economic harm (*Barlow v. Collins,* 1970), and injury to aesthetic interests (*Lujan v. Defenders of Wildlife,* 1972). Injuries that the court has held insufficient to afford standing include stigmatization by a governmental policy of granting tax-exempt status to private schools that discriminate on the basis of race (*Allen v. Wright,* 1984) and a threat to marital happiness because state abortion laws force a choice between refraining from normal sexual relations and endangering the wife's health (*Roe v. Wade,* 1973).

Mere existence of an injury is not enough. A plaintiff must also show that the injury was caused by the governmental action of which he or she complained and is likely to be redressed by the requested relief. Originally treated as a single test in which one or the other must be proved in *Warth v. Seldin* (1975), causation and redressability later became two separate tests, each of which must be established, in *Allen v. Wright.* The concepts are closely enough related that ordinarily either both or neither will be met. *Simon v. Eastern Kentucky Welfare Rights Organization* (1976), for example, involved a challenge to an Internal Revenue Service (IRS) regulation reducing the amount of free medical care that tax-exempt hospitals were required to provide. Plaintiffs argued that they were injured by the denial of needed medical care. The Court nevertheless denied standing because it was "purely speculative" whether the plaintiffs' loss of medical services could be traced to the IRS ruling and because there was no substantial likelihood that victory in the case would ensure the plaintiffs received the hospital care they sought.

No Third-Party Claims

The legal rights and interests asserted must be those of the plaintiff, not those of a third person not a party to the lawsuit. In *Warth v. Seldin* (1975), taxpayers of Rochester, New York, sought to challenge allegedly discriminatory zoning in the suburb of Penfield, alleging that they were injured by higher property-tax rates resulting from Rochester's need to provide additional low-income housing. The Court refused to allow the Rochester taxpayers to assert the constitutional rights of low-income minorities allegedly excluded from Penfield.

Four well-established exceptions exist. First, a third-party claim will be allowed when the third party is unlikely to be able to sue or have an incentive to do so. In *Griswold v. Connecticut* (1965), a physician charged with distributing contraceptives to a married couple was permitted to raise the substantive due process rights of the couple, and in *Powers v. Ohio* (1991), a black criminal defendant convicted by an all-white jury was permitted to raise the rights of black jurors excluded from the jury. Second, a third-party claim may also be allowed when there is a close relationship between the plaintiff and the third party. In *Pierce v. Society of Sisters* (1925), a religious school was permitted to raise the constitutional rights of its students and their parents when the state attempted to require that children attend public school. Third, an association will be permitted to assert the rights of its members, as in *National Association for the Advancement of Colored People v. Alabama* (1958).

A fourth exception to the third-party rule is the overbreadth doctrine. In First Amendment cases, a litigant has been permitted to make a facial challenge to a statute even though the law, if narrowly construed, could constitutionally prohibit the litigant's activity. Such a facial challenge is permitted when the law appears to be overly broad and thus possibly having a chilling effect on constitutionally protected activity. In *Schad v. Borough of Mount Ephraim* (1981), an adult bookstore was prosecuted for presenting nude dancing in an area where the zoning laws excluded all live entertainment. The Court, even while assuming that nude dancing was not protected by the First Amendment, still allowed the store owner to raise in defense the First Amendment rights of others to present constitutionally protected live entertainment.

Other Prudential Requirements

The Court will ordinarily deny standing when a plaintiff's only injury is as a taxpayer or citizen asserting an interest in having the government obey the law. In *Frothingham v. Mellon* (1923), the Court denied standing to a taxpayer who challenged the constitutionality, under the Tenth Amendment, of the Federal Maternity Act of 1921. Although the improper expenditure of taxpayers' money may arguably amount to an injury to an individual taxpayer, her interest was "comparatively minute and indeterminable." In *Schlesinger v. Reservists Committee to Stop the War* (1974), the Court held that plaintiffs in their capacity as U.S. citizens lacked the capacity to challenge, under Article I, section 6, of the Constitution, the practice of allowing members of Congress to hold commissions in the armed forces reserves. In *Flast v. Cohen* (1968), the Court created a narrow exception by allowing standing when the taxpayer alleged that Congress was violating a particular constitutional prohibition, such as the establishment clause of the First Amendment, rather than merely exceeding its delegated powers, as in *Frothingham.*

In cases where a claim is brought under a federal statute and the plaintiff is not directly subject to the contested regulatory action, the Court has established an additional requirement: that the right or interest the plaintiff is attempting to vindicate be within the zone of interests protected or regulated by the statute. The Court stated in *Clarke v. Securities Industries Association* (1987) that the zone-of-interests requirement is not meant to establish a high barrier for plaintiffs and that it is the defendant who bears the burden of proving the congressional intent to preclude judicial review in such cases. This is an example of a congressional waiver of a prudential requirement. The Court's willingness to find standing to challenge an administrative action under a statute, while it would likely deny standing to such a general claim brought under the Constitution, is a reflection of the Court's concern with judicial restraint and its proper role vis-à-vis the other branches.

A Controversial Doctrine

Standing is among the most analyzed and most criticized of judicial doctrines. The Court's treatment of it over the years has been called incoherent, erratic, and bizarre. It has even been suggested that there should be no standing doctrine at all, that the question of standing is part of the merits of the litigant's claim. Much of the problem stems from the Court's inability to develop a consistent philosophy of standing and to relate it to a view of the proper role of the judiciary in a system of checks and balances and of the proper role of a national judiciary in a federal system. Although there is much to be said for the efforts of, particularly, the Burger Court (1969-1986) to respect the separation of powers and to avoid unnecessary judicial intervention in the affairs of the other branches of government, it should be recognized that an overly narrow view of standing will deny legitimate litigants their day in court.

William V. Dunlap

Further Reading

Fairly detailed surveys of the standing doctrine may be found in the standard general treatises on U.S. constitutional law. A particularly comprehensive and useful example is the four-volume work by Ronald D. Rotunda and John E. Nowak, *Treatise on Constitutional Law: Substance and Procedure* (2d ed. Vol 1. St. Paul, Minn.: West Publishing, 1992). A briefer review is available in Rotunda and Nowak's one–volume edition, *Constitutional Law* (7th ed. St. Paul, Minn.: Thomson/ West, 2004). Other reliable single-volume treatises include Erwin Chemerinsky's *Constitutional Law, Principles and Policies* (New York: Aspen Law & Business, 1997) and Charles Alan Wright's *The Law of Federal Courts* (St. Paul, Minn.: West Publishing, 1994). Lawrence H. Tribe's *American Constitutional Law* (3d ed. Mineola, N.Y.: Foundation Press, 2000) offers a somewhat different organizational perspective.

Most of the serious analysis and criticism of the doctrine is to be found in the law reviews. Among the more interesting and influential commentaries is Antonin Scalia's defense (before he became a Supreme Court justice) of a narrow concept of standing in "The Doctrine of Standing as an Essential Element of the Separation of Powers," *Suffolk Law Review* 17 (1983), and two arguments for a broader approach, Mark Tushnet's "The New Law of Standing, a Plea for Abandonment," *Cornell Law Review* 62 (1977) and William Fletcher's "The Structure of Standing," *Yale Law Journal* 98 (1988). A well-reasoned critique of the ban on generalized grievances can be found in Donald Doernberg's "We the People: John Locke, Collective Constitutional Rights, and Standing to Challenge Government Action," *California Law Review* 73 (1985). A particularly interesting and creative proposal helped to shape the view of a generation of law students such as Christopher D. Stone, who wrote "Should Trees Have Standing?—Toward Legal Rights for Natural Objects," *Southern California Law Review* 45 (1972).

See also Advisory opinions; *Baker v. Carr*; *Clinton v. City of New York*; *Griswold v. Connecticut*; Judicial review; *National Association for the Advancement of Colored People v. Alabama*; *Pierce v. Society of Sisters*; Political questions; *Roe v. Wade*; Separation of powers; *Wisconsin v. Yoder*; Zoning.

State Action

Description: Actions for which the state government has some responsibility, whether by causing, requiring, or sanctioning their occurrence. Synonymous with "under the color of state law."

Significance: For the Supreme Court to find discrimination unconstitutional under the Fourteenth Amendment, the unequal treatment must be demonstrated to be the product of an action supported by the power or authority of the state. Otherwise, the discrimination is considered private, unreachable by the Court.

The Fourteenth Amendment, adopted in 1868, sought to provide equal protection for newly freed African Americans. The amendment stipulates that "No state shall . . . deny to any person . . . the equal protection of the laws." Shortly after its adoption, the Supreme Court had to define precisely who the state was for purposes of barring discriminatory action. Politically, the Court was asked whether the amendment could be used to end private discrimination.

In *Ex parte Virginia* (1880), the Court ruled that the Fourteenth Amendment barred government officials and agencies, in this case a judge, from denying equal protection of the laws. However in the

Civil Rights Cases (1883), the Court ruled narrowly, stating that only discrimination involving a state action could be called unconstitutional. It also rejected the Civil Rights Act of 1875, which barred private discrimination in inns, public conveyances, and places of public amusement. This gave way to the doctrine of separate but equal facilities. Blacks and whites were separated in many places of public accommodation, schools, parks, theaters, restaurants, and hotels.

An Expanded Reading

Not until after World War II did the Court begin to use the doctrine of state action to eliminate private discrimination. In *Shelley v. Kraemer* (1948), the Court prohibited the use of restrictive covenants. The deed provision in this case prohibited the sale of property to buyers of "the Negro or Mongolian race." The Court stated that although the discrimination occurred at the hands of private individuals, the agreements of these individuals were supported by state enforcement and thus sanctioned by state action. The actions of state courts and judicial officers in their official capacities to enforce these covenants was regarded as state action under the Fourteenth Amendment.

In the aftermath of *Shelley v. Kraemer*, the Court continued to provide relief to litigants by expanding its interpretation of the state action doctrine. In *Burton v. Wilmington Parking Authority* (1961), the Court found a private restaurant that refused to serve African Americans a state actor under the Fourteenth Amendment. The Eagle Coffee Shoppe was located in a public parking building owned and operated by the Wilmington Parking Authority, an agency of the state of Delaware. The state leased the land to the restaurant and provided parking for its patrons, thereby creating a symbiotic relationship between the state and the private business. In the Court's opinion, the Eagle Coffee Shoppe was therefore a state actor and under the scope of the equal protection clause of the Fourteenth Amendment.

Congress was next to use the state action doctrine to combat discrimination. It comprehensively addressed a variety of discriminatory practices with the passage of the Civil Rights Act of 1964. The commerce clause was employed as the legal authority supporting the act, thereby circumventing the need to prove that a party was a state actor before invoking Fourteenth Amendment protections. Title II outlawed discrimination in places of public accommodation. In *Heart of Atlanta Motel v. United States* (1964) and *Katzenbach v. McClung* (1964), the Court upheld the reach of the Civil Rights Act on commerce clause grounds.

A Contraction

Under Warren E. Burger, the Court limited the scope of the doctrine of state action. In *Adickes v. S. H. Kress and Co.* (1970), the Court applied the doctrine to a restaurant that refused to serve a white person in the company of blacks. However, in 1971 the Court narrowed the scope of the state action doctrine in ruling that the City of Jackson, Mississippi, could close a public swimming pool rather than allow African Americans to swim there. The high-water mark of limiting the state action doctrine was in *Moose Lodge v. Irvis* (1972), when the Court found no state action involved in a private club's refusal to serve African Americans, despite the fact that the state issued the club its liquor license. The majority argued that receiving benefits or services from the state was not enough to classify a private discriminator as a state actor for purposes of Fourteenth Amendment application. The once broad scope of state action was limited to allow some private discrimination to lie beyond the reach of the Fourteenth Amendment.

In *Jones v. Alfred H. Mayer Co.* (1968), the Court reasoned that the Civil Rights Act of 1866 and even the Thirteenth Amendment were more useful tools in regulating private discrimination than the Fourteenth Amendment. In *Jones*, the Court argued that these two provisions prohibited private and public discrimination in the sale of property. After this case, many suits involving private schools, employment, and racial harassment were resolved without involving the doctrine of state action.

Priscilla H. Machado

Further Reading

Berger, Raoul. *The Fourteenth Amendment and the Bill of Rights.* Norman: University of Oklahoma Press, 1989.

Curtis, Michael Kent. *No State Shall Abridge: The Fourteenth Amendment and the Bill of Rights.* Durham, N.C.: Duke University Press, 1986.

Hensley, Thomas R., Christopher E. Smith, and Joyce A. Baugh. *The Changing Supreme Court: Constitutional Rights and Liberties.* St. Paul, Minn.: West Publishing, 1997.

Killenbeck, Mark R., ed. *The Tenth Amendment and State Sovereignty: Constitutional History and Contemporary Issues.* Lanham, Md.: Rowman & Littlefield, 2002.

Kluger, Richard. *Simple Justice.* New York: Vintage Books, 1976.

Nagel, Robert F. *The Implosion of American Federalism.* New York: Oxford University Press, 2002.

Noonan, John Thomas. *Narrowing the Nation's Power: The Supreme Court Sides with the States.* Berkeley: University of California Press, 2002.

Schwartz, Bernard. *Super Chief.* New York: New York University Press, 1983.

See also *Civil Rights Cases*; Civil Rights movement; Equal protection clause; Federalism; Fourteenth Amendment; *Heart of Atlanta Motel v. United States*; Housing discrimination; *Shelley v. Kraemer*; States' rights and state sovereignty.

States' Rights and State Sovereignty

Description: Constitutional argument that state governments possess sovereignty, autonomous governing power that approximates the authority and status of the federal government.

Significance: After the Articles of Confederation went into effect in 1781, the states began to assert a degree of independence from the federal government. The Supreme Court's interpretation of states' rights was not consistent, although policy making in the United States tended to be more local and diverse and less national and uniform.

The states' rights argument dates back to the founding of the United States and the first national constitution, the Articles of Confederation. The articles were drafted by delegates of the "states in Congress assembled" and explicitly provided for state sovereignty: "Each state retains its sovereignty, freedom, and independence." The U.S. Constitution of 1789, however, makes no mention of sovereignty, implies popular sovereignty in the Preamble's invocation of "We the people," and explicitly declares national supremacy in Article VI: "This Constitution, and the Laws of the United States which shall be made in Pursuance thereof . . . shall be the supreme Law of the Land . . . , any Thing in the Constitution or Laws of any State to the Contrary notwithstanding." The first Congress in 1789 proposed what came to be the Tenth Amendment in order to pacify the antifederalists, the states' rights advocates who opposed the Constitution of 1789. This amendment's language still serves as the principal constitutional grounds for states' rights arguments: "The powers not delegated to the United States by the Constitution, nor prohibited by it to the States, are reserved to the States respectively, or to the people."

Determining States' Rights

For two hundred years, constitutional questions have arisen when the national government's delegated powers and states' reserved powers have come into actual or potential conflict. Peaceful resolution of these disagreements required a legitimate and authoritative decision maker, and the candidates were the involved state or the national government (Congress or the Supreme Court). With few exceptions, the Court emerged as the final arbiter of states' rights in conflict with federal law. For example, in *McCulloch v. Maryland* (1819), the great nationalist, Chief Justice John Marshall, in the opinion for the Court, wrote that the supremacy clause of Article VI prevented Maryland from taxing the Second Bank of the United States. Two years later in *Cohens v. Virginia* (1821), the Court held that it and not the highest state court had final say on the meaning of the U.S. Constitution in a case involving a state conviction for selling federal lottery tickets.

Similarly in *Cooper v. Aaron* (1958), the Court said in a school desegregation case that it, not Arkansas officials, was "supreme in the exposition of the law of the Constitution." Some exceptions to the Court's primacy in determining the boundaries of states' rights and federal authority have been the Union's military dominance in the Civil War, Congress's authority to decide when general federal regulations apply to the states, and state supreme courts' decision-making power over matters of purely state law.

Rejection of Radical States' Rights

John C. Calhoun, an American statesman and author who died in 1850, provided the nation's most systematic and philosophical treatment of states' rights. His theory of the "concurrent majority" posited that no action of the national government would be legitimate unless each separate interest represented in Congress would forgo its inherent right of veto and assent to the policy. States' rights corollaries of this theory were that the states are sovereign, and as such, they adopted the Constitution and could repudiate the national compact whenever it would be in their interest.

This kind of states' rights argument was presented to the Court in *McCulloch* by Luther Martin, counsel for Maryland and an ardent states' rights advocate. According to Martin, Maryland could tax the Second Bank of the United States because the states are "truly sovereign" and "possess supreme dominion." The response of the Court, written by Chief Justice Marshall, was that the Constitution was the creation of the sovereign people, not of the states, and it was therefore superior to the states. In *Texas v. White* (1869), the Court again had occasion to rule on the theory that a state could renounce its membership in the Union. The Court rejected radical state sovereignty in ruling that the Constitution "looks to an indestructible Union." Therefore, Texas was not legally capable of secession.

Era of Dual Federalism

National supremacy rulings such as *McCulloch* and *Cohens* did not go uncontested. Strains of states' rights theory were present on the Court during the mid-nineteenth century chief justiceship of Roger Brooke Taney, but it was not until the early twentieth century that the Court gave support to a full-blown theory of states' rights known as "dual federalism."

Probably the high-water mark of this brand of states' rights was *Hammer v. Dagenhart* (1918). In this case, the Court found that an attempt by Congress to prohibit the labor of children in factories and mines violated the Tenth Amendment. The Court's rationale was that employment in these industries was a local matter reserved to state regulation by the Tenth Amendment.

Dual federalism was the term given to the Court's theory that the Constitution created a system of dual supremacy: The national government was supreme in the exercise of its delegated powers, but the states were equally supreme in their exercise of reserved powers over local matters. The Court's narrow interpretation of the reach of delegated powers, for example, the power to regulate interstate commerce, in effect defused the supremacy clause of Article VI. It was not until *United States v. Darby Lumber Co.* (1941) that the Court overruled *Hammer* and said that the Tenth Amendment was not a check on the delegated powers of Congress. With the *Darby* decision, Marshall was in ascendancy and Calhoun in decline. The Court had entered a new jurisprudential period of economic nationalism in which federal regulatory power repeatedly displaced states' rights.

Judicial New Federalism

The administration of President Richard M. Nixon gave rise to the phrase "new federalism," the policy that the national executive and legislative branches should take steps to move power from the federal government back to the states. Subsequent presidential administrations continued to advocate new federalism policies.

The Court became part of this spirit when it initiated a period of "judicial new federalism" in *National League of Cities v. Usery* (1976). In this case, the Court declared that the Tenth Amendment prevented the federal Fair Labor Standards Act (1938), which contained minimum-wage and maximum-hour regulations, from being applied to state and local governments. Although the federal government could apply these general regulatory measures to businesses operating in interstate commerce, it could not apply such regulations to states acting in their governmental capacities. The heart of the Court's reasoning was that federal regulation of states struck at the states' integrity by impairing their ability to carry out their core governmental functions. The *Usery* rule was the Court's recognition once again of Tenth Amendment-based states' rights.

With judicial new federalism, the Court was saying something different from its "dual federalism" formulation of states' rights. With dual federalism, the Court said that the Tenth Amendment freed states to regulate local matters free from federal interference. With judicial new federalism, the Court said that the Tenth Amendment prevented application of a general federal regulatory measure to a state's "integral operations" which were the essence of "state sovereignty." After struggling for nine years to sort out what were and were not "attributes of state sovereignty" to determine what could be regulated by the federal government, the Court brought this era of states' rights to an end in *Garcia v. San Antonio Metropolitan Transit Authority* (1985). The Court overruled *Usery,* saying that its Tenth Amendment rationale had turned out to be "unworkable." Henceforth, the Court said, members of Congress and not the justices would decide when states' rights were a check on federal regulatory power.

Era of Dual Sovereignty

Writing the Court's official opinion in *Tafflin v. Levitt* (1990), Justice Sandra Day O'Connor held that the Constitution establishes "a system of dual sovereignty between the states and the federal government." In his dissent in *Garcia,* Justice William H. Rehnquist said that the *Usery* rule of states' rights was "a principle that will, I am confident, in time again command the support of a majority of this Court." His prophecy essentially came true in *New York v. United States* (1992). In that case, the Court considered the application to the states of a congressional enactment, the Low-Level Radioactive Waste Policy Act of 1980. To encourage the states to provide disposal sites, Congress gave the states a choice between two mandates: accept the ownership and resulting liability for radioactive waste or regulate it according to federal guidelines. The Court ruled that both options violated the Tenth Amendment. Borrowing from *The Federalist* (1788), the *New York* majority said that the Constitution "leaves to the several States a residuary and inviolable sovereignty."

This core of state sovereignty, the Court said, is violated when Congress commands state legislatures to legislate. In *New York,* the Court did not overrule *Garcia,* distinguishing *Garcia*'s approval of a general federal law being applied to a state from *New York*'s condemnation of a direct federal mandate to a state legislature. Five years later, *Printz v. United States* (1997) extended the *New York* rule to a federal mandate to state administrative officials and gave this states' rights principle the name of "dual sovereignty." The issue in *Printz* was the constitutionality of the mandate of the federal Brady Handgun Violence Prevention Act (1993) that county and municipal chief law-enforcement officers conduct a background check of would-be purchasers of handguns. To void the law, the majority used the Tenth Amendment principle of "dual sovereignty," which represented the Framers' intention to preserve "the States as independent and autonomous political entities." The *Printz* rule was categorical and absolute, thus "no case-by-case weighing of the burdens or benefits is necessary." The combined states' rights legacy of *New York* and *Printz* was that the "Federal Government may neither issue directives requiring the States to address particular problems, nor command the States' officers, or those of their political subdivisions, to administer or enforce a federal regulatory program." Apparently left undisturbed by *Printz*, however, was the holding of *South Dakota v. Dole* (1987) that the federal government could continue to use grants of money "with strings attached" to entice the states to do what the federal government could not directly mandate.

Modern States' Rights Analysis

In *New York*, Justice Sandra Day O'Connor wrote for the majority: "In the end, just as a cup may be half empty or half full, it makes no difference whether one views the question at issue in this case as one of ascertaining the limits of the power delegated to the Federal Government under the affirmative provisions of the Constitution or one of discerning the core of sovereignty retained by the States under the Tenth Amendment." Her point was that either analysis—the content of delegated powers or the content of reserved powers—could lead to the same end, enhanced states' rights. After *New York*, the Supreme Court used both approaches. In *Printz*, the majority stressed the Tenth Amendment in voiding the Brady Act. And in *United States v. Lopez* (1995), the Court focused on the limits of Congress's delegated powers in voiding the Gun-Free School Zones Act of 1990. In *Lopez*, the Court said that Congress's power to regulate interstate commerce extended only to "commercial" matters, which did not include guns at school.

New State Constitutionalism

A contemporary development in states' rights is a state supreme court using its state constitution to give greater protection to a fundamental right than that accorded the same right by the U.S. Supreme Court using the U.S. Constitution. The rationale for this practice is a long-standing principle of states' rights: the independent and adequate state grounds doctrine. In essence, this doctrine means that a state supreme court decision grounded solely in state law is final because the Supreme Court has no jurisdiction to review it. A corollary of the doctrine is that a state supreme court, compared with the U.S. Supreme Court, can be more protective, but never less protective, of an individual right.

Some applications of this states' rights doctrine have been state supreme courts acting opposite the U.S. Supreme Court to permit students to collect signatures on political petitions in shopping malls, to allow challenges to school funding schemes based on local property taxes, and to provide enhanced protection from police searches of automobiles.

James J. Lopach

Further Reading

Readers might begin with either of two general works on the relationship between the states and the federal government: Robert F. Nagel's *The Implosion of American Federalism* (New York: Oxford University Press, 2002) or John Thomas Noonan's *Narrowing the Nation's Power: The Supreme Court Sides with the States* (Berkeley: University of California Press, 2002). Another way to begin a study of states' rights is by looking at the theory's roots in the United States before 1787.

For extended discussion of the antifederalists' arguments and the Founders' motives and compromises, see Alpheus T. Mason's *The States' Rights Debate: Antifederalism and the Constitution* (New York: Oxford University Press, 1972) and Raoul Berger's *Federalism: The Founders' Design* (Norman: University of Oklahoma Press, 1987). The standard original source for explaining the Framers' intent for state autonomy is *The Federalist* (1788) by Alexander Hamilton, James Madison, and John Jay. Readers should pay special attention to the tensions between Nos. 39, 27, and 44.

A full appreciation of the states' rights doctrine must include some familiarity with its radical expression, which is detailed in John C. Calhoun's *A Disquisition on Government* (Indianapolis, Ind.: Bobbs-Merrill, 1953) and in *The Nullification Era* (New York: Harper & Row, 1967), edited by William W. Freehling. The eminent constitutional scholar Edward S. Corwin provides a clear exposition of the doctrinal evolution of national supremacy to dual federalism and back to national supremacy in *The Commerce Power Versus States Rights* (Princeton, N.J.: Princeton University Press, 1936).

The demise of the *Usery* era and a justification for the new dual sovereignty era is found in Martin H. Redish's "Doing It with Mirrors: *New York v. United States* and Constitutional Limitations on Federal Power to Require State Legislation," *Hastings Constitutional Law Quarterly* (1993): 593. Erwin Chemerinsky's large *Federal Jurisdiction* (4th ed. New York: Aspen, 2003) gives detailed analysis on all aspects of the complex topic. Jodie Lynn Boduch presents a relatively short and readable introduction to the topic in *States' Rights* (San Diego: Greenhaven Press, 2006).

SEE ALSO Commerce, regulation of; Federalism; *Garcia v. San Antonio Metropolitan Transit Authority*; *McCulloch v. Maryland*; *Printz v. United States*; State action; Tenth Amendment.

Statutory Interpretation

DESCRIPTION: Judicial determining of the meaning of statutes enacted by a legislature.

SIGNIFICANCE: Although the Supreme Court's function of interpreting the Constitution receives more attention, many, perhaps even a majority, of the cases before it that arise from federal courts involve questions of statutory interpretation.

Much federal and state law is based on statutes enacted by legislatures. Indeed, because little federal common law exists, almost all federal law except constitutional law is statutory. Article I of the Constitution states that a federal statute must be approved by a majority of the House of Representatives and of the Senate, then be signed by the president. If the proposed statute is vetoed by the president, it can still become law if two-thirds of both the House and the Senate vote to enact it.

Statutes cannot be completely clear in all circumstances, and many statutes are quite vague and do not precisely specify legal rights and responsibilities. Therefore, courts must interpret statutes in deciding cases. The Supreme Court is the final authority on the meaning of federal statutes; however, if Congress and the president disagree with the Court's interpretation of a statute, they can amend it so as to nullify the Court's interpretation. The Supreme Court, however, is not the ultimate arbiter of the meaning of state statutes. This task is performed by state supreme courts. Many, perhaps even a majority, of the cases that reach the Supreme Court from the federal courts involve the interpretation of federal statutes rather than the Constitution.

The approaches to interpreting statutes can be sorted into three major categories: textualism, intentionalism, and purposivism. Textualism focuses on the ordinary meaning of the words used in the statute. Intentionalism attempts to find the collective "intent" of the legislators who enacted the statute, often by consulting the legislative history of the statute, that is, the various documents produced when the legislature was considering the statute. Purposivism requires judges to determine the general purpose of the statute and adopt interpretations that further the statute's general purpose. From its inception, the Supreme Court has generally rejected textualism. After its decision in *Rector of Holy Trinity Church v. United States* (1892), the Court increasingly relied on legislative history. In the late 1980's and the 1990's, Justices Antonin Scalia and Clarence Thomas vigorously argued that the Court should adopt a textualism approach and disregard legislative history when interpreting statutes.

Bernard W. Bell

Further Reading

Mikva, Abner J., and Eric Lane. *An Introduction to Statutory Interpretation and the Legislative Process.* New York: Aspen Law & Business, 1997.

Oleszek, Walter J. *Congressional Procedures and the Policy Process.* Washington, D.C.: Congressional Quarterly, 1996.

Popkin, William D. *Materials on Legislation: Political Language and the Political Process.* Westbury, N.Y.: Foundation Press, 1997.
Scalia, Antonin. *A Matter of Interpretation: Federal Courts and the Law—An Essay.* Edited by Amy Gutmann. Princeton, N.J.: Princeton University Press, 1997.
Watry, Ruth Ann. *Administrative Statutory Interpretation: The Aftermath of "Chevron v. Natural Resources Defense Council."* New York: LFB Scholarly Publications, 2002.

See also Advisory opinions; Common law; Constitutional interpretation; Scalia, Antonin; Stewart, Potter; Thomas, Clarence; Treaties.

John Paul Stevens

Identification: Associate justice (December 19, 1975-)
Nominated by: Gerald R. Ford
Born: April 20, 1920, Chicago, Illinois
Significance: A justice known for independence and skepticism toward established doctrines, Stevens has demonstrated a strong commitment to civil liberties and the protection of the least powerful persons in society.

Raised in a prominent Hyde Park, Chicago, family, John Paul Stephens attended the University of Chicago, graduating Phi Beta Kappa in 1941. During World War II, he earned a Bronze Star for his service as a code breaker in the Navy. While studying law at Northwestern University, he was editor in chief of the law review and graduated first in his class in 1947. Through the following two years he served as law clerk for Justice Wiley B. Rutledge, Jr., and then worked for a private law firm from 1948 until 1950. Next, he served as associate counsel for the House Judiciary Committee's subcommittee on monopoly power. From 1952 through 1970, he was partner in a private law firm. During these busy years he also found time to lecture on antitrust law at the Northwestern University School of Law and at the University of Chicago Law School.

In 1969, Stevens first attracted public attention while serving as *pro*

John Paul Stevens. (Courtesy, the Supreme Court Historical Society)

bono counsel on the Illinois Supreme Court's special committee investigating a scandal that resulted in the resignation of two corrupt judges. In 1970, Richard M. Nixon appointed him to the United States Court of Appeals for the Seventh Circuit. During his five years on the Seventh Circuit, Stevens had a moderately conservative record.

Appointment to the Supreme Court

On November 12, 1975, following the resignation of Justice William O. Douglas, President Gerald R. Ford nominated Stevens as his replacement. With the 1976 presidential election drawing near, Ford, as an unelected incumbent president, had promised to look seriously at qualified women when choosing a Supreme Court nominee. However, Stevens, a sitting federal judge with distinguished experience but a low political profile, appeared to be an ideal choice. The American Bar Association Committee on the Federal Judiciary gave Stevens its highest recommendation. He was praised as a "lawyer's lawyer" and a "judge's judge." At his confirmation hearings, when asked whether he was liberal or conservative, he answered: "I would not label myself, Senator."

Feminist leaders expressed disappointment at Stevens's appointment. Margaret Drachsler of the National Organization for Women told the Senate Judiciary Committee that Stevens had "consistently opposed women's rights" in his appellate court opinions. Representative Bella Abzug also questioned the nominee's "sensitivity to women's rights." Nan Aron, president of the Women's Legal Defense Fund, criticized Stevens's refusal to regard sex as a suspect classification deserving of the Court's strictest scrutiny. Stevens's supporters answered that he had voted in favor of plaintiffs in more than 73 percent of the sex discrimination cases in which he had participated.

On December 17, 1975, the Senate confirmed Stevens's appointment by a vote of ninety-nine to none. Two days later, Stevens took the oath of office and became the Court's 101st member.

Jurisprudence and Decisions

Stevens's jurisprudence has often been characterized as idiosyncratic, and frequently he defended lonely and eccentric positions on issues. He has routinely published more dissents and concurring opinions than his fellow justices. Skeptical about abstractions and arguing that legal doctrines tend to simplify complex issues, he advocated the method of focusing on the circumstances of particular cases and controversies. He has been a skilled and lucid writer, and his opinions have been recognized for having literary quality.

During his early years on the Burger Court, Stevens was usually classified as a moderate conservative, but by the time that William H. Rehnquist became chief justice in 1986, Stevens was more often voting with the Court's liberal wing. By the mid-1990's, he was commonly described as the most liberal member of the Court. Stevens has been a fierce opponent of discrimination based on race, gender, and ethnicity. For many years he condemned affirmative action programs, as in *Regents of the University of California v. Bakke* (1978). He insisted that the 1964 Civil Rights Act prohibited all preferences based on race. Gradually his views changed, and he joined the majority in

Johnson v. Santa Clara County (1987), the first case in which the Court approved a voluntary sex-based affirmative action program. Dissenting in *Adarand Constructors v. Peña* (1995), he wrote that the nation's history of race discrimination justified strong remedial action. In *Grutter v. Bollinger* (2003), he joined the 5-4 majority in accepting race-based preferences aimed at achieving diversity.

In cases alleging discrimination under the equal protection clause, Stevens became a critic of the Court's precedents requiring proof of intent rather than asking whether policies have discriminatory effects. Although concurring in *Washington v. Davis* (1976), he challenged the distinction between discriminatory intent and discriminatory impact, arguing that this distinction tended to uphold policies that work to the disadvantage of minorities. In *McCleskey v. Kemp* (1986), he rejected the majority's holding that racial disparity in death sentences did not violate the equal protection clause because of a lack of intent. He joined the dissent, which argued that a significant risk of discrimination should be enough to establish a constitutional violation.

In many cases, Stevens criticized the Court's use of three different levels of judicial scrutiny: strict scrutiny, minimal scrutiny, and intermediate scrutiny. Since there is "only one equal protection clause," he argued that there should only be one standard of review. In *Cleburne v. Cleburne Living Center* (1985), he explained that all government classifications should be evaluated on the basis of a "rational basis" test, requiring that an impartial lawmaker would believe that the classification serves a legitimate public purpose that outweighs the harm done to members of the disadvantaged class.

In cases involving restraints on expression, Stevens's record was somewhat mixed. In *Young v. American Mini Theatres* (1976), he endorsed strict zoning ordinances that restricted sexually oriented businesses to designated neighborhoods. Gradually, he came to adhere to a libertarian approach to pornography, even voting to overthrow a federal law outlawing computer-generated child pornography in *ACLU v. Ashcroft* (2004). As a patriotic veteran, nevertheless, he dissented when the Court voted five to four to recognize the constitutional right of flag-burning in *Texas v. Johnson* (1989).

By the early twenty-first century, Stevens could usually be counted on to support left-of-center positions. Writing for the majority in *Rasul v. Bush* (2004), he ruled that aliens detained in a military base in another country had the right to seek habeas corpus relief in federal civilian courts. In *Roper v. Simmons* (2005), he voted to disallow the execution of minors convicted of murder. Having dissented in *Bowers v. Hardwick* (1986), when a 5-4 majority ruled that the Constitution did not protect a freedom to engage in homosexual acts, he gladly joined the 5-4 majority of *Lawrence v. Texas* (2003), which overturned that ruling. In addition, he wrote a strong dissent in *Bush v. Gore* (2000), criticizing the five conservative justices who stopped the Florida recount and ensured the outcome of the presidential election of 2000.

Through 2006, Stevens continued to participate actively on the Court as he entered his late eighties. To pass the record of Oliver Wendell Holmes as the oldest serving justice, he would have to stay on the Court until February 23, 2011.

Joseph A. Melusky
Revised and updated by the Editor

Further Reading

Bader, William H., and Roy M. Mersky, eds. *The First One Hundred Eight Justices.* Buffalo, N.Y.: William S. Hein, 2004.

Canon, Bradley C. "Justice John Paul Stevens: The Lone Ranger in a Black Robe." In *The Burger Court: Political and Judicial Profiles,* edited by Charles M. Lamb and Stephen C. Halpern. Urbana: University of Illinois Press, 1991.

Hensley, Thomas R. *The Rehnquist Court: Justices, Rulings, and Legacy.* Santa Barbara, Calif.: ABC-Clio, 2006.

Italia, Bob, and Paul Deegan. *John Paul Stevens.* New York: ABDO, 1992.

Manaster, Kenneth. *Illinois Justice: The Scandal of 1969 and the Rise of John Paul Stevens.* Chicago: University of Chicago Press, 2001.

Sickels, Robert Judd. *John Paul Stevens and the Constitution: The Search for Balance.* University Park: Pennsylvania State University Press, 1988.

Tushnet, Mark. *A Court Divided: The Rehnquist Court and the Future of Constitutional Law.* New York: W. W. Norton, 2005.

Yarbrough, Tinsley. *The Rehnquist Court and the Constitution.* New York: Oxford University Press, 2000.

See also Burger, Warren E.; *Bush v. Gore*; Dissents; Equal protection clause; Gender issues; Nominations to the Court; Rehnquist, William H.

Potter Stewart

Identification: Associate justice (May 15, 1959-July 3, 1981)
Nominated by: Dwight D. Eisenhower
Born: January 23, 1915, Jackson, Michigan
Died: December 7, 1985, Hanover, New Hampshire
Significance: A member of the Supreme Court under both Earl Warren and Warren E. Burger, Stewart served as an independent voice on the Court for twenty-two years, making contributions in the areas of criminal justice reform, search and seizure laws, capital punishment, gender discrimination, and civil rights.

Potter Stewart was born in Jackson, Michigan, the son of a wealthy Cincinnati lawyer, James Garfield Stewart, and his wife, Harriet Potter Stewart. Stewart's father served as the mayor of Cincinnati for nine years and later was appointed to the Ohio Supreme Court. His mother worked diligently to reform city government and served as the president of the League of Women Voters. Everyone in the family, including Stewart himself, assumed that he would become a lawyer as an adult. After receiving his high school education at a private school in Connecticut, Stewart enrolled at Yale, graduating in 1937. He also attended Yale Law School, serving as the editor of the law journal.

After graduation from law school, Stewart began working for a corporate law firm in New York City. His career was interrupted, however, by the beginning of World War II (1941-1945). As a naval officer, Stewart served on ships in the Atlantic and Mediterranean during the war.

After the war, Stewart practiced law briefly in New York before returning to Cincinnati. In addition to working as a trial lawyer, he entered politics and was elected to the city council. In 1954 Stewart was appointed to the Sixth Circuit Court of Appeals by President Dwight D. Eisenhower, making Stewart the youngest judge serving in a federal court at that time.

In October, 1958, Eisenhower appointed Stewart to the Supreme Court while the Senate was on recess. Consequently, Stewart began working on cases before his confirmation hearings. On May 5, 1959, the Senate confirmed his appointment. The Court was evenly divided between liberals and conservatives at that time, and Stewart often found himself being described as the swing vote. Court watchers found it difficult to predict Stewart's vote on any given issue. Although he was a Republican, Stewart could not be identified with any political ideology. Rather, Stewart said, he consistently tried to decide cases based solely on their Constitutional merits and legal reasoning.

Potter Stewart. (Harris and Ewing/ Collection of the Supreme Court of the United States)

He told biographers that he wanted to be remembered as a "good lawyer who did his best."

Civil and Other Rights

The Fourth Amendment to the U.S. Constitution states, in part, that "The right of the people to be secure in their persons, houses, papers, and effects against unreasonable searches and seizures shall not be violated and no Warrants shall issue, but upon probable cause,. . . particularly describing the place to be searched, and the person or things to be seized." Interpretations of the amendment vary concerning what constitutes a "place" and what "things" may be seized. In his opinion for *Katz v. United States* (1967), Stewart wrote that the Fourth Amendment "protects people, not places." Consequently, something as abstract as a conversation can be considered a "thing" that cannot be seized without a warrant, and a phone booth can be considered a "place." In this and several other cases, Stewart applied his careful legal mind to further strengthening and defining this amendment.

Although Stewart was a strong proponent of states' rights, he nonetheless made important decisions regarding civil rights. In writing the majority opinion for *Jones v. Alfred H. Mayer Co.* (1968), Stewart stated that the 1866 Civil Rights Act made it illegal to refuse to sell or rent property on the basis of the buyer's or renter's race. In an earlier case, Stewart voted to prohibit Birmingham, Alabama, police from using antiloitering laws to prevent civil rights demonstrations. On the other hand, Stewart's states' rights beliefs often placed him in opposition to challenges to voting practices designed to limit the rights of African American voters to register to vote. He believed that a state's electoral system belonged to the state, although he supported the 1965 Voting Rights Act.

Stewart consistently voted in favor of strengthening and supporting the right to free speech. He is best known for his stand on obscenity laws. In the Burger Court, he was often the dissenting voice, refusing to join with the majority on its strengthening of obscenity laws. Further, in a very famous 1971 case, *New York Times Co. v. United States,* Stewart ruled against the United States in its case against *The New York Times* for its publication of the Pentagon Papers. These papers were government documents, leaked to the press by an anti-Vietnam War activist. In addition, Stewart wrote several decisions on First Amendment rights of public employees, including teachers and low-level government workers.

Diane Andrews Henningfeld

Further Reading

Bader, William H., and Roy M. Mersky, eds. *The First One Hundred Eight Justices.* Buffalo, N.Y.: William S. Hein, 2004.

Barnes, Catherine. *Men of the Supreme Court: Profiles of the Justices.* New York: Facts On File, 1978.

Bendiner, Robert. "The Law and Potter Stewart: An Interview with Justice Potter Stewart." *American Heritage,* December, 1983, 98-104.

Cushman, Clare, ed. *The Supreme Court Justices: Illustrated Biographies, 1789-1993.* Washington, D.C.: Congressional Quarterly, 1993.

Friedman, Leon. "Potter Stewart." In *The Justices of the United States Supreme Court, 1789-1978: Their Lives and Major Opinions,* edited by Leon Friedman and Fred L. Israel. Vol. 5. New York: Chelsea House, 1978.

Schwartz, Bernard. *A History of the Supreme Court.* New York: Oxford University Press, 1993.

Tushnet, Mark. *A Court Divided: The Rehnquist Court and the Future of Constitutional Law.* New York: W. W. Norton, 2005.

Urofsky, Melvin I. *The Warren Court: Justices, Rulings, and Legacy.* Santa Barbara, Calif.: ABC-Clio, 2001.

_______., ed. *The Supreme Court Justices.* New York: Garland, 1994.

Yarbrough, Tinsley E. *The Burger Court: Justices, Rulings, and Legacy.* Santa Barbara, Calif.: ABC-Clio, 2000.

See also Burger, Warren E.; Civil Rights movement; *Katz v. United States*; *New York Times Co. v. United States*; States' rights and state sovereignty; Warren, Earl.

Harlan Fiske Stone

IDENTIFICATION: Associate justice (March 2, 1925-July 2, 1941), chief justice (July 3, 1941-April 22, 1946)
NOMINATED BY: Calvin Coolidge and Franklin D. Roosevelt
BORN: October 11, 1872, Chesterfield, New Hampshire
DIED: April 22, 1946, Washington, D.C.
SIGNIFICANCE: As an associate justice, Stone established a bedrock doctrine for judicial responsibility in the area of civil rights and promoted a philosophy of judicial self-restraint. Power struggles and discord among several strong-willed associate justices lessened the effectiveness of his tenure as chief justice.

Harlan Fiske Stone was born in New Hampshire but grew up near Amherst, Massachusetts, where his family moved when he was two

Harlan Fiske Stone. (Harris and Ewing/ Collection of the Supreme Court of the United States)

years old. His father's family, longtime farmers and community leaders, traced their roots in America to Simon Stone, who had emigrated from England in 1635. Stone graduated from Amherst College, where he was president of his class, in 1894 and from Columbia Law School in 1898.

Upon his admission to the bar, Stone worked as an attorney in various New York City firms and taught law as an adjunct professor at Columbia. In 1910 he was named dean of its law school and juggled academe with a successful law practice until 1923, when he resigned as dean to become a partner and head of the litigation department at Sullivan & Cromwell, a Wall Street law firm. After only one year, however, he left this lucrative position when his former college classmate and fellow Republican, President Calvin Coolidge, appointed him attorney general—at a substantial cut in pay. As part of his duties, Stone reorganized the Federal Bureau of Investigation, which had been despoiled by corruption, and appointed J. Edgar Hoover as its head.

Justice Stone

In January, 1925, Coolidge again looked to Stone to fill a vacancy, this time by nominating him to the Supreme Court. He was confirmed on February 5, 1925, and began a tenure in which he was the first justice to occupy all nine seats on the Court's bench, which are assigned according to seniority. Appointed as chief justice by President Franklin D. Roosevelt in 1941, he served until April 22, 1946, when, after collapsing at the bench, he died.

Although Stone was a Republican and Roosevelt a Democrat, Stone was an early supporter of Roosevelt's New Deal legislation. Stone and Justices Louis D. Brandeis and Benjamin N. Cardozo formed a tenacious minority who believed that the Court was inappropriately trying to limit the legislature's power to regulate the economy. Stone recorded his views in a particularly strident dissent after the Court struck down the Agricultural Adjustment Act of 1933, virtually accusing his fellow jurors of appropriating the roles and responsibilities of the legislature and outlining the importance of judicial self-restraint. The next year, after Roosevelt first tried to enlarge the Court, then appointed new, more liberally minded members as a result of some key retirements, the tide began to turn in favor of the

New Deal, and Stone became part of the majority on such decisions.

The next issue in which Stone played a pivotal role was in the still fledgling struggle for the civil rights of minority groups. In the fourth footnote in his opinion in *United States v. Carolene Products Co.* (1938), he argued that the Court should set aside the practice of judicial self-restraint in the face of legislation that infringed on constitutionally established rights for racial, political, or religious minorities. Frequently considered one of the most important footnotes in constitutional history, it established the doctrine of preferred freedoms, which ordains that certain rights are indeed inalienable and must be accorded special protection by the Court. In *Minersville School District v. Gobitis* (1940), he upheld these views as the lone dissenting vote in a case between a school district and two children who, as practicing Jehovah's Witnesses, refused to salute the U.S. flag. The Court supported the school district's action to expel the children. In part because of Stone's arguments against such a position, it was overturned in a similar case three years later.

Chief Justice Stone

After Charles Evans Hughes retired as chief justice in July, 1941, Roosevelt chose Stone as his successor, in part as a gesture of unity between political parties as war approached and in part as a reward for Stone's unstinting support of New Deal legislation. The Court included a number of strong-minded, highly intellectual justices, among them Hugo L. Black, William O. Douglas, Felix Frankfurter, and Robert H. Jackson. Stone proved unequal to the task of mediating the bitter differences that arose among these and the other associate justices as they faced the challenging and difficult issues that arose during World War II (1941-1945). The five years he served as chief justice are often regarded as the most openly combative in Court history.

Jane Marie Smith

Further Reading

Bader, William H., and Roy M. Mersky, eds. *The First One Hundred Eight Justices.* Buffalo, N.Y.: William S. Hein, 2004.

Lief, Alfred, ed. *Public Control of Business: Selected Opinions by Harlan Fiske Stone.* Buffalo, N.Y.: W. S. Hein, 1996.

Mason, Alpheus T. *Harlan Fiske Stone: Pillar of the Law.* New York: Viking, 1968.

_______. *The Supreme Court from Taft to Burger.* Baton Rouge: Louisiana State University Press, 1979.

Renstrom, Peter G. *The Stone Court: Justices, Rulings, and Legacy.* Santa Barbara, Calif.: ABC-Clio, 2001.

_______. *The Taft Court: Justices, Rulings, and Legacy.* Santa Barbara, Calif.: ABC-Clio, 2003.

Steamer, Robert J. *Chief Justice: Leadership and the Supreme Court.* Columbia: University of South Carolina Press, 1986.

Urofsky, Melvin I. *Division and Discord: The Supreme Court Under Stone and Vinson, 1941-1953.* Columbia: University of South Carolina Press, 1997.

White, G. Edward. *The American Judicial Tradition: Profiles of Leading American Judges.* New York: Oxford University Press, 1976.

See also Brandeis, Louis D.; Cardozo, Benjamin N.; *Carolene Products Co., United States v.*; Douglas, William O.; Frankfurter, Felix; Hughes, Charles Evans; Jackson, Robert H.; Judicial self-restraint; New Deal; Taft, William H.

Joseph Story

Identification: Associate justice (February 3, 1812-September 10, 1845)

Nominated by: James Madison

Born: September 18, 1779, Marblehead, Massachusetts

Died: September 10, 1845, Cambridge, Massachusetts

Significance: As a Supreme Court ally of Chief Justice John Marshall, Story contributed to the early formation of constitutional law in the United States, particularly in determining the appellate role of the Court in civil cases.

Joseph Story graduated with honors from Harvard University in 1798 and was admitted to the Essex County bar in 1801. A Democratic-Republican, he was elected to the Massachusetts House of Representatives in 1805 and to the U.S. Congress as a Representative from Essex South in 1808. His vote to repeal Thomas Jefferson's Embargo Act (1807) alienated him from the president and from his party.

As Story's political career faltered, his reputation in the courts gained distinction. He was a shrewd and exceptionally well-versed lawyer, particularly in commercial law, and his arguments before the federal courts persuaded many Republicans of his suitability to serve on the Supreme Court. When Justice William Cushing died in 1810, President James Madison, mindful of the rift between Jefferson and Story, reluctantly nominated Story after his first three choices declined the offer. At the age of thirty-two, Story became the youngest justice to serve on the Supreme Court. He served until his death, nearly thirty-four years later.

The Marshall-Story Alliance

Confirming Jefferson's suspicions, Story allied himself with Chief Justice John Marshall, whose aim was to forge a strong federal Court with broad jurisdiction and the power to strike down any legislative act that violated the Constitution. Constitutional law was in its infancy, and Marshall's agenda, though effectively implemented, lacked the weight of precedence and legal argument. Story drew from common law, natural law, and commercial law and wrote brilliantly articulated decisions supporting Marshall's more intuitive (and political) reasoning.

A land dispute, ruled on by the state of Virginia's chief justice Spencer Roane in 1810, was appealed to the Supreme Court. Marshall, himself involved in the suit, recused himself from hearing the case, and Story overturned the decision of the state court. Roane, in turn, ruled that the federal court's decision was unconstitutional. The case was returned to the Supreme Court in 1816. "It is the case . . . and not the court, that gives the jurisdiction," Story wrote in his decision, defending section 25 of the Judiciary Act of 1789 against Roane's assertion of state sovereignty. *Martin v. Hunter's Lessee* (1816) established the supremacy of the federal court in questions of federal law, even in civil cases that arise in state courts.

Story's opinions extended constitutional protections to private corporations under the contract clause (notably in *Dartmouth Col-*

lege v. Woodward, 1819) and sought to protect private property from takings by state governments. His expansive interpretation of laws has been criticized as tortured, but such adaptation of an older body of law to the new republic undoubtedly built and preserved the coequal status of the Supreme Court among the three branches of the federal government.

Years of Dissent

His opinions defending the "natural" rights of individuals and corporations against intrusion by the states became a desperate series of bitter dissents after the death of Marshall. President Andrew Jackson nominated Roger Brooke Taney to be the new chief justice, a move many believed would be the undoing of the Marshall Court's nationalistic gains. Story, now in the Court's minority, had few victories during his last decade on the Court. In *Charles River Bridge v. Warren*

Joseph Story. (Art & Visual Materials, Special Collections Department, Harvard Law School Library)

Bridge (1837), Taney ruled that the monopoly interest granted to the original bridge company could be revoked in the interest of the community, while Story staunchly defended the "implied" guarantee against competition of the original contract.

Story's personal abhorrence of slavery conflicted with his belief in its constitutional legitimacy. His single notable win on the Taney Court was in the *United States v. The Amistad* (1841), in which a group of Africans taken aboard a Spanish slave ship overthrew their captors and landed in the American courts. Story wrote the majority opinion that upheld the lower court's ruling and freed the Africans, reasoning that at the time of the incident they were victims of kidnapping and not lawful merchandise. In *Prigg v. Pennsylvania* (1842), however, Story concurred with the Court and dismissed a charge of kidnapping against a bounty hunter who had reclaimed an escaped slave, under the provisions of federal law, in violation of a state law. Though he suggested that states were under no obligation to aid in the apprehension of fugitive slaves, his opinion gave fugitive slave laws and slavery constitutional standing that they had not until then formally enjoyed.

As a dissenter, Story's influence on the decisions of the Court was not great, though his opinions remained of interest to constitutional scholars. It was as an educator that he sought to perpetuate his judicial philosophies. He returned to Harvard in 1829 as Dane Professor at Harvard Law School, where he greatly influenced the development of university-based law education in the United States. His *Commentaries* on the law (1832-1845) were long considered essential to an American legal education.

Janet Alice Long

Further Reading

Bader, William H., and Roy M. Mersky, eds. *The First One Hundred Eight Justices.* Buffalo, N.Y.: William S. Hein, 2004.

Clinton, Robert, Christopher Budzisz, and Peter Renstrom, eds. *The Marshall Court: Justices, Rulings, and Legacy.* Santa Barbara, Calif.: ABC-Clio, 2007.

Huebner, Timothy S. *The Taney Court: Justices, Rulings, and Legacy.* Santa Barbara, Calif.: ABC-Clio, 2003.

Irons, Peter. *A People's History of the Supreme Court.* New York: Viking, 1999.

McClellan, James. *Joseph Story and the American Constitution: A Study in Political and Legal Thought with Selected Writings.* Norman: University of Oklahoma Press, 1990.

Story, William Wetmore. *Life and Letters of Joseph Story, Associate Justice of the Supreme Court of the United States, and Dane Professor of Law at Harvard University.* 1851. 2 vols. Union, N.J.: Lawbook Exchange, 2000.

Watson, Alan. *Joseph Story and the Comity of Errors: A Case Study in Conflict of Laws.* Athens: University of Georgia Press, 1992.

See also Appellate jurisdiction; Constitutional interpretation; Cushing, William; Johnson, William; Marshall, John; Slavery; Taney, Roger Brooke.

William Strong

Identification: Associate justice (March 14, 1870-December 14, 1880)

Nominated by: Ulysses S. Grant

Born: May 6, 1808, Somers, Connecticut

Died: August 19, 1895, Lake Minnewaska, New York

Significance: Strong wrote the Court majority opinion that upheld the Legal Tender Act of 1862 and the constitutional opinion that African Americans had a right to not be discriminated against in the selection of jurors.

After graduating from Yale Law School in 1828, William Strong practiced law in Pennsylvania from 1832 to 1847. From 1847 to 1851 he served two terms in the U.S. House of Representatives. In 1857 he was elected to the Pennsylvania Supreme Court. He remained on the bench until 1868, when he resigned to return to his private law practice.

In 1870, President Ulysses S. Grant nominated Strong and Joseph P. Bradley to the Supreme Court. Many congressmen believed

William Strong. (Mathew Brady/ Collection of the Supreme Court of the United States)

that the nominations were a Court-packing scheme by Grant because of the *Legal Tender Cases* (1870) before the Court. In the Legal Tender Act of 1862, Congress declared that paper money issued during the Civil War by the federal government was legal tender for all debts. The constitutionality of this declaration was challenged on February 7, 1870, the same day that Strong and Bradley were nominated, and the Court declared the Legal Tender Act unconstitutional. However, upon rehearing the case in 1871, the Court reversed itself. Strong and Bradley provided the swing votes, and Strong wrote the majority opinion. Strong became regarded as an articulate opinion writer for the Court.

Alvin K. Benson

See also Bradley, Joseph P.; Chase, Salmon P.; Civil War; Opinions, writing of; Waite, Morrison R.

Sunday Closing Laws

DESCRIPTION: State or local laws that close all but essential businesses on Sundays to promote rest and the common welfare of the nation.

SIGNIFICANCE: In 1961 the Supreme Court ruled that these laws have a secular purpose and therefore do not violate the establishment of religion clause in the Constitution.

The first Sunday closing laws, or blue laws, went into effect in colonial America and were expressly designed to enable people to celebrate the Christian Sabbath. After the Civil War, businesses began to challenge the laws by, for example, publishing a newspaper on Sunday. In the late nineteenth century, labor unions and Sabbatarians joined forces to preserve Sunday as a common day of rest.

The Supreme Court has consistently upheld the Sunday laws. In *Petit v. Maryland* (1900), the Court ruled that cutting hair did not constitute a work of necessity or charity and therefore forbade a barber shop from operating on Sunday. In 1961 the court ruled on four Sunday closing law cases. *Gallagher v. Crown Kosher Super Market of Massachusetts* and *Braunfeld v. Maryland* involved challenges by Jewish merchants. The Court denied that the owners of these Jewish businesses, who closed on Saturday for religious reasons, suffered substantial harm from being forced to close on Sunday. In *McGowan v. Maryland* and *Two Guys from Harrison-Allentown v. McGinley*, the Court rejected the claim that Sunday closing laws promoted one religion over another and found that they did not violate the equal protection clause of the Fourteenth Amendment. The Court found that the law did not aid a particular religion but rather had a secular purpose, promoting a day of common rest and recreation for workers. Eighteen states recognize Sunday closing laws subject to local enforcement.

Dale W. Johnson

SEE ALSO Fifth Amendment; Fourteenth Amendment; General welfare clause; Religion, establishment of; Religion, freedom of.

George Sutherland

IDENTIFICATION: Associate justice (October 2, 1922-January 17, 1938)
NOMINATED BY: Warren G. Harding
BORN: March 25, 1862, Stoney Stratford, Buckinghamshire, England
DIED: July 18, 1942, Stockbridge, Massachusetts
SIGNIFICANCE: Sutherland was the most intellectually able of a conservative bloc of justices who reaffirmed earlier tenets of individualism and limited government during the 1920's and 1930's.

Born in England, George Sutherland immigrated with his parents to Utah before his second birthday. His parents came as Mormon converts; however, his father, Alexander—variously a miner, storekeeper, and justice of the peace—renounced Mormonism shortly after arriving in the United States. In his teens, Sutherland worked as a clothing store clerk, a mining recorder, and a Wells Fargo agent. In 1879 he entered Brigham Young Academy (later, Brigham Young University), where he was greatly influenced by the school's president, Karl G. Maeser, a thoroughgoing believer in nineteenth century individualist philosophy. After graduation in 1881, Sutherland attended one term at the University of Michigan law school, where he absorbed the natural rights philosophy of Thomas McIntyre Cooley.

POLITICAL CAREER

After returning to Utah, Sutherland quickly acquired a large legal practice and proved so politically adept that his earlier opposition to the Church of Jesus Christ of Latter-day Saints (Mormon) did not hinder his election as a Republican state senator in 1896. (Sutherland's own religion seems to have been a vague, if optimistic, theism.) By 1901 Sutherland had been elected to the U.S. House of Representatives, and in 1905 he became a U.S. senator from Utah. In Congress, Sutherland was noted for his interest in labor legislation (especially seamen's rights) and for his support of woman suffrage and the federal judiciary.

Defeated for reelection in 1916, Sutherland practiced law in Washington, D.C., was elected president of the American Bar Association, and became an adviser to Republican presidential candidate Warren G. Harding. In 1922 President Harding named Sutherland to the Supreme Court; the Senate confirmed him by acclamation—and without discussion—on the day of his appointment. Sutherland found the Court under William H. Taft both personally and philosophically congenial. He sympathized with the judicial conservatism of the majority, and his amiable personality quickly won the friendship even of ideological opponents.

Restriction of Government Power

Sutherland's first major decision, *Adkins v. Children's Hospital* (1923), struck down a District of Columbia law establishing a board to set minimum wages for women sufficient to "maintain them in good health and to protect their morals." Ruling in favor of a woman whose job had been lost to a man, Sutherland argued that no board

George Sutherland. (Library of Congress)

could determine the wage necessary to preserve health and morals and that forcing employers to pay wages without regard to the value of their employees' work was a "naked, arbitrary exercise of power." Predictably, the opinion aroused the ire of Progressives and organized labor, but it revealed Sutherland as a formidable exponent of economic conservatism, individual liberty, and the restriction of governmental power.

Sutherland's decisions continued to champion the individual against governmental regulation. In *Tyson v. Banton* (1927), he wrote for a majority who voided a New York law against ticket scalping. Fearing that such laws might lead to governmental price fixing "as a mere matter of course," Sutherland maintained that theaters were not affected with a public interest and that therefore, sale of their tickets was outside regulatory purview. Likewise, in *Liggett v. Baldridge* (1928), the Court, through Sutherland, ruled unconstitutional a Pennsylvania law intended to shelter old businesses from competition by prohibiting anyone who was not a pharmacist from owning a drugstore.

In perhaps his most widely applauded decision, *Powell v. Alabama* (1932)—the first Scottsboro case, a contemporary cause célèbre—Sutherland set aside the conviction of a young black defendant accused of raping a white girl. His decision declared the Sixth Amendment's guarantee of counsel to those accused of a capital crime to be an "inherent right" and combined a historical survey of due process with long passages from the trial transcript, which revealed (at best) an inappropriate casualness in providing legal representation for unsophisticated teenagers in an intensely hostile environment.

On the other hand, Sutherland voted against individual rights in cases in which he believed they were outweighed by the national interest. Thus, in *United States v. Macintosh* (1931), his opinion denied citizenship to a conscientious objector. Likewise, in *United States v. Curtiss-Wright Export Corp.* (1936), he granted the president broad, extraconstitutional powers to regulate foreign affairs against the interest of private corporations.

The Court vs. the New Deal

The ruling in the *Curtiss-Wright* case was especially surprising in the light of the hostility accorded to the domestic innovations of the

Depression era by the majority of the Court. Liberals soon dubbed Sutherland and three fellow conservative justices—Pierce Butler, James C. McReynolds, and Willis Van Devanter—the Four Horsemen (an allusion to biblical agents of destruction) because of their firm opposition to the New Deal. In *Home Building and Loan Association v. Blaisdell* (1934), Sutherland ruled that Minnesota's emergency postponement of mortgage payments violated the obligation of contract and in *Carter v. Carter Coal Co.* (1936), he declared that an attempt by Congress to institute wage and price controls in the coal industry was unconstitutional because production of coal remained outside its power to regulate under the commerce clause.

Emboldened by the margin of his reelection victory in 1936, President Franklin D. Roosevelt struck at the Court for having gutted major New Deal legislation. In 1937 he proposed to tip the ideological balance of the Court by adding an additional justice for every member over the age of seventy who refused to retire. Sutherland, who was nearing seventy-five and was ready to step down, decided to retain his seat until the Court seemed out of danger. The Court-packing plan proved unpopular and was defeated by Congress. However, Sutherland's decision in *Adkins* was overturned in *West Coast Hotel Co. v. Parrish* (1937)—the famous "switch in time that saved nine." Sutherland wrote a vigorous dissent. Then, in January, 1938, he submitted his resignation.

Sutherland's constitutional jurisprudence, with its emphasis on restricting governmental power, was at least as compatible with the intent of the Framers as that of his successors, but it quickly fell out of favor in the mid-twentieth century. Despite (or perhaps because of) his thoughtful, philosophical justification for economic conservatism and individual liberty, Sutherland eventually became the most overruled justice in the history of the Court.

John Austin Matzko

Further Reading

Arkes, Hadley. *The Return of George Sutherland: Restoring a Jurisprudence of Natural Rights*. Princeton, N.J.: Princeton University Press, 1994.

Bader, William H., and Roy M. Mersky, eds. *The First One Hundred Eight Justices*. Buffalo, N.Y.: William S. Hein, 2004.

Burner, David. "George Sutherland." In *The Justices of the United States Supreme Court, 1789-1978: Their Lives and Major Opinions,* edited by Leon Friedman and Fred L. Israel. Vol. 3. New York: Chelsea House, 1980.

Murphy, Paul. *The Constitution in Crisis Times, 1918-1969.* New York: Harper & Row, 1972.

Parrish, Michael E. *The Hughes Court: Justices, Rulings, and Legacy.* Santa Barbara, Calif.: ABC-Clio, 2002.

Paschal, Joel Francis. *Mr. Justice Sutherland: A Man Against the State.* Princeton, N.J.: Princeton University Press, 1951.

Renstrom, Peter G. *The Taft Court: Justices, Rulings, and Legacy.* Santa Barbara, Calif.: ABC-Clio, 2003.

See also Butler, Pierce; Contract, freedom of; Court-packing plan; Hughes, Charles Evans; McReynolds, James C.; New Deal; Taft, William H.; Van Devanter, Willis.

Swann v. Charlotte-Mecklenburg Board of Education

Citation: 402 U.S. 1
Date: April 20, 1971
Issue: School integration and busing
Significance: The Supreme Court decided that federal courts may order local school boards to use extensive busing plans to desegregate schools whenever racial segregation had been supported by public policy.

When the Supreme Court invalidated freedom of choice plans in *Green v. County School Board of New Kent County* (1968), it announced that it would examine desegregation plans to see if the "transition to unitary schools" was proceeding at an adequate pace. This transition was especially difficult to achieve in large metropolitan areas where residential segregation commonly existed on a de facto basis. The sprawling school district of the Charlotte metropolitan area in North Carolina had been under a court-ordered desegregation plan for several years. Approximately 30 percent of the students were African American, of which about half were attending schools that were integrated to some degree. In conformity with *Green,* the federal district court ordered a more ambitious desegregation plan, involving the transportation of some thirteen thousand students between the predominantly white regions and regions with large black concentrations. The controversial plan required the purchase of one hundred new buses and an annual operating budget of $500,000.

Writing for a unanimous Court, Chief Justice Warren E. Burger emphasized the authority of the federal courts to provide remedies for the present consequences of past de jure segregation. While recognizing that residential segregation based entirely on personal choice did not violate the equal protection clause of the Fourteenth Amendment, Burger contended that the federal courts had broad equity power whenever segregation had been sanctioned or even encouraged by governmental policy. If governmental responsibility for segregation were established, the courts would then have the authority to use busing and other appropriate tools to achieve nonsegregated schools. Although Burger wrote that every school was not required to reflect the racial composition of the school district, he nevertheless approved of "the very limited use of mathematical ratios." The opinion indicated that courts would not be allowed continually to reorder new busing plans on the basis of changing de facto residential patterns within a region.

The ambiguities of the *Swann* decision resulted from strong disagreements and extensive negotiations among the justices. Because Burger had first argued against the busing plan in conference, some justices were angry when Burger chose to write the official opinion in the case. *Swann*'s emphasis on the de facto/de jure distinction meant that most southern schools had the affirmative duty to achieve integration. Elsewhere, federal courts would have the authority to order busing remedies if there was a finding of some governmental involvement in promoting segregation, as in *Keyes v. Denver School District No. 1* (1973).

Thomas Tandy Lewis

Further Reading

Friedman, Leon, ed. *"Brown v. Board": The Landmark Oral Argument Before the Supreme Court.* New York: New Press, 2004.

Schwartz, Bernard. *Swann's Way: The School Busing Case and the Supreme Court.* New York: Oxford University Press, 1986.

See also Burger, Warren E.; Equal protection clause; Race and discrimination; School integration and busing; Segregation, de facto; Segregation, de jure; State action.

Noah H. Swayne

Identification: Associate justice (January 27, 1862-January 24, 1881)

Nominated by: Abraham Lincoln

Born: December 7, 1804, Frederick County, Virginia

Died: June 8, 1884, New York, New York

Significance: The first of Abraham Lincoln's five Supreme Court appointees, Swayne was chosen because of his strong unionist sentiment. He supported the administration's war efforts during and after the Civil War.

Born in Virginia, Noah H. Swayne moved to Ohio after earning his law degree. He spent several years serving as a state legislator and U.S. attorney. With the death of Justice John McLean, Swayne's strong abolitionist views and loyalty to the Republican Party brought him to President Abraham Lincoln's attention.

Appointed to fill the vacancy on the Supreme Court, Swayne took office in January, 1862, and quickly became a consistent vote in favor of the Civil War and toward nationalistic policies of a more powerful federal government. Yet his support consisted of joining opinions rather than writing his own or leading the Court with his views. He joined the Court's opinion in the *Prize Cases* (1863), which upheld the initial decision by Lincoln to have the Union navy blockade Southern ports. After the war, he continued to support the Lincoln administration's wartime measures by dissenting in *Ex Parte Milligan* (1866). In *Milligan,* the Court struck down the use of military courts in noncombat areas where civilian courts remained open. He also dissented in *Cummings v. Missouri* (1867) and *Ex parte Garland* (1867). In both cases, the Court struck down loyalty oaths for state officials and employees in areas once controlled by Confederate governments.

Swayne's nationalism was reflected in his broad interpretation of the Fourteenth Amendment restricting the powers of state governments. He dissented in the first Court case interpreting the amendment, the *Slaughterhouse Cases* (1873), in which the Court upheld a slaughterhouse monopoly against the contention that it violated the liberty rights of state citizens. In his dissent, Swayne supported a broad reading of the Fourteenth Amendment so as to restrict state regulatory power. He sought to use the Bill of Rights and the protections found there to protect state citizens from violation of their rights by state governments.

Part of Swayne's loyalty to the Lincoln administration was attrib-

Noah H. Swayne. (Handy Studios/ Collection of the Supreme Court of the United States)

uted to his desire to become chief justice. After the death of Chief Justice Roger Brooke Taney in 1864, Swayne gathered congressional and administration support for his being promoted to the vacancy. However, lack of any substantive record for Swayne and the absence of any leadership skills caused Lincoln to nominate Salmon P. Chase. After Chase's death in 1873, Swayne made another attempt at promotion, but his advanced age, sixty-nine, caused President Ulysses S. Grant to pass him over. With the chief justiceship beyond his reach, Swayne continued his unimpressive tenure, writing no memorable or landmark decisions during his almost nineteen years on the Court. In declining mental and physical health, he resigned in 1881.

Douglas Clouatre

Further Reading

Bader, William H., and Roy M. Mersky, eds. *The First One Hundred Eight Justices.* Buffalo, N.Y.: William S. Hein, 2004.

Fairman, Charles. *Mr. Justice Miller and the Supreme Court.* Cambridge, Mass.: Harvard University Press, 1939.

Friedman, Leon, and Fred L. Israel, eds. *The Justices of the United States Supreme Court: Their Lives and Major Opinions.* 5 vols. New York: Chelsea House, 1997.

Huebner, Timothy S. *The Taney Court: Justices, Rulings, and Legacy.* Santa Barbara, Calif.: ABC-Clio, 2003.

Lurie, Jonathan. *The Chase Court: Justices, Rulings, and Legacy.* Santa Barbara, Calif.: ABC-Clio, 2004.

Silver, David M. *Lincoln's Supreme Court.* Urbana: University of Illinois Press, 1956.

Stephenson, Donald Grier, Jr. *The Waite Court: Justices, Rulings, and Legacy.* Santa Barbara, Calif.: ABC-Clio, 2003.

See also Chase, Salmon P.; Federalism; Fourteenth Amendment; *Milligan, Ex parte*; *Slaughterhouse Cases*; Waite, Morrison R.

Symbolic Speech

DESCRIPTION: Communication by means other than oral speech or the printed word, usually through objects or actions that have some special significance, such as picketing, burning flags or draft cards, marching, and wearing protest armbands.

SIGNIFICANCE: The Supreme Court held that nonverbal forms of expression are as fully protected as traditional means of expression when they are peaceful and pose no threat to public order; however, when they contain elements that might disrupt the peace or otherwise pose a threat to the community, they are subject to reasonable regulation.

The Supreme Court gradually developed a theory of how the First Amendment applies to so-called "symbolic speech." However, no doubt reflecting the complexity of the issue and the infinite forms that such expression may take, it did so on a case-by-case basis that left the exact boundaries concerning what forms of nonverbal communication are completely protected somewhat vaguely defined. Nonetheless, the Court has increasingly made clear that peaceful forms of nonverbal expression, just as with more traditional forms of expression, may not be forbidden on the basis of content, although reasonable regulations, if their intent is not to suppress, may be imposed on such communications.

FLAGS

The Court's first symbolic speech case was *Stromberg v. California* (1931), a conviction under a California law, passed during the Red Scare of 1919, that banned the display of red flags in an attempt to suppress procommunist organizations. The Court struck down the law on the grounds that to forbid the display of emblems used to foster even "peaceful and orderly opposition" to government was an unconstitutional violation of the First Amendment. This ruling clearly foretold the general direction of later Court decisions in the symbolic speech area, namely that nonverbal expression that was peaceful and served as a functional equivalent of ordinary speech or press was, from a constitutional standpoint, equivalent to them. It clearly established the general principle that symbols such as flags could legally be used to peacefully express political opposition. It also specifically contained the seeds of the Court's holdings in *Texas v. Johnson* (1989) and *United States v. Eichman* (1990) that peaceful flag burning and other forms of flag desecration for the purpose of expressing political protest were fully protected.

The Court's second important symbolic speech case also involved flags. In *West Virginia State Board of Education v. Barnette* (1943), the Court, citing *Stromberg* among other precedents, overruled its own decision in *Minersville School District v. Gobitis* (1940). It held that compulsory public school flag salutes and Pledge of Allegiance requirements were unconstitutional, on the grounds that a child required to attend public schools could not, without violating the First Amendment, be forced by public authorities to verbally or symbolically express sentiments "not in his mind." In rhetoric since cited by many scholars as among the most important and eloquent ever uttered by the Court, Justice Robert H. Jackson declared, "Compulsory unification of opinion achieves only the unanimity of the graveyard" and that it seemed "trite but necessary to say that the First Amendment to our Constitution was designed to avoid these ends by avoiding these beginnings." Jackson stated that the case was difficult not because of the principles involved but because the flag involved was that of the United States. He declared:

> Freedom to differ is not limited to things that do not matter much. That would be a mere shadow of freedom. The test of its substance is the right to differ as to things that touch the heart of the existing order. If there is any fixed star in our constitutional constellation, it is that no official, high or petty, can prescribe what shall be orthodox in politics, nationalism, religion, or other matters of opinion.

Extensions of Protection

In other rulings, the Court extended the mantle of First Amendment protection to many other forms of symbolic speech, including the right to peacefully picket in labor disputes in *Thornhill v. Alabama* (1940) and to peacefully march in support of civil rights in *Cox v. Louisiana* (1965). In a widely publicized 1969 case, *Tinker v. Des Moines In-*

dependent Community School District, the Court upheld the right of schoolchildren to wear black armbands to express opposition to the Vietnam War, an activity that the Court termed "closely akin to 'pure speech'" and thus "entitled to comprehensive protection under the First Amendment" as long as it threatened no disruptions. The Court declared that "undifferentiated fear or apprehension of disturbance is not enough to overcome the right to freedom of expression" and that to justify suppression of expression, the government would have to show that its action was "caused by something more than a mere desire to avoid the discomfort and unpleasantness that always accompanies an unpopular viewpoint."

Court justices not only viewed such nonverbal expression as still essentially communicative in nature but also pointed out that symbolic speech might be the only way for the relatively powerless to gain public attention. In *Milkwagon Drivers Union v. Meadowmoor Dairies* (1941), the Court stated, "Peaceful picketing is the working man's means of communication." Justice William O. Douglas, dissenting in *Adderley v. Florida* (1966), noted, "Conventional means of petitioning may be, and often have been, shut off to large groups of our citizens [because] those who do not control television and radio, those who cannot afford to advertise in newspapers or circulate elaborate pamphlets may have only a more limited type of access to public officials."

Furthermore, the Court suggested that highly unorthodox and symbolic speech might especially deserve protection because it could communicate in an emotive way that ordinary speech and writing could not. Therefore, in *Cohen v. California* (1971), the Court overturned the conviction of a man who wore a jacket bearing the words "Fuck the Draft," declaring that words "are often chosen as much for their emotive as their cognitive force," and that "we cannot sanction the view that the Constitution, while solicitous of the cognitive content of individual speech, has little or no regard for that emotive function which, practically speaking, may often be the more important element of the overall message sought to be communicated."

The Court increasingly made clear that, just as ordinary written and oral political expression can virtually never be criminalized based on its content, neither can symbolic political speech be restricted on such grounds. In *Schacht v. United States* (1970), the Court struck down a law that forbade the unauthorized use of military uniforms in dramatic productions only when such use "tended to discredit" the military, and in *Boos v. Barry* (1988), it voided a law that banned picketing close to embassies only when the picket signs tended to bring the foreign government target into public "odium" or "disrepute."

UNPROTECTED EXPRESSIVE CONDUCT

However, in other symbolic speech cases, the Court declared that symbolically expressive conduct is not always as protected by the First Amendment as is pure speech. Therefore, in *Cox v. Louisiana*, the Court rejected the idea that the First Amendment and other constitutional provisions afforded "the same kind of freedom to those who would communicate ideas by conduct such as patrolling, marching and picketing on streets and highways" as was provided "to those who communicate ideas by pure speech."

In *United States v. O'Brien* (1968), the Court upheld a conviction under a 1965 law that outlawed draft card burning, noting, "We cannot accept the view that an apparently limitless variety of conduct can be labeled 'speech.'" Although the 1965 law was clearly intended to suppress dissent (failure to possess a draft card was already illegal and the congressional debate on the law was filled with references to draft card burners as filthy beatniks, communist stooges, and traitors), the Court upheld it on the strained grounds that it was designed not to hinder free expression but simply to foster the effective functioning of the draft (a purpose that required for its credibility the assumption that the draft administration retained no copies of the information contained on individuals' draft cards).

In *O'Brien*, the Court for the first time attempted to establish guidelines for determining when conduct could be constitutionally regulated if it was combined with an expressive element. In short, the Court held that restrictions on mixed conduct/expression could be upheld if the regulation was within the government's constitutional power and furthered an important or substantial governmental interest that did not involve the suppression of free expression and "if the incidental restriction on alleged First Amendment freedoms is no greater than is essential to the furtherance of that interest." As applied twenty years later to flag desecration, one of the most contentious symbolic speech issues to ever arise, the *O'Brien* guidelines were held to require the protection of protest flag burning on the grounds that the reason behind attempts to outlaw such expression involved the suppression of free expression.

The Court's ruling in *Schenck v. Pro-Choice Network of Western New York* (1997) suggests that further symbolic speech cases will continue to be decided on a case-by-case basis and that the basis of the Court's ruling may continue to be difficult to determine. In *Schenck,* the Court upheld the constitutionality of a fifteen-foot fixed buffer zone banning antiabortion activists from protesting and distributing literature around the driveways and entrances to an abortion clinic but struck down a fifteen-foot "floating" buffer around clients and staff entering or leaving the clinic. It held that the first restriction was justified to ensure public safety and order and burdened speech no more than necessary to achieve that goal, but the second restriction burdened "more speech than is necessary to serve the relevant governmental interests."

Robert Justin Goldstein

Further Reading

Farish, Leah. *"Tinker v. Des Moines": Student Protest.* Springfield, N.J.: Enslow, 1997.

Goldstein, Robert Justin. *Flag Burning and Free Speech: The Case of "Texas v. Johnson."* Lawrence: University Press of Kansas, 2000.

_______. *Saving "Old Glory": The History of the American Flag Desecration Controversy.* Boulder, Colo.: Westview Press, 1995.

Johnson, John. *The Struggle for Student Rights: "Tinker v. Des Moines" and the 1960's.* Lawrence: University Press of Kansas, 1967.

Tedford, Thomas. *Freedom of Speech in the United States.* State College, Pa.: Strata Publishing, 1997.

Welch, Michael. *Flag Burning: Moral Panic and the Criminalization of Protest.* New York: Aldine de Gruyter, 2000.

See also Black, Hugo L.; Cold War; Flag desecration; Speech and press, freedom of; *Texas v. Johnson*; Time, place, and manner regulations; *Tinker v. Des Moines Independent Community School District*; Vietnam War; *Virginia v. Black*; *Wisconsin v. Mitchell.*

William H. Taft

IDENTIFICATION: Twenty-seventh president of the United States (1909-1913), chief justice (July 11, 1921-February 3, 1930)

NOMINATIONS TO THE COURT: Six, all confirmed

NOMINATED BY: Warren G. Harding

BORN: September 15, 1857, Cincinnati, Ohio

DIED: March 8, 1930, Washington, D.C.

SIGNIFICANCE: Taft was the only person to serve as both president and chief justice of the United States. As president, he appointed six members to the Court, including a chief justice.

William H. Taft came from a distinguished Ohio family. His father, Alphonso Taft, served as secretary of war and then attorney general in President Ulysses S. Grant's cabinet. Even as a youth, Taft wanted

William H. Taft. (Deane Keller/Collection of the Supreme Court of the United States)

Taft's Appointments to the Court During His Presidency

Year	*Nominee*	*Result*
1910	Charles Evans Hughes	confirmed
1910	Edward Douglas White	confirmed
1910	Horace Harmon Lurton	confirmed
1911	Willis Van Devanter	confirmed
1911	Joseph Rucker Lamar	confirmed
1912	Mahlon Pitney	confirmed

to become a chief justice. He graduated from Yale University in 1878 and from Cincinnati Law School in 1880.

Taft was assistant prosecuting attorney of Hamilton County, Ohio, from 1881 to 1883. He was elected to the Ohio superior court in 1887. President Benjamin Harrison appointed Taft U.S. solicitor general in 1890 and later named him to the U.S. Sixth Circuit Court. In 1900 President William McKinley appointed Taft to head a commission to end U.S. military rule in the Philippine islands. In 1901 Taft became the first U.S. civil governor of the Philippines. Taft declined President Theodore Roosevelt's offers to appoint him to the Supreme Court as an associate justice, pleading the need to finish his work in the Philippines. In reality, he was holding out for appointment as chief justice. Taft eventually served Roosevelt as secretary of war. He also oversaw construction of the Panama Canal.

As President

In 1908 Roosevelt lobbied for Taft's nomination as the Republican Party's presidential candidate. Taft defeated Democrat William Jennings Bryan to become the twenty-seventh president of the United States. To him, being president was an honor, but his ambition was to become chief justice. During his presidency, he appointed six justices—more than any president since George Washington. He appointed Horace H. Lurton, Charles Evans Hughes, Edward D. White, Willis Van Devanter, Joseph R. Lamar, and Mahlon Pitney. He appointed the sixty-six-year-old White chief justice, hoping he would die in office and thus create the opportunity for the next president to appoint him chief justice. White died in May of 1921. His death led the way for Taft's appointment as chief justice.

Taft sought reelection in 1912. However, his reelection bid failed when former President Roosevelt split with the Republican Party and launched his own candidacy under the Progressive (Bull Moose) Party banner. The split divided the Republican vote, helping Democrat Woodrow Wilson win the election. In 1913 Taft became a professor of law at Yale University.

As Chief Justice

In 1921 President Warren G. Harding, a Republican, appointed Taft chief justice to replace White, who had died. White, who was half-blind and deaf, stayed in office so that a Republican president could appoint Taft chief justice. Taft inherited a strongly divided Court with a rapidly growing backlog of cases. Under his leadership, the Court's operations were streamlined. The reforms included reducing the number of allowable appeals, simplifying Court procedures and rules, and speeding up judicial decisions. In 1922 Taft created the Judicial Conference of the United States to coordinate the work of the federal judiciary's many courts.

Taft's judicial and presidential decisions earned him a reputation as a learned constitutional conservative with a scrupulous respect for property rights. However, Taft acknowledged the need for ordered change to alleviate social and economic inequities. For Taft, the law was a tool to control societal change. He advocated using the strong arm of the judiciary to resist the attacks of unrestrained popular power. Taft thought that the role of the judiciary was to balance the U.S. constitutional system that distributed power to the different branches of the government. Taft believed the Court was best qualified to adjust judicial machinery and legal rules to society's current needs.

While Taft was chief justice, Congress enacted the Judges Act of 1922, which helped relieve the burgeoning workload of the Court. Taft's masterstroke, however, was his lobbying Congress to pass the Judges Act of 1925. It gave the Court greater power to decide which cases it would hear and allowed it to give prompt attention to constitutional questions.

Taft said one of the most significant opinions he ever authored for the majority was *Myers v. United States* (1926). The decision upheld a president's authority to remove a postmaster without the consent of the Senate. Taft repeatedly sought to minimize dissent by "massing the Court" into a conservative majority. His conservative views contrasted sharply with the liberal philosophies of Justices Oliver Wendell Holmes and Louis D. Brandeis.

Late in his tenure as chief justice, Taft was increasingly frustrated with the dissents of Holmes and Brandeis, especially in labor-management disputes and cases involving the prohibition of liquor. Taft believed dissenting opinions unnecessarily slowed the work of the courts. As chief justice, Taft wrote 253 of the 1,596 opinions delivered by the Court between 1921 and 1930. Taft also successfully lobbied Congress to allocate funds for construction of the first Supreme Court building.

Taft's major contribution to the Court and the nation's legal system was in innovations in judicial administration rather than major shifts in legal thought or philosophy. Some historians rank Taft on a par with Oliver Ellsworth, who created the Judiciary Act of 1789 that organized the U.S. judicial system. Taft persuaded Congress to give the Court virtually unlimited discretion to decide which cases it would review. Some historians call Taft the first "modern" chief justice because he successfully expanded and redefined the duties of the chief justice.

Fred Buchstein

Further Reading

Burton, David H. *Taft, Holmes, and the 1920's Court: An Appraisal.* Cranbury, N.J.: Associated University Presses, 1998.

_______. *William Howard Taft in the Public Service.* Malabar, Fla.: Krieger, 1986.

Cushman, Clare, ed. *The Supreme Court Justices—Illustrated Biographies, 1789-1993.* Washington, D.C.: Congressional Quarterly, 1993.

Mason, Alpheus Thomas. *William Howard Taft: Chief Justice.* New York: Simon & Schuster, 1964.

Ragan, Allen E. *Chief Justice Taft.* Columbus, Ohio: Ohio Historical Society, 1938.

Renstrom, Peter G. *The Taft Court: Justices, Rulings, and Legacy.* Santa Barbara, Calif.: ABC-Clio, 2003.
Shoemaker, Rebecca S. *The White Court: Justices, Rulings, and Legacy.* Santa Barbara, Calif.: ABC-Clio, 2004.

See also Chief justice; Hughes, Charles Evans; Judicial activism; Moore, Alfred; Nominations to the Court; Pitney, Mahlon; Presidential powers; Van Devanter, Willis; White, Edward D.

Takings Clause

Date: 1791
Description: Provision in the Fifth Amendment that prohibits the taking of private property for public use unless the owner is appropriately compensated.
Significance: The takings clause is one of the most important and vigorously contested constitutional provisions, at the center of numerous cases before the Supreme Court. The clause pits fundamental capitalist principles of private ownership against the doctrines of state sovereignty and the public good.

The U.S. Constitution contains a number of provisions that seek to protect private ownership of property and property rights more generally. Chief among these is the takings clause of the Fifth Amendment. The clause provides that "private property [shall not] be taken for public use without just compensation." In including this provision, the Framers paid respect to a long-standing, basic individual right with roots in seventeenth century English legal tradition.

The takings clause seeks simultaneously to protect the property rights of individuals—crucial to the United States' capitalist economic system and its cultural value of individualism—and to ensure that the state is able to acquire private property when necessary in order to promote the public good. In other words, it is not a person's *property* that is inviolable; rather, a person is entitled to the *value* of that property in the event that the state has a compelling need to acquire ("take") it. Such state takings of property (usually land) follow the principle of eminent domain—essentially, that the government retains the ultimate right to secure private property for the good of the state because the existence of the state is a precondition of property itself. However, while the principles of eminent domain and just compensation work together neatly under the concept of the takings clause, the business of defining what specific instances warrant the exercise of eminent domain and what level of compensation is just, is fraught with controversy. The Supreme Court has issued a number of landmark decisions on these questions over the years.

Condemnation

Governments exercise eminent domain—that is, they take private property through a process of "condemnation"—in order to advance projects deemed to be in the interest of the public or the government. For example, state and local governments exercise eminent domain over private property that stands in the way of a planned road expansion, a proposed state building, a public works project such as a dam, or any of a number of other projects. Such condemnation of property typically is construed as a taking and thus requires payment of fair market value to the property owner. Eminent domain can be exercised by all levels of government, as well as some quasi-governmental entities such as public utilities.

Disputes may arise over what constitutes the fair market value for a property that is taken by the government through condemnation, but the principle of eminent domain is well established and seldom open to a constitutional challenge. As long as just compensation is provided, the threshold for a valid exercise of eminent domain is relatively low.

Sometimes a government may seize property without providing just compensation. For example, a number of laws at the state and federal level provide for the forfeiture of a person's assets under certain circumstances, including conviction for specified crimes. For example, federal laws permit the forfeiture of certain property, including boats and homes, that were purchased with illicit drug proceeds. Such laws have been challenged as unconstitutional, but generally it is the Eighth Amendment (which prohibits "excessive fines") that is invoked. Because seizures of this type are considered penalties, they do not require compensation.

There are several other circumstances under which the government can seize property without granting compensation. In certain cases, a government may destroy private property in order to preserve public health and safety. For example, the Court has long upheld the right of the state to demolish structures posing a fire hazard as in *Bowditch v. Boston* (1880), to destroy diseased trees that threaten the health of other trees as in *Miller v. Schoene* (1928), or otherwise to abate nuisances, all without compensation. In these cases, property is *not* seized for public use; rather, the state is performing a remediation action where a property owner has failed to meet requirements specified in laws and ordinances.

The takings issue becomes much more complicated when a government seeks not outright condemnation of property but rather to restrict its use. Regulating the use of property is a fundamental and indispensable facet of a government's police powers. Land-use restrictions of various kinds have long been a recognized prerogative of government.

For example, federal, state, and local governments impose habitability standards for housing, hotels, mobile homes, and other structures. Local governments typically zone different sections of land under their jurisdiction for different uses, such as housing, retail businesses, or parks in order to impose order and promote compatible uses. Some such zoning ordinances restrict liquor stores or adult bookstores from areas near churches or schools. Zoning may also be used to restrict residential construction from floodplains and other hazardous areas. Local ordinances may limit noise from a factory or amphitheater in order to preserve quiet for nearby neighborhoods. Land developers may be required to provide open space for habitat conservation or public recreation. Easements may be required to facilitate public access to natural resources such as shorelines or parks. In these and myriad other ways, government exercises a long-accepted right to restrict the use of property.

Regulatory Takings

Governmentally imposed restrictions on the use of property, such as zoning restrictions, can be construed as "regulatory takings" when new restrictions are imposed on a piece of property after a person has purchased it. Presumably restrictions that exist on a property at the time of its purchase are reflected in the purchase price, and thus no governmental compensation is necessary.

The idea that regulatory (nonphysical) takings require compensation has evolved slowly and remains controversial. Until the early 1900's most courts rejected the argument, made by some property owners, that postpurchase regulatory takings warranted compensation under the Fifth Amendment. For example, in *Euclid v. Ambler Realty Co.* (1926), the Court rejected a property owner's argument that he deserved compensation for a local zoning ordinance that banned industrial development on his land. The Court held that the restriction was a valid exercise of police powers exercised by the government for legitimate reasons. *Euclid* thus upheld the constitutionality of zoning ordinances. At about this time, the Court began to recognize the possibility that zoning and other land-use regulations, if restrictive enough, could indeed amount to takings deserving of just compensation. For example, in *Nectow v. City of Cambridge* (1928), the Court considered another ordinance prohibiting industrial development. In this case, the ordinance would permit only residential development on land under contract to be sold for industrial use. The Court found that the ordinance amounted to a taking because it allowed for "no practical use" of the particular parcel.

Many naturally sought guidance on identifying the point at which an otherwise legitimate government exercise of police powers becomes a taking under the Fifth Amendment. The issue was addressed, albeit incompletely, in the Court's opinion in *Pennsylvania Coal Co. v. Mahon* (1922). In that case, the first to address nonphysical takings, the Court found that "Government hardly could go on" if every governmental regulation that diminished the value of property had to be accompanied by compensation. Rather, "some values are enjoyed under an implied limitation and must yield to the police power." At the same time, however, "the implied limitation must have its limits or the contract and due process clauses are gone." In this case, the Court held that restrictions that prevented coal mining on a particular piece of property made that property virtually worthless, and therefore the owner deserved compensation. Justice Louis D. Brandeis issued a dissenting opinion, however, highlighting some difficult and controversial aspects to the Court's attempt at balancing public and private interests. Brandeis's dissent presaged many of the debates that would come into full bloom a half-century later.

For many decades after the 1920's the Court largely avoided takings cases, leaving them to be resolved by state and federal courts. Allowing for some variation among states and regions, legal development during much of the century generally took a fairly conservative approach to the takings clause, emphasizing the need for compelling, often extraordinary state interests in order to effect a taking without compensation. In the 1980's and 1990's, however, the Court heard and decided a number of landmark cases that generally had the effect of strengthening the government's ability to pursue regulatory takings, particularly with the goal of advancing environmental protection.

Balancing

In the 1980's the Court identified two major criteria for determining whether a taking had occurred. This approach, which the Court set forth in *Agins v. City of Tiburon* (1980), called for considering whether the restriction still permitted an economically practical use of the property and whether the regulation advanced a legitimate state interest. This approach is typically referred to as "balancing of public benefit against private loss." In the *Agins* decision, the Court determined that a local zoning ordinance that restricted but did not prohibit residential development did not constitute a taking.

It is important to note that denying a property owner the "highest and best" use of his or her property is not adequate grounds for a takings claim. Certainly a regulation eliminating all practical economic use would be considered a taking. This was illustrated in *Whitney Benefits v. United States* (1989), which held that federal legislation that deprived a mining company of all economic use of its property amounted to a taking without just compensation. Similarly, in *Lucas v. South Carolina Coastal Council* (1992), the Court found that the denial of a beachfront building permit effectively prohibited all economic use of the land and thus amounted to a taking deserving of compensation. (*Lucas* allowed an exception for nuisance abatement.) Aside from such extreme cases as *Whitney* and *Lucas*, however, it is somewhat difficult to establish whether a regulatory action or zoning ordinance permits "economically viable use." One case that did so is *Goldblatt v. Hempstead* (1962), wherein the Court found that an ordinance that effectively prohibited the operation of a gravel pit did nevertheless allow for other, economically viable uses for the property. A similar conclusion was arrived at in *Agins.*

In another landmark case from the 1980's, the Court ruled in *First English Evangelical Lutheran Church of Glendale v. County of Los Angeles* (1987) that even a temporary taking requires just compensation. In this case, a church sought to rebuild some structures on its property that were destroyed in a flood. The county, however, had adopted an interim ordinance preventing construction (including reconstruction) of buildings on the floodplain where the church's buildings had been located. The Court found that a taking, such as that created by the county ordinance, requires just compensation even when the taking is temporary. This decision closed a potential loophole of long-lived, though putatively temporary, land-use restrictions.

Open Space and Environment

The increasing concern with environmental issues in the latter part of the twentieth century was accompanied by greater governmental regulation of private property to provide open space and public access to natural resources. Although the Court has generally supported such goals as legitimate public purposes, it has also had occasion to identify circumstances in which takings have resulted, thus requiring just compensation. For example, in *Kaiser Aetna v. United States* (1980), the Court held that requiring a landowner to provide public access to a private pond amounted to a taking deserving of just compensation. The Court pushed this decision further in Nollan v. California Coastal Commission (1987), holding that a state agency's demand for a coastal easement on private property amounted to a regulatory taking that required just compensation. In the case of *Nollan,* it was a public resource (the coastline of the Pacific Ocean), rather than a private pond, for which public access was required.

It would seem that the Court accepted a broad range of resource-related goals as legitimate grounds for the exercise of eminent domain. At the same time, the Court seemed to be viewing open space requirements and demands for easements as bona fide takings requiring just compensation. A distinction was generally drawn for open space requirements imposed on land developers whose proposed development would itself generate a need for such open space. For example, a housing development on agricultural land would increase the population of the area, thus arguably creating a need to preserve and create access to some open space, such as parks or greenbelts. Requirements for such environmental impact-mitigating measures might therefore not warrant compensation. However, in *Dolan v. City of Tigard* (1994), the Court struck down a city's requirement that a hardware store owner dedicate a portion of property for a trail in order to be permitted to expand the store. The Court held that the city had not satisfactorily established that the requirement was needed to offset any anticipated increase in traffic from the expansion. Dolan thus underscored the need to link mitigating measures to the actual impacts of a proposed project.

Later Decisions

In the late 1990's the Court seemed to continue its support for environmentally based regulatory takings, while maintaining or even expanding the requirement that such takings, when significant, require just compensation. The state has a right to insist on property restrictions that protect the environment, the Court seemed to say, but the state must be willing to pay when these restrictions significantly restrict use.

A major case from this period was *Suitum v. Tahoe Regional Planning Agency* (1997). In this case, a property owner sought to build a home on an undeveloped lot she had purchased fifteen years earlier. The lot, in Nevada near Lake Tahoe, fell under the jurisdiction of the Tahoe Regional Planning Agency (TRPA). The agency, charged with protecting environmental quality in the Lake Tahoe Basin, prohibited the development as likely to cause unacceptable environmental damage. TRPA essentially denied all economic use and offered as compensation "transferable development rights." Such rights could not be used to build on Suitum's lot but could be sold to a different landowner in the Tahoe basin where such development would not be prohibited. By purchasing those rights, the property owner could build a larger structure than otherwise allowed.

Suitum had been told by a lower court that her case was not "ripe"—that she had not accepted and tried to sell the transferrable development rights. However, the Supreme Court held that Suitum's case was indeed ripe and must be decided by the District Court of Nevada.

The Court's interpretation of the takings clause in *Kelo v. City of New London* (2005) ignited a firestorm of criticism. In an attempt to repair a declining economy, a city government had decided to use its powers of eminent domain to require property owners to sell their land, which was then turned over to private developers who were expected to increase local jobs and promote economic development. Some of the affected property owners did not want to sell and sued the city, arguing that the use of eminent domain for private development was not authorized by the Fifth Amendment, which specified that private property could be "taken for public use." By a 5-4 margin, the Supreme Court ruled in favor of the city. Defending the ruling, Justice John Paul Stevens broadly interpreted the term "public use" as synonymous with a "public purpose," and he emphasized that the taking of property was part of the city's development plan to counter the economic difficulties of the city. The *Kelo* decision infuriated homeowners throughout the country, and Minnesota and other states passed legislation prohibiting the use of the takings clause for private development.

Transferable development rights are one of a number of the sometimes innovative, sometimes complicated, and frequently controversial approaches that were developed by various governmental bodies in order to regulate land use without running afoul of the Fifth Amendment. Other approaches involve development fees, open space dedications, habitat conservation plans, and statutory compensation programs.

Steve D. Boilard
Updated by the Editor

Further Reading

One of the most focused recent works on the Supreme Court's treatment of takings is provided in George Skouras's *Takings Law and the Supreme Court: Judicial Oversight of the Regulatory State's Acquisition, Use, and Control of Private Property* (New York: P. Lang, 1998). For theoretical overviews of the broader subject of property rights, see Polly J. Price's *Property Rights: Rights and Liberties Under the Law* (Santa Barbara, Calif.: ABC-Clio, 2003) and Tom Bethell's *The Noblest Triumph: Property and Prosperity Through the Ages* (New York: St. Martin's Press, 1998).

Among general works on legal issues associated with property rights (including treatments of takings), see Jan Laitos's *Law of Property Rights Protection: Limitations on Governmental Powers* (Gaithersburg, Md.: Aspen Law and Business, 1998). On the subject of environmentally motivated takings, see Robert Meltz et al., *The Takings Issue: Constitutional Limits on Land Use Control and Environmental Regulation* (Washington, D.C.: Island Press, 1998), and Robert Innes et al., "Takings, Compensation, and Endangered Species Protection on Private Lands," *Journal of Economic Perspectives* (Summer, 1998): 35-52. A somewhat critical assessment of regulatory takings is provided by Gideon Kanner in "Just Compensation Is by No Means Always Just," *The National Law Journal* (March 24, 1997): A23.

The Congressional Budget Office has put out a very understandable overview of regulatory takings, describing the current system for handling regulatory takings claims and evaluating various proposals for changing that system. See *Regulatory Takings and Proposals for Change* (Washington, D.C.: Congressional Budget Office, 1999).

See also Bill of Rights; Brandeis, Louis D.; Constitutional interpretation; Environmental law; Fifth Amendment; *Kelo v. City of New London*; Zoning.

Roger Brooke Taney

Identification: Chief justice (March 28, 1836-October 12, 1864)
Nominated by: Andrew Jackson
Born: March 17, 1777, Calvert County, Maryland
Died: December 1, 1864, Washington, D.C.
Significance: Although Taney is ranked by many scholars as one of the great chief justices, his reputation is marred by his support of the rights of slaveholders.

Roger Brooke Taney was born into a wealthy Maryland family that farmed tobacco. He studied law and entered Maryland politics. As a member of the Federalist Party, he advocated some government participation in the nation's economic development. However, his southern background often led him to take a strong states' rights position on many issues.

With the collapse of the Federalist Party, Taney became a Democrat and follower of Andrew Jackson. In 1831 Jackson appointed Taney to the office of attorney general. Initially a supporter of the Bank of the United States, Taney became a vigorous opponent of that institution by the 1820's. His role in Jackson's attack on the bank resulted in Taney's leaving the government. Jackson, however, was indebted to Taney for his efforts, and when the opportunity arose, he nominated him for the position of associate justice of the Supreme Court in 1835. The senate failed to act on the nomination. Later that same year, Jackson nominated Taney to fill the chief justice's office

Roger Brooke Taney. (Mathew Brady/ Collection of the Supreme Court of the United States)

left vacant by John Marshall's death. Although considerable opposition to Taney remained, the Senate confirmed him by a vote of twenty-nine to fifteen.

Chief Justice

Some observers feared that Taney would undo Marshall's legacy of a strong judiciary that favored nationalism over states' rights. Taney's decision in *Charles River Bridge v. Warren Bridge* (1837), which significantly revised the legal interpretations of contracts, ran contrary to Marshall's views and heightened concerns over the direction of the Court. Taney's decisions in *New York v. Miln* (1837) and *Briscoe v. Bank of the Commonwealth of Kentucky* (1837) also deviated from precedents established during Marshall's tenure. In the long run, however, Taney merely refined Marshall's nationalist outlook, arguing that the states and the federal government shared many powers and that in those areas of divided sovereignty, states were free to act as long as they did not violate federal laws.

Taney changed some of the traditions of the Court. Justices had long shared the same boardinghouse, a practice that Taney abandoned. He also allowed associate justices to write majority opinions in important cases, a responsibility that Marshall usually reserved for himself.

Slavery

Taney presided over the Court during a period when slavery and its expansion into the western territories became divisive issues in American life. Taney, who regarded slavery as a necessary evil that might one day fade away, had freed the slaves that he had inherited. Nonetheless, he was a staunch supporter of the rights of slaveholders and typically favored the power of the states over the federal government in regard to that issue. The Court had a proslavery majority during most of Taney's tenure, a fact reflected in its many decisions concerning slavery.

In *Groves v. Slaughter* (1841), a case involving the importation of slaves for sale in Mississippi, Taney wrote a concurring opinion in which he maintained that the federal government had no authority over matters involving slavery and the states. However, in his concurring opinion in *Prigg v. Pennsylvania* (1842), Taney argued that the Fugitive Slave Act of 1793 obliged government officials in free states to cooperate in the capture and return of fugitive slaves to their owners. This opinion revealed that Taney was willing to use federal laws to compel state action in those cases in which those laws supported the institution of slavery.

Taney's most famous decision, and the one that damaged his historical reputation, came in the 1857 case of *Scott v. Sandford.* In his opinion, Taney maintained that African Americans, whether free or enslaved, were not citizens of the United States. This ruling was in keeping with an opinion he had offered as attorney general regarding the right of states to prohibit the entry of free blacks. In that instance, Taney had declared that African Americans did not have rights because they were not regarded as citizens by the authors of the Constitution.

Taney's opinion in *Scott* unleashed a storm of controversy and contributed to the coming of the Civil War. It also destroyed Taney's final years on the Court. Already in poor health and grieving from the loss of his wife and daughter to yellow fever in 1835, Taney now received abuse and contempt for his ruling. Nonetheless, he remained on the Court. Although he was a unionist opposed to secession, Taney used his position to attack President Abraham Lincoln and the federal government during the war, including a publicly released brief that condemned the Emancipation Proclamation as unconstitutional. The embittered Taney died in 1864 believing that the power of the Court had been disastrously undermined by Lincoln's wartime exercise of executive power.

Legal scholars recognize Taney as one of the most effective chief justices in the nation's history. His willingness to revise Marshall's nationalist legacy allowed for a measure of flexibility in the law that promoted economic development. However, Taney's unwavering defense of slavery and the inconsistencies in his political philosophy that resulted from that defense have become the foundation for the general public's understanding of, and to a great degree contempt for, Taney.

Thomas Clarkin

Further Reading

Bader, William H., and Roy M. Mersky, eds. *The First One Hundred Eight Justices.* Buffalo, N.Y.: William S. Hein, 2004.

Fehrenbacher, Don E. *The Dred Scott Case: Its Significance in American Law and Politics.* New York: Oxford University Press, 2001.

Friedman, Leon, and Fred L. Israel, eds. *The Justices of the United States Supreme Court: Their Lives and Major Opinions.* 5 vols. New York: Chelsea House, 1997.

Huebner, Timothy S. *The Taney Court: Justices, Rulings, and Legacy.* Santa Barbara, Calif.: ABC-Clio, 2003.

Steiner, Bernard C. *Life of Roger Brooke Taney: Chief Justice of the Supreme Court.* Westport, Conn.: Greenwood Press, 1970.

Swisher, Carl Brent. *Roger B. Taney.* New York: Macmillan, 1935.

See also Civil War; Contracts clause; *Scott v. Sandford*; Slavery; Story, Joseph.

Tennessee v. Garner

Citation: 471 U.S. 1

Date: March 27, 1985

Issue: Use of force by the police

Significance: The Supreme Court held that a police officer may use deadly force only when there is probable cause to believe that the suspect poses an immediate threat of death or physical harm to the officer or to others.

In 1974 a fifteen-year-old boy, Edward Garner, broke a window to enter an unoccupied house in Memphis, Tennessee. Two officers intercepted the suspect in the back of the house. By shining a flashlight, the officers were "reasonably sure" that the suspect was young and unarmed. When he was about to escape over a fence, one of the officers shot him in the back. The officer had acted in accordance with Tennessee's fleeing felon statute, which authorized all means necessary to stop a suspected felon. The decedent's father, nevertheless, won a damage award against the officers and the city.

By a 6-3 vote, the Supreme Court struck down the relevant portion of the Tennessee law. In the majority opinion, Justice Byron R. White wrote that apprehending a suspect "is a seizure subject to the reasonableness requirement of the Fourth Amendment." The majority found no reasonable justification for officers to use deadly force against a suspect who did not appear to be armed and dangerous. After the *Garner* decision was issued, half of the states had laws that were unconstitutional because of a lack of restraint on the use of force while attempting to arrest a nondangerous suspect.

Thomas Tandy Lewis

See also Due process, procedural; Fourth Amendment; Police powers; White, Byron R.

Tenth Amendment

Date: 1791

Description: Amendment to the U.S. Constitution and part of the Bill of Rights that reserves for the states those powers not delegated to the federal government by the Constitution.

Significance: The Supreme Court's decisions involving the Tenth Amendment were not always consistent. At times the amendment was criticized as redundant and at others reaffirmed as a valuable part of the Constitution.

The Tenth Amendment protects the reserved powers of the state, those not delegated to the federal government by the U.S. Constitution. The First Congress received numerous requests to include a means of protecting the reserved powers of the states. These concerns arose in many quarters during the Constitutional Convention of 1787 and ratification process, especially among the Antifederalists, who feared that an overbearing national government would assume the authority of the states. Article II of the Articles of Confederation had contained explicit provisions for protecting states, initiating a system whereby "each state retains its sovereignty." Various early state constitutions included provisions outlining the primacy of states in the confederal arrangement.

TEXT OF THE TENTH AMENDMENT

The powers not delegated to the United States by the Constitution, nor prohibited by it to the States, are reserved to the States respectively, or to the people.

FEDERALISTS AND ANTIFEDERALISTS

The most popular form of amendment requested during the state ratification conventions and proposed to the First Congress concerned a reserved powers clause. The defenders of the Constitution argued that such a provision was unnecessary. James Madison suggested in No. 39 of *The Federalist* (1788) that each state was "a sovereign body," bound only by its voluntary act of ratification. Other Federalists at the Virginia ratifying convention, including James Wilson, Alexander Hamilton, and John Marshall, held that such a provision was already present in the Constitution and that the new government would have only the powers delegated to it.

Opposition to and suspicion of the proposed Constitution on the grounds that it would infringe on the privileged status of the states was widespread. The defenders of state authority viewed the states as the repository of reserved power, and many believed that states were invested with an equal capacity to judge infractions against the federal government. In the Virginia ratifying convention, George Nicholas and Edmund Randolph, members of the committee reporting the instrument of ratification, noted that the Constitution would have only the powers "expressly" delegated to it. If Federalists disagreed with the stress on state authority, they generally viewed a reserved power clause as innocuous, and Madison included such a provision among the amendments he introduced in 1789.

In the First Congress, Elbridge Gerry, a Founder and Antifederalist elected to the House of Representatives, introduced a proposal reminiscent of the Articles of Confederation, leaving to the states all powers "not expressly delegated" to the federal government. Gerry's proposal was defeated, in part because of concerns about the similarity between the language of his amendment and that of the articles.

Others who took a states' rights or strict constructionist view of the Constitution, including Thomas Jefferson, persisted in defending state power. Before ratification of the Tenth Amendment, Jefferson advised President George Washington that incorporating a national bank was unconstitutional, basing his opinion on the amendment. Jefferson would later compose the Kentucky Resolutions, which defended the states as the sovereign building blocks of the American nation and noted that the states retained a means of protection when threatened. To describe the process of state action, Jefferson supplied a new term, nullification, to note the immediacy and severity of the "remedy" necessary to prohibit the federal government from absorbing state authority.

Defenders of the federal government, sometimes described as nationalists or loose constructionists, argued that Congress must assume more power if the needs of the country were to be met. Most prominent among the advocates of increased federal authority was Hamilton. For Hamilton, the Tenth Amendment was unnecessary as the political order already protected states. The Constitution, according to the nationalists, already contained provisions for the exercise of federal power, including the necessary and proper clause and supremacy clause.

The Court and the Amendment

The Supreme Court addressed the controversy in *McCulloch v. Maryland* (1819). The Court upheld the constitutionality of a national bank, even though such an institution was not specified in the Constitution. In dismissing a strict delineation of state and federal authority, the Court, under the leadership of Marshall, extended the powers of Congress at the expense of the states. However, the Marshall Court also affirmed the notion that police powers belonged exclusively to the states. Under Chief Justice Roger Brooke Taney, the Court assumed more of a strict constructionist posture.

With the Civil War and Reconstruction, the authority and influence of the federal government were greatly increased. The role of the Tenth Amendment was essentially disregarded as federal troops occupied southern states and Congress provided governance. The authority of the states continued to suffer, resulting in part from a series of Court decisions in the twentieth century. In *Champion v. Ames* (1903), the Court affirmed a congressional act that prohibited the sale of lottery tickets across state lines as an effort to limit gambling. Before *Champion*, decisions regarding gambling were made by the states. The decisions of the Court were not consistent, and it soon adopted a view of the relationship between states and the federal government that allowed each to be authoritative in its own sphere, exempting "state instrumentalities" from federal taxation. In *Hammer v. Dagenhart* (1918), the Court ruled in favor of state power in terms of commerce. The Tenth Amendment would, however, suffer its most severe criticism in *United States v. Darby Lumber Co.* (1941). In this decision, Chief Justice Harlan Fiske Stone discredited the amendment as "redundant" and a "constitutional tranquilizer and empty declaration."

Stone's dismissal of the amendment turned out not to be permanent. During the 1970's, the Burger and Rehnquist Courts began looking to the Tenth and Eleventh Amendments to construct a "new federalism," resurrecting limits on Congress's power to regulate the states. The first major case was *National League of Cities v. Usery* (1976). In a 5-4 margin in that decision, the Court ruled that the Tenth Amendment outweighed the commerce clause, so that Congress had no power to apply the federal minimum wage to employees of states and local governments. Nine years later, however, Justice Harry A. Blackmun changed his position in *Garcia v. San Antonio Metropolitan Transit Authority* (1985), resulting in a 5-4 vote to overturn the *Usery* ruling.

The Court's official opinion in *Gregory v. Ashcroft* (1991), written by Justice Sandra Day O'Connor, defended the states' autonomy under the doctrine of "dual sovereignty," based primarily on the Tenth and Eleventh Amendments. O'Connor further asserted a "plain statement rule" with two-prongs: First, Congress must clearly articulate its intent to extend a law to the states; second, Congress must outline which activities are targeted under federal law. *Gregory*'s limits on federal power would reappear in many subsequent cases, including *New York v. United States* (1992), in which the Court struck down the part of the Low-Level Radioactive Waste Policy Act that required states to "take title" of nuclear waste at the request of the generator of the waste. The Court concluded that the "take title" provision crossed the line between regulation and "commandeering" the states' legislative processes, thus violating the Tenth Amendment. In *Printz v. United States* (1997), the Court again found that Congress had unconstitutionally intruded on state sovereignty in the portion of the Brady Act that required local law-enforcement officers to run background checks on hand gun purchasers.

Despite the justices' expansive reading of the Tenth Amendment, Congress retained substantial powers to enforce laws affecting the states. In *Reno v. Condon* (2000), for example, the Court unanimously upheld the Driver's Privacy Protection Act of 1994, which restricted the states' disclosure of personal information on drivers licenses without consent. Chief Justice William H. Rehnquist explained that the disclosure of such information was clearly a matter of interstate commerce. In *Raich v. Gonzales* (2005), the Court upheld, by a 6-3 margin, federal enforcement of the Controlled Substances Act of 1970, which outlawed all uses of marijuana, even in states that legalized the substance for certain forms of medical use. Arguing that the law was consistent with the Tenth Amendment, Justice John Paul Stevens observed that marijuana consumption was part of a "class of activities" that substantially affected the regulation of interstate commerce—one of Congress's enumerated powers."

H. Lee Cheek, Jr.
Updated by the Editor

Further Reading

Berger, Raoul. *Federalism: The Founders' Design.* Norman: University of Oklahoma Press, 1987.

Calhoun, John C. "A Discourse on the Constitution and Government of the United States." In *Union and Liberty: The Political Philosophy of John C. Calhoun,* edited by Ross M. Lence. Indianapolis, Ind.: Liberty Fund, 1992.

Hickok, Eugene W., Jr., ed. "The Original Understanding of the Tenth Amendment." In *The Bill of Rights.* Charlottesville: University of Virginia Press, 1991.

Killenbeck, Mark R., ed. *The Tenth Amendment and State Sovereignty: Constitutional History and Contemporary Issues.* Lanham, Md.: Rowman & Littlefield, 2002.

Lofgren, Charles A. "The Origins of the Tenth Amendment, History, Sovereignty, and the Problems of Constitutional Intention." In *Constitutional Government in America,* edited by Ronald K. L. Collins. Durham, N.C.: Carolina Academic Press, 1980.

McAffee, Thomas, and Jay Bybee. *Powers Reserved for the People and the States: A History of the Ninth and Tenth Amendments.* Westport, Conn.: Greenwood Press, 2006.

Nagel, Robert F. *The Implosion of American Federalism.* New York: Oxford University Press, 2002.

Noonan, John Thomas, Jr. *Narrowing the Nation's Power: The Supreme Court Sides with the States.* Berkeley: University of California Press, 2002.

See also Bill of Rights; Constitutional interpretation; *Darby Lumber Co., United States v.*; Federalism; *McCulloch v. Maryland*; *Printz v. United States*; *Raich v. Gonzales*; State action; States' rights and state sovereignty; Stone, Harlan Fiske; Taney, Roger Brooke.

Terry v. Ohio

Citation: 392 U.S. 1
Date: June 10, 1968
Issues: Stop and frisk rule; search and seizure
Significance: The Supreme Court upheld stop and frisk procedures in the first of a long series of cases.

Chief Justice Earl Warren, writing for an eight-member majority, upheld Terry's conviction and an Ohio law allowing stop and frisk procedures. These procedures allow a police officer to stop people on the street and pat them down to see if they are carrying weapons. In *Terry,* the police officer patted down two persons he suspected of "casing" a store before robbing it. The men had paced back and forth in front of a store a dozen times in front of the police before the officer stopped them. Finding both men armed with pistols, the officer arrested them. The Supreme Court ruled it was proper to admit the guns into evidence in the trial. This was the first in a series of cases dealing with various stop and frisk procedures. Justice William O. Douglas dissented, finding the police behavior intrusive.

Richard L. Wilson

See also Bill of Rights; Due process, procedural; *Ferguson v. City of Charleston*; Fourth Amendment; *Mapp v. Ohio*; Search warrant requirement; Warren, Earl.

Texas v. Johnson

Citation: 491 U.S. 397
Date: June 21, 1989
Issues: Symbolic speech; flag desecration
Significance: The Supreme Court directly struck down state flag desecration laws.

A member of the Communist Party burned the U.S. flag outside the Republican National Convention during a presidential election year in violation of Texas's statute banning desecration of the flag. By a 5-4 vote, the Supreme Court struck down the Texas statute on the grounds that the burning of the U.S. flag was a form of symbolic speech protected by the First Amendment. The Court looked rather heavily to the motives for the flag burning and decided that the act was really a form of political protest. Some scholars thought that the Court's position would have been more readily defensible if it had relied on a distinction between thought and action, which would have been an easier test to follow than one that relied on the flag burner's motives.

The Court's decision set off a howl of protest across the nation. People began calling for a constitutional amendment to exempt flag burning from First Amendment protection, but this effort failed in Congress because of concerns about the dangers involved in amending the Bill of Rights. Congress did attempt to overcome the Court's objections with a statute, the Flag Protection Act of 1989. The Court struck down the federal statute as it had the Texas statute in *United States v. Eichman* (1990).

Richard L. Wilson

Further Reading

Goldstein, Robert Justin. *Flag Burning and Free Speech: The Case of "Texas v. Johnson."* Lawrence: University Press of Kansas, 2000.

Miller, J. Anthony. *"Texas v. Johnson": The Flag Burning Case.* Springfield, N.J.: Enslow, 1997.

Welch, Michael. *Flag Burning: Moral Panic and the Criminalization of Protest.* New York: Aldine de Gruyter, 2000.

See also *Brandenburg v. Ohio*; Flag desecration; *Gitlow v. New York*; National security; *Schenck v. United States*; Symbolic speech; *Tinker v. Des Moines Independent Community School District*; *Virginia v. Black.*

Thirteenth Amendment

Date: 1865

Description: Amendment to the U.S. Constitution in 1865 that abolished slavery and allowed Congress to enact legislation enforcing the ban on slavery.

Significance: The Supreme Court used the Thirteenth Amendment to recognize Congress's power to enact laws aimed at combating racial discrimination by private individuals and businesses in property transactions and contracts.

Text of the Thirteenth Amendment

Section 1. Neither slavery nor involuntary servitude, except as a punishment for crime whereof the party shall have been duly convicted, shall exist within the United States, or any place subject to their jurisdiction.

Section 2. Congress shall have power to enforce this article by appropriate legislation.

After the end of the Civil War, in December, 1865, the Thirteenth Amendment was ratified, abolishing slavery in the United States. Section 1 of the amendment prohibited slavery, and section 2 gave Congress the power to enact legislation to enforce the prohibition on slavery. The Supreme Court initially examined the Thirteenth Amendment in the *Civil Rights Cases* (1883). Congress had enacted the Civil Rights Act of 1875, which barred racial discrimination in public accommodations, such as hotels, theaters, and railroads, and the Court was called on to decide whether Congress possessed the authority to prohibit discrimination by private individuals and businesses. The Court concluded that Congress's power under section 2 of the amendment was limited to legislation concerning slavery and involuntary servitude and that racial discrimination in public accommodations was a separate issue.

The Court had little reason to reexamine the Thirteenth Amendment until the Civil Rights movement of the 1960's pushed all segments of government to address the country's continuing problem

African Americans in Richmond, Virginia, celebrating Emancipation Day—the anniversary of the abolition of slavery—during the early twentieth century. (Library of Congress)

of racial discrimination. In *Jones v. Alfred H. Mayer Co.* (1968), the Court examined a statute that remained on the books from the Civil Rights Act of 1866. The law required that all citizens have the same rights as white people to buy and sell property. Although in 1883 the Court had distinguished private discrimination from slavery, in 1968 it saw congressional action against racial discrimination as part of an effort to eliminate the vestiges of slavery. According to Justice Potter Stewart's majority opinion in the *Jones* case, "When racial discrimination herds men into ghettos and makes their ability to buy property turn on the color of their skin, then it too is a relic of slavery."

In a later decision, *Runyon v. McCrary* (1976), the Court followed the same approach in endorsing another statute derived from the Civil Rights Act of 1866. In *Runyon,* the Court declared that the Thirteenth Amendment gave Congress the power to enact legislation barring racial discrimination in the formation of contracts. Through the Court's interpretation of the Thirteenth Amendment, Congress gained an important tool for enacting legislation aimed at eliminating several forms of unequal treatment practiced by private individuals and businesses.

Christopher E. Smith

Further Reading

Anastaplo, George. *The Amendments to the Constitution: A Commentary.* Baltimore, Md.: Johns Hopkins University Press, 1995.

Farber, Daniel A., William N. Eskridge, Jr., and Philip P. Frickey. *Constitutional Law: Themes for the Constitution's Third Century.* St. Paul, Minn.: West Publishing, 1993.

Foner, Eric. *Reconstruction: America's Unfinished Revolution, 1863-1877.* New York: Harper & Row, 1988.

Scaturro, Frank J. *The Supreme Court's Retreat from Reconstruction: A Distortion of Constitutional Jurisprudence.* Westport, Conn.: Greenwood Press, 2000.

Tsesis, Alexander. *The Thirteenth Amendment and American Freedom: A Legal History.* New York: New York University Press, 2004.

See also *Civil Rights Cases*; Civil War; Fifteenth Amendment; Peonage; Race and discrimination; Reconstruction; Slavery; Stewart, Potter.

Clarence Thomas

Identification: Associate justice (November 1, 1991-)
Nominated by: George H. W. Bush
Born: June 23, 1948, Pin Point, Georgia
Significance: The second African American to become a justice of the Supreme Court, Thomas has been one of the most consistently conservative justices to serve on the Court since the New Deal era.

A descendant of Georgia slaves, Clarence Thomas grew up speaking the Geechee dialect, a mixture of English and several West African languages. At the age of two, his father left his mother, and a few years thereafter he and his brother moved to Savannah, Georgia, to live with grandparents, who instilled in him the values of hard work, self-reliance, and ambition. He was a good student in high school, and after graduating cum laude at the College of the Holy Cross, he attended the Yale University Law School, graduating in 1974. There has been inconclusive debate about whether he benefited from affirmative action policies during his education.

After his graduation, Thomas became an assistant attorney general for Missouri attorney general John Danforth. Three years later he joined the Monsanto Corporation's law firm. In 1979, Danforth, then a U.S. senator, hired Thomas as a legislative assistant. Two years later Thomas was appointed assistant secretary for civil rights in the Department of Education by President Ronald Reagan. From 1982 to 1990, Thomas served as chairman of the Equal Employment Opportunity Commission (EEOC). At the EEOC, he established a conservative reputation as a result of his attempts to limit affirmative action programs, particularly the use of racial and ethnic preferences.

Appointment to the Supreme Court

In 1990, President George H. W. Bush appointed Thomas to the court of appeals for the District of Columbia. The next year, after Justice Thurgood Marshall announced his retirement, President Bush, looking for a conservative African American as his successor, nominated Thomas on July 8, 1990.

The confirmation hearings for Thomas created great controversy and unprecedented public interest. Liberal and civil rights organizations denounced the nomination. The American Bar Association rated Thomas between "qualified" and "not qualified." When grilled by the Democrats on the Senate Judiciary Committee, Thomas often appeared evasive, even more than most other candidates. His liberal critics expressed skepticism about his answers, especially his claim never to have discussed the abortion issue in law school. Just as it was beginning to appear that he would be relatively easily confirmed toward the end of the hearings, University of Oklahoma law professor and former EEOC attorney Anita Hill accused Thomas of having practiced sexual harassment. Denying her accusations, Thomas charged his critics of conducting "a high-tech lynching for uppity-blacks." On October 15, 1991, the U.S. Senate confirmed him to the Supreme Court by a 52-48 vote, the closest margin of approval in more than a century.

Justice Clarence Thomas (right) with Justices Antonin Scalia (left) and David Souter (center) in early 2006. (AP/Wide World Photos)

Jurisprudence and Decisions

Thomas's constitutional jurisprudence combined a commitment to natural rights with the doctrines of "textualism" and "originalism," focusing on the literal words of the text informed by the original intent of its framers. In addition, Thomas demonstrated a strong commitment to individualism and strong distrust of federal power and modern secularism. His views most often coincided with those of Justice Antonin Scalia, except that Thomas was less inclined to defer to the precedents of the Court (called the doctrine of *stare decisis*).

Advocating color-blind governmental policies, Thomas found nothing wrong with de facto racial segregation, insisting that only de jure (or state-enforced) segregation was unconstitutional. In his concurrence in *Missouri v. Jenkins* (1995), he wrote that the goal of integration falsely "assumed that blacks could not get ahead on their own." He consistently opposed all race-based preferences, declaring in *Adarand Constructors v. Peña* (1995) that there is no "racial paternalism exception to the principle of equal protection." When examining race-based policies for university admissions in *Grutter v. Bollinger* (2003), he rejected the rationale of racial diversity as "a faddish slogan of the cognoscenti." Likewise, he wrote a long concurrence in *Holder v. Hall* (1994), opposing special efforts to establish electoral districts dominated by minorities, which he denounced as "nothing short of a system of 'political apartheid.'"

Concerning the constitutional right of privacy, Thomas has frequently declared that the Fourteenth Amendment protects only those "liberty interests" that were "deeply rooted in the nation's history." Thus, he agreed with the Court's ruling that government may not prohibit married persons from purchasing contraceptives. In *Planned Parenthood of Southeastern Pennsylvania v. Casey* (1992), in contrast, he joined the dissenters who insisted that the Constitution did not protect a woman's right to have an abortion. Dissenting in *Lawrence v. Texas* (2003), when the Court struck down a Texas law outlawing homosexual practices, he wrote that the law was "uncommonly silly" but not unconstitutional.

Thomas has firmly supported states' rights under the Tenth Amendment, while concomitantly taking a narrow view of Congress's powers under the commerce clause. In *United States v. Lopez* (1995), he joined the majority in holding that states may not regulate local activities, such as firearms in school zones. In a concurrence, he wrote that the New Deal Court had "drifted far from the original understanding of the commerce clause." Likewise, in *Printz v. United States* (1997), he found that the Brady Bill violated both the commerce clause and the Tenth Amendment. He further argued that the bill might violate the Second Amendment, which conferred a "personal right" to keep and bear arms.

Thomas has almost always agreed with the pro-law-and-order perspective. Applying the Eighth Amendment narrowly in *Hudson v. McMillan* (1992), he dissented, arguing that the beating of a prison inmate by three guards did not amount to cruel and unusual punishment. In *Roper v. Simmons* (2005), he disagreed with the majority's view on the unconstitutionality of executing minors. In *Rasul v. Bush* (2004), he again joined the dissenters who wanted to deny habeas corpus relief in federal court to foreign citizens held at the U.S. military base in Guantanamo, Cuba.

On other issues as well, Thomas could normally be counted on to vote for the conservative viewpoint. In *Zelman v. Simmons-Harris* (2002), for example, he supported a lowering of the wall between church and state by enthusiastically endorsing the use of tax-supported vouchers for use in parochial school. In cases such as *Kelo v. City of New London* (2005), he construed the takings clause of the Fifth Amendment as providing broad protection for private property. In the controversial case, *Bush v. Gore* (2000), he joined with the majority's decision to stop the recount of popular votes in Florida, a decision that his critics found to be inconsistent with his theories of federalism and the Constitution's original understanding.

Thomas Tandy Lewis

Further Reading

Bader, William H., and Roy M. Mersky, eds. *The First One Hundred Eight Justices.* Buffalo, N.Y.: William S. Hein, 2004.

Davis, Richard. *Electing Justice: Fixing the Supreme Court Nomination Process.* New York: Oxford University Press, 2005.

Foskett, Ken. *Judging Thomas: The Life and Times of Clarence Thomas.* New York: HarperCollins, 2005.

Gerber, Scott Douglas. *First Principles: The Jurisprudence of Clarence Thomas.* New York: New York University Press, 1999.

Greenya, John. *Silent Justice: The Clarence Thomas Story.* Ft. Lee, N.J.: Barricade Books, 2001.

Hensley, Thomas R. *The Rehnquist Court: Justices, Rulings, and Legacy.* Santa Barbara, Calif.: ABC-Clio, 2006.

Marcosson, Samuel A. *Original Sin: Clarence Thomas and the Failure of the Constitutional Conservatives.* New York: New York University Press, 2002.

Mayer, Jane, and Jill Abramson. *Strange Justice: The Selling of Clarence Thomas.* New York: Houghton Mifflin, 1994.

Smith, Christopher, and Joyce Baugh. *The Real Clarence Thomas: Confirmation Veracity Meets Performance Reality.* San Francisco: Peter Lang, 2000.

Thomas, Andrew P. *Clarence Thomas: A Biography.* San Francisco: Encounter Books, 2001.

See also *Bush v. Gore*; *Hudson v. Michigan*; Marshall, Thurgood; Nominations to the Court; Rehnquist, William H.; Senate Judiciary Committee; Thomas-Hill hearings.

Thomas-Hill Hearings

Date: 1991

Description: The confirmation hearings of Supreme Court nominee Clarence Thomas, which became a nationally televised spectacle after charges of sexual harassment were made against Thomas by Anita Hill.

Significance: The hearings sparked intense national debate over issues of racism, sexism, and political gamesmanship. The public humiliation suffered by both Hill and Thomas opened debate on the nature and fairness of the Senate confirmation process.

After the resignation of Supreme Court Justice Thurgood Marshall, the first African American to serve on the Court, President George H. W. Bush sought to fill the vacancy with another African American.

Marshall, however, had been a leading advocate of the Civil Rights movement and the last staunchly liberal justice from the Warren era. Bush's nominee, Clarence Thomas, would be his predecessor's political and philosophical opposite.

Thomas was a Yale graduate and possessed a distinguished résumé, including the chairmanship of the Equal Employment Opportunity Commission (EEOC) and service as a judge on the federal court of appeals. He was also one of a number of black intellectuals who challenged the merits of affirmative action. Critics charged that his tenure at the EEOC had been marked by a reluctance to pursue civil rights complaints, and his judicial record demonstrated his willingness to throw out many of the liberal decisions of the earlier Supreme Court. These were political concerns, however, in a political climate that favored Thomas's views, and no charge of unethical conduct stood up under investigation.

Anita Hill had served under Thomas at the EEOC and had maintained an amicable relationship with her former boss. During the judiciary committee's confirmation investigation, Hill confided that Thomas had pressured her for dates and made crude, sexually charged remarks to her while he was her boss. This information was leaked to the media after the judiciary committee had voted to send the nomination to the full Senate. A second hearing was convened to examine the charges.

On October 11, the first day of the second round of hearings, Thomas angrily denied the charges, and he was treated with deference by the committee. Hill, however, was barraged with accusations and insinuations by senators and witnesses. Senator Joseph Biden seemed unable to prevent the degeneration of the televised proceedings into a quasi-judicial brawl.

Thomas's characterization of the second hearing as a "high-tech lynching" provoked the greatest reaction from the African American community, outraging many blacks with the implication that blacks themselves and their liberal white allies were figuratively lynching an "uppity" black because of his conservatism. The viciousness of the attacks on Hill, for feminists, seemed to illustrate perfectly the very reason most victims of sexual harassment do not bring charges against their harassers.

Thomas, though confirmed, began his service on the Supreme Court tainted by Hill's accusation. Judiciary hearings operate without standards of evidence or the rules that govern court proceedings. Biden's committee could not determine the truth of the matter but could merely vote based on their impression of Thomas's character and the political desirability of seating him on the Court.

Janet Alice Long

Further Reading

Brock, David. *The Real Anita Hill.* New York: Free Press, 1993.

Davis, Richard. *Electing Justice: Fixing the Supreme Court Nomination Process.* New York: Oxford University Press, 2005.

Greenya, John. *Silent Justice: The Clarence Thomas Story.* Ft. Lee, N.J.: Barricade Books, 2001.

Thomas, Andrew Peyton. *Clarence Thomas: A Biography.* San Francisco: Encounter Books, 2001.

Thomas, Clarence. *Confronting the Future: Selections from the Senate Confirmation Hearings and Prior Speeches.* Introduction by L. Gordon Crovitz. Washington, D.C.: Regnery Gateway, 1992.

See also Nominations to the Court; Senate Judiciary Committee; Thomas, Clarence.

Smith Thompson

Identification: Associate justice (February 10, 1824-December 18, 1843)

Nominated by: James Monroe

Born: January 17, 1768, Amenia, New York

Died: December 19, 1843, Poughkeepsie, New York

Significance: As a Supreme Court justice, Thompson defended states' rights against the power of the federal government. He also defended the right of groups of Native Americans to be considered sovereign nations.

Smith Thompson began practicing law in 1793 and served on the New York State Supreme Court from 1802 to 1818. President James

Smith Thompson. (Albert Rosenthal/ Collection of the Supreme Court of the United States)

Monroe appointed him secretary of the navy in 1818 and nominated him to the Supreme Court on December 8, 1823. He was confirmed by the Senate on December 19 and took office on February 10, 1824.

In *Ogden v. Saunders* (1827), Thompson joined with the majority in defending the right of a state to follow its own rather than federal bankruptcy laws, until the two systems actually conflicted. In *Kendall v. United States ex rel. Stokes* (1838), Thompson wrote the majority opinion, upholding the right of a District of Columbia court to order an official of the executive branch to perform a duty. This decision limited the authority of the president.

In *Cherokee Nation v. Georgia* (1831), Thompson dissented from the majority by regarding the Cherokee as a sovereign nation, with the right to be heard in the Court. Although initially rejected, this idea was soon accepted by the Court in *Worcester v. Georgia* (1832).

Rose Secrest

SEE ALSO Marshall, John; Native American sovereignty; States' rights and state sovereignty; Taney, Roger Brooke; *Worcester v. Georgia.*

Time, Place, and Manner Regulations

DESCRIPTION: Permissible forms of prior restraint not based on content of expression that regulate when, where, and how expression may occur freely.

SIGNIFICANCE: The Supreme Court usually considers the validity of time, place, and manner regulations in view of the forum in which the regulations are applied. Expressive activity occurring in a public, rather than private, forum receives the highest First Amendment protection.

In *Heffron v. International Society for Krishna Consciousness* (1981), Supreme Court Justice Byron R. White identified four characteristics of a valid time, place, and manner regulation: first, the restriction must be content neutral; second, the restriction must serve a significant governmental interest; third, the restriction must be no broader than would accomplish its purpose; and fourth, alternative means must exist to communicate the expression that is limited by the regulation. All four of the characteristics must be present for the regulation to be valid.

TIME, PLACE, AND MANNER

The Court has allowed to stand ordinances that restrict loud noises at night when people are likely to be asleep and broadcast regulations that restrict indecent programming to safe-harbor hours, between 10:00 P.M. and 6:00 A.M., when children are less likely to be in the audience.

The Court makes decisions regarding place according to the forum in which an activity occurs: a traditional public forum, a designated public forum, public property that is not a public forum, or private property. Traditional public forums are places that are accepted as sites where speeches may be made and people may assemble. Examples include public parks, street corners, and sidewalks.

Speeches occurring in traditional public forums receive the highest First Amendment protection. In *Lovell v. City of Griffin* (1938), the Court made it clear that public streets are public forums. The city of Griffin, Georgia, had an ordinance requiring written permission from the city manager before distributing information in any form. The city argued that First Amendment protection applied to only the publication of information, not its distribution, but Chief Justice Charles Evans Hughes refuted that argument in the opinion he wrote for the Court.

Designated public forums are places specifically provided by the government for communication, assembly, and similar uses. These include government-owned auditoriums, meeting halls, fairgrounds, and student newspapers open to all students. Communication occurring in designated public forums receives First Amendment protection, but not as much as that occurring in traditional public forums; therefore, it is more subject to time, place, and manner regulations.

Some types of public property are not considered public forums and are closed to expressive activity on the part of the general public. Examples include airport concourses, prisons, and military bases. Private property is not a public forum; owners may decide who uses the property for expressive activity.

In *Grayned v. Rockford* (1972), the Court applied time, place, and manner regulations to demonstrations next to a school in session, saying the nature of the place, including the pattern of its typical activities, dictates the kinds of regulations of time, place, and manner that are reasonable. In its decision, the Court indicated that silent expression in a public library might be appropriate, although making a speech in the area where patrons are reading would not be. The manner of expression should be compatible with the normal activity of a particular place at a particular time.

Problems in Application

When time, place, and manner regulations were applied to commercial or religious speech (*Metromedia v. San Diego*, 1981) or obscene or indecent language, the Court generally found these restrictions invalid because they were content based. The same line of reasoning was used to invalidate the Communication Decency Act of

1996 (*Reno v. American Civil Liberties Union*, 1996). The Court generally frowns on ordinances that rely on the discretion of community officials to decide whether speech is allowed (*Schneider v. New Jersey*, 1939) because these deliberations often require officials to evaluate speech based on content.

In *Madsen v. Women's Health Center* (1994), the Court applied the third prong of the 1981 validity test in considering whether an injunction directed at protesters at an abortion clinic was narrowly tailored enough to accomplish its goals without restricting more expression than necessary. The Court decided that a 36-foot buffer zone around clinic entrances and a driveway was permissible and not over broad, but that a 300-foot buffer zone around the residences of clinic employees and a 300-foot no-approach zone around the clinic were over broad, and therefore impermissible.

Alisa White Coleman

Further Reading

Dudley, William, ed. *Mass Media.* San Diego: Thomson/Gale, 2005.

Edelman, Rob, ed. *Freedom of the Press.* San Diego: Greenhaven Press, 2007.

Gillmor, Donald, Jerome Barron, and Todd Simon. *Mass Communication Law: Cases and Comment.* 6th ed. Belmont, Calif.: Wadsworth, 1998.

Hebert, David L. *Freedom of the Press.* Detroit: Greenhaven Press, 2005.

Pember, Don. *Mass Media Law.* Boston: McGraw-Hill, 1999.

Snepp, Frank. *Irreparable Harm: A Firsthand Account of How One Agent Took on the CIA in an Epic Battle over Free Speech.* Lawrence: University Press of Kansas, 2001.

Teeter, Dwight, Don Leduc, and Bill Loving. *Law of Mass Communications: Freedom and Control of Print and Broadcast Media.* 11th ed. New York: Foundation Press, 2004.

See also Assembly and association, freedom of; First Amendment; Public forum doctrine; Speech and press, freedom of; Symbolic speech.

Tinker v. Des Moines Independent Community School District

CITATION: 393 U.S. 503
DATE: February 24, 1969
ISSUE: Symbolic speech
SIGNIFICANCE: The Supreme Court's decision strengthened the rights of freedom of speech and symbolic speech for students.

Three Des Moines, Iowa, students protested the Vietnam War by wearing black armbands to school in violation of the school's policy. After they were suspended, the students challenged the policy, claiming it denied them their First Amendment rights. Justice Abe Fortas wrote the opinion for the 7-2 majority, voiding the school's policy. The Supreme Court held that the wearing of armbands, absent any other behavior that might subject the students to discipline, was an acceptable form of protest. It found no relation between the regulation and school discipline and stated that student opinions could not be confined to those officially approved. Justices Potter Stewart and Byron R. White concurred, and Justices Hugo L. Black and John M. Harlan II dissented.

Richard L. Wilson

SEE ALSO *Brandenburg v. Ohio*; First Amendment; *Gitlow v. New York*; *Schenck v. United States*; Speech and press, freedom of; Symbolic speech; *Texas v. Johnson*; Time, place, and manner regulations.

Thomas Todd

IDENTIFICATION: Associate justice (May 4, 1807-February 7, 1826)
NOMINATED BY: Thomas Jefferson
BORN: January 23, 1765, King and Queen County, Virginia
DIED: February 7, 1826, Frankfort, Kentucky
SIGNIFICANCE: Supreme Court justice Todd was an authority on land law and supported the power of the federal government over the states.

Thomas Todd. (Albert Rosenthal/ Collection of the Supreme Court of the United States)

Thomas Todd moved to Kentucky, then part of Virginia, in 1784. When Kentucky became a state in 1792, he was chosen as clerk of the legislature. He became clerk of the state supreme court in 1799, was appointed a judge on the court in 1801, and became its chief justice in 1806. President Thomas Jefferson nominated him to the Supreme Court on February 28, 1807. He was confirmed by the Senate on March 3 and took office on May 4.

Todd wrote only twelve opinions, all but one dealing with land law, in which he was an expert. In *Vowles v. Craig* (1814), Todd decided that a seller could not reclaim land after it had been sold, even if the original survey had been in error. In *Preston v. Browder* (1816), he upheld the right of a state to restrict land claims within Native American territory. In *Robinson v. Campbell* (1818), he denied a state the power to question the validity of previously established land titles.

In addition to this specialty, Todd supported Chief Justice John Marshall in a series of important cases that established the authority of the federal government over the states.

Rose Secrest

See also Federalism; Marshall, John; States' rights and state sovereignty.

Right to Travel

Description: Citizens' right to move into, out of, among, and within states, foreign nations, and lesser political and geographic entities.

Significance: The Supreme Court has interpreted the right to travel to apply to important questions of whether newly arrived citizens can vote and receive welfare and other benefits, without first being residents of states for a specified period of time. The right to travel is also involved in questions of whether citizens are allowed to travel freely to and from foreign nations.

The right to travel has been long recognized in Anglo-American law. An article of England's Magna Carta (1215) recognized the right to foreign travel. The Articles of Confederation expressly guaranteed "free ingress and egress" from one state to another because the nation's founders recognized that freedom of interstate movement follows from the recognition of nationhood. However, although the right to travel was an implicit right during the founding and settling of the American colonies and the westward expansion, it was not explicitly stated in the U.S. Constitution.

Nineteenth Century

The modern right to travel has its roots in the Supreme Court's interpretation of the commerce clause of the Constitution in the nineteenth century. In *Crandall v. Nevada* (1868), the Court invalidated a law that taxed the owner of for-hire vehicles for each passenger whom he transported out of state. It ruled that the right to travel from state to state came with national citizenship. The Court noted that the federal government was formed so that those living in the United States could be one people in one common country, with members of this one community having the right to pass through every part of it without interference.

For much of U.S. history, issues surrounding the right to travel were linked to the enslavement of African Americans. Before the Civil War, slave owners claimed the right to travel with their slaves to states and territories where slavery was prohibited while still retaining full property rights to their slaves. In 1857 this right was upheld by the Court in *Scott v. Sandford.* In the *Slaughterhouse Cases* (1873), the right to travel, as a right of national citizenship, was strengthened by its protection under the privileges or immunities clause of the Fourteenth Amendment.

The Twentieth Century

In *Edwards v. California* (1941), the Court invalidated, as a violation of the commerce clause, a state law that prohibited individuals from bringing into the state any indigent who was not a resident of the state. The Court significantly expanded the right to travel in *Shapiro v. Thompson* (1969) by viewing it as a fundamental right under the equal protection clause of the Fourteenth Amendment. (A fundamental right is any right that the Court has stated is guaranteed explicitly by, or implicitly from, the Constitution.) The Court ruled that the right to travel prohibits a state from setting durational residency requirements that must be met before new arrivals can receive welfare payments. Durational residency requirements require persons to show that in addition to being a bona fide resident of a state, they have resided in the location for a specific period of time. The Court reasoned that the nature of the federal union and the guarantee of personal liberty gave each citizen the right to travel throughout the United States without unreasonable restrictions.

In later cases, the Court struck down other durational residency requirements as violations of the fundamental right to travel. In *Memorial Hospital v. Maricopa County* (1974), the Court invalidated laws requiring new arrivals to meet durational residency requirements before receiving basic medical services. The Court noted that medical services are a basic necessity of life; their denial to a new resident who is indigent, when they are available to other residents who are similarly situated as to the objectives of the law, effectively penalizes a person's right to travel.

In 1999 the Court affirmed the right to travel. In *Saenz v. Roe* (1999), the Court invalidated a section of a federal law, the Personal Responsibility and Work Opportunity Act of 1996, that expressly authorized any state, for one year, to pay new arrivals benefits based on the amount they received in the state from which they came. The Court noted that the right to travel embraces three different components: the right to enter and leave another state; the right to be treated as a welcome visitor while temporally present in another state, and for those residents who elect to become permanent residents, the right to be treated like other citizens of that state.

Most important, in *Saenz*, the Court returned to the *Slaughterhouse Cases* to say that the rights of newly arrived citizens are protected by their status as both state and U.S. citizens, which are plainly identified in the Fourteenth Amendment privileges and immunities clause. The Court emphasized that because the right to travel embraces a citizen's right to be treated equally in his or her new state of residence, a discriminatory classification is itself a penalty. The Court drew upon *Zobel v. Williams* (1982) to say that the Fourteenth Amendment expressly equates citizenship with residence and does not tolerate a hierarchy of subclasses of similarly situated citizens based on the location of their prior residences.

Permitted Durational Residency Requirements

State durational residency requirements are permitted if a compelling government interest has been demonstrated. In *Dunn v. Blumstein* (1972), the Court found long durational residency requirements before permitting voting unconstitutional because such requirements interfered with the fundamental right to vote and penalized the fundamental right to travel. A state can require voters to be bona fide residents for a period of time before permitting them to vote, usually no more than fifty days. In *Sosna v. Iowa* (1975), the Court did not view a one-year residency requirement before a new resident could get a divorce as a denial of the right of travel. The Court noted that unlike the welfare recipients in *Shapiro*, the voters in *Dunn*, or the indigent patients in *Maricopa*, the new arrivals in *Sosna* were not irretrievably foreclosed by Iowa's one-year waiting period from getting a divorce. In *Vlandis v. Kline* (1973), the Court found a compelling government interest in allowing one-year residency requirements before students could receive reduced tuition at state universities. However, in *Supreme Court of New Hampshire v. Piper* (1985), the Court outlawed a one-year residency requirement before lawyers could be admitted to practice in a state. In the 1990's scholars have attempted, without success, to apply the right to travel to tightened airline security, to limits on intrastate travel from police enforcement tactics, and to movement among the states to secure abortions.

The government may seek to restrict citizens from traveling between the United States and specified foreign nations, if the restrictions are not based on the beliefs of the citizens seeking to travel. In *Aptheker v. Secretary of State* (1964), the Court invalidated a section of the Subversive Activities Control Act of 1950 that made it unlawful for any "knowing" member of a communist organization to use a passport. However, government efforts to restrict travel to and from nations for reasons of foreign relations and national security, for the most part, have not been successful.

Ronald Kahn

Further Reading

Aleinikoff, Thomas Alexander. *Semblances of Sovereignty: The Constitution, the State, and American Citizenship.* Cambridge, Mass.: Harvard University Press, 2002.

Cohen, William. "Equal Treatment for Newcomers: The Core Meaning of National and State Citizenship." *Constitutional Commentary* 1 (1984): 9-19.

Fried, Charles. *Saying What the Law Is: The Constitution in the Supreme Court.* Cambridge, Mass.: Harvard University Press, 2004.

Kahn, Ronald. *The Supreme Court and Constitutional Theory, 1953-1993.* Lawrence: University Press of Kansas, 1994.

Labb, Ronald M., and Jonathan Lurie. *The Slaughterhouse Cases: Regulation, Reconstruction, and the Fourteenth Amendment.* Lawrence: University Press of Kansas, 2003.

Poppe, Matthew. "Defining the Scope of the Equal Protection Clause

with Respect to Welfare Waiting Periods." *University of Chicago Law Review* 61 (1994): 291-323.
Porter, Andrew C. "Toward a Constitutional Right to Intrastate Travel." *Northwestern University Law Review* 86 (1992): 820-857.

SEE ALSO Commerce, regulation of; Fourteenth Amendment; Privileges and immunities; *Slaughterhouse Cases.*

Treaties

DESCRIPTION: Binding, normally written, international agreements between or among governments of states and/or intergovernmental organizations.

SIGNIFICANCE: Under the U.S. Constitution, the treaty process is mainly the concern of the executive and legislative branches of government. The Supreme Court must regard treaties entered into by the United States as the supreme law of the land, unless a conflict arises with the Constitution or a subsequent statute.

It should be noted that the U.S. Constitution itself takes the form of a treaty and required the ratification of the conventions of nine states to enter into force. In dealing with treaties, the Supreme Court is guided by the language of the Constitution and by long-standing practice that has emerged between the executive and legislative branches. The treaty clause of the Constitution is found in Article II, section 2. It stipulates that the president "shall have Power, by and with the Advice and Consent of the Senate, to make Treaties, provided two thirds of the Senators present concur." The Court's judicial power, as defined in Article III, section 2, extends to "all Cases . . . under this Constitution, the Laws of the United States, and Treaties made or which shall be made, under their authority." Finally, the supremacy clause of Article VI of the Constitution stipulates that "This Constitution, and the Laws of the United States which shall be made in Pursuance thereof; and all Treaties made, or which shall be made, under the Authority of the United States, shall be the supreme Law of the Land." This is the extent of the language in the Constitution regarding treaties. It establishes that the president is the chief maker of treaties and that the Senate exercises a role of advice and consent. The Court has no direct role in the treaty-making process, other than in interpreting treaties and statutes in cases brought before it and deferring to and applying them as the supreme law of the land.

The Constitution does not actually define the term "treaty." At the time of the Constitutional Convention, however, treaties were understood to include any international agreement duly entered into by heads of state. Indeed, from the standpoint of international law, any agreement the president enters into binds the United States, regardless of whether it is formally referred to as a treaty or any one of three dozen other terms, including charter, convention, covenant, and pact. However, a distinction in the internal practice of the United States emerged from the outset in the practice of presidents and the Senate. This distinction is rooted in the fact that although the Constitution does not define the term "treaty," it does stipulate that the president has the power to make a treaty with the consent of the Senate. The Constitution does not forbid a president from entering into agreements with other governments without the consent of the Senate. Although such an agreement would not be a treaty under the language of the Constitution, it would nonetheless still constitute binding international law. Such agreements are referred to as "executive agreements."

Executive Agreements and Treaties

In the United States, both executive agreements and treaties were routinely entered into by presidents. Presidents brought treaties before the Senate for its advice and consent before they formally ratified them. However, presidents also entered into agreements as they saw fit in conducting U.S. foreign policy, without the formal advice and consent of the Senate. Indeed the Senate acquiesced in this presidential practice as it has no constitutional authority to negotiate with foreign states and the president is better equipped and constitutionally authorized to conduct foreign relations and make treaties. In addition, for many routine matters of foreign affairs, the Senate can be easily overwhelmed with unnecessary work related to the treaty approval process.

In early practice, presidents brought major agreements to the Senate for approval, using executive agreements much less frequently. In the twentieth century, however, and especially after World War II, the use of executive agreements has skyrocketed, along with the number of international agreements. For every treaty entered into, nearly twenty executive agreements are signed. Proliferation in the use of executive agreements eventually caused Congress to pass the Case Act in 1972. This act attempted to ensure timely presidential consultation with Congress in the exercise of the treaty-making power through executive agreements.

The Case Act, reflecting long-standing actual practice, distinguished between congressional-executive agreements, in which a president seeks prior or subsequent authority by a joint resolution of both legislative chambers to negotiate and sign agreements, and sole or pure executive agreements, which the president enters into without any senatorial action or joint legislative approval. The Case Act requires the president to advise Congress in writing of all such agreements, even of agreements the president believes must be kept secret to protect national security, although these need not be transmitted with public notice.

Although the Court did not enter into the struggles by Congress to ensure its proper advisory role in the treaty-making process, as this is properly a matter of adjustment between the executive and legislative branches, it formally acknowledged in the *United States v. Pink* (1942) that executive agreements are as valid as treaties in their domestic effects. It also ruled that the president and Congress may distinguish between treaties and executive agreements. In the case of *Weinberger v. Rossi* (1982), the Court determined that Congress, in using the term "treaty" in a statute intended to prohibit discrimination against U.S. nationals seeking overseas employment at U.S. military bases unless permitted by a treaty, actually meant to include both formal Article II treaties requiring senatorial approval *and* executive agreements. By actual practice, Congress had tolerated presidential executive agreements with foreign governments that permitted discrimination against U.S. nationals in favor of foreign nationals who sought employment overseas, and the Court upheld the president's authority under both the Constitution and the congressional statute and practice to enter into such an agreement.

The Supremacy Clause

The Court has spoken definitively on the issue concerning the constitutional provision that treaties are the supreme law of the land and that they take precedence over prior federal statutes and the legislative enactments of the various states. In the case of *Missouri v. Holland* (1920), the Court held that a treaty between the United States and Great Britain on behalf of Canada regulating the hunting of migratory birds took precedence over Missouri statutes permitting the hunting of Canadian migratory geese. Especially telling in this case was that federal game wardens had previously attempted to enforce a federal statute regulating the hunting of migratory birds. Missouri successfully challenged this federal intrusion on grounds that it violated the reserved rights of states under the constitution to regulate such matters. However, when the president of the United States entered into a treaty with Great Britain and when Congress enacted a statute to enforce this treaty obligation, the situation changed. When Missouri again challenged the federal government's right to enforce federal statutes that conflicted with its own state law, the Court held that the federal government, and its agent Holland, had acted constitutionally.

The court cited the supremacy clause, which stipulates that treaties are the supreme law of the land. Because only the federal government—not the states—has treaty powers, treaties automatically take precedence over conflicting provisions of state law. In this case, the treaty regulating migratory birds had been given domestic legal effect through the passage of an implementing federal statute. What the latter alone could not accomplish constitutionally was constitutionally valid when effected pursuant to a treaty obligation.

Complications

Under international law, any treaty (or executive agreement) is binding on states and takes precedence over any prior or subsequent domestic law. Governments, from the standpoint of international law, may not use domestic legislation as a means of avoiding international treaty obligations. In U.S. practice, however, problems arise because the Court has held that treaties (like statutes) that violate the Constitution are invalid and that a statute that conflicts with a prior treaty supersedes the latter. Therefore, conflicts may arise between U.S. international obligations and internal legal requirements. In the case of *Reid v. Covert* (1957), the Court held that military wives who killed their husbands on U.S. foreign military bases had a constitutional right under the Fifth and Sixth Amendments to an indictment by a civilian grand jury and to a trial by jury of their peers. These rights, the Court held, were superior to either the federal statute or the executive agreements that called for courts-martial under the Uniform Code of Military Justice in such cases. This case clearly asserted the superiority of the Constitution over the terms of a treaty.

Whereas the *Missouri v. Holland* case illustrated that a treaty takes precedence over the prior legislation of states, the Court consistently held that a treaty may be abrogated in whole or in part by subsequent federal statutes. The Court routinely ruled, as in *Reid v. Covert,* that it is bound to apply whichever treaty or statute is most recent in time. Under the Constitution, treaties and statutes are treated in full parity as sources of law and obligation. Therefore, when a conflict in law arises between a treaty and a statute, the Court will apply the most recently enacted one. When the statute is the most recent and controlling source, this may place the United States in dereliction of its international obligations and may require it to pay due compensation; however, from the standpoint of domestic law, the statute would take precedence over the treaty. To avoid such problems, the Court attempts to resolve apparent conflicts between treaties and statutes so as to give effect to both, as it asserted in *Whitney v. Robertson* (1888).

Though the Court does on occasion rule in matters involving treaties, the power and practice of making treaties falls within the purview of the political and policy-making branches. The Court was not intended by the Constitution to exercise an aggressive oversight role in matters that so directly relate to national security, the national interest, and the challenge of fashioning effective foreign policy in the face of changing needs. Therefore, the president has exercised the lead role in this area to varying degrees with a cooperative or rebellious Congress.

Robert F. Gorman

Further Reading

One place to start a study of this subject is with general reference works on treaties, such as Charles Phillips and Alan Axelrod's *Encyclopedia of Historical Treaties and Alliances* (2d ed. New York: Facts On File, 2005) and *U.S. Laws, Acts, and Treaties* (3 vols. Pasadena, Calif.: Salem Press, 2003), edited by Timothy L. Hall.

Although relatively few works focus on the Supreme Court's activity in the treaty-making area, numerous works on international law, constitutional law, and the U.S. political process cover the subject. One of the most comprehensive assessments is Randall W. Bland's *The Black Robe and the Bald Eagle: The Supreme Court and Foreign Policy, 1789-1960* (Bethesda, Md.: Austin & Winfield, 1998). Also useful is Louis Henkin's *Foreign Affairs and the Constitution* (Mineola, N.Y.: Foundation Press, 1996).

Two excellent international law texts containing chapters devoted to treaties and executive agreements in U.S. practice are Gerhard von Glahn's *Law Among Nations* (New York: Macmillan, 1997) and William R. Slomanson's *Fundamental Perspectives on International Law* (New York: West Publishing, 1995). A lengthy and classic treatment on the international law of treaties is A. McNair's *The Law of Treaties* (Oxford, England: Clarendon Press, 1961). Useful sections dealing with Supreme Court cases on the treaty powers can be found in treatments on U.S. constitutional law such as Ronald D. Rotunda and John E. Nowak's *Treatise on Constitutional Law: Substance and Procedure* (Vol. 1. St. Paul, Minn.: West Publishing, 1992), as well as Randall W. Bland and Joseph Brogan's *Constitutional Law and the United States* (Bethesda, Md.: Austin & Winfield, 1999).

See also Executive agreements; National security; Native American sovereignty; Native American treaties; Presidential powers.

Robert Trimble

IDENTIFICATION: Associate justice (June 16, 1826-August 25, 1828)
NOMINATED BY: John Quincy Adams
BORN: November 17, 1776, Augusta County, Virginia
DIED: August 25, 1828, Paris, Kentucky
SIGNIFICANCE: Known for his sound sense and legal knowledge, Trimble wrote sixteen majority opinions during his two years on the Supreme Court. His most important opinion upheld the right of states to make their own bankruptcy laws.

What formal education Robert Trimble obtained was from Bourbon Academy and Kentucky Academy, and he began practicing law in Paris, Kentucky, about 1800, specializing in land litigation. He was not admitted to the bar until 1803. The governor of Kentucky ap-

Robert Trimble. (Albert Rosenthal/ Collection of the Supreme Court of the United States)

pointed him a justice on the state court of appeals in 1807, but Trimble returned to his more profitable law practice in 1809. In 1817 President James Madison appointed Trimble as a justice of the federal district court.

In 1826 President John Quincy Adams nominated Trimble as an associate justice of the Supreme Court, and he was easily confirmed. In his first opinion, *Montgomery v. Hernandez* (1827), Trimble delineated procedures that the Court still follows. While serving on the Court, Trimble typically supported Chief Justice John Marshall, upholding the dominance of federal over state laws whenever the two conflicted. However, he broke with Marshall and wrote one of his best opinions in concurring with the majority in *Ogden v. Saunders* (1827), maintaining that states held jurisdiction over bankruptcy legislation. After only two years on the bench, Trimble died, ending a promising career.

Alvin K. Benson

See also Bankruptcy law; McLean, John; Marshall, John.

Willis Van Devanter

Identification: Associate justice (January 3, 1911-June 2, 1937)
Nominated by: William H. Taft
Born: April 17, 1859, Marion, Indiana
Died: February 8, 1941, Washington, D.C.
Significance: Although he wrote few opinions, Van Devanter was a key figure in the Court's conservative majorities in the 1920's and 1930's because of his mastery of procedural and jurisdictional questions.

Willis Van Devanter was born into a legal family, and attended Indiana Asbury University (later DePauw) and received his law degree from the Cincinnati Law School in 1881. Because his brother-in-law had been appointed chief justice of the territorial court in Wyoming, Van Devanter moved west in July, 1884. During the next thirteen years, he practiced law and became a force in Republican politics. He

Willis Van Devanter. (Harris and Ewing/ Collection of the Supreme Court of the United States)

was the city attorney of Cheyenne in 1887, was elected to the territorial legislature in 1888, and served as chief justice of Wyoming from 1889 to 1890. His close friendship with Senator Francis E. Warren aided his political rise. Van Devanter defended the cattlemen in the notorious Johnson County "war" over cattle rustling in 1892.

In 1897 Van Devanter became assistant attorney general in the Department of the Interior, where he dealt with Indian and land cases. President Theodore Roosevelt appointed him to the circuit court of appeals for the eighth circuit in 1903. President William H. Taft, at the urging of Senator Warren, nominated Van Devanter to the Supreme Court in late 1910. He was sworn in on January 3, 1911.

On the Court, Van Devanter experienced difficulty in writing opinions quickly, and talk of his writer's block was common in Washington legal circles. Nonetheless, he was an important force behind the scenes because of his knowledge of procedure and his ability to propose jurisdictional answers to complex issues. He played a large role in drafting the Judiciary Act of 1925. He was conservative in his opinions about economic regulation and reflected the Republican doctrines of the late nineteenth century. Among Van Devanter's notable opinions were the *National Prohibition Cases* (1920), which said that the Eighteenth Amendment was constitutional, and the case of *McGrain v. Daugherty* (1927), which sustained the power of Congress to conduct investigations. On the Court, he was held in high regard by his colleagues, and Chief Justice Taft regarded him as the most valuable member of the Court during his tenure.

By the 1930's Van Devanter had become one of the four conservative justices who consistently voted against the New Deal. That situation led President Franklin D. Roosevelt to propose his Court-packing plan in 1937, which would have expanded the Court's membership and filled it with justices favorable to New Deal measures. Van Devanter had been planning to retire for several years, but he timed his announcement to have the most damaging effect on Roosevelt's efforts. His retirement on May 18, 1937, undercut one of the major arguments of the plan—that justices were staying too long in their positions. With characteristic skill, Van Devanter helped achieve a final political victory when Roosevelt's plan failed.

Lewis L. Gould

Further Reading

Bader, William H., and Roy M. Mersky, eds. *The First One Hundred Eight Justices.* Buffalo, N.Y.: William S. Hein, 2004.

Bickel, Alexander M., and Benno Schmidt. *The Judiciary and Responsible Government, 1910-1921.* New York: Macmillan, 1984.

Friedman, Leon, and Fred Israel, eds. *The Justices of the Supreme Court: Their Lives and Major Opinions.* 5 vols. New York: Chelsea House, 1997.

Gould, Lewis L. *Wyoming: From Territory to Statehood.* Worland, Wyo.: High Plains, 1989.

Parrish, Michael E. *The Hughes Court: Justices, Rulings, and Legacy.* Santa Barbara, Calif.: ABC-Clio, 2002.

Renstrom, Peter G. *The Taft Court: Justices, Rulings, and Legacy.* Santa Barbara, Calif.: ABC-Clio, 2003.
Shoemaker, Rebecca S. *The White Court: Justices, Rulings, and Legacy.* Santa Barbara, Calif.: ABC-Clio, 2004.

See also Court-packing plan; Hughes, Charles Evans; New Deal; Opinions, writing of; Taft, William H.; White, Edward D.

Vietnam War

Date: 1965-1973
Description: U.S. military effort designed to aid South Vietnam in its fight against North Vietnam, a communist country.
Significance: The Supreme Court's actions on Vietnam War-related cases established major precedents regarding the freedoms of speech, press, and religion and the powers of Congress and the president to conduct foreign and defense policies.

The Vietnam War's length and controversial nature raised various constitutional questions. Appeals to the Supreme Court included cases pertaining to the freedom of speech, the relationship between the free exercise clause and military conscription, freedom of the press, and the constitutionality of the U.S. military effort in Vietnam. In some cases, the Court established new precedents and in others, refused to accept a case, often citing the doctrine of political questions.

Freedom of Speech

The Court decisions about the Vietnam War that had the broadest, most long-term effects were those that pertained to the freedom of speech. During antiwar demonstrations obscenities and symbolic actions were sometimes used to communicate opposition to the Vietnam War. In *United States v. O'Brien* (1968), the Court, by a vote of seven to one, ruled against David O'Brien, who had been convicted of violating a federal conscript law by burning his draft card in a symbolic protest. O'Brien claimed that his conviction violated his freedom of speech. The majority opinion, written by Chief Justice Earl

Warren, stated that Congress has broad constitutional powers to raise and maintain armed forces, including the process of conscription, which encompasses draft cards. More significantly, *O'Brien*'s long-term impact was to place certain restrictions on the freedom of speech, especially when litigants claimed that their symbolic actions were protected by the freedom of speech.

One year later, however, the Court ruled in favor of high school and junior high school students who used symbolism to protest against the Vietnam War in *Tinker v. Des Moines Independent Community School District* (1969). The Tinker children and other students wore armbands with peace symbols to silently protest the Vietnam War despite the fact that school officials had previously forbidden them to do so. These students were suspended unless they returned to school without the armbands. The students asserted that this punishment and policy violated their freedom of speech. By a vote of seven to two, the Court ruled in favor of the protesting students. The Court stated that public school students retained their freedom of speech rights as long as their use of speech did not prove to be disruptive. Also, the

The Supreme Court ruled on a number of issues regarding freedom of speech of antiwar activists, such as the group pictured here. It did not, however, rule on the constitutionality of the war itself. (Library of Congress)

majority opinion noted that school officials in this district had previously allowed other forms of symbolic political expressions, such as campaign buttons. Therefore, the disciplinary action against students wearing antiwar armbands seemed to be directed against symbolic protest against the Vietnam War rather than against any student's use of any symbol of political speech.

What was somewhat surprising in the *Tinker* case was the dissenting opinion of Justice Hugo L. Black. Earlier in his career on the Court, Black was often identified as an absolutist in his support of the freedom of speech; that is, he took the view that government policies should not limit "balanced" speech, at least oral speech, in any way. In *Tinker*, however, Black asserted that symbolic actions such as this had less protection under the First Amendment and that school officials needed to have broad discretionary authority to prevent, prohibit, and punish expressions that they believed could be disruptive.

In *Cohen v. California* (1971), the Court had to address Paul Cohen's symbolic protest against the Vietnam War in general and the draft in particular, in which he printed the words "Fuck the draft" on his jacket. The state of California convicted him for violating a state law prohibiting "disturbing the peace . . . by offensive conduct." The long-term significance of this decision was the definition of obscenity concerning First Amendment protection. The Court ruled in favor of Cohen, stating that Cohen's profanity was "vulgar" but not obscene because its purpose was to convey a political message. Asserting the value of political speech for constitutional protest, the Court ruled that states cannot prohibit and punish such provocative speech and that such speech should not be perceived and punished as an incitement to possible future violent actions. The Court further expanded the freedom of speech-related antiwar expressions by ruling in *Flower v. United States* (1972) that the military could not prohibit antiwar activists from accessing military bases that are open to the public.

The Draft

Although the Court, with the prominent exception of the *O'Brien* decision, generally ruled in favor of expressions of antiwar opinions, it also expanded and diversified military draft exemptions based on the free exercise and establishment clauses of the First Amendment.

Before the Vietnam War, the Court had generally deferred to and closely adhered to the few, limited, specific religious reasons why a person would be designated as a conscientious objector, and therefore, exempted from being drafted into the armed forces. Although Congress had apparently intended conscientious objector exemptions to be primarily applied to members of pacifistic denominations, such as the Quaker and Amish churches, the Court ruled in *United States v. Seeger* (1965) and *Welsh v. United States* (1970) that agnostics who demonstrated a sincere, consistent philosophy of opposition to war should also be granted conscientious objector status. In its most famous Vietnam War-era draft case, the Court ruled in favor of the famous professional boxer Muhammad Ali, formerly known as Cassius Clay. Ali claimed that he should be exempt from the draft as a conscientious objector because of his Nation of Islam (Black Muslim) beliefs. In *Clay v. United States* (1971), the Court ruled in his favor.

After expanding and diversifying legitimate grounds for conscientious objector status, the Court further clarified, and then limited this expansion in *Gillette v. United States* (1971). In *Gillette,* the Court rejected the claim of conscientious objector status for a man who cited the Roman Catholic doctrine of the just-war theory, that is, that a Catholic should refuse to participate in unjust wars. Gillette asserted his belief that the Vietnam War was an unjust war. The Court concluded that Congress did not violate the establishment clause or Gillette's free exercise rights by refusing to allow draft-eligible men to choose which wars they would participate in according to their professed religious or philosophical beliefs.

Other Issues

The most significant Court decision about the relationship between the Vietnam War and freedom of speech was *New York Times Co. v. United States* (1971), commonly known as the Pentagon Papers case. Daniel Ellsberg, an antiwar former employee of the Pentagon (the Department of Defense), provided several newspapers, including *The New York Times,* with copies of the documentary history of U.S. foreign and defense policy toward Vietnam. The administration of Richard M. Nixon tried to prevent the publication of the Pentagon Papers, but the Court allowed their publication. The Court concluded that the Nixon administration failed to prove that publishing such papers would endanger current or future national security.

Although the Court generally strengthened the protection of First Amendment freedoms in the cases related to the Vietnam War, it repeatedly refused to rule on the war's constitutionality. Although Congress had never declared war against North Vietnam, it did adopt the Gulf of Tonkin Resolution of 1964, a joint resolution that gave the president broad, discretionary power to conduct war in Southeast Asia. The Court refused to grant writs of *certiorari* and review the lower court cases of *Holtzman v. Schlesinger* (1973), *Orlando v. Laird* (1971), *Mora v. McNamara* (1967), and *Massachusetts v. Laird* (1970), all of which challenged the constitutionality of the Vietnam War.

Associate Justice William O. Douglas was the most emphatic, determined justice who wanted the Court to grant *certiorari* and rule on the constitutionality of the Vietnam War. He took the unusual action of writing an opinion criticizing the Court's denial of *certiorari* in *Massachusetts v. Laird*. However, most justices believed that the existence and conduct of the war were political questions, that is, specific policies and political issues that were not justiciable by the courts because they should be resolved within and between the other two branches of the national government.

The constitutional legacy of major Court decisions related to the Vietnam War is that they provided important, influential precedents for future cases, especially for freedom of speech cases that did not pertain to expressions of protest over foreign and defense policy. For example, the Court partially relied on the *O'Brien* precedent to uphold a public indecency and nudity law in *Barnes v. Glen Theatre* (1991). In *Barnes*, the majority opinion concluded that the *O'Brien* precedent for limiting First Amendment protection of expressive conduct justified state laws prohibiting entirely nude exotic dancing in bars, just as the Court had ruled in *Cohen* that Cohen's use of an expletive to criticize the Vietnam War era draft was not an incitement. According to the *Chaplinsky v. New Hampshire* (1942) fighting words precedent, the Court ruled in *Texas v. Johnson* (1989) that burning or desecrating the U.S. flag did not represent an incitement either.

Regarding the more specific issues of whether public or congressional acts of opposition to certain U.S. foreign policy decisions are unconstitutional, the Court has generally followed the Vietnam War-era practice of holding such disputes to be nonjusticiable political questions. In *Goldwater v. Carter* (1979), several members of Congress unsuccessfully challenged the constitutionality of President Jimmy Carter's decision to terminate a treaty with Taiwan without obtaining the advice or consent of the Senate.

Sean J. Savage

Further Reading

In *The Constitution and American Foreign Policy* (St. Paul, Minn.: West Publishing, 1989), Jean E. Smith provides a collection of major Court decisions about the Vietnam War and other foreign policy issues. Frederick L. Borch's *Judge Advocates in Combat: Army Lawyers in Military Operations from Vietnam to Haiti* (Washington, D.C.: Office of the Judge Advocate General and Center of Military History, United States Army, 2001) is an official government account of how military attorneys performed in foreign actions including the Vietnam War.

Samuel Walker's *In Defense of American Liberties* (New York: Oxford University Press, 1990) details the role the American Civil Liberties Union played in major Vietnam War-related cases, especially *Tinker. The Brethren* (New York: Simon & Schuster, 1979), by Bob Woodward and Scott Armstrong, is an excellent, detailed analysis of the Supreme Court, including actions during the Vietnam War. David M. O'Brien's book *Storm Center: The Supreme Court in American Politics* (7th ed. New York: W. W. Norton, 2005) examines several key cases related to the Vietnam War.

The constitutional law textbooks, Sheldon Goldman's *Constitutional Law: Cases and Essays* (New York: HarperCollins, 1991) and Ralph A. Rossum and G. Alan Taer's *American Constitutional Law* (New York: St. Martin's Press, 1991) provide examples of Court cases related to Vietnam War issues. The related topics of justiciability and the doctrines of political questions are examined in Philippa Strum's *The Supreme Court and Political Questions* (Tuscaloosa: University of Alabama Press, 1974) and Alexander M. Bickel's *The Least Dangerous Branch* (Indianapolis, Ind.: Bobbs-Merrill, 1962). *Reporting Vietnam: American Journalism, 1959-1975* (New York: Library of America, 2000), with an introduction by Ward Just, is a collection of important journalistic writings from the war.

See also *Certiorari*, writ of; Douglas, William O.; *New York Times Co. v. United States*; Political questions; Speech and press, freedom of; Symbolic speech; *Tinker v. Des Moines Independent Community School District*; War and civil liberties.

Fred M. Vinson

Identification: Chief justice (June 24, 1946-September 8, 1953)
Nominated by: Harry S. Truman
Born: January 22, 1890, Louisa, Kentucky
Died: September 8, 1953, Washington, D.C.
Significance: Vinson presided over the Supreme Court during the early years of the Cold War and a new era in racial equality. His opinions, though few, defended the federal government's national security actions and set the stage for the civil rights revolution.

Fred M. Vinson began his public career as a city attorney. In 1923 he was elected to Congress as a Democrat and served five uneventful years in a Republican-controlled House. Defeated in 1928, largely because he supported Al Smith for the presidency, he was reelected in 1930. With the coming of the New Deal, Vinson played a leading role in shaping the Social Security Act (1935) and supporting President Franklin D. Roosevelt's Court-packing plan. In 1938 Roosevelt rewarded Vinson by appointing him to the District of Columbia Court of Appeals and five years later asked him to become the director of the Office of Economic Stabilization and then director of War Mobilization and Reconversion. In 1945 President Harry S. Truman chose Vinson to be secretary of the treasury. After Chief Justice Harlan Fiske Stone died, Truman named Vinson the thirteenth chief justice, a position he held from June 24, 1946, until September 8, 1953, when he died of a massive heart attack.

Truman had hoped that Vinson would be able to lead the divided

Court, but he had only limited success because he had to work with strong personalities such as Hugo L. Black, Felix Frankfurter, and William O. Douglas, and he did not have the intellectual skills to guide and influence his colleagues as they struggled with constitutional issues raised by the Cold War and the emerging Civil Rights movement. Vinson allowed Frankfurter and Black to define and lead the debate over the incorporation to the states of the Bill of Rights, and though he was deeply concerned about questions of national security and racial equality, he wrote relatively few majority opinions.

National Security

During Vinson's tenure, the Cold War, the fear of communism, and the government's loyalty and security programs dominated the Court's docket. Vinson's two major opinions illustrate his support for these government programs and reveal his lack of sensitivity to claims of individual liberty. In *American Communications Association v. Douds* (1950), he avoided the free speech issue and upheld the constitutionality of section 9 of the Taft-Hartley Act (1947), which required labor union officers to sign noncommunist affidavits, because it was reasonably related to a congressional interest in protecting interstate commerce from the consequences of a politically motivated strike. Then in *Dennis v. United States* (1951), he directly confronted the First Amendment and affirmed the convictions of eleven Communist Party leaders for violating the Smith Act (1940), an antisubversive law. In his opinion for the Court, he purported to rely on the clear and present danger test, but he did not define it to require that speech be directly related to an actual attempt to overthrow the government by violence. Instead, he read the test to extend to a conspiracy to advocate the evil of violent overthrow and permitted speech to be proscribed, no matter how remote, because the gravity of that evil was so great.

Vinson's commitment to a strong federal government included a vigorous conception of the presidency, a view reflected in his dissent in *Youngstown Sheet and Tube Co. v. Sawyer* (1952). In this case, he rejected the Court's view that President Truman's seizure of the steel mills was an unconstitutional encroachment on the power of Congress to make law. Truman's action, he argued, was a response to a genuine emergency, preventing a strike that would have imperiled

Fred M. Vinson. (James Whitmore/ Collection of the Supreme Court of the United States)

the conduct of the Korean War, and was taken pursuant to his power as commander in chief and his duty to enforce congressional statutes authorizing seizure.

Racial Equality

The Court took decisive action against racial discrimination in education, housing, transportation, criminal justice, voting rights, and labor relations. A moderate on race relations, Vinson made his distinctive contribution to the struggle for racial equality when he wrote unanimous opinions for the Court in three major cases. In *Shelley v. Kraemer* (1948), he held that judicial enforcement of racially restrictive covenants violated the equal protection clause. Two years later, he handed down *Sweatt v. Painter* (1950) and *McLaurin v. Oklahoma State Regents for Higher Education* (1950) on the same day. In his *Sweatt* opinion, he acknowledged that the white University of Texas law school and the state's African American law school were not physically equal but declined to follow the separate but equal doctrine of *Plessy v. Ferguson* (1896), instead crafting a new equal protection standard based on intangible differences, "those qualities which are incapable of objective measurement." Based on this new standard, Vinson found that racial segregation in legal education violated the equal protection clause. In his *McLaurin* opinion, he applied his *Sweatt* definition of equality to physical racial barriers created within a formerly all-white graduate school and found that separate classroom, cafeteria, and library seating were inequalities that would handicap the ability of African Americans to receive an effective education.

Immediately after these decisions, the National Association for the Advancement of Colored People initiated five lawsuits involving segregated public elementary and secondary schools in Kansas, South Carolina, Virginia, Delaware, and the District of Columbia. In 1952 the Court heard oral arguments in all five, now known by the title of the Kansas case: *Brown v. Board of Education* (1954), but instead of deciding them, Vinson announced in June, 1953, that the cases would be reargued the following term. When the Court reheard the cases, Earl Warren, the new chief justice, presided. On May 17, 1954, the Warren Court handed down a unanimous opinion that relied on Vinson's *Sweatt* and *McLaurin* opinions to hold "separate educational facilities are inherently unequal."

William C. Green

Further Reading

Bader, William H., and Roy M. Mersky, eds. *The First One Hundred Eight Justices.* Buffalo, N.Y.: William S. Hein, 2004.

Belknap, Michal R. *The Vinson Court: Justices, Rulings, and Legacy.* Santa Barbara, Calif.: ABC-Clio, 2004.

Pritchett, C. Herman. *Civil Liberties and the Vinson Court.* Chicago: University of Chicago Press, 1954.

Rudko, Frances. *Truman's Court: A Study in Judicial Restraint.* Westport, Conn.: Greenwood Press, 1988.

St. Clair, James E. *Chief Justice Fred M. Vinson of Kentucky: A Political Biography.* Lexington: University Press of Kentucky, 2002.

Urofsky, Melvin. *Division and Discord: The Supreme Court Under Stone and Vinson, 1940-1953.* Columbia: University of South Carolina Press, 1997.

See also *Brown v. Board of Education*; Cold War; Equal protection clause; Opinions, writing of; Restrictive covenants; *Shelley v. Kraemer*; Smith Act; Warren, Earl; *Youngstown Sheet and Tube Co. v. Sawyer.*

United States v. Virginia

Citation: 516 U.S. 2264
Date: June 26, 1996
Issue: Sex discrimination
Significance: The Supreme Court held that an all-male, state-supported military academy must admit women.

Justice Ruth Bader Ginsburg wrote the opinion for the 7-1 majority in the case requiring Virginia Military Institute, an all-male, state-supported military academy, to admit women. Ginsburg found that Virginia failed to show a persuasive reason for excluding women. She rejected Virginia's proposed alternative, creating a women-only military academy, because the academy was unlikely to ever equal the quality of the existing institute. According to the Court, Virginia's remedy could not offer comparable benefits sufficient to meet the equal protection clause requirements. Ginsburg rejected as plain error the notion that a substantive comparability inquiry should be used. Chief Justice William H. Rehnquist concurred. Justice Clarence Thomas did not participate and Justice Antonin Scalia dissented.

Richard L. Wilson

See also Due process, procedural; Equal protection clause; Gender issues; Ginsburg, Ruth Bader; Military and the Court.

Virginia v. Black

CITATION: 538 U.S 343
DATE: September 11, 2002
ISSUES: Symbolic speech; hate speech
SIGNIFICANCE: In holding that government may not punish a person for burning a cross unless there is sufficient evidence of an intent to intimidate or threaten, the Supreme Court helped clarify what kind of hate speech may be proscribed.

Before *Virginia v. Black*, the Supreme Court's rulings on First Amendment protection of unpopular and dangerous ideas had left many questions unanswered. In *Chaplinsky v. New Hampshire* (1942), the Court had held that face-to-face "fighting words" and insults might be punishable. The Court in *R.A.V. v. City of St. Paul*, however, had overthrown a conviction for a cross burning, finding that the city ordinance violated the First Amendment because of its "viewpoint discrimination" and its failure to distinguish between protected and unprotected speech.

Virginia v. Black involved Barry Black and two other Ku Klux Klan members who were convicted separately of violating a Virginia statute that had made it a felony to burn a cross "with the intent of intimidating any person or group." The law specified that any such burning would be "prima facie evidence of intent to intimidate a person or group." The Virginia Supreme Court overturned the convictions based on the conclusion that the statute violated the First Amendment.

The U.S. Supreme Court held by a 6-3 majority that the statute was constitutional so long as it was construed to punish the act of cross-burning when the intent was to intimidate or threaten other persons. Writing for the majority, however, Justice Sandra Day O'Connor went on to explain that it would be unconstitutional to punish a cross-burner whose intent was simply to communicate a viewpoint, such as pride of ancestry, without implying any threat or intimidation. Based on this analysis, the conviction of Barry Black was overturned, whereas the convictions of the other two men were remanded to the lower courts for reexamination consistent with the Supreme Court's analysis of the law. Ironically, three of the more liberal justices held that the law was unconstitutional.

Thomas Tandy Lewis

See also First Amendment; Hate speech; Speech and press, freedom of; Symbolic speech.

Morrison R. Waite

Identification: Chief justice (March 4, 1874-March 23, 1888)
Nominated by: Ulysses S. Grant
Born: November 29, 1816, Lyme, Connecticut
Died: March 23, 1888, Washington, D.C.
Significance: During his fourteen years as chief justice, Waite stood firm for the understanding that the Reconstruction era amendments had not drastically altered the U.S. constitutional system.

Morrison R. Waite was chief justice during a time of great change in the United States. The meaning of freedom for the four million former slaves was still unsettled, although the nation had already begun its retreat from the promises of Reconstruction. Industry was growing rapidly, and big business attempted to use the Fourteenth Amendment, intended to protect the former slaves in all the rights of citizenship, to defend its property interests against government regulation. Therefore, the most important issues considered by the Waite Court were the meaning of the Reconstruction (or Civil War) amendments and the extent to which government could regulate corporate greed. Waite's judicial contribution can best be understood as an attempt to preserve the traditional system of dual federalism in which both state and national governments are sovereign in their own separate spheres. Waite's devotion to dual federalism was first apparent in *Minor v. Happersett* (1875), in which the Court ruled that the vote was not one of the privileges and immunities of national citizenship. Virginia Minor, therefore, had no right to vote under the Fourteenth Amendment. By construing the Fourteenth Amendment narrowly, Waite left a wide scope for state authority.

Waite's nomination by President Ulysses S. Grant was completely unexpected. Three previous candidates—political cronies of the scandal-ridden Grant administration—were unacceptable to the Senate. Although relatively unknown, Waite was a man of character and integrity. The son of a Connecticut state chief justice, Waite graduated from Yale in 1837, then studied law with his father before moving to Ohio. There he established a successful law practice, served as a Whig in the state legislature, and helped organize the state's Republican party. After the Civil War (1861-1865), he distinguished himself as a member of the Geneva Commission that settled claims involving the British-produced Confederate ship *Alabama.* Waite had no previous judicial experience and had never argued a case before the Court when he took his seat.

Morrison R. Waite. (Collection of the Supreme Court of the United States)

Civil Rights

Vilified for his narrow interpretations of the Enforcement Acts (1879-1871) and the Fourteenth and Fifteenth Amendments, Waite was accused of abandoning the former slaves to the mercies of their former owners. While his opinions in *United States v. Cruikshank* (1876) and *United States v. Reese* (1876) were indeed formalistic, looking to the letter rather than the spirit of the Enforcement Acts, it is unfair to say that Waite was unconcerned about the rights of African Americans. He was bound in *Cruikshank* by the Court's original interpretation of the Fourteenth Amendment in the *Slaughterhouse Cases* (1873), which had distinguished sharply between state and national citizenship and left the protection of ordinary rights to the states. Still, it was not clear exactly what the privileges and immunities of national citizenship were, and Waite had the opportunity in *Cruikshank* to read the Bill of Rights into the Fourteenth Amendment. Instead he favored the states, suggesting that there must be overt discriminatory state action in order for the federal government to protect the civil rights of the freed slaves. Locked into a traditional understanding of dual federalism, Waite missed the change in federal-state relations inherent in the Fourteenth Amendment.

However, Waite had not completely turned his back on the needs of the freed slaves. Although he declared two sections of the First Enforcement Act (May, 1870) unconstitutional in *United States v. Reese*, he nevertheless suggested that indictments that averred race as a factor in voting rights cases under the Fifteenth Amendment would be acceptable in federal court. In addition, Waite voted with the majority in *Ex parte Yarbrough* (1884), which demonstrated that Article I, section 4, of the U.S. Constitution protected the franchise in federal elections without reference to race. Therefore, Waite was not averse to federal protection of black voting rights, though he preferred a federal system in which states protected the rights of all citizens.

Overall, the Waite Court's civil rights decisions did not display the overt racism that was characteristic of the Fuller Court that followed it. The justices steered a middle course and ruled in the *Civil Rights Cases* (1883) that the Fourteenth Amendment allowed Congress to act when state, not private, actions interfered with an individual's due process and equal protection rights; however, they upheld the rights of African Americans when there was overt state discrimination as in *Strauder v. West Virginia* (1880). Waite's personal concern for African Americans is evident in the long hours he worked on the Peabody and Slater Funds, northern philanthropies that funded black schools and colleges in the South as well as scholarships for African Americans to study in the North and abroad. Clearly he believed education was the solution to the problems African Americans faced in the United States.

Economic Issues

Waite's preference for state-centered federalism made him amenable to state regulation of the economy in an era when the Court was moving toward the protection of big business under the due process clause of the Fourteenth Amendment. Waite's landmark opinion in *Munn v. Illinois* (1877), one of a series of Granger cases and the chief justice's best-known decision, upheld state power to regulate businesses "affected with a public interest." In the majority opinion, Waite stated that government regulation of fees charged by grain storage warehouses was not a deprivation of property without due process of law, demonstrating his clear preference for legislative over judicial regulation. Similarly in *Stone v. Farmers' Loan and Trust Co.* (1886), Waite found that government regulation of railroad rates did not constitute a "taking" of property without due process. However, Waite suggested in this opinion that the power of regulation had limits, a notion the Court would embrace with a vengeance in the 1890's when Waite was no longer on the bench.

Waite was a good, if not great, chief justice. He is underrated today for two reasons: civil rights decisions that became unpopular after the Civil Rights movement, however much they reflected the tenor of his time, and a lackluster writing style. However, Waite's character, integrity, and leadership abilities helped restore a dignity to the Court that had been lacking ever since the *Scott v. Sandford* (1857) decision.

Lou Falkner Williams

Further Reading

Bader, William H., and Roy M. Mersky, eds. *The First One Hundred Eight Justices.* Buffalo, N.Y.: William S. Hein, 2004.

Howard, John R. *The Shifting Wind: The Supreme Court and Civil Rights from Reconstruction to Brown*. Albany: State University of New York Press, 1999.

Magrath, C. Peter. *Morrison R. Waite: The Triumph of Character.* New York: Macmillan, 1963.

Stephenson, D. Grier. "The Chief Justice as Leader: The Case of Morrison R. Waite." *William and Mary Law Review* 14 (1973).

_______. *The Waite Court: Justices, Rulings, and Legacy*. Santa Barbara, Calif.: ABC-Clio, 2003.

See also *Civil Rights Cases*; *Cruikshank, United States v.*; Fifteenth Amendment; Fourteenth Amendment; *Munn v. Illinois*; Reconstruction; *Slaughterhouse Cases*; State action.

Wallace v. Jaffree

Citation: 472 U.S. 38

Date: June 4, 1985

Issue: Separation of church and state

Significance: Applying an expansive interpretation of the establishment clause of the First Amendment, the Supreme Court struck down a state law that authorized schools to devote a minute of silence for "meditation or voluntary prayer."

The majority of the public, especially in the South, disagreed with *Engel v. Vitale* (1962), which had banned formal prayers from the public schools. In 1978 the Alabama legislature authorized the schools to devote one minute of silence "for meditation." In 1981 the legislature amended the law to authorize the period "for meditation or voluntary prayer." In 1982 the legislature authorized teachers to lead "willing students" in oral prayers. In response to the laws, Ishmael Jaffree, an outspoken humanist and father of six children, complained that public officials were subjecting his children to indoctrination and pressures to participate in religious conduct. As expected, the federal courts quickly ruled that the 1982 law was unconstitutional.

In *Wallace v. Jaffree*, the Supreme Court justices voted six to three that the 1981 law also violated the establishment clause. Justice John Paul Stevens's opinion for the majority analyzed the law according to the first criterion of the *Lemon* test (developed in *Lemon v. Kurtzman*, 1971), which meant that the law must be invalidated if it was motivated entirely by the purpose of advancing religion. From the record, Stevens found that the legislature's only motivation was to "endorse prayer as a favored practice." In a concurring opinion, Justice Sandra Day O'Connor emphasized that neutral moments of silence were constitutional. In a strong dissent, Justice William H. Rehnquist argued that the intent of the First Amendment was merely to prohibit establishment of a national church or laws preferring one sect over another. Similarly, Chief Justice Warren E. Burger wrote that it was almost "ridiculous" to suggest that silent prayers could lead to an established religion, and he referred to *Marsh v. Chambers* (1983), in which the Court had allowed formal prayer rituals in legislative sessions.

Thomas Tandy Lewis

See also *Abington School District v. Schempp*; Burger, Warren E.; *Epperson v. Arkansas*; *Lee v. Weisman*; Religion, establishment of; Stevens, John Paul.

War and Civil Liberties

Description: During periods of armed conflict and fear of war, the U.S. government has often restricted and even curtailed the liberties and rights guaranteed in the U.S. Constitution.

Significance: In wartime, when persons have challenged the government's denial of constitutional rights, especially the rights to free expression and fair trials, many justices of the Supreme Court have given civil liberties less emphasis than national security.

The civil liberties contained in the U.S. Constitution were designed to protect citizens against abuses of power by government. The Bill of Rights sets limits on the government's power to regulate an individual's speech, religion, and political activities. In addition, it provides the government with certain procedures to ensure that individuals accused of crimes are treated fairly. The Constitution also empowers the government to pursue legitimate goals, one of the most important of which is defense of the nation. As the guardian of the Constitution, the Supreme Court has frequently been called upon to decide cases in which the government's ability to wage war has come into conflict with the civil liberties of its citizens.

When the Bill of Rights was ratified, attitudes about liberties and rights were much more limited than in later periods of history. During an undeclared naval war with France, for example, Congress passed the Sedition Act of 1798, which codified the English common law of seditious libel, making it a crime punishable by imprisonment or fine to speak disparagingly of the national government or national leaders. Supreme Court justices, while on circuit, presided over trials in which persons were sentenced to prison for their speech. Although most jurists of the time considered the Sedition Law constitutional because it did not authorize prior restraint of expression, the

Dust clouds enveloping Lower Manhattan after hijacked airliners were flown into the towers of the World Trade Center, causing both buildings to collapse on September 11, 2001. (www.bigfoto.com)

law became very unpopular, especially after its denunciation in the Kentucky and Virginia Resolutions, written by Thomas Jefferson and James Madison. During the War of 1812 (1812-1814) and the Mexican War (1846-1848), national leaders apparently saw no need to pass another such law.

The Civil War

During the course of the Civil War (1861-1865), President Abraham Lincoln, taking a narrow view of individual liberties, issued executive orders to suspend the writ of habeas corpus, to seize newspapers critical of the government's policies, and to conduct military trials of civilians. Because the federal courts had not routinely heard claims of civil liberties violations, relatively few cases reached the Court. When they did arrive, Chief Justice Roger Brooke Taney, a southerner, was one of Lincoln's strongest critics.

In the case of *Ex parte Merryman* (1861), which involved a pro-Confederate political leader arrested under Lincoln's suspension of habeas corpus, Chief Justice Taney filed an opinion condemning the arrest as unconstitutional, arguing that only Congress had authority to suspend the writ. However, the majority of justices refused to join the opinion, and Congress later defended Linclon by passing a habeas corpus statute. After Clement Vallandigham was tried in a military court and banished beyond Confederate lines, he petitioned the Supreme Court for a review of his conviction. In *Ex parte Vallandigham* (1864), the Court responded that based on the Judiciary Act of 1789, it lacked jurisdiction to review military proceedings.

In 1866, after the Civil War ended, the Court finally issued a ruling on the constitutionality of military trials of civilians in *Ex parte Milligan.* Lambdin P. Milligan had been tried by a military commission in Indiana on charges of conspiring to seize Union munitions. Strongly rejecting the government's argument that the Bill of Rights could be suspended in time of war, the Court held that Milligan had been deprived of his constitutional right to a trial by jury. As long as the civilian courts continued to operate, the Court held, military trials of civilians were prohibited. Ironically, Republican liberals at the time denounced the *Milligan* ruling because President Andrew Johnson used it as a justification to reduce military authority in the occupied

South. Most commentators regard *Milligan* as a constitutional landmark, although the Court did not refer to it as a binding precedent during World War II.

World War I

During World War I, Congress enacted the Espionage Act of 1917, which included criminal punishments for anyone making false reports to help the enemy or anyone seeking to interfere with military operations or the draft. An amendment of 1918, commonly called the Sedition Act, further punished the uttering or printing of any "disloyal" language. Under this draconian legislation, the government reported a total of 877 convictions out of 1,956 prosecutions. The first case to come before the Court was *Schenck v. United States* (1919), which involved a defendant found guilty of distributing leaflets that encouraged young men to resist the military draft. The Court upheld Schenck's conviction, saying that his ideas posed a "clear and present danger" of leading to the results that Congress had the constitutional right to prevent.

In *Debs v. United States* (1919), the Court upheld the conviction of a prominent Socialist leader Eugene V. Debs for delivering a speech denouncing the war that, in the Court's view, had the tendency to promote illegal acts against the war effort, even though Debs did not explicitly advocate illegality. Likewise, in *Abrams v. United States* (1919), the Court upheld, by a 7-2 vote, a sentence of twenty years imprisonment for distributing leaflets that urged people to oppose American efforts to undermine Russia's Bolshevik Revolution. In an eloquent dissent, Justice Oliver Wendell Holmes declared that the government under the First Amendment could only punish "speech that produces or is intended to produce a clear and imminent danger" of substantive harm. He denied that such a danger existed from "the surreptitious publishing of a silly leaflet by an unknown man."

World War II

The Supreme Court's commitment to civil liberties was severely tested during World War II (1941-1945). In 1942, President Franklin D. Roosevelt signed Executive Order 9066, authorizing the forced evacuation of about 110,000 persons of Japanese ancestry. Despite the protections of the Fifth Amendment, the internees were deprived of liberty without being charged of any wrongdoing. Many lost their homes and businesses. The government argued that some Japanese Americas remained loyal to their ancestral homeland and therefore posed a threat to national security, and that it was impossible to separate the loyal from the disloyal. In *Korematsu v. United States* (1944), the Court upheld the forced relocation by a 6-3 vote. Writing for the majority, Justice Hugo L. Black uncritically accepted the arguments of military leaders; ironically, he affirmed that restrictions of a single racial group should be given "the most rigid scrutiny."

In reviewing prosecutions of alleged war criminals, the Stone Court usually deferred to the wishes of the executive branch. In *Ex parte Quirin* (1942), the Court unanimously upheld the use of secret military commissions in the convictions of eight German saboteurs captured in the United States. The Court quickly concluded that Congress had authorized the commissions in Article of War 15, showing little concern about the procedures used. The justices declared that despite the 1866 *Milligan* precedent, the saboteurs were not entitled to civilian trials because they were enemy belligerents (even though one of the men had been a naturalized U.S. citizen).

In *Haupt v. United States* (1947), the Supreme Court upheld a treason conviction based on evidence that the defendant had done no more than shelter his son. When upholding the very hasty military conviction of a Japanese general charged with failure to prevent war crimes in the Philippines in the case of *In re Yamashita* (1946), Chief Justice Harlan Fiske Stone, speaking for seven justices, rejected the two dissenters' concern about the lack of any due process required by the Fifth Amendment. In *Duncan v. Kahanamoku* (1946), which involved the use of military tribunals for prosecuting civilians in what was then the territory of Hawaii, the Court eventually held that the use of the tribunals violated Hawaii's organic law. However, reflecting the Court's determination not to hinder the war effort, the Court did not issue the decision until two years after the termination of martial law. Even then, the Court carefully avoided any reference to constitutional rights or to *Milligan.*

In comparison with its actions during the previous world war, the Court was not faced with the task of reviewing mammoth assaults on free expression. The Roosevelt administration did not prosecute large numbers of people for speech or press violations under either the Smith Act of 1940 or the Espionage Act of 1940. However, the Court did decline to review a few cases in which individuals were punished for illegal advocacy, most notably the sensational case of eighteen communists convicted in Minnesota in 1941 under the Smith Act. More typical, however, was the case of *Hartzel v. United States* (1944), in which the Court overturned an Espionage Act conviction for the distribution of profascist literature, finding insufficient evidence that the defendant had intended to impede the U.S. war effort. Likewise, in *Keegan v. United States* (1945), it concluded that the evidence was too meager to sustain the conviction of German American Bund members for conspiracy to oppose the draft. Perhaps the most important free expression precedent during the war was *West Virginia State Board of Education v. Barnette* (1943), which upheld the constitutional right of schoolchildren not to participate in salute-the-flag ceremonies.

The Cold War, 1946-1991

After World War II, government prosecutors vigorously pursued communist leaders under the Smith Act, which threatened up to ten years imprisonment for any person who "advocates, abets, advises, or teaches" the desirability of a violent revolution. Chief Justice Fred M. Vinson as well as other members of the Court were fearful of internal subversion, perhaps influenced by Senator Joseph McCarthy's anticommunist crusade during the Korean War (1950-1953). In a 6-2 decision, the Court upheld the Smith Act convictions of eleven communist leaders in *Dennis v. United States* (1961), emphasizing the "gravity of the evil" and applying the so-called "grave and probable danger test."

After the Korean War ended in 1953, the justices began to moderate their fears of communist subversion. Setting aside the convictions of fourteen communists leaders in *Yates v. United States* (1957), the majority opinion stated that convictions must be based on advocacy of action and not advocacy of belief, which made convictions difficult under the Smith Act. In *Peters v. Hobby* (1955), the Court reinstated federal employees who had been discharged under the loyalty-security program. In *Watkins v. United States* (1957), the Court put limits on the extent to which congressional committees could require witnesses to answer personal questions.

During the late 1950's, Justices Felix Frankfurter and John Marshall Harlan appeared to become more fearful of subversion. In *Barenblatt v. United States* (1959), the Court retreated from *Watkins* and upheld the conviction for contempt of a witness who had refused to answer questions to the House Committee on Un-American Activities (HUAC). The justices voted five to four to sustain a Smith Act conviction in *Scales v. United States* (1961), although they insisted that any convictions must be based on evidence of active participation in a subversive group.

During the Vietnam War (1965-1973), in contrast to its actions during most other U.S. wars, the Court actually expanded constitutional liberties. In the seminal case of *Brandenburg v. Ohio* (1968), the Court held that advocacy of violence could only be punished when it was intended and likely to provoke "imminent lawless action." The Court's ruling in *Tinker v. Des Moines Independent Community School District* (1969) recognized that public school students had a constitutional right to display antiwar symbols as long as there was no disruption of normal school activities. Refusing to endorse a "prior restraint of expression" in *New York Times Co. v. United States* (1971), the Court rejected the government's attempt to suppress publication of the Pentagon Papers in the name of national security.

Terrorism, Afghanistan, and Iraq

As in other times of fear and war, the terrorist attacks on the United States of September 11, 2001, caused many Americans to become more concerned about national security than about their civil liberties. Seven days after the attacks, Congress passed an Authorization to use Military Force, empowering the president to "use all necessary and appropriate force" against terrorists and their supporters. A few weeks later, Congress passed passed the Patriot Act, which made it easier for executive agencies to gather and share information about persons in the United States. Civil libertarians were highly critical of these statutes, especially since some provisions resembled bills of attainder.

Civil libertarians denounced President George W. Bush's executive order authorizing the National Security Agency (NSA) to monitor, without obtaining warrants, conversations among Americans and among suspected terrorists abroad, contrary to legislation requiring that warrants first be obtained by the Federal Intelligence Surveillance Act (FISA). The Bush administration responded that its policy was justified by the inherent powers of the president as well as by Congress's endorsement of a war against terrorism. Civil libertarians were outraged with the Bush Administration's domestic surveillance policies. In 2006, it remained uncertain whether the Supreme Court would be called on to decide the constitutionality of Bush's policies.

Meanwhile, the Court faced decisions about whether to review cases involving the detaining of persons (both citizens and noncitizens) suspected of giving support to terrorists. After invading Afghanistan in 2001, President Bush ordered an ambitious military operation against Iraq in 2003. The administration endorsed a policy of detaining large numbers of persons suspected of either being terrorists or cooperating with terrorist groups. Many prisoners naturally sought habeas corpus relief in U.S. federal courts. Yaser Hamdi, an American citizen raised in Saudi Arabia and accused of cooperating with the enemy in Afghanistan, was imprisoned for over two years in the United States as an "enemy combatant," without being charged and without the right of habeas corpus. In *Hamdi v. Rumsfeld* (2004), however, the Court held that the due process clause guaranteed all citizens the right to a "fair opportunity" to contest their detention before neutral magistrates, and that Hamdi had either to be tried for a specific crime or be released. An arrangement was worked out through which Hamdi renounced his citizenship and was returned to Saudi Arabia.

An issue of greater significance was the fate of five hundred foreign citizens held on suspicion of supporting terrorism at the U.S. naval base in Guantanamo, Cuba. The government claimed that these alien prisoners on foreign soil did not have any privilege of seeking habeas corpus relief in the federal courts, emphasizing that the naval base, which was located in a foreign country, did not fall under the jurisdiction of U.S. federal courts. When finally reviewing several habeas corpus petitions in *Rasul v. Bush* (2004), the Court rejected the government's position by a 6-3 vote. Speaking for the majority, Justice John Paul Stevens concluded that federal courts held jurisdiction over the "territory over which the United States exercises exclusive jurisdiction and control." In addition, he wrote that the right to habeas corpus was not dependent upon citizenship status, observing that for three hundred years the English common law had extended the privilege to any person held by the government. In 2006, it was expected that the right of habeas corpus relief would eventually force the government to choose between either releasing or prosecuting at least some of the Guantanamo detainees.

The Bush administration made plans to use special military commissions for the trials of aliens who could be charged with crimes of war. The commissions were established under a presidential order of 2003. By early 2006, ten detainees at Guantanamo had been formally charged. The Supreme Court reviewed the case of one of these defendants, Salim Ahmed Hamdan, a Yemeni national accused of conspiracy to commit terrorism. Its 5-3 decision, *Hamdan v. Rumsfeld* (2006), rendered the administration a major setback, as it held that the special commissions were illegal under both the Geneva Convention and the Uniform Code of Military Justice (UCMJ). The majority of justices concluded that the Authorization for the Use of Military Force (AUMF) had not authorized the president to create special commissions, and even if such commissions were to have congressional support, they would have to include all the procedures of the UCMJ and the Geneva Convention. Stevens firmly rejected the administration's policy of denying the detainees the protections of the Geneva Convention based on the claim that they were not lawful combatants fighting in uniform for a foreign country. Stevens argued that all detainees were entitled to the convention's full protections until a court decided they were not prisoners of war. From the Bush administration's perspective, the only good thing about the *Hamdan* decision was that it did not actually require the release of any of the detainees.

Philip R. Zampini
Revised and updated by the Editor

Further Reading

Baker, Thomas, and John Stack, eds. *At War with Civil Rights and Liberties.* New York: Rowland & Littlefield, 2005.
Cole, David. *Terror and the Constitution: Sacrificing Constitutional Freedom in the Name of National Security.* New York: New Press, 2006.
Irons, Peter. *Justice at War.* New York: Oxford University Press, 1983.
Neely, Mark E. *The Fate of Liberty: Abraham Lincoln and Civil Liberties.* New York: Oxford University Press, 1991.
Rehnquist, William H. *All the Laws but One: Civil Liberties in Wartime.* New York: Alfred A. Knopf, 1998.
Stone, Geoffrey. *Perilous Times: Free Speech in Wartime.* New York: W. W. Norton, 2004.
Wilson, Richard A. *Human Rights in the "War on Terror."* New York: Cambridge University Press, 2005.
Yoo, John. *The Powers of War and Peace: The Constitution and Foreign Affairs after 9/11.* Chicago: University of Chicago Press, 2005.

See also Bill of attainder; Civil War; Cold War; Espionage acts; *Hamdan v. Rumsfeld*; Japanese American relocation; Military and the Court; National security; Speech and press, freedom of; Vietnam War; War powers; World War II.

War Powers

Description: The constitutional and political authority to protect the nation from its enemies and to place U.S. military forces abroad in hostile situations.

Significance: The vagueness of the parts of the Constitution dealing with war powers caused the president and Congress to disagree about their interpretation. The Supreme Court ruled on a number of cases involving the legitimate use of military force in foreign lands.

Article I, section 8, of the U.S. Constitution grants Congress the power to tax and spend for the common defense, to declare war, to raise and support armies and a navy, and to make rules for the governance of such forces. The Constitution (Article II, section 2) makes the president commander in chief and gives him or her the power to make treaties and appoint ambassadors with the advice and consent of the Senate. Although Congress has the power to declare war, from the nation's beginnings, presidents have claimed the authority to place military troops abroad and to wage war. The United States has been involved in only five declared wars: the War of 1812, the Mexican War (1846-1848), the Spanish-American War (1898), World War I (1917-1918), and World War II (1941-1945). Of those, only the War of 1812 was actively debated by Congress before a formal declaration of war was made. Nevertheless, military troops have been deployed more than two hundred times in various military actions abroad.

In *Bas v. Tingy* (1800), the Supreme Court recognized that Congress could authorize war both by a formal declaration and by passing statutes that recognized a state of "limited," "partial," or "imperfect" conflict. A sharply divided court upheld President Abraham Lincoln's blockade of Confederate ports in the *Prize Cases* (1863), stating that while Lincoln did not have the power to initiate a war, he did have the authority to meet force with force without any special legislative authority. The Court gave further support to presidential power in the conduct of foreign affairs in *United States v. Curtiss-Wright Export Corp.* (1936) and *United States v. Belmont* (1937), asserting that the president was the sole representative of the nation in its foreign relations and affairs.

The aftermath of World War II saw the rise of the United States to world power status and the development of permanent standing armies, factors not anticipated by the Framers of the Constitution. Beginning with the administration of President Franklin D. Roosevelt, presidents have argued for an expansive reading of the executive war powers to meet the needs of national security in the nuclear age. With few exceptions, the federal courts have been unwilling to involve themselves in the conflict between the legislative and executive branches over the exercise of war powers, calling the issue a political question and inappropriate for judicial resolution. Central to the war powers debate has been the legality and applicability of the War Powers Act of 1973, which sets time and communications requirements upon any military troop deployment by the president.

Timothy S. Boylan

Further Reading

Dirck, Brian R. *Waging War on Trial: A Handbook with Cases, Laws, and Documents.* Santa Barbara, Calif.: ABC-Clio, 2003.
Ely, John Hart. *War and Responsibility.* Princeton, N.J.: Princeton University Press, 1993.
Fisher, Louis. *Presidential War Power.* Lawrence: University Press of Kansas, 1995.
Moore, James. *Bush's War for Reelection: Iraq, the White House, and the People.* New York: John Wiley & Sons, 2004.
Ng, Wendy L. *Japanese American Internment During World War II: A History and Reference Guide.* Westport, Conn.: Greenwood Press, 2002. Comprehensive reference source on the internment years.
Woodward, Bob. *Bush at War.* New York: Simon & Schuster, 2002.

See also *Curtiss-Wright Export Corp., United States v.*; *Hamdan v. Rumsfeld*; Japanese American relocation; Military and the Court; National security; Presidential powers; Vietnam War; War and civil liberties; World War II.

Earl Warren

Identification: Chief justice (October 5, 1953-June 23, 1969)
Nominated by: Dwight D. Eisenhower
Born: March 19, 1891, Los Angeles, California
Died: July 9, 1974, Washington, D.C.
Significance: Under Warren's leadership, the Supreme Court forged new doctrines in equal justice and fair trial procedures and altered the character of representation in the political system. The Warren Court's due process revolution produced profound changes in the law and transformed the way society perceived civil liberties and civil rights.

The son of Scandinavian immigrants, Earl Warren grew up in Bakersfield, California, where his father was a railroad worker. Warren attended the University of California, Berkeley, where he received his law degree in 1914. After briefly serving as an officer in the army in

Earl Warren. (Supreme Court Historical Society)

World War I, he began work in the office of the Alameda County district attorney and became identified with the Republican Party.

In 1926 Warren was elected district attorney for Alameda County, a position he held for thirteen years. He quickly made a name for himself as a racket-buster, and a 1931 survey of U.S. district attorneys declared Warren the best in the United States. He was elected attorney general of California in 1938 and modernized the office during his four-year term. As the state's attorney general at the beginning of World War II, Warren was a strong advocate of the forced evacuation of persons of Japanese ancestry from the West Coast—an action he later regretted. In 1942 he was elected governor and served for an unprecedented three terms, once being nominated by both major parties under California's old system of cross-filing.

As governor, Warren was an able administrator who reorganized the state government and secured the passage of reform legislation that built highways, modernized the hospital system, improved state prisons, and made the University of California system the envy of other states. He endeared himself to liberal groups by taking stands against racial prejudice and urging increased social security benefits including improved old-age and unemployment benefits. The popularity of his administration made him a national figure in the Republican Party, and he was Thomas Dewey's running mate in the 1948 presidential election. In 1952, Warren played a key role in the latter stages of Dwight D. Eisenhower's presidential campaign. After the election, Eisenhower promised Warren appointment to the Supreme Court upon the first vacancy that might occur. Eisenhower's attorney general, Herbert Brownell, held further discussions with Warren about accepting an appointment as solicitor general until there was an opening on the Court.

Appointment to the Court

Warren had accepted an offer to be solicitor general in the Eisenhower administration when on September 8, 1953, Chief Justice Fred M. Vinson suddenly died of a heart attack. Eisenhower appointed Warren to the chief justiceship, and Warren took up his new duties at the beginning of the 1953 term. Because Congress was not in session at the time of his appointment, Warren was not confirmed by the Senate until March 1, 1954. Warren served on the Court until his retirement on June 23, 1969.

In 1963 under pressure from President Lyndon B. Johnson, Warren agreed to chair the special commission to investigate the assassination of President John F. Kennedy. The Warren Commission report was a controversial document, and the chief justice was criticized for participating in an extrajudicial assignment.

In June, 1968, Warren informed Johnson that he intended to retire as soon as a successor could be named. Johnson nominated Associate Justice Abe Fortas. When alleged financial misconduct by Fortas was revealed, his nomination was withdrawn, and Warren agreed to stay on until the next president could name his successor. Warren presided at the opening of the 1968 term, and when Richard M. Nixon was elected president, the chief justice repeated his offer of resignation but preferred to wait until the end of the term. Nixon accepted Warren's suggestion, and eventually nominated Warren E. Burger, who was confirmed by the Senate and took the oath of office on the day of Warren's retirement on June 23, 1969.

Equal Protection

During Warren's first term, the Court ruled on the constitutionality of racially segregated schools in *Brown v. Board of Education* (1954). The justices had heard the case argued in the preceding term but had asked for re-argument to address the applicability of the Fourteenth Amendment's equal protection clause. Warren presided over a Court divided over the issues of the case with four justices apparently opposed to overruling the separate but equal doctrine enunciated in *Plessy v. Ferguson* (1896). Displaying the leadership and straightforward defining of issues that were to characterize his chief justiceship, Warren won over the other justices, and a unanimous Court declared that separate facilities were inherently unequal. At his first *Brown* conference, Warren defined the issue in moral terms: *Plessy* could be sustained only on the premise that blacks were inferior to whites, and he did not grant that premise. At the same time, Warren cautioned that remedies should be determined in the future and with the participation of representatives of the affected states. Warren's opinion for the Court was in many ways the watershed constitutional case of the century. By finding segregation in violation of the equal protection clause, the Court put the nation on a new path in race relations. It also signaled that if the other branches of government defaulted in their responsibilities, the Court would ensure that constitutional rights were protected.

In the next term, in *Brown II* (1955) Warren wrote a decree to implement an end to segregated schools that was gradual and mindful of local conditions. The Court, following Warren's lead, subsequently struck down every segregation law challenged before it and ruled such separation invalid in all public buildings, housing, transportation, and recreational and eating facilities. When Governor Orval Faubus of Arkansas challenged the Court's authority to enforce its *Brown* mandates, Warren rallied all of the justices to affix their names to the opinion in *Cooper v. Aaron* (1958), which affirmed the supremacy of the Court's interpretation of the constitution.

Fair Representation

Warren called *Baker v. Carr* (1962) the most vital decision during his tenure on the Court and the apportionment revolution that followed the most important achievement of the Warren Court. In *Colegrove v. Green* (1946), the Court had refused to rule on legislative apportionment, which Justice Felix Frankfurter declared was a political question to be decided by elected representatives and therefore not justiciable. In 1961 when urban voters in Tennessee challenged the apportionment of seats in the state legislature as contrary to equal protection, however, the Warren Court, in *Baker*, entered what Frankfurter had termed the political thicket. Justice William J. Brennan, Jr., writing for the majority, held that such cases were indeed justiciable under the Fourteenth Amendment.

In a series of cases that followed, the Court changed the character of U.S. politics by requiring that all citizens be represented equally in state legislatures and in Congress. The judiciary put an end to traditional malapportionment reflecting rural bias because there was no other feasible way to correct the constitutional command of voting equality. In *Wesberry v. Sanders* (1964), the Court ruled that congressional apportionment schemes should be based on the criterion of one person, one vote. In *Reynolds v. Sims* (1964), which required representation based on population in both branches of a state legislature, Warren maintained that it was unconstitutional to overweight the value of some voters and underweight the value of others.

Due Process Revolution

Until the 1960's, the Court had been hesitant to incorporate Bill of Rights protections to apply to the states through the due process clause of the Fourteenth Amendment. Beginning with *Mapp v. Ohio* (1961), however, the Warren Court selectively incorporated most of the protections afforded the accused before the bar of justice. The *Mapp* decision held that the exclusionary rule that bars evidence obtained in violation of the Fourth Amendment's ban on unreasonable searches and seizures applies in state as well as federal cases.

Fifth Amendment protections against self-incrimination were incorporated in *Malloy v. Hogan* (1964) and against double jeopardy in *Benton v. Maryland* (1969). The Warren Court incorporated most of the provisions of the Sixth Amendment, including the right to counsel in felony prosecutions in *Gideon v. Wainwright* (1963); confrontation clause protections in *Pointer v. Texas* (1965); the right to a speedy trial in *Klopfer v. North Carolina* (1967) by an impartial jury in *Parker v. Gladden* (1966) with compulsory processes for obtaining witnesses in *Washington v. Texas* (1968); and the right to a trial by jury in criminal cases in *Duncan v. Louisiana* (1968). The Eighth Amendment prohibition against cruel and unusual punishment was applied to the states in *Robinson v. California* (1962).

In a series of decisions, the Warren Court restrained the process of state law enforcement from investigation through arrest and trial. Warren wrote for the Court in *Miranda v. Arizona* (1966), setting up clear rules that the police would have to follow during interrogations and declaring that any statements elicited in violation of these procedures would be inadmissible. Although the *Miranda* decision was criticized for restricting the efforts of law-enforcement officials, Miranda warnings, with their cluster of constitutional rights for those accused of crimes, became a part of police routines.

Other Rights

The Warren Court handed down several landmark First Amendment decisions. The ruling in *New York Times Co. v. Sullivan* (1964) established the actual malice test for libel suits by public officials and protected the rights of citizens to criticize official conduct of government officials. The Warren Court made the United States much less puritanical by its rulings on obscenity. In *Roth v. United States* (1957), the Court defined obscenity and empowered judges to see that the censorious did not go beyond prescribed parameters. In *National Association for the Advancement of Colored People v. Button* (1963), the Court found that the First and Fourteenth Amendments protect the right of association. In decisions made during the McCarthy Red Scare era, however, the Court had a mixed record of protecting free speech and association rights of communists or those accused of associating with communists. The Court's interpretation of the Smith Act (1940) in *Yates v. United States* (1957) and *Scales v. United States* (1961) severely restricted its usefulness in limiting communist activities.

Government-sponsored prayers in public schools were found to be inconsistent with the establishment clause in *Engel v. Vitale* (1962), as were Bible readings and the recitation of the Lord's Prayer in classes in *Abington School District v. Schempp* (1963). In both cases, the Court concluded that the challenged practices served sacred rather than secular purposes. *Engel* and *Schempp* initiated a continuing and volatile debate on school prayer.

Warren joined in the majority opinion in *Griswold v. Connecticut* (1965), which proclaimed a general right to privacy that the Court would later extend to apply to the questions of abortion and gender discrimination. In privacy, as in the areas of other fundamental rights, the Warren Court's legacy influences the daily and public lives of Americans.

Leadership and Philosophy

Chief Justice Warren was a notable leader. An experienced administrator, he was accustomed to chairing meetings, managing agendas, and assigning tasks to others. Warren was particularly adept at conducting the conference. He came prepared with a knowledge of each case and forthrightly stated the facts and led discussion. Warren articulated and pressed on others the convictions on which he believed a majority decision should rest. The force generated by Warren's convictions about what was fair or equitable altered the meaning of technical debates on the Court. What counted in decision making was the conviction that a result was right. Warren used his political skills to induce the justices to follow his lead, and he personally was a guiding force in the landmark decisions during his tenure.

Warren did not have an overriding ideology or philosophy that directed his jurisprudence. He was a pragmatist who used the law to reach the result he favored in a given case. The values to which Warren adhered were traditional American ones such as family, morality, fairness, and equity. His concept of law applied equally to all parts of society: all races, citizens, different economic groups, prosecutors, and defendants. Warren's concern for equality was reflected in his racial discrimination, malapportionment, and criminal justice decisions. His dominant consideration was seeing that the right side prevailed in a given case. The rightness of a side was determined by his conception of social good. Therefore, Warren could be called a realist for whom neither rules nor logic produced court decisions. For this result-oriented justice, the outcome of a case mattered more than the reasoning behind the decision.

The chief justice joined Hugo L. Black and William O. Douglas in an activist approach to the role of the Court. He followed the idea of judicial restraint in economic areas, but he believed that the Bill of Rights required more active enforcement in civil liberties cases. For Warren, it was the duty of the Court to rectify individual instances of injustice, particularly when the victims suffered from racial, economic, or similar disadvantages. Warren attempted to ensure fairness and equity in all cases where they had not been secured by other government processes. If a constitutional requirement remained unenforced because of government's failure to compel obedience to it, the Court had to act. The Court had to step in because the political branches had not acted to support certain constitutional rights and the government could not or would not act to correct the situation.

For Warren, principle was more compelling than precedent. He was not afraid of change to enable public law to cope with rapid societal transformations. Conservative critics opposed Warren's judicial activism and his broad interpretation of the Bill of Rights. Other critics faulted his lack of scholarship or judicial craftsmanship. However, under the leadership of "Super Chief," as Justice Brennan fondly dubbed Warren, the Court brought the law more nearly in accord with the aspirations of the majority of the nation.

Theodore M. Vestal

Further Reading

Earl Warren is well served with fine studies, such as Melvin I. Urofsky's *The Warren Court: Justices, Rulings, and Legacy* (Santa Barbara, Calif.: ABC-Clio, 2001), Michal R. Belknap's *The Supreme Court Under Earl Warren, 1953-1969* (Columbia: University of South Carolina Press, 2005), and Christine L. Compston's *Earl Warren: Justice for All* (New York: Oxford University Press, 2001).

Ed Cray's *Chief Justice: A Biography of Earl Warren* (New York: Simon & Schuster, 1997) is a highly readable account of the life of the man of contradictions who "grew to meet the demands of each new job." A professor of journalism, Cray's work is informative and full of insights about Warren, but his analyses of cases are for the general reader. More satisfying in its legal analysis is Bernard Schwartz's *Super Chief: Earl Warren and His Supreme Court: A Judicial Biography* (New York: New York University Press, 1983), which begins with Warren's arrival at the Court and reveals the internal dynamics of the Court's handling of important cases and events. The most scholarly biography is by G. Edward White, who clerked for Warren in his retirement. White's *Earl Warren, A Public Life* (New York: Oxford University Press, 1982) portrays the chief justice in a series of episodes and elements of his life. *Earl Warren: The Judge Who Changed America* (Englewood Cliffs, N.J.: Prentice-Hall, 1979) by Jack H. Pollack describes Warren's career but does not analyze his jurisprudence.

Warren had almost completed a first draft of his memoirs when he died. *The Memoirs of Earl Warren* (Garden City, N.Y.: Doubleday, 1977) was published posthumously and contains comments on some events and cases, including *Brown.* John D. Weaver's *Warren: The Man, the Court, the Era* (Boston: Little, Brown, 1967) is well documented, but slightly less than half its length is devoted to Warren's judicial service. A less well-documented work is Leo Katcher's *Earl Warren: A Political Biography* (New York: McGraw-Hill, 1967), which was published before Warren's retirement from the Court and stresses his pre-Court years in California.

See also *Baker v. Carr*; *Brown v. Board of Education*; Burger, Warren E.; Chief justice; Due process, procedural; Due process, substantive; Equal protection clause; Fourteenth Amendment; Fundamental rights; Incorporation doctrine; Judicial activism; Libel; Obscenity and pornography; Privacy, right to; Representation, fairness of; Vinson, Fred M.

Bushrod Washington

IDENTIFICATION: Associate justice (November 9, 1798-November 26, 1829)

NOMINATED BY: John Adams

BORN: June 5, 1762, Westmoreland County, Virginia

DIED: November 26, 1829, Philadelphia, Pennsylvania

SIGNIFICANCE: Washington, a Federalist like many of his fellow Supreme Court justices, tended to join with the majority on the Court, although he expressed his opinion more openly as a circuit judge.

Bushrod Washington was the son of John Augustine Washington and Hannah Bushrod and the favorite nephew of President George Washington. He initially met John Marshall (later chief justice) during their legal studies at the College of William and Mary. Following his service as a cavalry officer under the Marquis de Lafayette, Washington read law with James Wilson (later associate justice) in Philadelphia.

Washington and Marshall served together in the Virginia Convention, held to adopt and ratify the U.S. Constitution. In 1798 at the urging of former president Washington, both men entered congressional campaigns as Federalists. When Justice Wilson died, President John Adams considered both Marshall and Washington to fill the vacancy. The associate justice position was first offered to Marshall but he chose to continue his congressional race. Washington abandoned his campaign to accept the appointment and, at age thirty-seven, became the youngest justice to that time. Three years later, Marshall accepted appointment as chief justice on the Court.

Justice William Johnson wrote that Washington and Marshall were "commonly estimated as one judge." However, in the Marshall Court, silent acquiescence in the majority opinion by dissenting justices was the normal practice. Washington publicly disagreed with the chief justice only eight times in their twenty-eight years of joint tenure and with Justice Joseph Story only five times in the fourteen years they were both on the Court. He disfavored dissenting opinions (writing only three), because he believed that such opinions diluted the au-

Bushrod Washington. (Collection of the Supreme Court of the United States)

thority and reputation of the Court. He also avoided concurring opinions except in *Dartmouth College v. Woodward* (1819). In many instances, he probably felt no need to dissent, as his Federalist principles about strong national government, property rights, the role of the Court, and economic regulation routinely prevailed.

Washington was known as a particularly conscientious and able circuit judge. He first rode circuit in the Deep South, then transferred to the Third Circuit covering New Jersey and Pennsylvania. Washington's acumen manifested itself more clearly in his circuit decisions, made away from the Court and its imposed norm of unanimity. In that role, he held that congressional power over bankruptcy was supreme and preempted state action in *Golden v. Prince* (1814), signed the writ of error that advanced *Martin v. Hunter's Lessee* (1816) to the Court, and presided over politically charged trials involving the Sedition Act of 1798 and over *United States v. Bright* (1809), the treason trial of a Pennsylvania militia officer ordered to prevent enforcement of the Court's decision in *United States v. Peters* (1809).

Before assuming the bench, Washington had collected and published opinions of the Virginia Court of Appeals. His interest in disseminating precedents and legal reasoning continued as he and his colleagues, especially Justice Story, regularly shared information about their circuit decisions. The justices thus were able to identify, and somewhat guide, issues that would eventually reach the Court.

Susan Coleman

Further Reading

Annis, David. *Mr. Bushrod Washington: Supreme Court Justice on the Marshall Court.* Notre Dame, Ind.: University of Notre Dame, 1976.

Bader, William H., and Roy M. Mersky, eds. *The First One Hundred Eight Justices.* Buffalo, N.Y.: William S. Hein, 2004.

Clinton, Robert, Christopher Budzisz, and Peter Renstrom, eds. *The Marshall Court: Justices, Rulings, and Legacy.* Santa Barbara, Calif.: ABC-Clio, 2007.

Custer, Lawrence B. "Bushrod Washington and John Marshall: A Preliminary Inquiry." *American Journal of Legal History* 4 (1960): 34-48.

Harrington, Matthew P. *Jay and Ellsworth, The First Courts: Justices, Rulings, and Legacy.* Santa Barbara, Calif.: ABC-Clio, 2007.

White, G. Edward. *The Marshall Court and Cultural Change, 1815-1835.* New York: Oxford University Press, 1991.

See also Baldwin, Henry; Johnson, William; Marshall, John; Second Amendment; Story, Joseph.

Washington v. Glucksberg

Citation: 521 U.S. 702

Date: June 26, 1997

Issue: Physician-assisted suicide

Significance: The Supreme Court held that the U.S. Constitution does not guarantee any right to have assistance in committing suicide.

In *Cruzan v. Director, Missouri Department of Health* (1990), the Supreme Court "assumed and strongly suggested" that the due process clause of the Fourteenth Amendment protects the traditional right of competent adults to refuse medical treatment, including life-support systems. Building on this substantive reading of the due process clause, the Ninth Circuit struck down Washington state's ban on assisted suicide, and it recognized that terminally ill competent adults have the right to hasten their deaths with medication prescribed by physicians.

The Supreme Court unanimously reversed the lower court's ruling. Speaking for a majority, Chief Justice William H. Rehnquist found that the decision to terminate medical treatment was fundamentally different from providing active assistance in a suicide. The use of substantive due process, he emphasized, should be limited to protecting those rights and liberties that are "deeply rooted in this Nation's history and traditions," and he noted that this tradition had almost universally rejected any notion of a right to commit suicide. Washington's law, moreover, furthered the state's legitimate interest in protecting human life.

Four justices, while concurring in Rehnquist's ruling, expressed more expansive views of individual rights to personal autonomy protected by substantive due process, recognizing some right to avoid pain and suffering.

Thomas Tandy Lewis

See also *Cruzan v. Director, Missouri Department of Health*; Die, right to; Due process, substantive; *Moore v. City of East Cleveland*; Rehnquist, William H.

James M. Wayne

IDENTIFICATION: Associate justice (January 14, 1835-July 5, 1867)
NOMINATED BY: Andrew Jackson
BORN: 1790, Savannah, Georgia
DIED: July 7, 1867, Washington, D.C.
SIGNIFICANCE: An expert in admiralty law, Wayne helped expand the power of the federal government over waterborne commerce as a Supreme Court justice. Although a Southerner and a defender of slavery, he supported the Union during the Civil War.

James M. Wayne began practicing law in 1810, served in the Georgia legislature from 1815 to 1817, and was mayor of Savannah from 1817 to 1819. He served as a local and state judge from 1819 to 1828, when he was elected to Congress. He was nominated to the Supreme Court

James M. Wayne. (Handy Studios/ Collection of the Supreme Court of the United States)

by President Andrew Jackson on January 6, 1835, confirmed by the Senate on January 9, and sworn in five days later.

Wayne's written opinions often dealt with admiralty law. In *Waring v. Clarke* (1847), he wrote the majority opinion, expanding federal authority over ocean commerce to include major inland waterways.

In *Scott v. Sandford* (1857), Wayne agreed with the majority that the federal government had no power to limit slavery in new territories. Despite this decision and although a Southerner, he later supported the Union during the Civil War (1861-1865). In the *Prize Cases* (1863), he agreed with the majority that President Abraham Lincoln had the authority to order a blockade of Confederate ports before Congress declared war. After the war, he opposed laws intended to punish former Confederates, in cases such as *Cummings v. Missouri* (1867).

Rose Secrest

See also Civil War; *Scott v. Sandford*; Slavery; Taney, Roger Brooke.

Webster v. Reproductive Health Services

Citation: 492 U.S. 490
Date: July 3, 1989
Issue: Abortion
Significance: The Supreme Court substantially expanded the ability of the states to place restrictions on the availability of abortion services.

In 1986 the state of Missouri enacted an abortion statute that included three major provisions: a preamble declaring that human life "begins at conception" and that "unborn children have protectable interests in life, health, and well-being"; a prohibition on the use of public facilities and personnel for performing abortions or for counseling a woman to obtain an abortion, with exceptions allowed to save the life of a pregnant woman; and a requirement for a viability test whenever a physician believed that a fetus was twenty weeks of gestational age. Because of recent changes on the Supreme Court, it appeared possible that the justices might use the case to overturn the *Roe v. Wade* (1973) precedent. Thus, pro-choice and pro-life groups filed seventy-eight *amicus curiae* briefs, the largest number ever submitted to the Court in a single case.

The Court responded in a fragmented and complex manner. By a 5-4 vote, the Court upheld all the provisions of the statute, but the majority could not agree on a united opinion. Speaking for a plurality of three, Chief Justice William H. Rehnquist acknowledged that the due process clause of the Fourteenth Amendment protected a "liberty interest" that included a woman's limited right to choose to terminate a pregnancy. However, Rehnquist applied the rationality test and insisted that the state's legitimate interest in protecting "potential human life" was of equal weight throughout the pregnancy. It appeared that such an approach would have allowed the states to enact almost any regulation to protect fetal life, even to the extent of making abortions illegal. Although Justice Sandra Day O'Connor voted with the majority, she continued to push her undue burden approach, which accepted the woman's fundamental right to an abortion until the development of fetal viability. Justice Antonin Scalia, in contrast, argued in favor of overturning *Roe* entirely. Harry A. Blackmun, joined by two other dissenters, argued that the statute violated a fundamental right as recognized in *Roe*. Also dissenting, Justice John Paul Stevens found that the preamble of the statute violated the First Amendment because it endorsed a particular religious view.

Although the *Webster* decision did not overturn *Roe*, it signaled that the Court was willing to approve quite restrictive regulations. In *Planned Parenthood of Southeastern Pennsylvania v. Casey* (1992), a controlling plurality of the justices endorsed the undue burden test as advocated by Justice O'Connor.

Thomas Tandy Lewis

See also Abortion; Birth control and contraception; Due process, substantive; Fundamental rights; Judicial scrutiny; *Planned Parenthood of Southeastern Pennsylvania v. Casey*; Privacy, right to; *Roe v. Wade*.

West Coast Hotel Co. v. Parrish

CITATION: 300 U.S. 379
DATE: March 29, 1937
ISSUE: Freedom of contract
SIGNIFICANCE: Abandoning its long-standing freedom of contract doctrine, the Supreme Court allowed states great discretion in regulating working conditions and protecting the rights of employees.

In 1935 Elsie Parrish, a resident of the state of Washington, was discharged from her job with the West Coast Hotel Company. She was being paid twenty-five cents an hour, which was significantly less than the state's minimum wage of $14.50 per week, set by a commission according to a 1913 law. Parrish sued the company for $216.19, which was the difference between the minimum wage and her actual wages during her employment. Although the Supreme Court had overturned a minimum-wage law for women as recently as *Morehead v. New York ex rel. Tipaldo* (1936), the Washington State supreme court ruled in favor of Parrish's claim. The hotel company appealed the judgment to the Supreme Court.

Less than two months after President Franklin D. Roosevelt announced his court-packing plan, the Court formally upheld the Washington court's ruling with a 5-4 vote. Justice Owen J. Roberts, who had voted to strike down a minimum-wage law in *Morehead,* joined the *West Coast Hotel* majority—the famous "switch in time that saved nine." Writing for the majority, Chief Justice Charles Evans Hughes argued that the liberty of the due process clause did not prohibit state government from using their police powers to establish reasonable regulations in the interests of the community. He found that it was entirely reasonable to restrict the freedom of contract in order to provide women with a living wage, a policy clearly related to the promotion of health and welfare. He also noted that an earlier Court had approved of maximum-hour legislation for women, and he could find no relevant difference between the regulation of hours and the regulation of wages.

West Coast Hotel was one of the major decisions of the so-called constitutional revolution of 1937. In effect, the landmark decision meant that the Court would henceforth give greater deference to the judgment of legislatures, and that it would no longer strike down labor regulations based on a substantive due process reading of the Fourteenth Amendment.

Thomas Tandy Lewis

See also Contract, freedom of; Court-packing plan; Due process, substantive; Hughes, Charles Evans; Roberts, Owen J.

Byron R. White

Identification: Associate justice (April 16, 1962-June 28, 1993)
Nominated by: John F. Kennedy
Born: June 8, 1917, Fort Collins, Colorado
Died: April 15, 2002, Denver, Colorado
Significance: A key figure on the Supreme Court under Warren E. Burger and William H. Rehnquist who, though viewed by many as something of an enigma, was often a swing vote. White wrote several important opinions regarding the power of the press and led the Court in crafting a good-faith exception to the exclusionary rule.

Byron R. White was a well-known football player at the University of Colorado, where he was given the nickname "Whizzer." He played professional football in 1938 for one season with the Pittsburgh Steelers and was named the National Football League rookie of the year. In 1939 he studied at Oxford as a Rhodes scholar, but his stay was cut short by the beginning of World War II (1941-1945). Upon his return from England, White entered Yale Law School and played football for two seasons (1940-1941) with the Detroit Lions. In May, 1942, he joined the U.S. Navy, serving in the Pacific theater as a naval intelligence officer and attaining the rank of lieutenant. After the war, he finished law school and clerked for Chief Justice of the United States Frederick Vinson during the October, 1946, term. After several years of private practice following his clerkship, he helped

Byron R. White. (Photograph by Joseph Bailey, National Geographic Society, Courtesy the Supreme Court of the United States)

organize John F. Kennedy's successful 1960 presidential campaign. Kennedy appointed White deputy attorney general in early 1961.

Appointment to the Court

White was the first of the two Supreme Court nominations Kennedy made. His nomination engendered little controversy. He served on the Court from 1962 until 1993. During that time, he participated in 807 cases that split the Court five to four (second only to Justice William J. Brennan, Jr.) and was in the majority in 65 percent of them. White joined the Court while Earl Warren was chief justice but was not a major figure in the Warren Court's rulings. He dissented from several of the Court's decisions expanding the rights of criminal defendants, most notably *Miranda v. Arizona* (1966). However, with the arrival of Chief Justice Warren Burger and Justices Harry A. Blackmun, Lewis F. Powell, Jr., and William H. Rehnquist between 1969 and 1971, White became a crucial swing vote and was assigned significant opinions. He retained this pivotal role when Rehnquist replaced Burger as chief justice. He was often viewed as a judicial conservative but differed sufficiently from conservatives such as Burger, Rehnquist, Powell, and Antonin Scalia to be difficult to characterize. For example, White's pro-national stance on federalism issues, pro-civil-rights position in voting rights and reapportionment cases involving racial minorities, and pro-labor views are some of the positions that served to distinguish him from the conservatives.

Legacy

White played a major role in the development of the Court's jurisprudence with respect to media law, the establishment of a good-faith exception to the exclusionary rule, and the Court's refusal to place constitutional limits on statutes categorizing people on the basis of their sexual preferences. He authored opinions for majorities or pluralities in several cases, rejecting claims by news organizations that they deserved special protection given their important role in informing the public, including *Branzburg v. Hayes* (1972), *In re Pappas* (1972), *United States v. Caldwell* (1972), *Herbert v. Lando* (1979), *Zurcher v. The Stanford Daily* (1978), and *Cohen v. Cowles Media Co.* (1991). White enjoyed less success in influencing the Court's defamation jurisprudence. He joined the majority in *New York Times Co. v. Sullivan* (1964), the font of many of the constitutional protections limiting defamation actions, but for the remainder of his career sought to limit *Sullivan*'s implications, objecting to the special constitutional protections for defamation defendants developed in succeeding cases, such as *Gertz v. Robert Welch* (1974).

White was dissatisfied with the breadth of the Court's exclusionary rule, which prevented the use of any evidence obtained in violation of a criminal defendant's constitutional rights. He eventually persuaded his colleagues to adopt a good-faith exception to the exclusionary rule, which allowed the introduction of evidence obtained in violation of a defendant's Fourth Amendment rights if the law-enforcement officers acted in reasonable reliance on a search warrant. White announced this good-faith exception in his opinion for the Court in *United States v. Leon* (1984). He also authored the opinion for the five-justice majority in *Bowers v. Hardwick* (1986), which held that the Constitution did not prohibit states from criminalizing sodomy. The case was viewed as establishing the principle that laws classifying people based on their sexual preferences should receive little judicial scrutiny.

Major Dissents

Two of White's most noteworthy dissents were in *Immigration and Naturalization Service v. Chadha* (1983) and *Roe v. Wade* (1973). In *Chadha,* White argued that the majority erred in striking down the legislative veto, the use of congressional resolutions to prevent an administrative regulation from taking effect. White's *Chadha* dissent reflected his broader view that Congress and the president were entitled to substantial leeway in structuring the relationships between the three branches of the federal government and, therefore, that separation of powers challenges to statutes should rarely be upheld. White dissented from *Roe,* in which the Court decided that some restrictions of women's ability to obtain abortions violated their constitutional right of privacy. After *Roe,* White regularly dissented from decisions that voided state laws limiting women's ability to terminate their pregnancies. White viewed *Roe* not only as wrong but also as an illegitimate judicial usurpation of power.

Bernard W. Bell

Further Reading

Bader, William H., and Roy M. Mersky, eds. *The First One Hundred Eight Justices.* Buffalo, N.Y.: William S. Hein, 2004.

Hensley, Thomas R. *The Rehnquist Court: Justices, Rulings, and Legacy.* Santa Barbara, Calif.: ABC-Clio, 2006.

Hutchinson, Dennis J. *The Man Who Once Was Whizzer White: A Portrait of Justice Byron R. White.* New York: Free Press, 1998.

Italia, Bob. *Byron White.* Edina, Minn.: Abdo & Daughters, 1992.

Schwartz, Bernard. *Super Chief, Earl Warren and His Supreme Court: A Judicial Biography.* New York: New York University Press, 1983.

Starr, Kenneth. "Justice Byron R. White: The Last New Dealer." *Yale Law Journal* 103, no. 1 (October, 1993): 37-41.

Urofsky, Melvin I. *The Warren Court: Justices, Rulings, and Legacy.* Santa Barbara, Calif.: ABC-Clio, 2001.

Yarbrough, Tinsley E. *The Burger Court: Justices, Rulings, and Legacy.* Santa Barbara, Calif.: ABC-Clio, 2000.

See also Burger, Warren E.; Exclusionary rule; Miranda rights; *New York Times Co. v. Sullivan*; Privacy, right to; Rehnquist, William H.; *Roe v. Wade*; Separation of powers.

Edward D. White

Identification: Associate justice (March 12, 1894-December 18, 1910), chief justice (December 19, 1910-May 19, 1921)

Nominated by: Grover Cleveland and William H. Taft

Born: November 3, 1845, near Thibodaux, Louisiana

Died: May 19, 1921, Washington, D.C.

Significance: During his twenty-seven years on the Supreme Court, White became the first associate justice elevated to chief justice. His legacy consists less of legal doctrine than of ceremonial procedure. White introduced the informal handshaking tradition before each Court conference to ameliorate ideological contentiousness.

The only native of Louisiana to serve on the Supreme Court, Edward D. White came from an elitist background. His father and grandfather were wealthy sugar planters whose careers joined politics and the law. His maternal grandfather was the first federal marshal of the District of Columbia and the U.S. Supreme Court. The Whites were lawyer politicians who worked to preserve their southern way of life through their legislative, executive, and judicial careers. Unlike his father and grandfather, White never received an academic degree, dropping out of Georgetown College in Washington, D.C., to join the Confederate army. Captured in 1863, he spent the remainder of the war in Louisiana as a paroled prisoner of war. After the war, he read law in New Orleans and was admitted to the state bar in 1868.

Following his family tradition, White soon became involved in legislative politics and was elected to the state senate in 1874. His father's friendship with the governor led to White's appointment in 1878 as an associate justice of the Louisiana supreme court. He

Edward D. White. (Albert Rosenthal/ Collection of the Supreme Court of the United States)

served in that capacity until rival political factions forced him from the bench in 1880. He was elected in 1891 to the U.S. Senate, where he served as the majority leader.

White became President Grover Cleveland's fourth choice to fill a vacancy on the Supreme Court. White was the first Democrat appointed since 1862 and the second Roman Catholic to serve on the Court. He served as associate justice from 1894 to 1910, when President William H. Taft appointed him the ninth chief justice, perhaps appointing an aged candidate to increase his own chances of succeeding the chief justice, as Taft did in 1921.

Critics expected a reactionary southerner, but White revealed himself as a nationalist and progressive conservative. He wrote approximately seven hundred majority opinions, ten concurring opinions, and thirty-three dissents. He established the judicial definition of a trust that is still used, and he set forth the rule of reason criterion in *Standard Oil Co. v. United States* (1911), which undermined the Sherman Antitrust Act of 1890 by promoting oligopoly. His distinction between "incorporated" and "unincorporated" territories was accepted in *Dorr v. United States* (1904), permitting imperialist gains, protecting sugar and tobacco interests, and limiting civil rights in new U.S. territories.

White was universally liked. Justice Charles Evans Hughes thought so highly of him that he hung White's portrait in his own home. A conservative Democrat, White was a close adviser to Taft at the same time he was friendly with the progressive wing of the Republican party, including Theodore Roosevelt. Ironically, though White institutionalized his geniality with the tradition of justices shaking hands before conferences and court sessions as a reminder that they could remain friends despite possibly disagreeing on cases, a common error among scholars is to credit his predecessor as chief justice with that legacy, based only on the supposed word of Felix Frankfurter, the Court's so-called Emily Post and one of its most disruptive personalities.

William D. Pederson

Further Reading

Bader, William H., and Roy M. Mersky, eds. *The First One Hundred Eight Justices.* Buffalo, N.Y.: William S. Hein, 2004.

Baier, Paul R. "'Father Chief Justice': E. D. White and the Constitution, A Play." *Louisiana Law Review* 58 (1998): 423-447.

Ely, James W., Jr. *The Fuller Court: Justices, Rulings, and Legacy.* Santa Barbara, Calif.: ABC-Clio, 2003.

Highsaw, Robert B. *Edward Douglass White: The Defender of the Conservative Faith.* Baton Rouge: Louisiana State University Press, 1981.

Pederson, William D. "U.S. Chief Justice Edward Douglass White and the Path to Judicial Power." In *Grassroots Constitutionalism,* edited by Norman Provizer and William D. Pederson. Lanham, Md.: University Press of America, 1988.

Shoemaker, Rebecca S. *The White Court: Justices, Rulings, and Legacy.* Santa Barbara, Calif.: ABC-Clio, 2004.

Umbreit, Kenneth B. *Our Eleven Chief Justices.* New York: Harper, 1938.

See also Chief justice; Fuller, Melville W.; Hughes, Charles Evans; Rule of reason.

Charles E. Whittaker

IDENTIFICATION: Associate justice (March 25, 1957-April 1, 1962)
NOMINATED BY: Dwight D. Eisenhower
BORN: February 22, 1901, Troy, Kansas
DIED: November 26, 1973, Kansas City, Missouri
SIGNIFICANCE: During five years on the Supreme Court, Whittaker functioned as a swing vote until forced to retire because of ill health.

Charles E. Whittaker was born on a farm near Troy, Kansas, in 1901. Press coverage of a notorious murder case sparked his interest in law, but he dropped out of school after the death of his mother. A few years later, he renewed his ambition to become a lawyer. He was admitted to law school on the condition that he complete his high school requirements during law school. He graduated as valedictorian of his class.

Charles E. Whittaker. (Abdon Dacud Ackad/Collection of the Supreme Court of the United States)

Whittaker was a successful lawyer in Kansas City, Missouri, for thirty years before becoming a judge. He represented many prominent businesses, including the *Kansas City Star* newspaper. The publisher of the *Star,* Roy Roberts, was a charter member of the group that encouraged Dwight D. Eisenhower to run for the presidency. With Roberts's support, Whittaker was appointed to the U.S. District Court for the Western District of Missouri and two years later to the Eighth Circuit Court of Appeals. Whittaker spent only nine months on the Eighth Circuit before Eisenhower named him to the Supreme Court.

Whittaker, although politically conservative, did not vote along strictly ideological lines. He decided each case on its individual merits, seeking to master the facts and to apply the law to those facts as neutrally as possible. This approach often made Whittaker a swing vote. Sometimes he would join more liberal members of the Court, such as in *Trop v. Dulles* (1958), in which the majority held that Congress could not take away a person's citizenship for wartime military desertion, but other times he joined the conservative members of the Court. Perhaps the most enduring of his opinions is his concurrence in *Gomillion v. Lightfoot* (1960), in which he applied the equal protection clause of the Fourteenth Amendment to voting rights. His view later became the dominant one on the Court.

Whittaker was hospitalized in 1962 because of physical and mental exhaustion. His strenuous work routine and the seriousness of his responsibilities as a member of the Court had taken a heavy toll on his mind and health. He retired from the Court and later became an arbitrator for General Motors in disputes with its dealers. He died in 1973 from heart failure.

Jeffrey E. Thomas

Further Reading

Bader, William H., and Roy M. Mersky, eds. *The First One Hundred Eight Justices.* Buffalo, N.Y.: William S. Hein, 2004.

Friedman, Leon. "Charles Whittaker." In *The Justices of the United States Supreme Court: Their Lives and Major Opinions,* edited by Leon Friedman and Fred L. Israel. Vol. 4. New York: Chelsea House, 1997.

Kohn, Alan C. "Charles Whittaker." In *The Supreme Court Justices: Illus-*

trated Biographies, 1789-1995, edited by Clare Cushman. 2d ed. Washington, D.C.: Congressional Quarterly, 1995.

Miller, Richard Lawrence. *Whittaker: Struggles of a Supreme Court Justice.* Westport, Conn.: Greenwood Press, 2002.

Smith, Craig Alan. *Failing Justice: Charles Evans Whittaker on the Supreme Court.* Jefferson, N.C.: McFarland & Co., 2005.

Urofsky, Melvin I. *The Warren Court: Justices, Rulings, and Legacy.* Santa Barbara, Calif.: ABC-Clio, 2001.

Woeste, Victoria Saker. "Charles Evans Whittaker." In *The Supreme Court Justices: A Biographical Dictionary*, edited by Melvin I. Urofsky. New York: Garland, 1994.

See also Citizenship; Resignation and retirement; Warren, Earl.

Whren v. United States

Citation: 517 U.S. 806

Date: June 10, 1996

Issues: Fourth Amendment; pretextual automobile stop; racial profiling

Significance: The Supreme Court ruled that the subjective motivations of police officers were irrelevant when stopping a car based on probable cause of a traffic violation, however minor.

Plainclothes District of Columbia officers working in a "high drug area" in an unmarked vehicle noticed a truck occupied by two young African Americans waiting at a stop sign for an unusually long period of time. The truck then turned without signaling and left the intersection at what the officers called an unreasonable speed. When the officers stopped the truck, presumably to warn the driver about possible traffic violations, they observed plastic bags that seemed to contain cocaine. The occupants of the truck were arrested and later convicted of violating federal drug laws. At trial, the defense lawyers unsuccessfully tried to have the evidence suppressed. They pointed out that the officers did not have probable cause, or even reasonable suspicion, to think that the truck contained contraband. Based on these circumstances, they argued that the justification for stopping the truck, given the circumstances, appeared to be pretextual. To prevent the police from using a very minor traffic violation as a pretext to investigate the possibility of other crimes on the basis of a vague suspicion, the defense lawyers asserted that the Fourth Amendment test for automobile stops should be whether an officer, acting reasonably, would have stopped the vehicle for the reason given.

The Supreme Court unanimously found that the police were justified in stopping the vehicle in the circumstances of the case. Delivering the opinion of the Court, Justice Antonin Scalia wrote that "the decision to stop an automobile is reasonable where the police have probable cause to believe that a traffic violation has occurred." He referred to precedents in which the Court had refused to entertain Fourth Amendment probable-cause challenges based on the subjective motivations of police officers. Although Scalia acknowledged that the U.S. Constitution prohibits selective law enforcement based on considerations such as race, he saw "no realistic alternative to the traditional common-law rule that probable cause justifies a search and seizure."

Civil libertarians worried that the *Whren* ruling was inconsistent with the spirit of the Fourth Amendment. They argued that the broad scope of ruling would allow the police to use traffic stops to investigate individuals without being able to articulate any reasonable cause, which might encourage practices such as "racial profiling." They noted that the police, after having made a stop, may frisk occupants for weapons based on reasonable suspicion, investigate suspicious containers in plain view, request consent searches without explaining the right to refuse, and use dogs to detect drugs without reasonable suspicion of any kind.

Thomas Tandy Lewis

See also Automobile searches; Bill of Rights; Exclusionary rule; Fourth Amendment; Scalia, Antonin; Search warrant requirement.

James Wilson

IDENTIFICATION: Associate justice (October 5, 1789-August 21, 1798)
NOMINATED BY: George Washington
BORN: September 19, 1742, Fifeshire, Scotland
DIED: August 21, 1798, Edenton, North Carolina
SIGNIFICANCE: One of the first six justices on the first Supreme Court, Wilson ended his career in disgrace.

Born into a poor farming family in Scotland, James Wilson received a university education at his family's expense because his parents hoped he would enter the ministry. After his father's death in 1763, Wilson decided that his options were limited in Scotland. Two years later, he emigrated to Philadelphia. There he studied law under John Dickinson, a leading figure in Pennsylvania politics. Wilson opened his own law offices in 1766.

In 1775 Wilson was elected to the Second Continental Congress. An advocate of American independence, Wilson signed the Declaration of Independence in 1776. He was a critic of the Articles of Confederation, and he took part in the 1787 Constitutional Convention. A proponent of a strong federal government, Wilson called for a powerful executive branch. However, he also supported democratic measures such as the direct election of senators. After the convention completed its work, Wilson played a key role in Pennsylvania's ratification of the Constitution.

Appointment to the Court

Wilson wanted to be chief justice of the United States, and asked President George Washington to offer him the position. When Washington chose John Jay instead, Wilson accepted an appointment as an associate justice.

His failure to become chief justice was mitigated by appointment to the faculty of the law school at the College of Philadelphia. He offered a successful series of lectures on his theory of law in 1790 and 1791; his audience for the first lecture included President Washington and Vice President John Adams. According to Wilson, God was the source of the law, which could be known when free individuals gave their consent to be governed. Thus, Wilson's conception of the law was in keeping with his advocacy of democratic institutions.

Although Wilson had a keen mind, he did not prove to be an influential or outstanding justice. His few written opinions were brief and reveal little about his political philosophy, which was surprising given his reputation for writing lengthy grand jury charges in his role as a circuit judge in Pennsylvania. It was in that capacity that Wilson refused to rule in a pension case involving William Hayburn, a veteran of the Revolutionary War. In a letter to Washington, Wilson and his fellow circuit judges argued that despite a congressional mandate, the court had no jurisdiction in the case. Legal historians point to *Hayburn's Case* (1792) as the first exercise of judicial review.

The only exception to Wilson's unexceptional performance on the Court was his 1793 ruling in *Chisholm v. Georgia*, which again evidenced his nationalism. In his decision, Wilson maintained that citizens of a state had the right to sue other states in federal court. Wilson rejected the notion that the states were sovereign and immune from such lawsuits, arguing that this notion of sovereignty would unconstitutionally limit the jurisdiction of the Court.

Wilson consistently supported the federal government in his actions both outside and inside the courtroom. In 1794 farmers in western Pennsylvania rebelled against federal excise taxes in what came to be known as the Whiskey Rebellion. After Wilson informed President Washington that a state of lawlessness existed, Washington called out the militia to suppress the rebellion. In the 1796 case of *Ware v. Hylton*, Wilson reaffirmed his belief in a strong central government when he ruled that treaties were superior to state laws.

Scandal and Decline

Financial problems intruded on Wilson's performance as a justice. He speculated in real estate, at one time so successfully that he was one of the wealthiest men in the United States. By the 1790's, however, Wilson was heavily in debt, which may have been why Washington refused to appoint him chief justice when that position became vacant in 1795 and again in 1796. Many observers hoped that Wilson would resign from the Supreme Court rather than face impeachment, which became increasingly possible as his financial status worsened. Wilson, however, had no intention of resigning, and remained convinced that he could prevent any efforts to impeach him.

Wilson was unable to visit several states because he feared he would he placed in debtors' prison. His world collapsed in 1797 when he was forced to leave Pennsylvania in order to avoid his creditors. He was briefly incarcerated in a New Jersey debtors' prison. Upon his release he moved to North Carolina, where he was again jailed for his debts. His son secured his release, but Wilson's health had failed. He contracted malaria and then suffered a stroke, finally dying in a North Carolina hotel room. Because his family could not afford to transport his remains to Pennsylvania, Wilson was buried in North Carolina.

Wilson's unimpressive performance as an associate justice and the scandalous financial difficulties of his final years clouded his reputation, making Wilson a largely forgotten figure for most of the nineteenth century. As Wilson received scholarly attention, however, his reputation rose. Constitutional scholars noted that many of his ideas regarding popular sovereignty and the role of the court later became central to the operation of the American government. In 1906 Wilson's remains were exhumed, and he was given a state burial in Philadelphia that several justices attended. Despite such recognition, the general public remains largely unaware of Wilson's contributions to American history.

Thomas Clarkin

Further Reading

Bader, William H., and Roy M. Mersky, eds. *The First One Hundred Eight Justices.* Buffalo, N.Y.: William S. Hein, 2004.

Friedman, Leon, and Fred L. Israel, eds. *The Justices of the United States Supreme Court: Their Lives and Major Opinions.* 5 vols. New York: Chelsea House, 1997.

Harrington, Matthew P. *Jay and Ellsworth, The First Courts: Justices, Rulings, and Legacy.* Santa Barbara, Calif.: ABC-Clio, 2007.

Seed, Geoffrey. *James Wilson.* Millwood, N.Y.: KTO Press, 1978.

Smith, Charles Page. *James Wilson, Founding Father, 1742-1798.* Westport, Conn.: Greenwood Press, 1973.

See also *Chisholm v. Georgia*; Jay, John; Judicial review; Rutledge, John.

Wisconsin v. Mitchell

Citation: 509 U.S. 476
Date: June 11, 1993
Issue: Freedom of speech
Significance: The Supreme Court upheld the constitutionality of a state law that increased the sentence for a crime in which the defendant intentionally selected the victim on the basis of race, national origin, religion, sexual orientation, or similar characteristics.

In 1989 Todd Mitchell and several other young African Americans were discussing the white racism depicted in the film *Mississippi Burning,* and they became so angry that they attacked a white boy, leaving him unconscious for four days. Mitchell was convicted of aggravated assault, a crime for which Wisconsin law assigned a maximum sentence of two years' imprisonment. However, because the state's hate crime statute allowed for an enhanced punishment, Mitchell was sentenced to four years' imprisonment.

The main question before the Supreme Court was whether the hate crime statute violated the freedom of expression guaranteed by the First Amendment. The justices unanimously agreed that it did not. Speaking for the Court, Chief Justice William H. Rehnquist argued that the statute simply punished overt conduct and that violence had never been protected by the concepts of symbolic speech and expressive conduct. Under the statute, moreover, motive plays the same role as it does under antidiscrimination laws, which had survived constitutional challenge. Recognizing that people have a right to "bigoted speech," Rehnquist rejected the argument that the statute might have a chilling effect on such expressions, because only those persons contemplating acts of violence would need to worry about whether their speech might be used as evidence under the statute.

Thomas Tandy Lewis

See also Rehnquist, William H.; Speech and press, freedom of; Symbolic speech.

Wisconsin v. Yoder

CITATION: 406 U.S. 205
DATE: May 15, 1972
ISSUE: Freedom of religion
SIGNIFICANCE: Using the compelling interest standard, the Supreme Court held that a state could not require the children of some religious sects to attend high school.

Wisconsin's compulsory school-attendance law required children to attend public or private schools until the age of sixteen. The Old Order Amish Church was opposed to formal education beyond the eighth grade because such an environment promotes secular and competitive values contrary to the Amish way of life. After the eighth grade, however, Amish parents did provide additional career training and religious instruction in private homes. Jonas Yoder and another Amish parent were convicted and fined five dollars each for violating the law.

By a 6-1 margin, the Supreme Court found that application of the law to Amish parents was prohibited by the free exercise clause of the First Amendment. Writing for the Court, Chief Justice Warren E. Burger balanced the free exercise claims of the parents against the state's competing interest in educating children. Although the state's interest in education was of "the highest order," it was not absolute to the exclusion of all other interests. Burger emphasized the long history of Amish traditions and that the Amish alternative to education prepared young people to function effectively in later life. Referring to *Sherbert v. Verner* (1963), he noted that a law neutral on its face could be unconstitutional if it placed an undue burden on the free exercise of one's religious beliefs. Dissenting in part, Justice William O. Douglas wrote that the children themselves should have the choice of deciding whether or not to attend high school. In *Employment Division, Department of Human Resources v. Smith* (1990), the Court rejected the compelling interest standard in cases dealing with indirect burdens on religious conduct; thus, it is unclear whether *Yoder* continues as a binding precedent.

Thomas Tandy Lewis

Witnesses, confrontation of

See also *Boerne v. Flores*; Burger, Warren E.; *Employment Division, Department of Human Resources v. Smith*; First Amendment; *Good News Club v. Milford Central School*; Jay, John; Religion, freedom of; *Sherbert v. Verner.*

Confrontation of Witnesses

Description: The right, guaranteed by the U.S. Constitution's Sixth Amendment, of criminal defendants to have the witnesses against them testify in open court, face to face with them and the fact-finder, and to cross-examine those witnesses.

Significance: As interpreted by the Supreme Court, the provision prohibits the prosecution from using evidence such as video testimony, written statements, affidavits, transcripts, and second-hand accounts. Banned also are unreasonable limits on defense questioning of prosecution witnesses.

The Sixth Amendment's confrontation clause fosters reliability and fairness in federal and state prosecutions. It allows criminal defendants to confront witnesses against them in open court, under oath or affirmation, face to face, and to cross-examine these witnesses. The scope of its protections, which benefit criminal defendants, has been defined by Supreme Court decisions citing history, reason, and practicality.

Normally, words may not be reported by others or in writing—that is, the witness must appear—and may be cross-examined under the full panoply of courtroom safeguards. However, the defendants' entitlements are qualified. For example, the separate, long-standing evidentiary rule against hearsay has numerous exceptions permitting second-hand or reported evidence, most of which, if they are deemed "firmly rooted" (rational and historically traditional), the Court has gradually been incorporating into the confrontation clause as in *White v. Illinois* (1992) and *Bourjailly v. United States* (1987). Thus, excited utterances, statements to physicians, coconspirator statements during and furthering the conspiracy, and the like can be reported, though the person who spoke them is not at trial to be confronted.

These sorts of statements are presumed to be especially reliable and necessary. In *Idaho v. Wright* (1990), the Court ruled that some second-hand statements could be allowed if special facts demonstrated their reliability and necessity. In *Ohio v. Roberts* (1980), the Court ruled that sometimes the litigators must demonstrate the unavailability of the witness for appearance at trial before second-hand statements could be admitted as evidence.

Once witnesses *are* produced at trial, defendants' opportunity to cross-examine them may similarly be confined within reasonable limits. In *Montana v. Egelhoff* (1996), the Court ruled that, for example, the judge may apply normal exclusionary evidence rules, recognize privileges, or prohibit unduly prejudicial, harassing, time-consuming, or misleading questioning. If a witness becomes ill or dies after giving testimony but before full cross-examination, the testimony might still be allowed to stand. In *Maryland v. Craig* (1990), the Court determined that if a specific child-witness will suffer trauma from confronting his or her accused molester, the child may testify on one-way closed-circuit television, despite some infringement of the face-to-face requirement, provided there is full opportunity to put questions to the witness and all can see the screen.

Thus, the rights conferred by the confrontation clause are not absolute but are qualified by countervailing concerns and may amount merely to a strong preference.

Paul F. Rothstein

SEE ALSO Bill of Rights; Fifth Amendment; Jury, trial by; Self-incrimination, immunity against; Sixth Amendment.

Levi Woodbury

IDENTIFICATION: Associate justice (September 23, 1845-September 4, 1851)
NOMINATED BY: James K. Polk
BORN: December 22, 1789, Francestown, New Hampshire
DIED: September 4, 1851, Portsmouth, New Hampshire
SIGNIFICANCE: While serving on the Supreme Court, Woodbury wrote his most notable opinions in dissent, usually taking a states' rights, strict constructionist view of the Constitution. He vigorously supported the improvement of education.

Levi Woodbury graduated from Dartmouth in 1809, studied law at Litchfield Law School, and was admitted to the New Hampshire bar in 1812. In 1817 he was appointed to the state superior court and served until 1823, when he was elected governor of New Hampshire. From 1825 to 1831 he served in the U.S. Senate. President Andrew

Levi Woodbury. (Handy Studios/ Collection of the Supreme Court of the United States)

Jackson appointed him secretary of the Navy (1831-1834) and secretary of the Treasury (1834-1841). Woodbury provided strong opposition to the rechartering of the Bank of the United States, promoting instead the idea of an independent treasury. In 1841 he was again elected to the U.S. Senate.

President James K. Polk appointed Woodbury to the Supreme Court in 1845. In the *Passenger Cases* (1849), Woodbury argued that states could legally regulate admitted immigrants without violating the commerce clause. Although he personally opposed slavery, he insisted that slavery was a state, not a federal, matter. On the bench, he strongly advocated free public education, systematic teacher training, and public facilities for adult education. His solid reasoning and hard work made Woodbury a valuable, respected member of the Court.

Alvin K. Benson

See also Dissents; Opinions, writing of; States' rights and state sovereignty; Taney, Roger Brooke.

William B. Woods

Identification: Associate justice (January 5, 1881-May 14, 1887)
Nominated by: Rutherford B. Hayes
Born: August 3, 1824, Newark, Ohio
Died: May 14, 1887, Washington, D.C.
Significance: While on the Supreme Court, Woods wrote more opinions than any other associate justice. He was noted for his understanding of complicated issues, particularly the civil rights of African Americans, patent cases, and interpretation of the Fourteenth Amendment.

After graduating from Yale in 1845 and studying law in Newark, Ohio, William B. Woods was admitted to the Ohio bar in 1847. Between 1862 and 1866, he served in the Union army in the Civil War, seeing action at Shiloh, Chickasaw, Vicksburg, and in General William T. Sherman's march to the sea and rising to the rank of brigadier

William B. Woods. (Collection of the Supreme Court of the United States)

general. After the war, Woods went to Alabama and took an active part in the Reconstruction policies of the federal government.

In 1880 Woods was appointed to the Supreme Court by President Rutherford B. Hayes, becoming the first justice appointed from a Confederate state since 1853. Woods was a diligent worker, writing 207 opinions, most dealing with routine legal disputes involving patents, real property, and estate and trust cases. A few of his opinions touched on constitutional issues. In the *United States v. Harris* (1883), Woods asserted that the Fourteenth Amendment did not give Congress authority to enact laws that punished individuals for depriving other individuals of their civil rights. In *Presser v. Illinois* (1886), he maintained that the Second Amendment was applicable in federal but not state activities.

Alvin K. Benson

See also Fourteenth Amendment; Opinions, writing of; Reconstruction; Waite, Morrison R.

Worcester v. Georgia

Citation: 31 U.S. 515
Date: February 20, 1832
Issue: Native American sovereignty
Significance: The Supreme Court held that the federal government had exclusive jurisdiction over territories owned by Native Americans. It also recognized that the tribes retained significant claims to sovereignty.

The Reverend Samuel Worcester was a Christian missionary who was convicted and imprisoned for disobeying a Georgia law that required white men to have a state license to live in Indian territory. When Worcester appealed his conviction, the Supreme Court had clear jurisdiction to consider the case under a writ of error. By a 5-1 margin, the Court held that the Georgia law violated three legal principles: the commerce clause of the U.S. Constitution, the Cherokee treaties with the federal government, and the residual sovereignty rights of the Cherokee Nation. In a far-reaching opinion, Chief Justice John Marshall wrote that the Indian tribes remained "distinct, independent political communities," possessing their own territory and substantial elements of sovereignty within their boundaries.

Although the Court's order to free Worcester was ignored by Georgia's courts, he was eventually pardoned by the governor. The *Worcester* decision did not immediately help the Cherokee because it did not place any restrictions on the actions of the federal government. President Andrew Jackson, who disliked the decision, was in the process of using his authority to force the Cherokee to leave Georgia and go to Oklahoma—a mass migration known as the Trail of Tears. *Worcester*'s concept of limited Indian sovereignty proved to be very influential during the twentieth century.

Thomas Tandy Lewis

See also *Johnson and Graham's Lessee v. McIntosh*; Native American sovereignty; Native American treaties; States' rights and state sovereignty; Thompson, Smith.

Workload

DESCRIPTION: Burdens and responsibilities of the Supreme Court justices.

SIGNIFICANCE: The increase in the number of filings and the overall workload of the Court over the years resulted in much debate and a few changes.

The workload of the Supreme Court can be measured in part by the number of filings, or cases it is asked to decide. Filings rose from 51 in 1803, to 723 in 1900, and to 2,296 in 1960. By 1970 the number of filings had almost doubled, reaching 4,212. In 1990 the number of filings rose to 6,316, and in 1999 the number of cases topped 8,000. The workload may also be measured by the expanded burdens and responsibilities of each of the associate justices and the chief justice.

Reasons for Increased Filings

The number of filings increased because of population growth, the greater complexity of the United States' political, economic, and social systems, and congressional legislation that provided new bases on which individuals, interest groups, and governments could bring legal actions to federal courts, subject to appeal to the Supreme Court. Other factors include the Court's defining of new individual rights and new expansions of and limitations on government power through interpretation of the Constitution and its amendments.

In the first half of the nineteenth century, filings increased because of population growth, territorial expansion, and incremental growth in federal regulation. In the second half of that century, the Civil War, Reconstruction, industrialization, and the emergence of large corporations were primary sources of legal conflict that swelled the numbers of filings. In addition, the jurisdiction of federal courts was greatly expanded to include civil rights, habeas corpus appeals (appeals by citizens who argue their arrest is illegal under the Constitution), and an increase in the number of federal questions raised by the actions of states with the passage of the Fourteenth Amendment. The nationalization of the economy led to an increase in the number of cases that came to federal courts because parties who were from different states could go to federal court to resolve their problems. These are called diversity of citizenship cases.

In the early twentieth century, filings increased because of population growth, war contract cases, suits against the government, and congressional legislation and administrative regulations that made it easier for governments and special interest groups to appeal directly to the Court. In addition, Congress granted businesses the right to challenge government administrative decisions under expanding and more intricate antitrust and interstate commerce laws.

Responses to Increased Filings

Over the years Congress responded to the increased demand for Supreme Court action by limiting the types of cases that could be brought to federal courts and possibly be appealed to the Court and by expanding the number and complexity of courts below the Court, such as the tax court and intermediate circuit courts of appeals. Congress hoped that the demand for court action to settle conflicts among parties could be met below the Supreme Court. For example, in the Judiciary Act of 1891, Congress created intermediate federal appellate courts between the district courts and the Supreme Court, initially called circuit courts of appeals.

To meet what was perceived as a severe workload problem for the Court, Congress enacted the Judiciary Act of 1925. This law significantly reduced the number of cases that required a review by the Court. In place of mandatory rights to Court action, litigants had to file writs of *certiorari.* These writs permitted full discretion by the Court over which cases to decide. The Court could set its own agenda and choose for full hearing and written opinions only cases of national importance. In 1988 Congress repealed the few remaining mandatory appeals.

Another major response to the increased number of filings was to make the process through which the Court decides to hear cases more efficient, thus reducing the time that individual justices spent deciding which cases deserved Court action. This was accomplished by introducing the cert pool in 1972. Writs of *certiorari* are pooled and distributed among the law clerks of the participating justices. Each filing is read by a single law clerk, who writes a *certiorari* memo, which is circulated to all the justices who have contributed law clerks to the cert pool. Typically, each justice asks one of his or her clerks to read these memos and make recommendations. The Court also established procedures to reduce the number of frivolous *in forma pauperis* petitions from indigents who seek release from jail.

In the 1970's and 1980's the number of law clerks, secretarial staffers, and supporting administrative staffers, such as research librarians, was significantly increased, and computerized word processing became more commonly employed. In the 1940's under Chief Justice Harlan Fiske Stone, justices had one clerk, and the chief justice had two. Under Chief Justices Fred M. Vinson and Earl Warren, most justices had two or three clerks, and the chief justice had an additional clerk or two. Under Chief Justices Warren E. Burger and William H. Rehnquist, most justices had three or four clerks, and Burger had five and Rehnquist three.

Workload of Justices

With innovations in the processing of filings, increases in Court staffing, and the virtual abolishment of mandatory appeals, the number of filings may no longer be the most valid indicator of workload. A more useful way to think about the Court's workload may be to consider the burdens placed on the justices by the complex and time-consuming process through which cases are decided and opinions are written. The Court has nine justices, as it has since 1837, except for a few years in the Civil War decade.

When the Court decides to take a case for oral argument and written decision, justices must read briefs, attend oral arguments, hold conferences to discuss cases and vote, and write the institutional, usually majority, decision of the Court, as assigned by the chief justice. Justices also write concurring and dissenting opinions. Institutional, concurring, and dissenting opinions are circulated among the justices for their suggestions of changes in a time-consuming process in which justices seek support from fellow justices for their positions on the constitutional questions in a particular case.

Some scholars, notably David M. O'Brien, theorize that the Court's workload increased dramatically because of the decline in the institutional norm of consensus in Court decision making. After

Editorial cartoon in Puck *showing the Court's overworked justices in 1885.* (Library of Congress)

the 1940's, the number of unanimous institutional decisions declined, and the number of concurring opinions increased ten times. The number of dissents grew four times, and the number of separate opinions in which justices explain their personal views and why they partially concur in or dissent from the Court's opinion is seven times higher. In the 1990's, justices wrote twice as many opinions as they did fifty years ago.

However, while the number of opinions written by the justices increased, the number of cases taken for full oral argument and written signed opinions dramatically declined in the 1990's. In 1935 the Court decided about 150 cases on their merits. In the October, 1986, term, with a far larger number of filings, the Court decided only 145 cases on their merits. After 1986, as the number of cases on the Court's docket increased, the number of cases heard and decided by written opinions declined to 112 cases in the 1990 term, 84 in 1993, and 75 in 1995. However, the number of separate, concurring, and dissenting opinions continued to remain very high in the 1990's. In effect, the Court reduced its workload by reducing the number of cases it hears for oral argument and full written opinions. Some scholars argue the Court is taking too few cases to meet the increasing number of conflicts among the lower courts as to what the Constitution, state and federal law, and individual rights mean in a growing, diverse, more complex nation.

Perception and Response

Whether workload is viewed as a problem for the Court has changed over the years. In the 1970's and 1980's scholars such as Philip Kurland and Dennis Hutchinson argued that the Court's workload radically reduced the quality of its reasoning and the clarity of its decisions because of reductions in the time that the justices could debate, come to a compromise, and write decisions. They based their view on the opinion that the Court should make more unanimous or near unanimous decisions to ensure that it sends clear signals to lower courts, lawyers, governments, and all possible litigants. However, other scholars disagree with the view that the quality of Court decisions has deteriorated. They argue that such concerns about the quality of decisions have always existed and are either not valid or based on subjective standards of evaluation.

Many reforms have been proposed to meet the Court's workload problems. These have included a call by the 1971 Study Commission on the Caseload of the Supreme Court for a national court of appeals to select cases for the Court to review and a recommendation by the 1972 Commission on the Revision of the Federal Court Appellate System that a national court of appeals be set up to resolve intercircuit conflicts on cases recommended by the Court or U.S. courts of appeals. In 1983 Chief Justice Warren E. Burger supported legislation to establish an experimental intercircuit tribunal of the U.S. courts of appeals, consisting of judges drawn from the current courts of appeals to sit for a specified period of years to decide cases referred to it by the Court. In 1990 the Federal Courts Study Committee urged Congress to give the Court the authority, for an experimental period, to refer cases involving unresolved intercircuit conflicts to a randomly selected court of appeals sitting *en banc* (as a full bench), whose findings would be binding on all courts except the Supreme Court.

None of these reforms have taken place, perhaps because the Court is unlikely to want to relinquish its power to determine what cases it will decide. The addition of another tier of federal appellate courts or the establishment of a means through which petitions for action by the Court are sent to existing circuit courts of appeal might actually increase delay and reduce the clarity of the Court's decisions and interpretations. Such reforms also would reduce the power and authority of the Court and weaken its position as the apex of a hierarchical legal system, as the final decider of constitutional questions.

Given that the Court already introduced many internal reforms without undermining in a significant way the process of deciding which cases to take and the justices, like members of Congress and presidents, have a responsibility to continue the Court's power and authority under the doctrine of separation of powers, few additional external reforms may be possible. Given the history of reform efforts and the respect for the principle of separation of powers among members of all branches of government, the justices will have to approve any significant changes in the structure of the Court to meet workload problems, something they have not been willing to do throughout the Court's existence.

Ronald Kahn

Further Reading

Joan Biskupic and Elder Witt's *The Supreme Court at Work* (2d ed. Washington, D.C.: Congressional Quarterly, 1997) is an overview of the workings of the Court. Other useful overviews of Court workings include Timothy Russell Johnson's *Oral Arguments and Decision Making on the United States Supreme Court* (Albany: State University of New York Press, 2004), Maxwell L. Stearns's *Constitutional Process: A Social Choice Analysis of Supreme Court Decision Making* (Ann Arbor: University of Michigan Press, 2000), Drew Noble Lanier's *Of Time and Judicial Behavior: United States Supreme Court Agenda-Setting and Decision-Making, 1888-1997* (Selinsgrove, Penn.: Susquehanna University Press, 2003), and *The Supreme Court in Conference, 1940-1985: The Private Discussions Behind Nearly Three Hundred Supreme Court Decisions*, edited by Del Dickson (New York: Oxford University Press, 2001).

David M. O'Brien's *Storm Center: The Supreme Court in American Politics* (7th ed. New York: W. W. Norton, 2005) and "Join Three Votes, the Rule of Four, the Cert. Pool, and the Supreme Court's Shrinking Plenary Docket," *Journal of Law and Politics* 13 (1997): 779-808, are excellent analyses of the process of Supreme Court decision making with particular emphasis on the effect that the decline in adherence to the principle of unanimity and consensus has had on the workload problem. Richard Posner's *The Federal Courts: Challenge and Reform* (Cambridge, Mass.: Harvard University Press, 1996) superbly links the caseload problem to problems in the overall federal court system.

Philip Kurland and Dennis Hutchinson's "The Business of the Supreme Court, O.T. 1982," *University of Chicago Law Review* 50 (1983): 628-651, offers a critical analysis of how workload pressures affect the quality of Court decisions. H. W. Perry, Jr.'s *Deciding to Decide: Agenda Setting in the United States Supreme Court* (Cambridge, Mass.: Harvard University Press, 1991) explains workload issues in the light of reforms in the process through which the Court chooses cases for action. Finally, Lee Epstein, Jeffrey Segal, Harold J. Spaeth, and Thomas G. Walker's *The Supreme Court Compendium: Data, Decisions, and Developments* (3d ed. Washington, D.C.: CQ Press, 2003) is the best source on the number of filings and other statistics on the workload of the Supreme Court.

See also *Certiorari*, writ of; Chief justice; Clerks of the justices; Conference of the justices; Court-packing plan; Dissents; Housing of the Court; Oral argument; Rules of the Court.

World War II

Date: 1939-1945

Description: A conflict waged by Great Britain, France, the Soviet Union, and the United States against Germany, Italy, and Japan, formally declared in December, 1941. During the conflict, within the United States, numerous economic and other regulations came into force and some civil liberties were suspended or limited.

Significance: Many U.S. actions during this war, especially on the home front, were affected by and interpreted by the Supreme Court. These actions include war-making powers, emergency powers, economic controls, and the internment of Japanese Americans, both resident aliens and U.S. citizens of Japanese descent.

Late in the nineteenth century, Justice Stephen J. Field declared, "War seems to create—or leave unresolved—at least as many problems as it settles." Issues are raised when a nation is at war that would never be raised during times of peace. World peace was shattered by the German invasion of Poland in 1939. The Japanese attack on Pearl Harbor in Hawaii, the headquarters of the U.S. Pacific Fleet, on December 7, 1941, thrust the United States into its second world war within twenty-five years.

A major U.S. objective in World War II was to preserve the principle of constitutional government. Ironically, parts of that principle had to be sacrificed in order to preserve the whole. During World War II, the wheels of U.S. government had to be streamlined as part of the war effort. Early in 1942, in a lecture at Cornell University, Robert Cushman outlined three changes that he believed would result from that streamlining. The first was the relationship between the states and the federal government, in which the states would lose. Second was the relationship between Congress and the president, in which Congress would lose. The last change would be the impact on civil liberties, where individual citizens would lose to strengthen the nation as a whole. Cushman's predictions proved accurate, although surprisingly few of the changes rose to the need of a Supreme Court decision.

War-Making Powers

The Constitution carefully divides the war-making powers of Congress and of the president. Congress has the responsibility for raising and supporting military forces and the sole authority to declare war. The president is the commander in chief of all military forces and therefore has the authority to send them anywhere in the world. After President Franklin D. Roosevelt asked Congress, on December 8, 1941, for a declaration of war against Japan, each branch carried out its constitutional responsibilities.

One major issue involving war-making powers was the raising of military forces by involuntary means. Conscription was used during the Civil War and accepted as constitutional. However, during World War I, conscription was criticized as being involuntary servitude and therefore in violation of the Thirteenth Amendment. The Supreme

Court, in *Butler v. Perry* (1916) and in subsequent *Selective Draft Law Cases* (1918), differentiated between involuntary servitude and involuntary duty. In 1939 with war again raging in Europe, the possibility and constitutionality of a peacetime draft was discussed in the United States. By June, 1940, with France on the verge of collapse, eventual U.S. involvement in the war seemed certain.

President Roosevelt did not want the nation caught unprepared as in 1917, but knowing that a peacetime draft would arouse strong opposition, especially with the inborn American fear of a strong government, he appointed a private citizen task force to develop a plan. The group was led by Grenville Clark, a highly respected law partner of Elihu Root (secretary of war, 1901-1904). The plan was implemented with surprisingly little opposition or refusal to register, as in 1917. The Court resolved, in *Falbo v. United States* (1944), an issue involving a conscientious objector who had failed to report for alternate civilian service as ordered. Falbo's claim of ministerial exemption had been rejected by his draft board, but the Court refused to accept his appeal. Other draft-related problems, such as congressional expansion of the draft to include eighteen-year-olds, pre-Pearl Harbor fathers, and some farmworkers, the issue of African American soldiers in combat after D-day in 1944, and interpretation of fair deferment standards, were all resolved without further Court action. A related issue of national civilian service was raised by Clark and Roosevelt in 1944 but was rejected by Congress.

Military courts also became an issue during the war. In *Ex parte Quirin* (1942), the Court ruled that a military commission had the right to try eight German saboteurs who were captured with explosives on beaches in New York and Florida six months after Pearl Harbor. The Court in *In re Yamashita* (1946) upheld the right of the military to condemn a Japanese officer for war crimes. However, in *Duncan v. Kahanamoku* (1946), the Court refused to extend the power of military courts to include civilian crimes not related to the war.

Emergency Powers

The Constitution does not make specific provisions for emergency powers to be used by the executive branch of government. However, an issue that arose during World War II was the presidential use of emergency or discretionary funds. In 1943 Congress passed the Urgent Deficiency Appropriations Act. Section 304 of that act, initiated by the House Committee on Un-American Activities (HUAC), chaired by Representative Martin Dies (Democrat, Texas), suspended salary or compensation for three federal employees after November 15, 1943, unless by that date they were reappointed by the president with the advice and consent of the Senate. The named employees were Robert Morse Lovett, William E. Dodd, Jr., and Goodwin B. Watson. They were among thirty-nine federal employees attacked in a speech in the House by Representative Dies on February 1, 1943, as being "irresponsible, unrepresentative, crackpot radical bureaucrats" and affiliates of "communist front organizations."

Although the president did not reappoint Lovett, Dodd, and Watson, the agencies for which they worked kept them on the job after November 15, but without their salaries. The men later filed with the Court of Claims to recover their lost salaries on three grounds: that Congress has no power to remove executive employees, that section 304 violated Article I, section 9, clause 3, of the Constitution, which prohibits bills of attainder and ex post facto laws, and that it violated the due process clause of the Fifth Amendment. In *United States v. Lovett* (1946), the Court ruled that section 304 was in fact a bill of attainder and thus in violation of the Constitution. Lovett, Dodd, and Watson were entitled to receive their salaries and compensation after November 15, 1943.

Japanese Internment

After the United States declared war on Japan, President Roosevelt issued several executive orders that seriously affected the rights of any person of Japanese ancestry living in the United States, especially those living on the West Coast. The orders authorized the secretary of war to designate military areas within the United States and to limit individual rights in those areas. Congress soon ratified the president's action by authorizing curfew orders to protect vital war resources. On March 24, 1942, in accordance with the orders, the military commander of the Western Defense Command, Lieutenant General J. L. DeWitt, proclaimed the entire Pacific coast to be a military area and that all persons of Japanese descent must observe a curfew from 8:00 P.M. to 6:00 A.M.

Gordon Kiyoshi Hirabayashi was an American citizen and a student at the University of Washington in Seattle. After he was convicted of violating the curfew, he appealed on the grounds that the executive orders and the power delegated to military authorities were in violation of the Fifth Amendment. His case, *Hirabayashi v. United States* reached the Court in 1943. The Court, in an opinion written by Chief Justice Harlan Fiske Stone, unanimously upheld both the presidential orders and the curfew, basing the action on the great importance of the military installations on the West Coast and on the close ties that persons of Japanese descent had with their mother country. The decision viewed the curfew as a protective measure but did not answer the constitutional issues involved. Chief Justice Stone went so far as to say that racial discrimination was justified during times of war when applied to those who had ethnic affiliation with an invading enemy.

Military authorities eventually decided that people of Japanese descent must be evacuated from the West Coast. When voluntary evacuation failed, a new presidential order created the War Relocation Authority, which was given the task of relocating one hundred thousand people. Fred Korematsu, from San Leandro, California, was arrested for refusing evacuation. The American Civil Liberties Union chose him as a test case for the constitutionality of the presidential order. Like Hirabayashi, Korematsu was a U.S. citizen. The Court, in an opinion written by Justice Hugo L. Black in 1944, decided *Korematsu v. United States* on the same basis as Hirabayashi's but this time without a unanimous decision. Justice Black stated that compulsory evacuation was constitutionally suspect but was justified by the national emergency. In a case related to *Korematsu, Ex parte Endo* (1944), Justice William O. Douglas ordered the release of a Japanese American whose loyalty was never questioned. He argued that congressional approval of the War Relocation Authority was not a blanket approval for every individual case.

The Court treated the internment of Japanese Americans as an exercise of the government's emergency powers and saw the suspension of civil liberties as necessary in the interest of national security.

Economic Controls

Less than two months after the attack on Pearl Harbor, Congress passed the Emergency Price Control Act in order to prevent inflation that would hinder the war effort. In *Yakus v. United States* (1944), the Court ruled only on the manner in which Congress should achieve its goal, not on the goal itself. The Court upheld the power given by the act to the administrator of the Office of Price Administration to fix maximum prices and rents for a limited period of time, stating that sufficient standards had been established by Congress to ensure the just application of the law. Similar issues relating to economic controls followed the same pattern.

Glenn L. Swygart

Further Reading

An excellent beginning for a study of the Court and World War II is David B. Currie's *The Constitution in the Supreme Court: The Second Century—1888-1986* (Chicago: University of Chicago Press, 1990). Peter G. Renstrom's *The Stone Court: Justices, Rulings, and Legacy* (Santa Barbara, Calif.: ABC-Clio, 2001) is a comprehensive reference work on the Supreme Court under Chief Justice Harlan Fiske Stone, who served through the war years. Page Smith, in *Democracy on Trial* (New York: Simon & Schuster, 1995), presents a clear and detailed account of the Japanese internment issue. Wendy L. Ng's *Japanese American Internment During World War II: A History and Reference Guide* (Westport, Conn.: Greenwood Press, 2002) is a comprehensive reference source on the internment years.

A Democracy at War, by William L. O'Neill (New York: Free Press, 1993), discusses many economic issues relating to World War II. Legal issues at the beginning of the war are given in *The Impact of the War on America: Six Lectures by Members of the Faculty of Cornell University* (Ithaca, N.Y.: Cornell University Press, 1942). A classic edited by Stanley Kutler, *The Supreme Court and the Constitution: Readings in American Constitutional History* (2d ed. New York: Norton, 1977), gives insight into the Japanese internment and many other war-related issues. *Congressional Politics in the Second World War,* by Roland Young (New York: Columbia University Press, 1956), discusses many domestic issues that eventually required court action.

Gary Hess, in *The United States at War, 1941-1945* (Arlington Heights, Ill.: Harlan Davidson, 1986), gives a brief summary of the war and its impact on the United States. *American Constitutional History* (New York: Macmillan, 1989), with an introduction by Leonard Levy, gives an overview of the Court under Chief Justice Stone, 1941-1946, indicating the philosophy behind his decisions.

See also Bill of attainder; Cold War; Fifth Amendment; Japanese American relocation; *Quirin, Ex parte*; Stone, Harlan Fiske; Vietnam War; War and civil liberties; War powers.

Youngstown Sheet and Tube Co. v. Sawyer

Citation: 343 U.S. 579
Date: June 2, 1952
Issue: Presidential powers
Significance: During the Korean War, the Supreme Court disallowed the president's right to invoke emergency powers in order to seize and operate private businesses without prior congressional approval.

Fearful that a long strike would damage the war effort, President Harry S. Truman issued an executive order instructing the secretary of commerce to take over the steel plants and maintain full production. Although there was no statutory authority for the seizure, the president argued that the policy was valid under his inherent powers as president and commander in chief. The steel companies argued that the seizure was unconstitutional unless authorized by an act of Congress. They emphasized that Congress, in passing the Taft-Hartley Act (1947), had considered but rejected an amendment permitting the president to seize industrial facilities in order to resolve labor disputes.

By a 6-3 vote, the Supreme Court ruled in favor of the companies. Writing for the majority, Justice Hugo L. Black rejected Truman's defense based on the existence of an inherent executive power. Reflecting his desire to adhere closely to the text of the Constitution, Black wrote that "the Constitution is neither silent nor equivocal about who shall make laws which the President is to execute." In concurring opinions, several justices recognized an inherent executive power transcending the enumerated powers in Article II of the Constitution but joined the decision because Congress had specifically refused to give the president the kind of power that Truman had exercised. All members of the majority apparently agreed that Congress could have legitimately ordered or authorized the seizure of the steel mills. The three dissenters argued that presidents had been allowed to exercise similar emergency powers in the past.

The steel seizure case did not represent a complete repudiation of the theory of inherent presidential powers. The decision did make it clear, however, that the president is not invested with unbridled discretion in the name of national security. When examining the limits of executive actions, moreover, the Court indicated that it would consider both the explicit and the implicit will of Congress.

Thomas Tandy Lewis

See also Executive agreements; National security; Presidential powers; Separation of powers; War powers.

Zelman v. Simmons-Harris

Citation: 536 U.S. 639
Date: June 27, 2002
Issue: Public subsidies of religious schools
Significance: Continuing a permissive trend in the use of tax money for parochial schools, the Supreme Court approved an Ohio program of providing low-income families with tax-subsidized vouchers to pay for tuition at private schools.

As part of plan to increase educational opportunity, the legislature of Ohio enacted a statute with a Pilot Scholarship Program that provided vouchers for low-income students to attend private schools of their choice from kindergarten through the eighth grade, with the announced goal of improving academic achievement. During the 1990-2000 school year, 96 percent of the students participating in the program attended religiously affiliated schools, and 82 percent of the participating schools had religious affiliations. Susan Tave Zelman, Ohio's superintendent of public instruction, joined with other Ohio taxpayers to initiate a lawsuit alleging that the program violated the establishment clause of the First Amendment. The challengers prevailed in both the District Court and the Court of Appeals.

The lower courts based their decision on the three-pronged test in *Lemon v. Kurtzman* (1971), which required a secular purpose, a secular primary impact, and no "excessive entanglement" between government and religion. For some time, however, the Supreme Court had been applying the Lemon test permissively, with less and less insistence on a "high wall" of separation between church and state. In *Mueller v. Allen* (1983), the Court had upheld a Minnesota law permitting a tax deduction for tuition costs at private schools, even though 95 percent of the deductions were for attendance at parochial schools. More recently, in *Mitchell v. Helms* (2000), the justices by a 5-4 margin had upheld a federal program of providing religious schools with computers and other equipment, despite the likelihood that some equipment might be occasionally used for religious instruction.

In the *Zelman* case, the Supreme Court reversed the lower courts' rulings and upheld the constitutionality of the Ohio voucher program. Speaking for a 5-4 majority, Chief Justice William H. Rehnquist reasoned the program was "entirely neutral with respect to religion." Developing a "private choice test," he argued that the Court's precedents had consistently recognized a distinction between government aid going directly to the schools and assistance going to private individuals who are given adequate secular options. He emphasized that the government had done nothing to encourage the students to attend parochial rather than nonreligious schools. In a strong dissent, Justice David H. Souter countered that the program involved the use of tax funds to subsidize religious indoctrination.

Although the *Zelman* decision created great controversy, it was unlikely that vouchers would be offered in many other places. Between 1970 and 2000, eight states held elections to decide the issue, and each time the voters rejected the proposal, usually by a vote of more than 65 percent.

Thomas Tandy Lewis

See also First Amendment; *Lemon v. Kurtzman*; Rehnquist, William H.; Religion, establishment of; Souter, David H.

Zoning

Description: Premier land-use regulation method in the United States, which divides urban areas into different sectors or zones, with different uses and regulations and requirements.

Significance: Most contested zoning legal issues were handled by one of the fifty state court systems and received final judgment in the state supreme courts; however, a few significant land-use cases found their way to the U.S. Supreme Court.

The police power, which is the right of government to regulate public health, safety, and welfare, gives zoning its legitimacy. State constitutions and statutes enable local governments to create their own zoning ordinances. Some states also created state zoning laws. The exact limits of the zoning power may seem fluid in time and place. Zoning power is ultimately what the courts determine. Conservative courts tend to limit the zoning power, and liberal courts tend to expand it.

Euclid v. Ambler Realty Co. (1926) was one of the most significant legal decisions by the Supreme Court in the history of zoning. Chief Justice George Sutherland concluded that each community had the right and responsibility to determine its own character. Zoning was a valid use of the police power as long as it did not disturb the orderly growth of the region or the nation. Justice Sutherland wrote,

> But this village, though physically a suburb of Cleveland, is a separate municipality, with powers of its own and authority to govern itself. . . . The will of its people determines, not that industrial development shall cease at its boundaries, but that such development shall proceed between fixed lines.

The Court made it clear that a municipality may determine the nature of development within its boundaries and plan and regulate the use of land as the people within the community may consider it to be in the public interest. Justice Sutherland introduced the concept that a community must also relate its plans to the area outside its own boundaries. Thus, the Court sustained a village zoning ordinance that prevented Ambler Realty from building a commercial structure in a residential zone. This case first established the constitutionality of all parts of comprehensive zoning.

The courts continued to support the rights of municipalities to zone, and conventional "Euclidean zoning" became almost universal in both urban and suburban areas. The power to zone as well as to use other, more flexible land-use controls, has an ideological dimension because it conflicts with the ability of property owners to use their property as they see fit. Typically, zones have been devoted to commercial, industrial, and residential uses, with different density requirements and other regulations.

Relationship to Taking Cases

In *First English Evangelical Lutheran Church of Glendale v. County of Los Angeles* (1987), the Court ruled that if landowners had been unduly burdened by land-use control regulations, they should be compensated by the government. Before this case, it was understood that a property owner might sue to have a regulation overturned. However, it was not required that compensation be paid for losses incurred while the regulation was actually in force. The Court's decision hinged on the last sentence of the Fifth Amendment, "nor shall private property be taken for public use, without just compensation." Undue restriction of use in the Court's view met the meaning of the word "taken" and therefore required compensation. Eventually when the case was sent back to a lower court, it was found that the taking had not occurred and that the church was not entitled to compensation. Despite the lower court's decision, the Court's ruling meant that a government might be forced to pay a large judgment if its actions were found to constitute a taking. Some feared the possibility that local governments might have to pay large judgments to litigants who could prove that zoning power had been overused.

Later, in *Lucas v. South Carolina Coastal Council* (1992) and *Dolan v. City of Tigard* (1994), the Court upheld the limiting of the government's authority to restrict the specific uses to which privately owned land could be devoted. For example, one opinion in the *Lucas* decision suggested that the one instance in which there might not need to be compensation (even though the property owner was deprived of all property use) was if that use might violate an established nuisance law. Some authorities speculated that the legal basis of zoning might be trimmed back to being totally dependent on nuisance law. Land-use regulations in *Hadacheck v. Sebastian* (1915) had evolved from nuisance law but had been expanded well beyond these limited origins to a much more extensive notion of the public interest.

Aesthetics and Exclusionary Zoning

Many legal experts believe that zoning and other police power regulations may not be adopted when their sole basis lies in aesthetics. Proponents of this theory cite *Welch v. Swasey* (1909) and decisions rendered by most of the state supreme courts. However, this view was challenged in *Berman v. Parker* (1954), in which Justice William O. Douglas, speaking for the unanimous Court opinion, stated, "If those who govern the District of Columbia decide that the Nation's Capital should be beautiful as well as sanitary, there is nothing in the Fifth Amendment that stands in the way." However, this case involved an effort to enjoin condemnation to preserve the natural beauty of urban renewal property. The Court was not confronted with a case in which police power was exercised in the form of a zoning ordinance and in which no compensation was paid. However, state courts have applied *Berman* in zoning cases. Douglas clearly affirmed that citizens need not tolerate an unsightly community and may take legal steps to change it.

Restrictive covenants, which discriminate against minority groups through race-based zoning ordinances, were declared unconstitutional by the Court in 1927 in *Buchanan v. Warley*. A Louisville, Kentucky, ordinance regulated the occupancy of city blocks; people of color could not reside in blocks where greater numbers of dwellings were occupied by whites and vice versa. This use of the police power was a violation of the Fourteenth Amendment because it prevented the use of property and deprived its owner of use without due process.

Years later the Court held in *Arlington Heights v. Metropolitan Housing Development Corp.* (1977) that a zoning ordinance does not necessarily violate the Constitution by restricting minority and low-income people; it must be shown that there was a deliberate exclusionary intention.

G. Thomas Taylor

Further Reading

Crawford, Clan. *Strategy and Tactics in Municipal Zoning.* Englewood Cliffs, N.J.: Prentice-Hall, 1979.

Davy, Benjamin. *Essential Injustice: When Legal Institutions Cannot Resolve Environmental and Land Use Disputes.* Wien, N.Y.: Springer, 1997.

Frizell, David J. *Land Use Law.* 3d ed. Eagan, Minn.: Thomson/West Group, 2005.

Kelly, Eric D. "Zoning." In *The Practice of Local Government Planning,* edited by Frank So. Washington D.C.: International City Management Association, 1988.

McAvoy, Gregory. *Controlling Technocracy: Citizen Rationality and the NIMBY Syndrome.* Washington, D.C.: Georgetown University Press, 1999.

Mandelker, Daniel R. *Land Use Law.* 5th ed. Newark, N.J.: LexisNexis, 2003.

Nelson, Robert H. *Zoning and Property Rights: An Analysis of the American System of Land-Use Regulation.* Cambridge, Mass.: MIT Press, 1980.

Price, Polly J. *Property Rights: Rights and Liberties Under the Law.* Santa Barbara, Calif.: ABC-Clio, 2003.

See also Fifth Amendment; Fourteenth Amendment; *Kelo v. City of New London*; Police powers; Restrictive covenants; Sutherland, George; Takings clause.

Appendixes

Time Line of the U.S. Supreme Court

Semicolons separate events occurring on the same dates.

1789 (Sept. 24) First Judiciary Act creates federal court system; President George Washington appoints John Jay chief justice and John Rutledge, William Cushing, Robert Harrison (who declines), James Wilson, and John Blair, Jr., associate justices. (Oct. 5) Wilson is sworn in. (Oct. 19) John Jay is sworn in.

1790 *United States Reports* begins publication. (Feb. 2) Supreme Court opens its first session; Cushing and Blair are sworn in as associate justices. (Feb. 8) Washington appoints James Iredell to the Court. (Feb. 15) Rutledge is sworn in as associate justice. (May 12) Iredell is sworn in as associate justice.

1791 (Mar. 5) Rutledge resigns from the Court to head South Carolina's top court. (Aug. 5) Washington gives Thomas Johnson a recess appointment to the Court. (Oct. 31) Washington formally nominates Johnson. (Nov. 7) Senate confirms Johnson's nomination.

1792 (Aug. 6) Johnson is sworn in as associate justice.

1793 (Jan. 16) Justice Johnson resigns. (Feb. 27) Washington appoints William Paterson to the Court; nomination is withdrawn the next day. (Mar. 4) Washington again nominates Paterson; Senate confirms nomination the same day. (Mar. 11) Paterson is sworn in.

1795 (June 29) Chief Justice Jay resigns to enter politics. (July 1) Washington appoints John Rutledge to replace Jay. (Aug. 12) Rutledge is sworn in without Senate confirmation. (Oct. 25) Justice Blair resigns. (Dec. 15) Senate rejects Rutledge's nomination.

1796 (Jan. 27) Cushing declines Washington's promotion to chief justice after serving one week in that position. (Jan. 26) Washington nominates Samuel Chase to the Court; Senate confirms nomination the next day. (Feb. 4) Chase is sworn in. (Mar. 3) Washington nominates Oliver Ellsworth as chief justice; Senate confirms nomination the next day. (Mar. 8) Ellsworth is sworn in.

1798 (Aug. 21) Justice Wilson dies. (Aug. 28) Adams gives Bushrod Washington a recess appointment to the Court. (Nov. 9) Washington is sworn in. (Dec. 19) Adams formally nominates Washington to the Court; Senate confirms nomination the next day.

1799 (Feb. 4) Bushrod Washington is sworn in as associate justice. (Oct. 20) Justice Iredell dies. (Dec. 4) Adams nominates Alfred Moore to the Court. (Dec. 10) Senate confirms Moore's nomination.

1800 (Apr. 21) Moore is sworn in as associate justice. (June 6) John Marshall becomes secretary of state. (July 18) Former justice Rutledge dies. (Aug. 31) Former justice Blair dies. (Dec. 15) Chief Justice Oliver Ellsworth resigns. (Dec. 19) John Jay declines President John Adams's offer of reappointment to the Court.

1801 Adams appoints John Marshall chief justice. (Jan. 27) Senate confirms Marshall's nomination. (Feb. 4) Marshall is sworn in; he remains secretary of state until replaced by James Madison on May 2. (Feb. 13) Second Judiciary Act creates six new circuit courts.

1804 Chief Justice Marshall publishes the first volume of his five-volume biography of George Washington. (Jan. 26) Justice Alfred Moore resigns. (Mar. 12) House of Representatives votes to impeach Justice Chase. (Mar. 22) Jefferson nominates William Johnson to the Court; Senate confirms nomination two days later. (May 8) Johnson is sworn in.

1806 (Sept. 9) Justice Paterson dies. (Nov. 10) President Thomas Jefferson gives Brockholst Livingston a recess appointment to the Court. (Dec. 13) Jefferson formally nominates Livingston to the Court. (Dec. 17) Senate confirms Livingston's nomination.

1807 (Jan. 20) Livingston is sworn in as associate justice. (Feb. 28) President Jefferson nominates Thomas Todd to the court and he is confirmed by the Senate the following month. (May 4) Todd is sworn in.

1810 (Sept. 13) Justice Cushing dies. (Oct. 15) Former justice Moore dies.

1811 (Jan. 2) President James Madison nominates Levi Lincoln to the Court; Senate confirms nomination the next day, but Lincoln declines appointment. (Feb. 4) Madison nominates Alexander Wolcott to the Court. (Feb. 13) Senate rejects Wolcott's nomination. (June 19) Justice Chase dies. (Nov. 15) Madison nominates Joseph Story and Gabriel Duvall to the Court; Senate confirms both nominations three days later. (Nov. 23) Duvall is sworn in.

1812 (Feb. 3) Story is sworn in as associate justice.

1823 (Mar. 18) Justice Livingston dies. (Sept. 1) President James Monroe gives Smith Thompson a recess appointment to the Court. (Dec. 8) Monroe formally nominates Thompson to the Court; Senate confirms nomination three days later.

1824 (Feb. 10) Thompson is sworn in as associate justice.

1826 (Feb. 7) Justice Todd dies. (Apr. 11) President John Quincy Adams nominates Robert Trimble to the Court. (May 9) Senate confirms Trimble's nomination. (June 16) Trimble is sworn in as associate justice.

1828 (Aug. 25) Justice Trimble dies. (Dec. 17) Adams nominates John J. Crittenden to succeed Trimble, but Senate takes no action on nomination.

1829 (Mar. 6) President Andrew Jackson nominates John McLean to the Court; Senate confirms him the next day. (May 17) Former chief justice Jay dies. (Nov. 26) Justice Washington dies.

1830 (Jan. 4) Jackson nominates Henry Baldwin to the Court; Senate confirms nomination two days later. (Jan. 11) McLean is sworn in as associate justice. (Jan. 18) Baldwin is sworn in.

1834 (Aug. 4) Justice William Johnson dies.

1835 (Jan. 14) Justice Gabriel Duvall resigns. (Jan. 6) Jackson nominates James M. Wayne to the Court; Senate confirms nomination three days later. (Jan. 14) Wayne is sworn in. (July 6) Chief Justice Marshall dies. (Dec. 28) Jackson appoints Roger Brooke Taney chief justice and Philip P. Barbour an associate justice.

1836 (Mar. 15) Senate confirms Taney's and Barbour's nominations. (Mar. 28) Taney is sworn in as chief justice. (May 12) Barbour is sworn in as associate justice.

1837 (Mar. 3) Judiciary Act creates three new circuits and adds two seats to the Supreme Court, raising total to nine justices; Jackson nominates William Smith and John Catron to the Court. (Mar. 8) Smith declines nomination; Catron is confirmed by Senate. (Apr. 22) President Martin Van Buren makes John McKinley a recess appointment to the Court. (May 1) Catron is sworn in. (Sept. 18) Van Buren formally nominates McKinley to the Court. (Sept. 25) Senate confirms McKinley's nomination.

1838 (Jan. 9) McKinley is sworn in as associate justice.

1841 (Feb. 25) Justice Barbour dies. (Feb. 26) Van Buren nominates Peter V. Daniel to the Court. (Mar. 2) Senate confirms Daniel's nomination, but Daniel does not join Court until following January.

1842 (Jan. 10) Daniel is sworn in as associate justice.

1843 (Dec. 19) Justice Thompson dies.

1844 (Jan. 9) President John Tyler nominates John C. Spencer to the Court. (Jan. 31) Senate rejects Spencer's nomination. (Mar. 6) Former justice Duvall dies. (Mar. 13) Tyler nominates Reuben H. Walworth to the Court. (Apr. 21) Justice Baldwin dies. (June 5) Tyler nominates Edward King to the Court, but Senate takes no action to confirm appointment. (June 17) Tyler withdraws Walworth nomination after Senate fails to act.

1845 (Jan. 23) Tyler withdraws King nomination after Senate twice fails to take confirmation action. (Feb. 4) Tyler nominates Samuel Nelson to the Court. (Feb. 7) Tyler nominates John M. Read to the Court, but Senate takes no action. (Feb. 27) Nelson is sworn in. (Sept. 10) Justice Story dies. (Dec. 20) President James K. Polk nominates Levi Woodbury to the Court. (Dec. 23) Polk nominates George W. Woodward to the Court.

1846 (Jan. 3) Senate confirms Woodbury's nomination, and Woodbury is sworn in. (Jan. 22) Senate rejects Woodward's nomination. (Aug. 3) Polk nominates Robert Grier to the Court. (Aug. 4) Senate confirms Grier's nomination. (Aug. 10) Grier is sworn in.

1851 (Sept. 4) Justice Woodbury dies. (Sept. 22) President Millard Fillmore gives Benjamin R. Curtis a recess appointment to the Court. (Oct. 10) Curtis is sworn in. (Dec. 11) Fillmore formally nominates Curtis to the Court; nine days later, Senate confirms appointment.

1852 (July 19) Justice McKinley dies. (Aug. 16) Fillmore nominates Edward A. Bradford to the Court, but Senate never acts on nomination.

1853 (Jan. 10) Fillmore nominates George E. Badger to the Court, but Senate never acts on nomination. (Feb. 24) Fillmore nominates William C. Micou to the Court, but Senate ignores nomination. (Mar. 22) President Franklin Pierce nominates John A. Campbell to the Court; three days later, Senate confirms appointment. (Apr. 11) Campbell is sworn in.

1857 (Sept. 30) Justice Curtis resigns. (Dec. 9) President James Buchanan nominates Nathan Clifford to the Court.

1858 (Jan. 8) Senate confirms Clifford's nomination. (Jan. 21) Clifford is sworn in.

1860 The Supreme Court moves its operations to old Senate Chamber, which will remain its home for seventy-five years. (May 31) Justice Daniel dies.

1861 (Apr. 4) Justice McLean dies. (Apr. 30) Justice Campbell resigns to join Confederate government on the eve of the Civil War.

1862 (Jan. 22) President Abraham Lincoln nominates Noah H. Swayne to the Court. (Jan. 27) Swayne is sworn in. (July 16) Lincoln nominates Samuel F. Miller to the Court. (July 21) Miller is sworn in. (Oct 17) Lincoln gives David Davis a recess appointment. (Dec. 8) Senate confirms Davis's nomination. (Dec. 10) Davis is sworn in.

1863 (Mar. 3) Congress raises number of seats on the Court to ten. (Mar. 6) Lincoln nominates Stephen J. Field to the Court. (Mar. 10) Senate confirms Field's nomination. (May 20) Field is sworn in.

1864 (Oct. 12) Chief Justice Taney dies. (Dec. 6) Lincoln nominates Salmon P. Chase to succeed Taney; Senate confirms nomination same day. (Dec. 15) Chase is sworn in.

1865 (May 30) Justice Catron dies.

1866 (Apr. 16) President Andrew Johnson nominates Henry Stanbery to the Court, but Senate instead votes to eliminate Catron's unfilled seat.

1867 (July 5) Justice Wayne dies. (July 23) Congress reduces the Court from ten to seven seats to prevent Johnson from appointing new justices.

1869 (Apr. 10) Congress restores two seats to the Court, enabling Johnson's successor, President Ulysses S. Grant, to make new appointments; its Judiciary Act also gives justices retirement benefits for first time. (Dec. 15) Grant nominates Ebenezer R. Hoar to the Court. (Dec. 24) Edwin M. Stanton dies a few days after Senate confirms Grant's nomination of him as associate justice.

1870 (Jan. 31) Justice Grier retires. (Feb. 3) Senate rejects Hoar's nomination. (Feb. 7) Grant nominates William Strong and Joseph P. Bradley to the Court. (Mar. 14) Strong is sworn in. (Mar. 23) Bradley is sworn in. (Sept. 25) Former justice Grier dies.

1872 (Nov. 28) Justice Nelson retires. (Dec. 3) Grant nominates Ward Hunt to replace Nelson.

1873 (Jan. 9) Hunt is sworn in. (May 7) Chief Justice Chase dies. (Dec. 1) Grant nominates George H. Williams to the Court. (Dec. 13) Former justice Nelson dies.

1874 (Jan. 8) Williams asks for his nomination to be withdrawn. (Jan. 9) Grant nominates Caleb Cushing to the Court but withdraws nomination four days later. (Jan. 19) Grant then nominates Morrison R. Waite as chief justice; Senate confirms nomination two days later. (Mar. 4) Waite is sworn in. (Sept. 15) Former justice Curtis dies.

1877 (Mar. 4) Justice Davis resigns to enter Senate. (Oct. 16) President Rutherford B. Hayes nominates John Marshall Harlan to replace Davis. (Nov. 29) Senate confirms Harlan's nomination. (Dec. 10) Harlan is sworn in.

1879 (Mar. 3) Belva Ann Lockwood is admitted as the Court's first woman bar member.

1880 (Dec. 14) Justice Strong retires. (Dec. 15) Hayes nominates William B. Woods to replace Strong. (Dec. 21) Senate confirms Woods's nomination.

1881 (Jan. 5) Woods is sworn in as associate justice. (Jan. 24) Justice Swayne retires. (Jan. 26) President James Garfield nominates Stanley Matthews to replace Swayne, but Senate takes no action. (Mar. 14) Garfield renominates Matthews. (May 12) Senate confirms Matthews's nomination. (May 17) Matthews is sworn in. (July 25) Justice Clifford dies. (Dec. 19) President Chester Arthur nominates Horace Gray to replace Clifford; Senate confirms the nomination the next day.

1882 (Jan. 9) Gray is sworn in as associate justice. (Jan. 27) Justice Hunt retires. (Mar. 2) Roscoe Conkling declines Arthur's offer of seat on the Court. (Mar. 13) Arthur nominates Samuel Blatchford, whose nomination Senate confirms two weeks later. (Apr. 3) Blatchford is sworn in.

1884 (June 8) Former justice Swayne dies.

1886 (Mar. 24) Former justice Hunt dies. (June 26) Former justice Davis dies.

1887 (May 14) Justice Woods dies. (Dec. 6) President Grover Cleveland nominates Lucius Q. C. Lamar to the Court.

1888 (Jan. 16) Senate confirms Lamar's nomination; Lamar is sworn in two days later. (Mar. 23) Chief Justice Waite dies. (Apr. 30) Cleveland appoints Melville W. Fuller chief justice. (July 20) Senate confirms his nomination. (Oct. 8) Fuller is sworn in.

1889 (Mar. 12) Former justice Campbell dies. (Mar. 22) Justice Matthews dies. (Dec. 4) President Benjamin Harrison appoints David J. Brewer to replace Matthews. (Dec. 18) Senate confirms Brewer's nomination.

1890 (Jan. 6) Brewer is sworn in as associate justice. (Oct. 13) Justice Miller dies. (Dec. 23) Harrison appoints Henry B. Brown to Miller's seat; Senate confirms the nomination six days later.

1891 Circuit Court of Appeals Act creates appeals courts that reduce Supreme Court caseload and relieve justices from having to ride circuits. (Jan. 6) Brown is sworn in as associate justice.

1892 (Jan. 22) Justice Bradley dies. (July 19) Harrison appoints George Shiras, Jr., to Bradley's seat; Senate confirms the nomination one week later. (Oct. 10) Shiras is sworn in.

1893 (Jan. 23) Justice Lamar dies; Harrison nominates Howell E. Jackson to replace him the next day. (Feb. 18) Senate confirms Jackson's nomination. (Mar. 4) Jackson is sworn in. (July 7) Justice Blatchford dies. (Sept. 19) President Grover Cleveland nominates William B. Hornblower to replace Blatchford.

1894 (Jan. 15) Senate rejects Hornblower's nomination. (Jan. 23) Cleveland nominates Wheeler H. Peckham. (Feb. 16) Senate rejects Peckham's nomination. (Feb. 19) Cleveland nominates Edward D. White, whose nomination Senate confirms the same day. (Mar. 12) White is sworn in.

1895 (Aug. 8) Justice Jackson dies. (Aug. 19) Former justice Strong dies. (Dec. 3) Cleveland nominates Rufus W. Peckham to replace Strong; Senate confirms nomination six days later.

1896 (Jan. 6) Peckham is sworn in as associate justice.

1897 (Dec. 1) Justice Field retires. (Dec. 16) President William McKinley nominates Joseph McKenna to replace Field.

1898 (Jan. 21) Senate confirms McKenna's nomination. (Jan. 26) McKenna is sworn in.

1899 (Apr. 9) Former justice Field dies.

1902 (Sept. 15) Justice Gray dies. (Aug. 11) President Theodore Roosevelt gives Oliver Wendell Holmes a recess appointment to the Court. (Dec. 2) Roosevelt formally appoints Holmes, whose nomination Senate confirms the same day. (Dec. 8) Holmes is sworn in as associate justice.

1903 (Feb. 23) Justice Shiras retires. (Mar. 2) Roosevelt appoints William R. Day to replace Shiras. (Feb. 23) Senate confirms Day's nomination. (Mar. 2) Day is sworn in.

1906 (May 28) Justice Brown retires. (Dec. 3) Roosevelt appoints William H. Moody to the Court. (Dec. 12) Senate confirms Moody, who is sworn in five days later.

1908 Brief on constitutionality of Oregon law submitted to the Court by attorney Louis D. Brandeis launches new era in constitutional interpretation.

1909 (Oct. 24) Justice Peckham dies. (Dec. 13) President William Howard Taft nominates Horace H. Lurton to replace Peckham; Senate confirms Lurton's nomination one week later.

1910 (Jan. 3) Lurton is sworn in as associate justice. (Mar. 28) Justice Brewer dies. (July 4) Chief Justice Fuller dies. (Apr. 25) Taft appoints Charles Evans Hughes to replace Brewer; Senate confirms Hughes's nomination one week later. (Oct. 10) Hughes is sworn in as associate justice. (Nov. 20) Justice Moody retires. (Dec. 12) Taft promotes Justice White to chief justice and nominates Willis Van Devanter and Joseph R. Lamar to the Court; Senate confirms White's nomination the same day and Van Devanter's and Lamar's nominations three days later. (Dec. 19) White is sworn in as chief justice.

1911 Congress formally abolishes old circuit courts. (Jan. 3) Van Devanter and Lamar are sworn in as associate justices. (Oct. 14) Justice Harlan dies.

1912 (Feb. 19) Taft nominates Mahlon Pitney to the Court. (Mar. 13) Senate confirms Pitney, who is sworn in five days later.

1914 (July 12) Justice Lurton dies. (Aug. 19) President Woodrow Wilson appoints James C. McReynolds to Lurton's seat; Senate confirms McReynolds's nomination ten days later. McReynolds is sworn in.

1916 (Jan. 2) Justice Lamar dies. (Jan. 28) Wilson appoints Louis D. Brandeis to replace Lamar and become first Jewish justice on the Court. (June 1) Senate confirms Brandeis, who is sworn in four days later. (June 10) Justice Hughes resigns. (July 14) Wilson appoints John H. Clarke to replace Hughes; Senate confirms Clarke's nomination ten days later. (Aug. 1) Clarke is sworn in.

1917 (July 2) Former justice Moody dies.

1921 (May 19) Chief Justice White dies. (June 30) President Warren G. Harding appoints former president William H. Taft chief justice; Senate confirms Taft's nomination the same day. (July 11) Taft is sworn in.

1922 (Sept. 5) Harding appoints George Sutherland to the Court; Senate confirms Sutherland's nomination the same day. (Sept. 18) Justice Clarke resigns. (Oct. 2) Sutherland is sworn in. (Nov. 13) Justice Day retires. (Nov. 23) Harding nominates Pierce Butler to the Court, but Senate takes no action. (Dec. 5) Harding renominates Butler, whose nomination Senate confirms sixteen days later. (Dec. 31) Justice Pitney retires.

1923 (Jan. 2) Butler is sworn in as associate justice. (Jan. 24) Harding appoints Edward T. Sanford to the Court; Senate confirms Sanford's nomination five days later. (Feb. 5) Sanford is sworn in. (July 9) Former justice Day dies.

1924 (Aug. 2) Former justice Shiras dies. (Dec. 9) Former justice Pitney dies.

1925 New Judiciary Act greatly reforms entire appeals process and broadens Supreme Court's powers to select areas in which to make rulings. (Jan. 5) Justice McKenna retires; President Calvin Coolidge appoints Harlan Fiske Stone to succeed him the same day. (Feb. 5) Senate confirms Stone's nomination. (Mar. 2) Stone is sworn in.

1926 (Jan. 27) Senate approves U.S. participation in Permanent Court of International Justice in The Hague, Netherlands; however, U.S. reservations on participation are rejected by that court. (Nov. 21) Former justice McKenna dies.

1929 (May 13) Former justice Hughes is appointed to Permanent Court of International Justice at The Hague.

1930 (Feb. 3) Chief Justice Taft retires; President Herbert Hoover appoints former justice Hughes as his successor the same day. (Feb. 13) Senate confirms Hughes, who is sworn in on Feb. 24. (Mar. 8) Taft and Justice Sanford die on same day. (Mar. 21) Hoover nominates John J. Parker to replace Sanford. (May 7) Senate rejects Parker's nomination. (May 9) Hoover nominates Owen J. Roberts to the Court; Senate confirms Roberts's nomination eleven days later. (June 2) Roberts is sworn in.

1932 Work begins on first building to be occupied exclusively by the Supreme Court. (Jan. 12) Justice Holmes retires. (Feb. 15) Hoover nominates Benjamin N. Cardozo to replace Holmes; Senate confirms Cardozo's nomination nine days later. (Mar. 14) Cardozo is sworn in.

1935 The Court makes new Supreme Court building its permanent home. (Mar. 6) Former justice Holmes dies. (Oct. 7) Court opens its first session in its new building.

1937 (Feb. 5) President Franklin D. Roosevelt recommends adding more justices to the Court when seventy-year-old justices refuse to retire. (Mar. 1) Congress votes full pay to justices who retire after reaching seventy. (June 2) Justice Van Devanter retires. (Aug. 12) Roosevelt appoints Hugo L. Black to the Court; Senate confirms his nomination five days later. (Aug. 19) Black is sworn in.

1938 (Jan. 15) Roosevelt appoints Stanley F. Reed to the Court. (Jan. 17) Justice Sutherland retires. (Jan. 27) Senate confirms Reed's nomination. (Jan. 31) Reed is sworn in. (July 9) Justice Cardozo dies.

1939 (Jan 5.) Roosevelt appoints Felix Frankfurter to the Court. (Jan. 17) Senate confirms Frankfurter's nomination. (Jan. 30) Frankfurter is sworn in. (Feb. 13) Justice Brandeis retires. (Mar. 20) Roosevelt appoints William O. Douglas to the Court. (Apr. 4) Senate confirms Douglas's nomination. (Apr. 17) Douglas is sworn in. (Nov. 16) Justice Butler dies.

1940 (Jan. 4) Roosevelt appoints Frank Murphy to the Court; Senate confirms the nomination twelve days later. (Jan. 18) Murphy is sworn in.

1941 (Feb. 1) Justice McReynolds retires. (Feb. 8) Former justice Van Devanter dies. (June 12) Roosevelt nominates Justice Stone to replace Chief Justice Hughes, who retires on July 1; Roosevelt also appoints James F. Byrnes and Robert H. Jackson as associate justices; Senate confirms Byrnes's nomination the same day. (June 27) Senate confirms Stone's nomination. (July 3) Stone is sworn in. (July 7) Senate confirms Jackson's nomination. (July 8) Byrnes is sworn in. (July 11) Jackson is sworn in. (Oct. 5) Former justice Brandeis dies.

1942 (July 18) Former justice George Sutherland dies. (Oct. 3) Justice James F. Byrnes resigns.

1943 (Jan. 11) Roosevelt appoints Wiley B. Rutledge, Jr., to the Court. (Feb. 8) Senate confirms Rutledge, who is sworn in on Feb. 15

1944 (Oct. 22) Lucile Loman becomes first woman law clerk to work for a Supreme Court justice.

1945 (July 31) Justice Roberts resigns. (Sept. 18) President Harry S. Truman appoints Harold H. Burton to replace Roberts; Senate confirms his nomination the next day. (Oct. 1) Burton is sworn in.

1946 (Apr. 22) Chief Justice Stone dies. (June 6) Truman nominates Fred M. Vinson to replace Stone; Senate confirms the nomination two weeks later. (June 24) Vinson is sworn in. (Aug. 24) Former justice McReynolds dies.

1948 (Aug. 27) Former chief justice Hughes dies. (Sept. 1) William T. Coleman becomes the Court's first black law clerk.

1949 (July 19) Justice Murphy dies. (Aug. 2) Truman nominates Tom C. Clark to the Court; Senate confirms Clark's nomination sixteen days later. (Aug. 24) Clark is sworn in. (Sept. 10) Justice Rutledge dies. (Sept. 15) Truman nominates Sherman Minton to the Court; Senate confirms Minton's nomination on Oct. 4. (Oct. 12) Minton is sworn in.

1953 (Sept. 8) Chief Justice Vinson dies. (Oct. 2) President Dwight D. Eisenhower makes Earl Warren a recess appointment as chief justice; Warren is sworn in three days later.

1954 (Jan. 11) Eisenhower formally nominates Warren as chief justice. (Mar. 1) Senate confirms Warren's nomination; Warren is sworn in again the next day. (Oct. 9) Justice Jackson dies. (Nov. 9) Eisenhower nominates John M. Harlan II to replace Jackson, but Senate takes no action.

1955 (Jan. 10) Eisenhower renominates Harlan. (Mar. 16) Senate confirms Harlan's nomination. (Mar. 2) Congress raises salaries of justices to $35,000 per year. (Mar. 28) Harlan is sworn in as associate justice. (May 17) Former justice Roberts dies.

1956 (Oct. 15) Justice Minton retires; Eisenhower makes William J. Brennan, Jr., a recess appointment the same day; Brennan is sworn in the next day.

1957 (Jan. 14) Eisenhower formally nominates Brennan to the Court. (Feb. 25) Justice Reed retires. (Mar. 2) Eisenhower nominates Charles E. Whittaker to the Court. (Mar. 19) Senate confirms Brennan's and Whittaker's nominations; Brennan is sworn in on Mar. 22, Whittaker on Mar. 25.

1958 (Aug. 21) Senate narrowly defeats Jenner-Butler Bill, a House attempt to limit the Court's powers. (Oct. 13) Justice Burton retires. (Oct. 14) Eisenhower gives Potter Stewart a recess appointment as associate justice; Stewart is sworn in on same day. (Dec.) John Birch Society mounts effort to impeach Chief Justice Warren.

1959 (Jan. 17) Eisenhower formally nominates Stewart to the Court. (May 5) Senate confirms Stewart's nomination; Stewart is sworn in on May 15.

1962 (Apr. 1) Justice Whittaker retires. (Apr. 3) President John F. Kennedy appoints Byron R. White to the Court; Senate confirms the nomination on Apr. 11, and White is sworn in on Apr. 16. (Aug. 28) Justice Frankfurter retires. (Aug. 31) Kennedy nominates Arthur J. Goldberg to the Court. (Sept. 25) Senate confirms Goldberg, who is sworn in on Oct. 1.

1964 (Oct. 28) Former justice Burton dies.

1965 (Feb. 22) Former justice Frankfurter dies. (Apr. 9) Former justice Minton dies. (July 25) Goldberg resigns from the Court to become ambassador to United Nations. (July 28) President Lyndon B. Johnson appoints Abe Fortas to the Court. (Aug. 11) Senate confirms Fortas's nomination. (Oct. 4) Fortas is sworn in.

1967 (June 12) Justice Clark retires from the Court after his son, Ramsey Clark, is appointed attorney general. (June 13) Johnson nominates Thurgood Marshall to become first African American justice. (Aug. 30) Senate confirms the nomination. (Oct. 2) Marshall is sworn in.

1968 (June 26) Johnson nominates Justice Fortas to succeed Warren as chief justice and announces intention to nominate William H. Thornberry to the associate justice seat vacated when Justice Fortas becomes chief justice. (Oct. 1-4) Johnson withdraws both nominations after Fortas is publicly charged with financial improprieties

1969 (May 14) Justice Fortas resigns from the Court. (May 21) President Richard M. Nixon nominates Warren E. Burger as chief justice. (June 9) Senate confirms Burger's nomination. (June 23) Burger is sworn in, and Chief Justice Warren retires. (Aug. 18) Nixon nominates Clement Haynsworth, Jr., to the Court. (Nov. 21) Senate rejects Haynsworth's nomination.

1970 (Jan. 19) Nixon nominates G. Harrold Carswell to the Court. (Apr. 8) Senate rejects Carswell's nomination. (Apr. 15) Nixon nominates Harry A. Blackmun to the Court. (May 12) Senate confirms Blackmun's nomination. (June 9) Blackmun is sworn in. (Dec. 3) House subcommittee rejects Congressman Gerald Ford's impeachment charge against Justice Douglas.

1971 (Sept. 17) Justice Black retires. (Sept. 23) Justice Harlan retires. (Sept. 25) Former justice Black dies. (Oct. 22) Nixon nominates William H. Rehnquist and Lewis F. Powell, Jr., to the Court. (Dec. 6-10) Senate confirms Powell's and Rehnquist's nominations. (Dec. 29) Former justice Harlan dies.

1972 (Jan. 7) Rehnquist and Powell are sworn in as associate justices. (Apr. 9) Former justice Byrnes dies.

1973 (Nov. 26) Former justice Whittaker dies.

1975 (Nov. 12) Justice Douglas retires. (Nov. 28) President Gerald R. Ford nominates John Paul Stevens to the Court. (Dec. 17) Senate confirms Stevens's nomination. (Dec. 19) Stevens is sworn in.

1980 (Jan. 19) Former justice Douglas dies. (Apr. 2) Former justice Reed dies. (Nov.) Justices stop using "Mr." before their names when signing opinions.

1981 (July 3) Justice Stewart retires. (July 7) President Ronald Reagan nominates Sandra Day O'Connor to the Court. (Sept. 21) Senate confirms the nomination; O'Connor is sworn in as first woman justice on the Court on Sept. 25.

1985 (Aug. 18) Eileen F. Cincotta becomes the Court's first woman police sergeant. (Dec. 7) Former justice Stewart dies.

1986 (June 17) Reagan announces that Chief Justice Burger is resigning; he promotes Justice Rehnquist to succeed him and nominates Antonin Scalia to succeed Rehnquist as associate justice. (Sept. 17) Senate confirms both nominations. (Sept. 26) Chief Justice Burger retires as Scalia and Rehnquist are sworn into office.

1987 (June 26) Justice Powell retires. (July 1) Reagan nominates Robert H. Bork to succeed Powell. (Oct. 23) Senate rejects Bork's nomination. (Oct. 29) Reagan instead nominates Douglas H. Ginsburg, who withdraws his nomination a week later. (Nov. 24) Reagan next nominates Anthony M. Kennedy.

1988 (Feb. 3) Senate confirms Kennedy's nomination. (Feb. 18) Kennedy is sworn in. (Nov. 19) Congress's Judicial Improvements and Access to Justice Act limits types of cases that the Supreme Court is required to hear on appeal.

1989 (Jan. 20) Justice O'Connor issues oath of office to Vice President Dan Quayle, becoming first woman justice to participate in a presidential inauguration.

1990 (July 20) Justice Brennan retires. (July 25) President George Bush nominates David H. Souter to succeed him. (Oct. 2) Senate confirms Souter's nomination. (Oct. 9) Souter is sworn in.

1991 (June 27) Justice Marshall retires. (July 1) Bush nominates Clarence Thomas to succeed him. (Oct. 15) Senate confirms Thomas's nomination. (Nov. 1) Thomas is sworn in.

1993 (June 29) Justice White retires. (June 14) President Bill Clinton nominates Ruth Bader Ginsburg to the Court. (Aug. 3) Senate confirms Ginsburg's nomination. (Aug. 10) Ginsburg is sworn in.

1994 (Mar. 13) Clinton nominates Stephen G. Breyer to fill seat vacated by Justice Blackmun. (June 30) Blackmun retires. (Aug. 3) Breyer is sworn in.

1995 (June 25) Former chief justice Burger dies.

1997 (July 24) Former justice Brennan dies.

2005 (July 1) Justice O'Connor announces her retirement. (July 19) President George W. Bush nominates John Roberts to fill O'Connor's vacancy. (Sept. 3) Before Roberts is confirmed, Chief Justice Rehnquist dies of cancer, and Bush changes Roberts's nomination to fill the chief justice vacancy. (Sept. 29) Roberts is confirmed by the Senate and joins the Court as chief justice. (Oct. 3) Bush nominates Harriet Meyers to fill O'Connors's associate justice seat. (Oct. 27) Meyers withdraws after great public criticism. (Oct. 31) Bush instead names Samuel A. Alito, Jr., as O'Connor's successor.

2006 (Jan. 31) Justice O'Connor retires; after being confirmed, Alito is sworn in as the 110th justice of the Supreme Court.

Glossary

Absolutism, First Amendment. Literal interpretation of the words "no law" in the amendment as prohibiting any governmental limits on the listed rights.

Abstention. Doctrine or policy under which the federal courts delay or refrain from ruling in state cases until the issues have been definitely resolved by the state courts.

Acquittal. Finding that a criminal defendant is not guilty.

Actual malice. Libel in which material was published with knowledge that it was false or with reckless disregard toward its truthfulness.

Adjudication. Process of reaching a decision in a court of law.

Adversarial system. Judicial system, such as that of the United States, in which two opposing parties confront each other in a court of law.

Affidavit. Written statement of facts made voluntarily under oath or affirmation.

Affirm. To uphold a decision made by a lower court.

Amicus curiae brief. Latin for "friend of the court." A document filed by a person or organization not directly involved in the litigation in order to supply arguments and evidence supporting one side of the dispute.

Appeal. Process of bringing a decision of a lower court to a higher court for a review of the judgment.

Appellant. Party that loses in a lower court and attempts to have the judgment reversed in a higher court.

Appellee. Party that prevails in the lower court and then responds when the case is taken to a higher court by an appellant.

Arraignment. Early stage of the criminal process in which charges are read to a defendant and he or she enters a plea of guilty, not guilty, or *nolo contendere.*

Association, freedom of. Fundamental right to associate with other people and organizations without unwarranted government restrictions.

Attorney-client privilege. Right of a person not to disclose any matters discussed with an attorney in the course of professional consultation.

Balancing test. Judicial approach in which a court weighs the relative importance of competing legal principles and governmental interests.

Bifurcated trial. Division of a trial into separate phases for determining guilt and punishment.

Bill of attainder. Legislative act inflicting punishment without a trial on named individuals or the members of a group.

Broad construction. Interpretation that goes beyond the literal meaning of the words in a legal text.

Burden of proof. Obligation of presenting enough evidence to establish the truthfulness of an assertion.

Capital offense. Felony that may be punished by the death penalty.

Case law. Rules and principles derived from judicial decisions, including constitutional and statutory interpretations.

Censorship. Narrowly defined, a governmental action preventing something from being published or said; broadly defined, any governmental restriction on expression.

Certification, writ of. Relatively rare procedure in which a lower court requests a higher court to rule on specific legal questions in order to apply the law correctly.

Certiorari. Latin for "to make certain." A writ in which a higher court orders an inferior court to send up the record of a particular case.

Checks and balances. Constitutional arrangement that puts limits on the powers of each of the three branches of government in order to prevent an excessive concentration of power.

Citation. Standard form used to indicate where to find a statute or a court case. For example, the citation of *Mapp v. Ohio* is 367 U.S. 643 (1961), indicating that the case is found in volume 367 of *United States Reports* beginning on page 643.

Civil infraction. Noncriminal violation of a law, such as a minor traffic violation.

Civil law. Laws that relate to relationships among private parties, in contrast to criminal law. Also, the legal tradition derived from Roman law, in contrast to the common-law tradition.

Civil liberties. Freedoms from government control or restraint, especially those freedoms guaranteed in the Bill of Rights.

Civil rights. Positive rights protected by the government, especially those rights found in the equal protection clause of the Fourteenth Amendment and the Civil Rights laws.

Civil rights laws. Federal and state statutes designed to prevent invidious discrimination in areas such as employment, education, public accommodations, and voting rights.

Class-action suit. Lawsuit brought in behalf of all persons sharing similar circumstances with those of the plaintiff.

Clear and convincing evidence. Intermediate standard of proof that is more demanding than "preponderance of evidence" and less demanding than "beyond a reasonable doubt."

Comity. Principle by which the courts of one jurisdiction accept the validity of the judicial proceedings of another jurisdiction.

Commerce. Broad term that refers to trade, traffic, transportation, communication, or intercourse by way of trade or traffic.

Commerce clause. Statement in Article I of the Constitution that gives Congress the authority to regulate commerce among the states, with foreign countries, and with the Native American tribes.

Common law. Ever-changing body of principles and rules that have evolved from prevailing customs and judicial decisions rather than from legislative statutes.

Compelling interest. Interest of the highest order; required by government to justify suspect classifications or restrictions on fundamental rights.

Comstock laws. Series of nineteenth century statutes, promoted by Anthony Comstock, which made it a crime to send "indecent" or "obscene" materials, including information about family planning, through the U.S. mail.

Concurrent jurisdiction. Judicial authority that is shared by different courts of law, especially between federal and state courts.

Concurring opinion. Written statement of a judge or justice who agrees with the decision of the majority but writes separately in order to emphasize a particular matter or to disagree with the reasoning used in the opinion of the court.

Confrontation clause. Sixth Amendment right of a criminal defendant to observe the testimony of prosecution witnesses and to cross-examine these witnesses.

Consent decree. Court-enforced agreement that is reached by the mutual consent of all parties to a lawsuit.

Conspiracy. Crime in which two or more persons make plans to commit a specific criminal act.

Constitution. Supreme law of a country defining the structures and prerogatives of governmental institutions and the legal rights of individuals.

Constitutional courts. Those federal courts established by Congress under the authority of Article III, section 1, of the U.S. Constitution.

Construction. Synonym for interpretation.

Contempt of court. Failure to carry out a court order, or an action that obstructs, embarrasses, or shows disrespect for a court of law.

Continuance. Delay of a judicial proceeding.

Counsel. Lawyer authorized to represent a party.

Courts of appeals. At the federal level, those constitutional courts having appellate jurisdiction over decisions by district courts except in the few cases in which there is a right to a direct appeal to the Supreme Court.

Crime. Positive or negative act considered as a wrong against society and classified as either a misdemeanor or a felony.

Criminal law. Body of law defining and providing for the punishment of crimes, in contrast to civil law, which applies to relationships between private parties.

Custodial interrogation. Questioning by the police of a suspect held in custody.

De facto. Latin for "in fact." An existing situation that arises from private decisions rather than governmental action. De facto segregation is considered beyond the jurisdiction of the courts because no state action is involved.

De jure. Latin for "by law." A condition that results from law or official governmental action.

De minimus. Matter not important enough to warrant adjudication.

Declaratory judgment. Judicial ruling declaring the legal rights of the parties to a dispute but not imposing any remedy or relief.

Defendant. Party being sued in a civil case or charged with a crime in a criminal case. At the appellate level, the party moved against is called the respondent or appellee.

Demurrer. Latin for "to object or delay." An objection by a defendant admitting the facts alleged by the plaintiff but contending that these facts do not justify a civil lawsuit or criminal charge.

Dicta. Statements in a judicial opinion that are not a part of the actual decision.

Dissenting opinion/dissent. Written statement by a judge or justice who disagrees with a decision reached by the majority.

District courts. In the federal system, the trial courts with original jurisdiction.

Diversity cases. Lawsuits involving parties residing in different states.

Docket. Schedule of cases awaiting action in a court.

Double jeopardy. Trying of a person twice for the same crime in the same jurisdiction.

Dual sovereignty (dual federalism). Theory of federalism that holds that the national and state governments are sovereign in their respective spheres, so that the national government must not invade a sphere reserved to the states by the Tenth Amendment.

Due process of law. Requirement that government must use fair and established procedures whenever it deprives a person of life, liberty, or property. Also, requirement that laws must be fair and reasonable in substance as well as in procedures.

Elastic clause (necessary and proper clause). Authority of Congress under Article I, section 8, to select any means appropriate to achieving the enumerated powers.

Eminent domain. Government's power to take property for a public purpose by providing just compensation.

Enumerated powers. Prerogatives given to the national government in Article I, section 8, of the Constitution.

Equity. Historically, a system of jurisprudence developed in England to supplement the common law by emphasizing principles of fairness rather than the letter of the law.

Establishment clause. Statement in the First Amendment prohibiting any direct governmental support or favoritism for religion or religious institutions.

Ex parte. Latin for "from one side." A hearing in which only one party to a dispute is present, especially a hearing to consider a petition for a writ of habeas corpus.

Ex post facto law. Latin for "from after the fact." A retroactive statute that criminalizes an action that was legal when it occurred or increases punishment for a criminal act after it was committed.

Excessive bail. Unreasonable large sum of money imposed as a requirement for a defendant to be released before a trial.

Exclusionary rule. Constitutional interpretation holding that evidence obtained by illegal means cannot be introduced by the prosecution in a criminal trial.

Exclusive jurisdiction. When only a particular court can hear a certain kind of case.

Exculpatory evidence. Information tending to exonerate a person of guilt or blame.

Exigent circumstances. Emergency situation demanding immediate action, such as allowing the police to enter into private property without a search warrant.

Federal question (national question). Legal issue that involves the U.S. Constitution, congressional legislation, or a treaty.

Federal system (federalism). Constitutional arrangement that distributes political powers between the national government and regional governments.

Felony. Serious crime that carries a possible penalty of at least a year in prison.

Fighting words doctrine. Idea that utterances addressed at a person are not protected by the First Amendment if they are inherently likely to provoke a violent response from an average addressee.

Free exercise clause. Guarantee in the First Amendment to believe and practice the religion of one's choice.

Frisk. Precautionary pat-down of a suspect for weapons in order to protect an officer and other persons.

Full faith and credit clause. Provision in Article IV of the Constitution requiring that states must recognize the records and legal proceedings of other states.

Fundamental rights. Those rights, regardless of whether they are explicitly mentioned in the Constitution, that the courts have decided are essential to liberty and human dignity, including First Amendment freedoms, the right to vote, and the right to privacy.

Gag order. Judge's instructions requiring certain parties to refrain from speaking publicly or privately about a particular trial.

Gerrymandering. Drawing of an election district in a strange shape in order to give an advantage to a political party or special interest.

Good faith exception. Exception to the exclusionary rule, so that the prosecution can introduce evidence acquired by the police in an invalid search and seizure when the police had good reason to believe the search was legal at the time.

Habeas corpus. From Latin for "you have the body." An order to a custodial officer to bring a person held in custody before a judge in order to explain the legal justification for holding the person.

Harmless error. Procedural or substantive mistake that does not affect the final result of a judicial proceeding.

Hate crimes. Crimes in which a victim is chosen on the basis of race, ethnicity, religion, gender, or sexual orientation.

Hate speech. Offensive communication expressing disdain for persons of ethnic, religious, or other social categories.

Hicklin test. Obsolete standard for judging obscenity, taken from *Regina v. Hicklin* (1886), that allowed government to proscribe a literary work if an isolated section might tend to "deprave and corrupt" children.

Higher law. Idea that principles of natural law take precedence over human laws, including the Constitution.

Hot pursuit. Situation in which a police officer is allowed to pursue a fleeing suspect into a protected area without a search warrant.

Immunity. Exemption from criminal prosecution in return for testimony in a criminal case.

In forma pauperis. Latin for "in the manner of a pauper." A waiver from court fees and certain legal expenses in order to allow a poor person to have access to a court of law.

In re. Latin for "in reference to." A designation used in judicial proceedings when there are no formal adversaries.

Inadmissible. Materials that under the established rules of law cannot be admitted as legal evidence.

Incitement standard. Doctrine that government cannot punish seditious speech unless it is directed at provoking illegal action that is likely to occur.

Incorporation (or absorption). Doctrine under which most provisions of the Bill of Rights have been "incorporated" or "absorbed" into the due process clause of the Fourteenth Amendment so that they are applicable to state and local governments.

Indictment. Formal charge issued by a grand jury against a person for a particular crime.

Inevitable discovery. Doctrine that illegally obtained evidence is admissible in a criminal trial if it appears inevitable that the evidence would have been discovered by legal means.

Information. Formal accusation of a crime issued by a prosecutor in order to initiate a criminal trial without a grand jury indictment. Because the grand jury requirement of the Fifth Amendment has never been incorporated, several states allow prosecutions to be initiated by information.

Inherent powers. Powers of an official or a government that derive from the concept of sovereignty and do not depend upon explicit provisions of a constitution or statutes.

Injunction. Judicial order prohibiting or requiring certain acts by designated persons.

Intermediate scrutiny. Judicial standard requiring government to justify a challenged policy by demonstrating its substantial relationship to an important government interest. Courts use the standard to scrutinize allegations of gender discrimination.

Interpretivism. Interpretative approach that attempts to determine the meanings conveyed by the text itself, without reference to nontextual considerations such as natural law or sociological theory.

Inventory search. Authority of the police to make an administrative listing of articles following the arrest of a person or the impoundment of a vehicle.

Jim Crow. System of laws in the South that required racial segregation, in effect from the late nineteenth century until passage of the Civil Rights laws of the 1960's.

Judgment of the court. Court's official ruling in a particular case or controversy, excluding the reasoning used in the ruling.

Judicial restraint. View that judges should be careful not to inject their own ideas about "good" or "wise" public policy in their decisions; as distinguished from "judicial activism."

Judicial review. 1) In American constitutional law, authority of a court to invalidate legislative and executive acts if they are inconsistent with constitutional principles. 2) In a general sense, the review of any issue by a court of law.

Jurisdiction. Legal authority of a court to hear and to decide a particular case or controversy.

Just compensation clause. Statement in the Fifth Amendment requiring that owners whose property is taken under the eminent domain power must be fairly compensated for their loss.

Justiciable question. Legal issue that can be appropriately and effectively decided in a court of law.

Lemon test. Based on an interpretation of the establishment clause in *Lemon v. Kurtzman* (1971), a three-part requirement that public aid to religious schools must have a secular purpose, a primary effect that neither advances or inhibits religion, and no excessive entanglement between government and religion.

Libel. Written defamation of another person's character or reputation.

Literacy tests. Requirement of a reading test in order to vote, generally used to prevent African Americans from voting in the South; now illegal.

Litigant. Party to a lawsuit.

Magistrate. Judge with minor or limited authority.

Mandamus, writ of. Latin for "we command." A court order directing a public official or organization to perform a particular duty.

Mandatory jurisdiction. Requirement of a court to hear a certain category of cases.

Miranda warning. Notice to a detained suspect by a police officer advising the person of the rights to remain silent and to have the assistance of counsel.

Misdemeanor. Crime with a maximum penalty of one year or less in jail; less serious than a felony.

Moot question. Status of a lawsuit that no longer involves a justiciable controversy either because the issue has been resolved or the conditions have so changed that the court is unable to grant the requested relief.

Natural rights. Idea that all governments at all times have the obligation of respecting basic human rights, either because of human nature or a divine purpose.

Necessary and proper clause. See **Elastic clause**.

Nolo contendere. Latin for "I do not contest it." A defendant's plea that has the effect of a guilty plea in a criminal case but does not constitute an admission of guilt that might be used in another case.

Non sequitur. Latin for "it does not follow." A conclusion that does not follow logically from the premises and facts.

Obiter dicta. Latin for "said in passing." Incidental statements in a court's opinion that are not necessary to support the decision and are not binding as precedent.

Obscenity. Sexually explicit materials that are not protected by the First Amendment according to the three-prong test of *Miller v. California* (1973).

Open fields doctrine. Principle that privacy rights under the Fourth Amendment do not apply to unoccupied areas outside a home's yard.

Opinion of the Court. Opinion endorsed by a majority or a controlling plurality of the participating justices. It both announces the decision and explains the rationale for the decision.

Ordinance. Most commonly refers to an enactment by a local government.

Original intent. Meaning of a document according to the person or persons who produced it. There is disagreement about whether modern courts should attempt to follow the original understanding of the Constitution.

Original jurisdiction. Authority of a court to conduct trials and decide cases in the first instance, as distinguished from appellate jurisdiction. The Supreme Court has original jurisdiction in cases involving foreign diplomats or states as parties.

Overbreadth doctrine. Principle that governmental policies that directly or indirectly restrict constitutional rights are unconstitutional unless they are narrowly tailored to advance a sufficiently important governmental interest.

Overrule. Action of a court that explicitly reverses or makes void an earlier decision about the same legal issue by the same court.

Penumbra. Theory that the Constitution casts partial shadows that expand constitutional protection to include broad values such as privacy; associated especially with Justice William O. Douglas.

Per curiam. Latin for "by the court." An unsigned or collectively written opinion by a court.

Peremptory challenge. Right of an attorney to exclude a prospective juror without explaining the reasons for doing so.

Petit jury. Jury, normally composed of twelve persons, that hears a trial and renders a verdict.

Petitioner. Party seeking relief in a court of law.

Petty (petit) offenses. Minor crimes that are punished by fines or short jail sentences. The Supreme Court has held that a jury trial is not required if the maximum penalty is less than six months.

Plain meaning rule. Principle that the words of constitutional and statutory texts should be interpreted according to the common meanings of ordinary language.

Plain view rule. Doctrine that allows a police officer to seize contraband that is readily visible to the officer's naked eye, so long as the officer is legally in the place where the contraband is observed.

Plaintiff. Party who initiates a civil action or sues to obtain a remedy for an injury.

Plea bargain. Agreement between a criminal defendant and a prosecutor whereby the defendant pleads guilty in return for a reduction in the charges or the recommended punishment.

Plenary consideration. When the Supreme Court gives full consideration for a case, including the submission of briefs and oral arguments.

Plurality opinion. Opinion that receives the highest number of votes in an appellate court but without a majority of the judges.

Police power. Recognized authority of the states to protect the public's safety, health, morality, and welfare. The national government has gradually acquired overlapping prerogatives by way of the commerce and welfare clauses.

Political question doctrine. Principle that the federal courts allow elected officials to resolve political controversies that do not involve constitutional issues.

Political speech. Communication about public affairs that is considered to have the highest level of First Amendment protection.

Pornography. Broad term that refers to sexually oriented materials ranging from constitutionally protected forms of "indecency" to unprotected "obscenity."

Precedent. Prior decision resolving a legal issue that serves as a model or guide for deciding cases involving the same or a similar issue.

Preemption. Doctrine that allows Congress to enact a statute that brings an area of authority under the primary or exclusive jurisdiction of the national government, even though the matter was previously under the jurisdiction of the states.

Preferred freedoms doctrine. Idea that First Amendment freedoms should have priority among constitutional rights and liberties. Although influential in the 1940's, the doctrine has generally been replaced by that of "fundamental rights."

Preponderance of evidence. Standard of proof in civil cases, requiring evidence that an assertion is more probable than a contrary assertion.

Preventive detention. Practice of denying bail to a person awaiting trial on the grounds that the person's release would endanger the public safety.

Prima facie. Latin for "at first sight." An argument that is sufficiently persuasive to prevail unless effectively refuted by the opposing side.

Prior restraint. Most extreme form of government censorship, restraining expression before its publication or broadcast.

Privacy, right of. Constitutionally protected liberty to engage in intimate personal conduct and to exercise personal autonomy without unjustified governmental interference.

Probable cause. Sufficient evidence to lead a reasonable person to conclude that it is highly likely that certain evidence will be found in a particular place or that a certain individual has probably committed a crime.

Probate. Court procedures for determining whether a will is valid or invalid.

Procedural due process. Constitutional requirement that the methods and procedures used in the enforcement of laws must be fair, such as the requirements of the Sixth Amendment.

Proportionality. Extent to which a particular punishment is 1) commensurate with the harm done in a criminal act or 2) proportional to the penalties given for other crimes of similar magnitude.

Public safety exception. Immediate threat to the public's safety that allows police officers to ask suspects particular questions before giving the Miranda warnings.

Punitive damages. In a civil suit, a monetary award that is added to payment for compensatory damages in order to punish the defendant and serve as a deterrent.

Rational basis test. Standard requiring that a challenged law must bear a reasonable relationship to a legitimate governmental interest. This test is used when a case does not involve a suspect classification or a fundamental right.

Real evidence. Actual object that is used as evidence, rather than a description by a witness.

Reapportionment. Redrawing of the boundaries of a voting district based on population.

Reasonable doubt. Degree of uncertainty that would lead a prudent person of sound mind to hesitate to make a decision of personal significance.

Reasonable expectation of privacy. Person's right to expect that activities in certain places are private, so that government agents cannot intrude in such places except under the provisions of the Fourth Amendment.

Reasonable suspicion. Objective circumstances that lead a prudent person to think that a person is likely involved in criminal activity; more than a hunch but less than probable cause.

Reasonableness. Legal standard attempting to determine what decisions and actions would be expected of a prudent and reasonably intelligent person within a particular set of circumstances.

Rebuttable presumption. Presumption in law that can be refuted by adequate evidence, as distinguished from an irrebuttable presumption that cannot be refuted by evidence.

Recuse. Decision of a judge not to participate in a case because of a conflict of interest or another disqualifying situation.

Regulatory taking. Government regulations that eliminate the useful value of private property, requiring compensation under the Fifth Amendment.

Remand. Superior court's decision to return a case to a lower court for additional action, usually with specific instructions about how to proceed.

Republican government. Political system with elected representatives and without hereditary rulers.

Reserved powers. Police powers retained by the states in the Tenth Amendment.

Respondent. Party against whom a legal action is taken.

Restrictive covenant. Contract that prohibits transfer of property to one or more classes of persons, usually minorities.

Reverse. Judgment of an appellate court setting aside a decision of a lower court.

Ripeness. Status of a case that is ready for adjudication by a court. An issue is not "ripe for review" before the Supreme Court unless there is an actual case or controversy and the parties have exhausted all other routes of appeal and resolution.

Rule of four. Principle that the Supreme Court will not review a case unless four justices vote to accept it.

Saving construction. Doctrine that the courts, given two plausible interpretations of a statute, will choose the one that allows the statute to be found constitutional.

Seditious speech. Communications intended to incite insurrection or overthrow of the government.

Selective incorporation. Practice of making applicable to the states those provisions of the Bill of Rights considered fundamental or essential to a regime of ordered liberty.

Self-incrimination. Declaration or action by which persons implicate themselves in a crime; prohibited by the Fifth Amendment and provisions of most state constitutions.

Separation of church and state. Interpretation of the First Amendment requiring a "wall of separation" between religion and government.

Separation of powers. Constitutional division of authority among the legislative, executive, and judicial branches of government.

Seriatim. Latin for "serially." The practice of each judge writing a separate opinion without a single "opinion of the court."

Sexual harassment. Type of discrimination in employment or education involving sexual advances or requests for sexual favors, interpreted as a violation the Civil Rights Act of 1964.

Slander. Speaking of false and malicious words that harm the reputation of another person or group.

Solicitor general. High official of the Department of Justice who argues the government's position before the Supreme Court.

Sovereign immunity. Principle of precluding lawsuits against a government without its consent.

Sovereignty. Supreme political authority that is exercised by an independent country. In addition to the sovereignty of the national government, the states and the Indian tribes retain sovereignty in particular spheres.

Standing to sue. Status of a party who has the right to bring legal action because of a direct harm.

Stare decisis. Latin for "let the decision stand." The doctrine, emphasized in the common-law tradition, that a legal issue settled in a judicial decision should be followed as precedent in future cases presenting the same issue. The Supreme Court is not required to practice the doctrine, especially in regard to constitutional issues.

State action. Official action by an agent of the state or "under color of state law." Such action is an essential element for "equal protection" and "due process" claims under the Fourteenth Amendment.

Statute. Generally applicable law enacted by a legislature, to be distinguished from constitutional law, common law, administrative law, or case law.

Strict construction. Literal or narrow reading of the words of a document, especially the Constitution.

Strict necessity, doctrine of. Doctrine that a court should consider a constitutional issue only when necessary to decide a particular case.

Strict scrutiny. Judicial approach for considering laws that abridge fundamental rights or utilize a suspect classification scheme involving race or national origin. When considering such laws, the courts require government to show that the law is narrowly tailored to advance a compelling state interest, so that laws usually do not survive strict scrutiny.

Subpoena. Latin for "under penalty." A judicial order requiring a person to appear before a grand jury, a court, or a legislative hearing.

Summary judgment. Court decision rendered without a full hearing or without the benefit of briefs.

Supremacy clause. Provision in Article VI of the Constitution declaring that the Constitution, with federal legislation and treaties consistent with it, is the supreme law of the land.

Suspect classification. Government categorization of people based on characteristics such as race or national origin, resulting in a special benefit or disadvantage.

Swing vote. Deciding vote in a 5-4 Supreme Court decision.

Symbolic speech. Act that expresses a message through means other than spoken or written language. An example is the desecration of the flag.

Textual analysis. Approach to interpretation that concentrates on the language in a legal text rather than on extratextual considerations.

Tort. Willful or negligent injury to a person or property, which is a common basis for a civil lawsuit.

Total incorporation. Judicial doctrine holding that all of the first eight amendments should be incorporated into the Fourteenth Amendment and thus applied to the states.

Ultra vires. Latin for "beyond powers." An action that goes beyond the legal authority of a person or agency performing it.

Unenumerated rights. Constitutionally protected rights not explicitly mentioned in the Constitution. Such rights are usually defended by the substantive due process doctrine or the Ninth Amendment.

Uniform Code of Military Justice (UCMJ). Code of laws enacted by Congress to govern people serving in the military.

Vagueness doctrine. Doctrine holding that a law violates due process principles if it is not written precisely enough to make it clear which actions are illegal.

Venue. Location where a legal proceeding takes place.

Vested rights. Long-established rights, especially property rights, which cannot be taken from a person without due process of law.

Viewpoint discrimination. Governmental exclusion of a category of expression when the exclusion is not reasonable in the light of the forum.

Voir dire. French for "to see, to speak." The process in which prospective jurors are questioned by attorneys or judges in order to select juries for trials.

Waiver. Voluntary and intentional relinquishment of a legal right. Citizens have the right to waive their rights, so long as there is no coercion by the police.

Warrant. Court order authorizing the police to make an arrest or conduct a search and seizure.

White primary. Primary election in the "one-party South" that prohibited participation by African Americans.

Writ. Written court order.

Yellow dog contract. Requirement, illegal since 1932, that an employee must agree not to join a labor union as a condition of employment.

Bibliography

Additional bibliographical information can be found in the Further Reading notes at the ends of more than 235 articles in the main text.

General Works on the Supreme Court

Ackerman, Bruce. *We the People 2: Transformations.* Cambridge, Mass.: Harvard University Press, 1998. Controversial book viewing the Supreme Court as essentially a political institution, arguing that in times of crisis the Court has been a participant in social movements that have produced constitutional revolutions.

Agresto, John. *The Supreme Court and Constitutional Democracy.* Ithaca, N.Y.: Cornell University Press, 1994. About one-third of this book is a historical analysis of the work of the Court, and the remainder discusses the Court's role in American political life, stressing its interaction with the other two branches.

Cooper, Phillip J. *Battles on the Bench: Conflict Inside the Supreme Court.* Lawrence: University Press of Kansas, 1999. Covering all eras of Supreme Court history, Cooper tells fascinating stories of large and small clashes among justices, with analysis of why and how the conflicts have occurred, and how they have often shaped decisions.

Faigman, David L. *Laboratory of Justice: The Supreme Court's Two-Hundred-Year Struggle to Integrate Science and the Law.* New York: Henry Holt, 2004. Argues that scientific beliefs have always influenced the Court's decisions and that the process has often been unsystematic and haphazard, as in the Court's early justification of racism and eugenics.

Hall, Kermit L., ed. *The Oxford Companion to the Supreme Court of the United States.* 2d ed. New York: Oxford University Press, 2005. This single-volume reference on the Court has more than a thousand articles by specialists that include biographies, studies of individual decisions, and major issues confronting the Court.

Hensley, Thomas, Christopher Smith, and Joyce Baugh. *The Changing Supreme Court: Constitutional Rights and Liberties.* 2d ed. Belmont: Thomson/Wadsworth, 2007. Scholarly and interesting text arranged topically, with both qualitative analysis and quantitative scales of liberal/conservative voting patterns of the justices.

Irons, Peter H. *A People's History of the Supreme Court.* New York: Penguin Books, 2000. Colorfully written and filled with insightful portraits of justices, lawyers, and litigants alike, this book praises the liberal justices for having advanced the principles of liberty and equality.

Levy, Leonard, and Kenneth Karst, eds. *Encyclopedia of the American Constitution.* 2d ed. 6 vols. New York: Macmillan Reference, 2000. These large volumes provide detailed accounts of doctrines, terms, and cases relating to the American Constitution and constitutional law, written by recognized scholars.

McCloskey, Robert G. *The American Supreme Court.* 2d ed. Chicago: University of Chicago Press, 1994. Presents a complete overview of the structure, functions, history, and direction of the Supreme Court and an appreciation of its role in the U.S. political and governmental system.

Maltzman, Forrest, et al. *Crafting Law on the Supreme Court: The Collegial Game.* New York: Cambridge University Press, 2000. Argues that the justices are constrained by the choices of the other justices, requiring them to make compromises and alliances in order to build majority opinions.

Maroon, Fred J., and Suzy Maroon. *The Supreme Court of the United States.* West Palm Beach, Fla.: Lickle Publishing, 1996. Contains 130 color photographs of the Supreme Court building—both inside and outside—a photo-essay on the progress of an appeal through the Court, and a brief history of the Court.

O'Brien, David. *Storm Center: The Supreme Court in American Politics.* 7th ed. New York: W. W. Norton, 2005. Informed introduction to the Supreme Court's role in debating and often deciding the legal outcomes of controversial issues.

Powers, Stephen, and Stanley Rothman. *The Least Dangerous Branch? Consequences of Judicial Activism.* Westport, Conn.: Greenwood Press, 2002. Two moderately conservative critics express their distrust of judicial power and dislike for the Court's ruling in cases of affirmative action, busing, prison reform, and criminal procedures.

Savage, David. *Guide to the U.S. Supreme Court.* 4th ed. Washington, D.C.: CQ Press, 2004. Comprehensive reference source on the Supreme Court, covering its origins, history, organization, procedures, justices, and major decisions.

Schwartz, Bernard. *A History of the Supreme Court.* New York: Oxford University Press, 1993. Excellent one-volume history of the Supreme Court with interesting descriptions of major justices and detailed descriptions of landmark decisions.

Semonche, John. *Keeping the Faith: A Cultural History of the U.S. Supreme Court.* Lanham, Md.: Rowman & Littlefield, 1998. Portraying the Supreme

Court as a guardian of the progressive values of liberty and equality, Semonche portrays the justices as "the high priests of the American civil religion."

Spaeth, Harold. *How the Supreme Court Decides Cases.* New York: Oxford University Press, 1996. Schwartz examines four major ways that cases are decided: leadership by a strong chief justice, leadership on given issues by forceful individual justices, general cooperation of justices dealing with a weak chief justice, and decision by vote switching.

_______. *Majority Rule or Minority Rule: Adherence to Precedent on the U.S. Supreme Court.* New York: Cambridge University Press, 2001. Asserts that quantitative data show that justices are rarely influenced by precedent, even though many justices, such as Sandra Day O'Connor, claim otherwise. Interesting from a methodological perspective.

Stephens, Otis H., Jr., and John M. Scheb. *American Constitutional Law.* 3d ed. Belmont: Thomson/Wadsworth, 2003. One of the best of the college textbooks, organized topically with a strong historical perspective, containing many selections from Supreme Court decisions.

Urofsky, Melvin I., and Paul Finkelman. *A March of Liberty: A Constitutional History of the United States.* 2d ed. 2 vols. New York: Oxford University Press, 2004. Written primarily to serve as a textbook for college courses, this is a readable and scholarly account of the Constitution and its interpretation by the Supreme Court.

Wiecek, William M. *Liberty Under Law: The Supreme Court in American Life.* Baltimore, Md.: Johns Hopkins University Press, 1988. This clear and succinct summary of the history of the Court is aimed at those who have no background in law. Its judgments about people and events are carefully considered, with some bias in favor of an activist Court.

Wrightman, Lawrence. *The Psychology of the Supreme Court.* New York: Oxford University Press, 2006. Using modern academic concepts and research, an eminent social psychologist's examination of the factors that influence behavior, including social background, appointment, role of the law clerks, the chief justice, and daily interaction with other justices.

Justices

Biskupic, Joan. *Sandra Day O'Connor: How the First Woman on the Supreme Court Became Its Most Influential Member.* New York: ECCO, 2005. Drawing on papers of justices and hundreds of interviews, this fascinating biography portrays the complexity of the woman who became the axis of many key decisions.

Compston, Christine. *Earl Warren: Justice for All.* New York: Oxford University Press, 2002. Relatively short biography with many illustrations, portraying Chief Justice Warren as a courageous man with strong moral commitments, written primarily for general readers.

Cray, Ed. *Chief Justice: A Biography of Earl Warren.* New York: Simon & Schuster, 1997. Based on personal papers and interviews of his associates, and long considered the most complete biography of Warren, it does not have as much legal analysis, however, as G. Edward White's *Earl Warren: A Public Life* (New York: Oxford University Press, 1982).

Friedman, Leon, and Fred L. Israel, eds. *The Justices of the United States Supreme Court: Their Lives and Major Opinions.* 5 vols. New York: Chelsea House, 1997. Interesting scholarly essays devoting about twenty-five pages to each justice. This latest edition has an essay on Justice Stephen Breyer.

Greenhouse, Linda. *Becoming Justice Blackmun.* New York: Henry Holt, 2005. Using Justice Harry A. Blackmun's voluminous records, *The New York Times*'s specialist on the Supreme Court has written a fascinating account of the debates within the Court and in the left-leaning direction of Blackmun's thinking.

Gunther, Gerhard. *Learned Hand: The Man and the Judge.* New York: Alfred A. Knopf, 1994. A former clerk to both judge Learned Hand and Chief Justice Earl Warren, Gunther explains why Hand—though he never sat on the U.S. Supreme Court—had a major impact on the Court's workings with the powerful opinions he wrote during his fifty-two years as a federal judge.

Hirsch, H. N. *The Enigma of Felix Frankfurter.* New York: Basic Books, 1981. Attempting to explain Frankfurter's evolution from a civil libertarian to an advocate of judicial restraint, Hirsch relies upon speculative psychoanalytic theories in this scholarly and valuable contribution.

Hockett, Jeffrey. *New Deal Justice: The Constitutional Jurisprudence of Hugo L. Black, Felix Frankfurter, and Robert H. Jackson.* New York: Rowman & Littlefield, 1996. Engrossing and well-researched analysis of President Franklin D. Roosevelt's most notable Court appointees that emphasizes their regional, cultural, and ideological disagreements.

Hutchinson, Dennis. *The Man Who Once Was Whizzer White: A Portrait of Justice Byron R. White.* New York: Free Press, 1998. Scholarly study of a competent justice who valued his privacy and attempted to make good decisions in particular cases rather than formulating constitutional doctrines or worrying about consistency.

Irons, Peter. *Brennan vs. Rehnquist: The Battle for the Constitution.* New York: Alfred A. Knopf, 1994. Fascinating comparative analysis of two strong ideological voices that dominated the Court for many years. However, while Irons consistently agrees with Brennan's views, he finds it difficult to be fair when discussing those of Rehnquist.

Jeffries, John C., Jr. *Justice Lewis F. Powell, Jr.* New York: Charles Scribner's Sons, 1994. Justice Powell's former clerk has written a penetrating analysis of how this moderately conservative justice was often the swing vote in important cases dealing with school desegregation, abortion, capital punishment, and racial preference in school admissions.

Marion, David E. *The Jurisprudence of Justice William J. Brennan, Jr.: The Law and Politics of Libertarian Dignity.* Lanham: Rowman & Littlefield, 1997. Marion contends that Brennan was the most important liberal justice of the twentieth century, emphasizing his great influence on political discourse and public policy.

Maveety, Nancy. *Justice Sandra Day O'Connor: Strategist on the Supreme Court.* Lanham, Md.: Rowman & Littlefield, 1996. Maveety provides a brief biographic introduction before embarking on a scrupulous analysis of how O'Connor reached her decisions and the tactics by which she made herself as influential as possible on the Court.

Murphy, Bruce Allen. *Fortas: The Rise and Ruin of a Supreme Court Justice.* New York: William Morrow, 1988. Fascinating tale of a man tricked into taking a seat on the Supreme Court, bringing ruin on himself by violating the separation of powers in principle and practice as well as by unethical financial dealings, and making possible the right-leaning trend of the Court after his time.

_______. *Wild Bill: The Legend and Life of William O. Douglas.* New York: Random House, 2003. Excellent account of the controversial libertarian and unique individualist who wrote more opinions and dissents than any other justice, while also having more marriages and surviving more impeachment attempts.

Newman, Roger K. *Hugo Black: A Biography.* New York: Pantheon Books, 1994. About half of this thorough biography is devoted to Justice Hugo L. Black's service on the Court as an effective defender of individual rights and liberties. Newman includes much detailed information about Black's life, including his youthful involvement with the Ku Klux Klan.

Newmyer, R. Kent. *John Marshall and the Heroic Age of the Supreme Court.* Baton Rouge: Louisiana State University, 2001. With a good balance between Marshall's private life and his jurisprudence, this work is recognized as the best one-volume biography on the "great chief justice."

_______. *Justice Joseph Story: Statesman of the Old Republic.* Chapel Hill: University of North Carolina Press, 1985. Describes the remarkable evolution of Joseph Story as a person and a legal thinker.

Polenberg, Richard. *World of Benjamin Cardozo: Personal Values and the Judicial Process.* Cambridge, Mass.: Harvard University Press, 1999. Well-written and detailed account that emphasizes Justice Cardozo's strong commitment to moral values.

Ross, Michael. *Justice of Shattered Dreams: Samuel Freeman Miller and the Supreme Court During the Civil War Era.* Baton Rouge: Louisiana State University Press, 2003. Excellent biography revealing that the author of the Court's decision in the *Slaughterhouse Cases* was a former slave owner who defended Abraham Lincoln's war policies and became a champion of African American rights.

Rossum, Ralph. *Antonin Scalia's Jurisprudence: Text and Tradition.* Lawrence: University Press of Kansas, 2006. Comprehensive and sympathetic analysis of the six hundred Supreme Court opinions and other writings of the witty, argumentative, and conservative justice.

St. Clare, James, and Linda Gugin. *Chief Justice Fred M. Vinson of Kentucky: A Political Biography.* Lexington: University Press of Kentucky, 2002. Study of an amiable chief justice who presided over the Court as it became embroiled in the critical issues of racial discrimination and freedom of expression.

Smith, Jean Edward. *John Marshall: Definer of a Nation.* New York: Henry Holt, 1996. One of the best of several biographies of the chief justice who is considered the most influential legal statesman to have served on the Supreme Court.

Stebenne, David L. *Arthur J. Goldberg, New Deal Liberal.* New York: Oxford University Press, 1996. In addition to a scholarly analysis of Goldberg's brief but significant tenure on the Supreme Court, this book provides a useful background account of postwar liberalism and Goldberg's work as general counsel to the United Steelworkers of America.

Strum, Philippa. *Louis D. Brandeis: Justice for the People.* Cambridge, Mass.: Harvard University Press, 1984. Attempts to reconcile some of the polarities of Justice Louis D. Brandeis's thought by portraying him as a person with Jeffersonian sensibilities who had to cope with the complexities of an age of rapid urban and industrial growth.

Thomas, Andrew Peyton. *Clarence Thomas: A Biography.* New York: Encounter Books, 2002. Highly critical biography that includes information about Justice Thomas's benefits from affirmative action, his discussions of *Roe v. Wade* before his confirmation, his two marriages, and his vexed relationship with Anita Hill.

Tushnet, Mark. *Making Constitutional Law: Thurgood Marshall and the Supreme Court, 1961-1991.* New York: Oxford University Press, 1997. Justice Marshall's former clerk, Tushnet argues that Thomas had more impact on civil rights before joining the Court than he did afterward and explores Marshall's growing frustrations on issues of busing and affirmative action.

Urofsky, Melvin I., ed. *Biographical Encyclopedia of the Supreme Court: The Lives and Legal Philosophies of the Justices.* Washington, D.C.: CQ Press, 2006. Useful scholarly essays about the justices and their views on jurisprudence.

_______. *Oliver Wendell Holmes: Sage of the Supreme Court.* New York: Oxford University Press, 2000. Scholarly study of Justice Holmes's personality, ideas, and writings, from his early life in Boston and courageous service during the Civil War through his thirty years on the Supreme Court.

Yarbrough, Tinsley. *John Marshall Harlan: Great Dissenter of the Warren Court.* New York: Oxford University Press, 1991. Impressively researched and gracefully written portrait of a moderately conservative justice whose lengthy, careful, and learned opinions were admired even by judicial lawyers who disagreed with his conclusions.

_______. *Judicial Enigma: The First Justice Harlan.* New York: Oxford University Press, 1995. Explores the discontinuity between Justice John Marshall Harlan's early life as a slave owner and his later liberal dissents in cases affecting civil rights and due process.

Court History

Belknap, Michal R. *The Supreme Court Under Earl Warren, 1953-1969.* Columbia: University of South Carolina Press, 2005. The best single volume on the justices and cases during one of the most significant periods in the history of the Supreme Court.

Casto, William A. *The Supreme Court in the Early Republic: The Chief Justiceships of John Jay and Oliver Ellsworth.* Columbia: University of South Carolina Press, 1995. Insightful study of a neglected period of Court history, the pre-John Marshall years, when the Court combined English law and colonial practice with the emergence of new legal doctrines and forms appropriate to the U.S. Constitution.

Ely, James M., Jr. *The Chief Justiceship of Melville W. Fuller, 1888-1910.* Columbia: University of South Carolina Press, 1995. An eminent law professor, Ely defends the thesis that Fuller and his fellow justices were not simply defenders of wealth and business interests but were motivated by a desire to preserve individual liberty, albeit conceived primarily in economic terms.

Huebner, Timothy. *The Taney Court: Justices, Rulings, and Legacy.* Santa Barbara: ABC-Clio, 2003. Useful account of the Court's decisions concerning slavery, federalism, and property rights from 1836 to 1864.

Keck, Thomas M. *The Most Activist Supreme Court in History: The Road to Modern Judicial Conservatism.* Chicago: University of Chicago Press, 2004. Despite conservatives' long-standing advocacy of judicial restraint, Keck finds that both liberal and conservative justices on the Rehnquist Court actively attempted to overturn legislation and precedents that they disliked.

Lazarus, Edward. *Closed Chambers: The Rise, Fall, and Future of the Modern Supreme Court.* New York: Penguin Books, 1999. Justice Harry A. Blackmun's former law clerk concentrates on capital punishment, race relations, and abortion to describe a sometimes dysfunctional court engaging in jealous and partisan bickering and rubber-stamping opinions written by clerks. Some of his contentions have been criticized as inaccurate.

Leuchtenberg, William E. *The Supreme Court Reborn: The Constitutional Revolution in the Age of Roosevelt.* New York: Oxford University Press, 1995. The work of a noted pro-New Deal historian, presenting a comprehensive description of the Court's turn from laissez-faire to activist government.

Levy, Leonard W. *Legacy of Suppression: Freedom of Speech and Press in Early American History.* Cambridge, Mass.: Harvard University Press, 1960. While arguing that the Alien and Sedition Acts of 1798 were probably consistent with the original understanding of the First Amendment, Levy gives low marks to both Federalists and Republicans on issues of civil liberties.

Lurie, Jonathan. *The Chase Court: Justices, Rulings, and Legacy.* Santa Barbara: ABC-Clio, 2004. Useful account of the work of the Court from 1864 to 1873.

McKenna, Marian. *Franklin Roosevelt and the Great Constitutional War: The Court-Packing Crisis of 1937.* New York: Fordham University Press, 2002. Portrays President Franklin D. Roosevelt as initiating a "reorganization of the federal judiciary" on the advice of Attorney General Homer Cummings with the support of a "grad coalition."

Murphy, Paul L. *The Constitution in Crisis Times, 1918-1969.* New York: Harper & Row, 1972. Critical analysis of the Supreme Court's treatment of civil liberties during wars and periods of concern for natural security.

Renstrom, Peter. *The Stone Court: Justices, Rulings, and Legacy.* Santa Barbara: ABC-Clio, 2003. Useful account of the work of the Court during World War II.

Scaturro, Frank J. *The Supreme Court's Retreat from Reconstruction: A Distortion of Constitutional Jurisprudence.* Westport, Conn.: Greenwood Press, 2000. Castigates the Court for not opposing the development of Jim Crow, arguing that the Court departed from the intent of the Framers of the Fourteenth and Fifteenth Amendments.

Schwartz, Herman, ed. *The Burger Court: Counter-Revolution or Confirmation?* New York: Oxford University Press, 1998. Impressive collection of writings about the Supreme Court and its controversial rulings during the often tumultuous period from 1969 to 1987, with writings by distinguished legal scholars and practitioners.

Silver, David M. *Lincoln's Supreme Court.* Urbana: University of Illinois Press, 1998. Classic study of President Abraham Lincoln's manipulation of the Supreme Court during the Civil War in order to attain maximum discretion.

Tushnet, Mark. *A Court Divided: The Rehnquist Court and the Future of Constitutional Law.* New York: W. W. Norton, 2005. Balanced work arguing that the rumors of a "Rehnquist Revolution" were highly exaggerated, in large part because of the conservative justices' strong disagreements on abortion and other social issues.

Urofsky, Melvin I. *Division and Discord: The Supreme Court Under Stone and Vinson, 1941-1953.* Columbia: University of South Carolina Press, 1997. Readable and often entertaining account of strong and combative justices on the Court wrestling with the issues associated with World War II and the Cold War.

Wiecek, William. *The History of the Supreme Court of the United States: The Birth of the Modern Constitution, 1941-1953.* New York: Cambridge University Press, 2006. Scholarly and highly detailed study of the important changes in the twelve years before Earl Warren became chief justice.

Woodward, Bob, and Scott Armstrong. *The Brethren: Inside the Supreme Court.* New York: Simon & Schuster, 1979. Based primarily on interviews with former clerks, the book provides informative and interesting and informative insight into the personalities and ideas of the justices during the first decade of the Burger Court.

Yarbrough, Tinsley. *The Burger Court: Justices, Rulings, and Legacy.* Santa Barbara: ABC-Clio, 2000. Part of the publisher's Supreme Court Handbooks Series, the book provides a balanced analysis of the rulings of the Court and their impact from 1969 until 1986.

The Court and Rights and Liberties

Abraham, Henry, and Barbara Perry. *Freedom and the Court: Civil Rights and Liberties in the United States.* 8th ed. Lawrence: University Press of Kansas, 2003. Readable, lively, and trustworthy text of how the Supreme Court has interpreted the Bill of Rights and the Fourteenth Amendment, providing both technical analysis and discussion of the human impact.

Abrams, Floyd. *Speaking Freely: Trials of the First Amendment.* New York: Penguin Books, 2006. Written by one of the premier First Amendment lawyers, the book has discussions of modern controversies such as campaign finance reform and rights of journalists, as well as comparison with other countries.

Alderman, Ellen, and Caroline Kennedy. *In Our Defense: The Bill of Rights in Action.* New York: Avon Books, 1991. Highly readable and compelling work that includes nineteen vignettes of real-life cases in which ordinary people have relied upon one or more of the liberties and rights guaranteed by the first ten amendments.

Alley, Robert. *The Constitution and Religion: Leading Supreme Court Cases on Church and State.* New York: Prometheus Books, 1998. This collection presents full texts of the most significant cases on the topic in a comprehensive and nonpartisan fashion and includes reference to debates on original intent.

Amar, Akhil Reed. *The Bill of Rights: Creation and Reconstruction.* New Haven, Conn.: Yale University Press, 2000. Historical approach, arguing that the

Reconstruction projects and particularly the Fourteenth Amendment transformed the Bill of Rights in applying to the states and in protecting the rights of minorities.

Ball, Howard. *The Supreme Court and the Intimate Lives of Americans: Birth, Sex, Marriage, Childrearing, and Death.* New York: New York University Press, 2004. Analysis of the controversial "liberty interest" issues, including abortion, parental rights, gay rights, the right to die, and physician-assisted suicides.

Barnett, Randy, ed. *The Rights Retained by the People: The History and Meaning of the Ninth Amendment.* Fairfax, Va.: George Mason University Press, 1989. Excellent collection of essays advocating a variety of interpretations about the most elusive of the first ten amendments.

Bartee, Alice F. *Privacy Rights: Cases Lost and Cases Won Before the Supreme Court.* New York: Rowman & Littlefield, 2006. Examines the arguments and processes behind eight historic decisions concerning four privacy issues: birth control, gay rights, abortion, and the right to die.

Bradley, Craig. *The Failure of the Criminal Procedure Revolution.* Philadelphia: University of Pennsylvania Press, 1993. Compared with other industrial countries, Craig argues that the piecemeal, case-by-case development of criminal procedures has produced a system that is overly complex and cumbersome. He advocates a comprehensive code that is nationally applicable.

Cortner, Richard C. *The Supreme Court and the Second Bill of Rights: The Fourteenth Amendment and the Nationalization of the Bill of Rights.* Madison: University of Wisconsin Press, 1981. Brilliant account of the development of the incorporation doctrine and its application to the first eight amendments.

Curtis, Michael Kent. *No State Shall Abridge: The Fourteenth Amendment and the Bill of Rights.* Durham: Duke University Press, 1990. Professor Curtis makes a strong case for the controversial thesis that the Republicans who framed the Fourteenth Amendment intended to make the first eight amendments—or at least most of their provisions—applicable to the states.

Davis, Abraham L., and Barbara Luck Graham. *The Supreme Court, Race, and Civil Rights: From Marshall to Rehnquist.* Thousand Oaks, Calif.: Sage Publications, 1995. Combines a narrative text with cases emphasizing the human dimensions of the politically disadvantaged in each historical era, with about three-quarters of the book devoted to the Court under Earl Warren, Warren E. Burger, and William H. Rehnquist.

Ely, James, Jr. *The Guardian of Every Other Right: The Constitutional History of Property Rights.* New York: Oxford, 1992. Scholarly and interesting account, with a great deal of information of topics such as the takings clause and the liberty of contract doctrine.

Epstein, Lee, and Thomas G. Walker. *Constitutional Law for a Changing America: Rights, Liberties, and Justice.* 5th ed. Washington, D.C.: CQ Press, 2003. Designed for undergraduate college students, this work combines an interesting and scholarly narrative with many selections from Supreme Court cases.

Foley, Michael. *Arbitrary and Capricious: The Supreme Court, the Constitution, and the Death Penalty.* New York: Praeger, 2003. Dispassionate history of almost one hundred rulings on capital punishment from 1878 to 2002, concluding that the quest for a fair and discrimination-free process remains as elusive as ever.

Glendon, Mary Ann. *Rights Talk: The Impoverishment of Political Discourse.* New York: Free Press, 1993. Polemical work arguing that a single-minded emphasis on individual legal entitlements has distracted from other values such as care, responsibility, and practical compromises.

Hall, Kermit, ed. *By and for the People: Constitutional Rights in American History.* Arlington Heights, Ill.: Harlan Davidson, 1991. Commemorating the bicentennial of the Bill of Rights, this volume brings together eleven concisely written articles about significant aspects of the amendments, each written by an authority in the field.

Hixson, Richard. *Pornography and the Justices: The Supreme Court and the Intractable Obscenity Problem.* Carbondale: Southern Illinois University Press, 1996. Chronological examination of how the Court has dealt with obscene material within the context of decision making in evolving social mores.

Howard, John R. *The Shifting Wind: The Supreme Court and Civil Rights from Reconstruction to Brown.* Albany: State University of New York Press, 1999. Study of how the Court allowed the establishment of Jim Crow segregation in the late nineteenth century and then worked gradually to dismantle it.

Kalven, Harry, Jr. *A Worthy Tradition: Freedom of Speech in America.* New York: Harper & Row, 1988. Scholarly account of cases dealing with free expression from 1919 to 1974.

Klarman, Michael J. *From Jim Crow to Civil Rights: The Supreme Court and the Struggle for Racial Equality.* New York: Oxford University Press, 2006. Detailed account of how the constitutional law on race changed from *Plessy v. Ferguson* (1896) to *Brown v. Board of Education* (1954).

Kopel, David, Stephen Halbrook, and Alan Korwin. *Supreme Court Gun Cases: Two Centuries of Gun Rights Revealed.* Phoenix, Ariz.: Bloomfield Press, 2004. Finding ninety-two relevant cases, this controversial book argues that the Supreme Court has recognized gun possession as a personal right.

Latzer, Barry. *Death Penalty Cases: Leading U.S. Supreme Court Cases on Capital Punishment.* Burlington, Mass.: Butterworth Heinemann, 1997. After an introductory chapter, Latzer presents excerpts from twenty-two cases between 1968 and 1991, omitting most footnotes and citations but preserving the essence of the arguments and reasoning.

Levy, Leonard. *The Establishment Clause: Religion and the First Amendment.* Durham: University of North Carolina Press, 1994. Written from a pro-separatist perspective, an eminent professor discusses the formation of the establishment clause and includes two thought-provoking chapters about Supreme Court decisions on cases involving aid to parochial schools, religious ceremonies, and nativity scenes.

Mackey, Thomas C. *Pornography on Trial: A Handbook with Cases, Laws, and Documents.* Santa Barbara: ABC-Clio, 2003. Well-written and organized handbook that can be used by researchers as well as students and general readers.

McKinnon, Catherine. *Only Words.* Cambridge, Mass.: Harvard University Press, 1996. The intellectual leader of feminine legal theory, McKinnon argues that the goal of equality justifies proscribing those forms of pornography that degrade or subordinate women.

Manfredi, Christopher P. *The Supreme Court and Juvenile Justice.* Lawrence: University Press of Kansas, 1997. Manfredi provides a readable and insightful historical treatment of the evolution of the juvenile court movement, with the weight of the treatment on discussions of *Kent v. United States* (1966) and *In re Gault* (1967).

Morgan, Richard E. *Disabling America: The "Rights Industry" in Our Time.* New York: Basic Books, 1984. Conservative attack on the Supreme Court's expansive interpretations of defendants' rights since the due process revolution of the Warren Court.

Murphy, Paul L. *The Meaning of Free Speech: First Amendment Freedoms from Wilson to Roosevelt.* Westport, Conn.: Greenwood Press, 1972. Excellent discussion of free-speech controversies during the two decades following World War I.

Noonan, John T., Jr., and Edward Gaffney, Jr. *Religious Freedom: History, Cases, and Other Materials on the Interaction of Religion and Government.* New York: Foundation Press, 2001. Valuable collection of more than nine hundred pages of documents and essays about religious freedom and governmental relationship to religion from the colonial period until the twenty-first century.

Peck, Robert S. *Libraries, the First Amendment, and Cyberspace: What You Need to Know.* Chicago: American Library Association, 1999. Written for librarians by a lawyer who specializes in First Amendment issues, this is a useful guide about topics like confidentiality laws, the exclusion of "indecent" materials, and inappropriate uses of the Internet.

Perry, Michael J. *We the People: The Fourteenth Amendment and the Bill of Rights.* New York: Oxford University Press, 2001. Denying that the modern Supreme Court has engineered a "judicial usurpation of politics," Perry generally defends the Court's application of the Fourteenth Amendment in the areas of racial segregation, affirmative action, abortion, and discrimination based on sex and sexual orientation.

Peters, Shawn. *Judging Jehovah's Witnesses: Religious Persecution and the Dawn of the Rights Revolution.* Lawrence: University Press of Kansas, 2000. Vivid analysis of the legal suppression of members of the Jehovah's Witnesses from 1938 to 1955 and how their struggle expanded civil liberties.

Price, Polly J. *Property Rights: Rights and Liberties Under the Law.* Santa Barbara: ABC-Clio, 2003. Historical account of the constitutional status of private property; written for a general audience.

Rehnquist, William. *All the Laws but One: Civil Liberties in Wartime.* New York: Alfred A. Knopf, 1999. In this interesting analysis that emphasizes the experiences of the Civil War and World War II, Chief Justice Rehnquist argues that wars necessitate a balancing between constitutional liberties and the demands of national security.

Saunders, Kevin. *Violence as Obscenity: Limiting the Media's First Amendment Protection.* Durham: Duke University Press, 1996. Argues that the definition of obscenity should be expanded to include explicit and offensive violence, which should be regulated because of its harm to society.

Savage, David. *The Supreme Court and Individual Rights.* Washington, D.C.: CQ Press, 2004. Written by an outstanding scholar, this is an excellent historical account current through the Court's 2002-2003 term.

Schwartz, Bernard. *The Great Rights of Mankind: A History of the American Bill of Rights.* New York: Roland & Littlefield, 1998. Perhaps the best short history about the first ten amendments, including summaries of major judicial interpretations through the Rehnquist Court.

Smith, Jeffrey. *War and Press Freedom: The Problem of Prerogative Power.* New York: Oxford University Press, 1999. Richly documented work about the restrictions on the press in the name of "national security" from the adoption of the First Amendment until the Gulf War of 1991. A professor of journalism, Smith argues that unrestricted freedom of the press is less dangerous than governmental suppression.

Smith, Rodney K. *Public Prayer and the Constitution.* Wilmington, Del.: Scholarly Resources, 1987. Cogent analysis of the Constitution's establishment clause, rejecting the idea of a "wall of separation" in favor or Madison's view that the government should neither promote nor proscribe religious observations.

Spitzer, Robert J. *The Right to Bear Arms: Rights and Liberties Under the Law.* Santa Barbara: ABC-Clio, 2001. History of the Second Amendment and its controversies, including the relevant opinions by the Supreme Court.

Stossen, Nadine. *Defending Pornography: Free Speech, Sex, and the Fight for Women's Rights.* New York: New York University Press, 2000. A former president of the American Civil Liberties Union, Stossen argues that pornography's good effects outweigh the bad—thus any attempt to censor pornography produces more evils than it prevents.

Urofsky, Melvin I., ed. *One Hundred Americans Making Constitutional History: A Biographical History.* Washington, D.C.: CQ Press, 2004. Collection of the stories, each in about two thousand words, about the key individuals whose cases resulted in Supreme Court decisions.

Volokh, Eugene. *First Amendment: Law, Cases, Problems, and Policy Arguments.* New York: Foundation Press, 2001. Exhaustive collection of documents and commentary related to the principles of the First Amendment.

Wallace, Jonathan, and Mark Manga. *Sex, Laws, and Cyberspace.* New York: M & T Books, 1996. Balanced work that examines the complex issues relating to free expression over the Internet, with suggested compromises for monitoring the Internet while preserving the values of the First Amendment.

Whitebread, Charles, and Paul Marcus. *Gilbert Law Summaries: Criminal Procedure.* 16th ed. New York: Harcourt Brace Jovanovich Legal and Professional Publications, 2004. Clearly written and concise reference summarizing the Supreme Court's rulings in all areas of criminal procedures.

Wilson, Donald Jackson. *Even the Children of Strangers: Equality Under the U.S. Constitution.* Lawrence: University Press of Kansas, 1993. Traces the complex meanings that have been attached to the notion of equal protection during its evolving treatment by the Supreme Court and uses the methodology of social sciences to establish an argument that entitlement to equal protection should always be presumed.

Constitutional Interpretation

Barber, Sotirios A. *The Constitution of Judicial Power: Defending the Activist Tradition.* Baltimore, Md.: Johns Hopkins University Press, 1997. Criticizing moral relativism, Barber argues that judicial activism is traceable to *The Federalist Papers* (1788) but must be properly rooted in a philosophy of moral realism to be sound and effective.

Berger, Raoul. *Government by Judiciary: The Transformation of the Fourteenth Amendment.* Cambridge, Mass.: Harvard University Press, 1977. A conservative defender of states' rights, Berger rejects the idea that the Framers of the Fourteenth Amendment meant to apply the first eight amendments to the states, and he criticizes the modern Supreme Court for failing to give proper weight to the Framers' intent.

Bickel, Alexander M. *The Least Dangerous Branch: The Supreme Court at the Bar of Politics.* New Haven, Conn.: Yale University Press, 1990. An eminent law professor who advocated judicial restraint, Bickel writes that *Marbury v. Madison* (1803) provided a somewhat shaky foundation for the practice of judicial review and argues that decisions opposed by the majority of the people will not endure in the long term.

Bobbitt, Philip. *Constitutional Fate: Theory of the Constitution.* New York: Oxford University Press, 1984. Systematic analysis of the nature of interpretation, considering six types of constitutional arguments: historical, textual, structural, prudential, doctrinal, and ethical.

Bork, Robert. *The Tempting of America: The Political Seduction of the Law.* New York: Macmillan, 1990. Scholarly but accessible critique of legal activism and a powerful and eloquent polemic cogently arguing the necessity of returning to the original intent of the authors of the Constitution. The tone of the work is sometimes angry.

Breyer, Stephen G. *Active Liberty: Interpreting our Democratic Constitution.* New York: Alfred A. Knopf, 2005. Disagreeing with Justice Antonin Scalia's emphasis on original intent and literalism, Justice Breyer argues that abstract conceptions like "due process" should be interpreted according to the broad democratic goals of the Constitution.

Cox, Archibald. *The Court and the Constitution.* Boston: Houghton Mifflin, 1987. This historically organized work reviews the issues and debates of various eras to demonstrate the process by which the Court continually keeps the Constitution a vital and creative instrument of government.

Dworkin, Ronald. *Freedom's Law: The Moral Reading of the Constitution.* Cambridge, Mass.: Harvard University Press, 1996. Series of essays by a liberal theorist advocating the use of abstract moral principles at the most general possible level in interpreting the text of the U.S. Constitution.

Ely, John Hart. *Democracy and Distrust: A Theory of Judicial Review.* New York: Oxford University Press, 1990. Important work of jurisprudence that advocates special judicial protection for democratic processes, including free expression, while favoring judicial restraint toward legislative choices. Ely rejects the substantive due process doctrine and denies that the Constitution protects a right to abortion.

Kahn, Ronald. *The Supreme Court and Constitutional Theory, 1953-1993.* Lawrence: University Press of Kansas, 1994. In an effort to revise and clarify the perceptions of the Court under Warren E. Burger, Kahn begins by refining and clarifying the essence of the Warren Court and then embarks on an illuminating comparison.

Leyh, Gregory, ed. *Legal Hermeneutics: History, Theory, and Practice.* Berkeley: University of California Press, 1992. Fourteen interesting essays with a diversity of viewpoints about the historical and philosophical assumptions about the nature of language and the art of interpretation.

Nelson, William E. *The Fourteenth Amendment from Political Principle to Judicial Doctrine.* Cambridge, Mass.: Harvard University Press, 1995. Nelson argues that the Framers of the Fourteenth Amendment wanted to affirm the public's long-standing rhetoric of equality, which gives support to the expansive interpretations of the equal protection clause during the twentieth century.

Posner, Richard A. *Problematics of Moral and Legal Theory.* Cambridge, Mass.: Harvard University Press, 1999. Posner, a brilliant judge known for his use of economic theory, argues that moral philosophy is too subjective to be useful in constitutional interpretation, and he endorses pragmatic and empirical conclusions based on concrete facts.

Scalia, Antonin. *A Matter of Interpretation: Federal Courts and the Law.* Princeton, N.J.: Princeton University Press, 1999. Justice Scalia condemns the idea of a "living Constitution," advocates constitutional interpretation based on textual analysis and a search for the original meaning—not subjective intent—and advocates the same approach in constitutional and statutory interpretations. The volume includes critiques by Lawrence Tribe and others.

Segal, Jeffrey, and Harold Spaeth. *Supreme Court and the Attitudinal Model Revised.* New York: Cambridge University Press, 2006. Criticizing the "legal model," two political scientists argue that the justices' ideological views on issues such as business regulation provide the best means for explaining and predicting their decisions.

Tribe, Lawrence, and Michael Dorf. *On Reading the Constitution.* Cambridge, Mass.: Harvard University Press, 1991. Brief defense of a broad and liberal interpretation of the Constitution, combining the common-law tradition, textual analysis, and concern for American values. Its discussions of the Ninth Amendment and *Bowers v. Hardwick* (1986) are especially interesting.

Wellington, Harry H. *Interpreting the Constitution: The Supreme Court and the Process of Adjudication.* New Haven, Conn.: Yale University Press, 1991. Covering a range of cases from 1803 to 1973, Wellington treats the Constitution as a living document and rejects the utility and even the possibility of interpreting it solely in terms of the original intent of its Framers.

Whittington, Kenneth. *Constitutional Interpretation: Textual Meaning, Original Intent, and Judicial Review.* Lawrence: University Press of Kansas, 2001. Cogent defense of moderate "originalism," insisting that it is possible to know some of the principles of the Framers of the Constitution. Whittington criticizes the subjectivism of contemporary postmodernism and deconstructionism.

Court Rulings

Baker, Liva. *Miranda: Crime, Law, and Politics.* New York: Atheneum, 1983. Detailed account that places the pivotal *Miranda v. Arizona* case within the context of sociopolitical conceptions about criminal behavior in the modern era.

Epps, Garrett. *To an Unknown God: Religious Freedom on Trial.* New York: St. Martin's Press, 2001. Detailed account of *Employment Division v. Smith*

(1990), in which Native American Al Smith's religious use of peyote led to decisions providing less protection for religious freedom.

Fehrenbacher, Don E. *The Dred Scott Case: Its Significance in American Law and Politics.* New York: Oxford University Press, 2001. Masterful examination of the Court's most infamous ruling, placing it within the legal aspects of the slavery controversy.

Fisher, Louis. *In the Name of National Security: Unchecked Presidential Power and the Reynolds Case.* Lawrence: University Press of Kansas, 2006. Examination of *United States v. Reynolds* (1953), which established the right of the federal government when sued to withhold evidence in the name of national security.

_______. *Nazi Saboteurs on Trial: A Military Tribunal and American Law.* Lawrence: University Press of Kansas, 2003. Study of the World War II case *Ex parte Quirin,* arguing that the justices yielded to public pressure in failing to protect due process rights.

Friendly, Fred W. *Minnesota Rag: The Dramatic Story of the Landmark Supreme Court Cast That Gave New Meaning to Freedom of the Press.* New York: Random House, 1981. A television executive and professor of journalism, Friendly has written a colorful account of *Near v. Minnesota* (1931), a landmark case in the evolution of freedom of the press.

Friendly, Fred W., and Martha Elliott. *The Constitution: That Delegate Balance.* New York: Random House, 1984. Written to accompany a television series, this volume includes sixteen well-written and interesting chapters, each of which is devoted to one or more Supreme Court cases involving a constitutional right.

Garrow, David. *Liberty and Sexuality: The Right to Privacy and the Making of "Roe v. Wade."* Berkeley: University of California Press, 1998. A model of topnotch journalism, this meticulously researched and carefully presented work is a vast treatment of the political and legal debate over abortion spanning more than fifty years.

Irons, Peter. *The Courage of Their Convictions: Sixteen Americans Who Fought Their Way to the Supreme Court.* New York: Penguin Books, 1988. This fascinating work portrays pivotal cases touching on religion, race, protest, or privacy, from *Minersville School District v. Gobitis* (1940) to *Bowers v. Hardwick* (1986). Includes a lengthy statement by a principal in each of the cases.

_______. *Justice at War: The Story of the Japanese-American Internment Cases.* Berkeley: University of California Press, 1993. A lawyer who helped reverse some of the convictions he discusses, Irons provides an exhaustive account of *Hirabayashi v. United States* (1943) and *Korematsu v. United States* (1944).

Kens, Paul. *Judicial Power and Reform Politics: The Anatomy of "Lochner v. New York."* Lawrence: University Press of Kansas, 1990. Informed and readable account of the famous case that came to symbolize the early Supreme Court's use of the substantive due process doctrine to overturn labor regulations.

Labbe, Ronald M. *The Slaughterhouse Cases.* Lawrence: University Press of Kansas, 2006. Detailed examination of the Court's narrow interpretation of the privileges or immunities clause of the Fourteenth Amendment that prevented application of the Bill of Rights to the states through a half century.

Lewis, Anthony. *Gideon's Trumpet.* New York: Vintage Books, 1989. Originally published in 1964, this is the fascinating story of Clarence Gideon who established the right of poor persons to counsel in felony cases.

_______. *Make No Law: The "Sullivan" Case and the First Amendment.* New York: Random House, 1992. As a reporter, Lewis covered the development of the *New York Times Co. v. Sullivan* case, the libel suit that expanded the right to criticize public officials.

Killenbeck, Mark R. *McCulloch v. Maryland.* Lawrence: University Press of Kansas, 2006. The case that established Congress's broad discretion when passing laws "necessary and proper" to its enumerated powers.

Patterson, James T. *"Brown v. Board of Education": A Civil Rights Milestone and Its Troubled Legacy.* New York: Oxford University Press, 2002. Following a concise narrative with a fascinating cast of characters, Patterson argues that some of the unintended consequences of the *Brown* decision have not helped African Americans.

Schwartz, Bernard. *Behind "Bakke": Affirmative Action and the Supreme Court.* New York: New York University Press, 1988. Superb recounting of the *Bakke* case (1978) with the legal background and issues embedded in it.

Smolla, Rodney. *Jerry Falwell v. Larry Flint: The First Amendment on Trial.* New York: St. Martin's Press, 1988. Scholarly but highly readable analysis of an important freedom of speech case, written by a recognized authority on the First Amendment.

Swanson, Wayne. *The Christ Child Goes to Court.* Philadelphia: Temple University Press, 1989. Interesting case study of the crèche case, *Lynch v. Donnelly* (1984), providing detailed information about the judicial process as well as the local politics of Rhode Island.

Joseph M. McCarthy
Thomas T. Lewis

Supreme Court Justices

Justices who have served on the Supreme Court, with their dates of tenure given in parentheses. Asterisks (*) indicate tenure dates of chief justices. Justices whose names are followed by two sets of dates served as both associate and chief justices. Crosses (†) after dates indicate terms of justices who died in office. For the justices' vital dates and other information, see the essays on individual justices.

Samuel A. Alito, Jr. (2006-   ) During his first term, supported exception to the exclusionary rule in *Hudson v. Michigan*; defended special military commissions in *Hamdan v. Rumsfeld*; favored presidential prerogatives and property rights.

Henry Baldwin (1830-1844†) Moderate northerner who supported states' rights and viewed slaves a private property; wrote a book about the Constitution.

Philip P. Barbour (1836-1841†) Defended sovereignty of states in *New York v. Miln* (1837) and other cases.

Hugo L. Black (1937-1971) Outspoken proponent of "total incorporation" of first eight amendments to states in *Adamson v. California* (1947; dissent); advocated literal interpretations; defended Japanese relocation in *Korematsu v. United States* (1944); staunch opponent of substantive due process, as in *Griswold v. Connecticut* (1965; dissent); absolutist on First Amendment; liberal on civil rights except in later cases.

Harry A. Blackmun (1970-1994) Strong defender of generic right to privacy in *Roe v. Wade* (1973) and *Bowers v. Hardwick* (1986; dissent); advocate of affirmative action in *Regents of the University of California v. Bakke* (1978; dissent); increasingly liberal views on criminal due process and capital punishment.

John Blair, Jr. (1790-1795) Asserted judicial review on circuit in *Hayburn's Case* (1792); supported right of nonresidents to sue states in *Chisholm v. Georgia* (1793).

Samuel Blatchford (1882-1893†) Author of earliest opinions defending privilege against self-incrimination in *Counselman v. Hitchcock* (1892); defender of emerging substantive due process doctrine in *Chicago, Milwaukee, and St. Paul Railway Co. v. Minnesota* (1890).

Joseph P. Bradley (1870-1892†) Author of first significant interpretation of Fourth and Fifth Amendments in *Boyd v. United States* (1886); defended statute prohibiting women to practice law in *Bradwell v. Illinois* (1873); dissented in *Slaughterhouse Cases* (1793).

Louis D. Brandeis (1916-1939) Coauthor of influential article on "privacy" in 1890; wrote famous "Brandeis Brief" for *Muller v. Oregon* (1908); argued that liberty of Fourteenth Amendment went beyond property rights to protect personal freedoms of Bill of Rights in *Gilbert v. Minnesota* (1920; dissent); applied freedom of speech to states in *Whitney v. California* (1927); wrote that wiretapping fell under Fourth Amendment in *Olmstead v. United States* (1928; dissent).

William J. Brennan, Jr. (1956-1990) Arguably most influential liberal voice of his period; defended judicial supremacy in *Cooper v. Aaron* (1958); expanded protection for press freedom in *Roth v. United States* (1957) and *New York Times Co. v. Sullivan* (1964); emphasized protection for symbolic speech in *Texas v. Johnson* (1989); defended heightened judicial scrutiny for gender-based classifications in *Craig v. Boren* (1976); opposed all capital punishment in *Gregg v. Georgia* (1976); consistently defended privacy rights, abortion rights, and affirmative action.

David J. Brewer (1890-1910†) Conservative who wrote that "this is a Christian nation" in *Holy Trinity Church v. United States* (1892); supported substantive due process doctrine but upheld protection for women workers in *Muller v. Oregon* (1908); defended right of reasonable profit in regulated industries in *Reagan v. Farmers' Loan and Trust Co.* (1894); usually defended racial segregation, as in *Berea College v. Kentucky* (1908).

Stephen G. Breyer (1994-   ) Usually liberal but nondoctrinaire positions on criminal procedures, generic privacy, abortion rights, affirmative action, and federalism; proposed right to die "with dignity" in *Washington v. Glucksberg* (1997); joined minority in *Bush v. Gore* (2000); defended Court's consideration of foreign materials.

Henry B. Brown (1891-1906) Author of notorious "separate but equal" doctrine in *Plessy v. Ferguson* (1896); defended property rights and substantive due process, but recognized limits of freedom of contract doctrine in *Holden v. Hardy* (1898).

Warren E. Burger (1969-1986*) Moderate who criticized but failed to reverse Warren-era expansion of constitutional rights; devised three-pronged test for establishment of religion cases in *Lemon v. Kurtzman* (1971); formulated three-pronged test for obscenity in *Miller v. California* (1973); held that "gag orders" in criminal trial were last resort in *Nebraska Press Association v. Stuart* (1976); upheld federal affirmative action program in *Fullilove v. Klutznick* (1980); allowed Internal Revenue Service to tax racially segregated schools in *Bob Jones University v. United States* (1983).

Harold H. Burton (1945-1958) Moderate known for careful research and well crafted opinions. An outspoken opponent of racial discrimination and segregation; upheld state prosecutions of noncapital felonies without appointed counsel in *Bute v. Illinois* (1948); usually voted to uphold anticommunist policies of Truman administration.

Pierce Butler (1923-1939†) One of the conservative "Four Horsemen"; wrote defense of liberty of contract doctrine in *Morehead v. New York ex rel. Tipaldo* (1936); defended constitutionality of prior restraint of press in *Near v. Minnesota* (1931; dissent), but strongly condemned use of wiretaps in *Olmstead v. United States* (1928).

James F. Byrnes (1941-1942) Judicial conservative who wrote sixteen majority opinions during his one term in office; strengthened constitutional right to travel in *Edwards v. California* (1941).

John A. Campbell (1853-1861) Southerner who defended states' rights and took moderate position on slavery, while concurring in *Dred Scott v. Sandford* (1857); resigned after Civil War began and served as assistant secretary of war; as counsel in *Slaughterhouse Cases* (1873), helped advance doctrine of substantive due process.

Benjamin N. Cardozo (1932-1938†) Defender of sociological jurisprudence in his book *The Nature of the Judicial Process* (1922); defended theory of "selective incorporation" of Bill of Rights in *Palko v. Connecticut* (1937); critic of freedom of contract doctrine and defender of legislative authority for economic regulations; applied general welfare clause in New Deal programs, as in *Helvering v. Davis* (1937).

John Catron (1837-1865†) Jacksonian Democrat who defended states' right and slavery; concurred in *Dred Scott v. Sandford* (1857) but strongly opposed southern secession.

Salmon P. Chase (1864-1873*†) Abolitionist who served as Abraham Lincoln's treasury secretary; defended loyalty oath requirements for office in *Cummings v. Missouri* (1967; dissent); defended constitutional right of women to practice law in *Bradwell v. Illinois* (1873); disagreed with majority's narrow interpretation of Fourteenth Amendment in *Slaughterhouse Cases* (1873); opposed greenbacks; denied right of secession in *Texas v. White* (1969).

Samuel Chase (1796-1811†) Signer of Declaration of Independence and ardent federalist; only eighteenth century justice to reject federal common law of crimes; frequently defended doctrine of judicial review and proposed natural law interpretation of Constitution in *Calder v. Bull* (1798); defendant in impeachment trial of 1805.

Tom C. Clark (1949-1967) Supporter of exclusionary rule on states in *Mapp v. Ohio* (1961); banned religious ceremonies in public schools, *Abington School District v. Schempp* (1963); broadened concept of conscientious objector in *United States v. Seeger* (1965); overturned criminal conviction because of prejudicial publicity in *Sheppard v. Maxwell* (1966); angered President Truman in steel seizure case.

John H. Clarke (1916-1922) Supporter of convictions under Espionage Act of 1918 in *Abrams v. United States* (1919); defended broad congressional powers to regulate business in *Hammer v. Dagenhart* (1922).

Nathan Clifford (1858-1881†) Author of opinion that Court could declare congressional statute unconstitutional on grounds other than constitutional text, in *Loan Association v. Topeka* (1874).

Benjamin R. Curtis (1851-1857) Enunciator of "selective exclusiveness" doctrine of congressional power to regulate commerce, *Cooley v. Board of Wardens of the Port of Philadelphia* (1852); wrote Court's first extended analysis of due process clause in *Murray's Lessee v. Hoboken Land and Improvement Co.* (1856); his strong dissent in *Dred Scott v. Sandford* (1857) produced so much rancor that he resigned.

William Cushing (1790-1810†) Supporter of early form of judicial review in *Ware v. Hylton* (1796).

Peter V. Daniel (1842-1860†) Virginian who consistently advocated states' rights and opposed expansion of federal authority; held expansive view of states' eminent domain power in *West River Bridge Co. v. Dix* (1849); wrote that freed blacks could not be citizens in *Dred Scott v. Sandford* (1857).

David Davis (1862-1877) Friend of Abraham Lincoln who wrote *Ex parte Milligan* (1866), which disallowed military trials when civil courts were available.

William R. Day (1903-1922) Advocate of states' rights under Tenth Amendment, as in *Hammer v. Dagenhart* (1916), which overturned federal child labor act; wanted to limit individual liberty of contract claims in *Lochner v. New York* (1905; dissent); established exclusionary rule in federal Fourth Amendment cases, *Weeks v. United States* (1914).

William O. Douglas (1939-1975) Outspoken iconoclast known for expansive view of individual liberties; endorsed students' right to refuse to salute the flag in *West Virginia State Board of Education v. Barnette* (1943); reluctantly supported Japanese relocation in *Korematsu v. United States* (1944); wrote controversial *Terminiello v. Chicago* (1949), which reversed the speaker's conviction for insulting hostile mob; opposed governmental restrictions on obscenity; argued right of privacy based on "penumbras" of Bill of Rights in *Griswold v. Connecticut* (1965); recognized claim of trees to standing to bring lawsuits in *Sierra Club v. Morton* (1972; dissent); sometimes called "Wild Bill."

Gabriel Duvall (1811-1835) One of first justices to hold strong antislavery views; supported decisions of John Marshall, except for dissent in *Dartmouth College v. Woodward* (1819); ill health during his last decade.

Oliver Ellsworth (1796-1800*) Helped arrange Great Compromise in 1787; main author of Judicial Act of 1789; supporter of general expansion of federal courts; ill during most of his tenure; died on diplomatic mission to France to end war.

Stephen J. Field (1863-1897) Zealous advocate of inalienable rights, especially property rights; crusader for substantive due process as means for protecting businesses from government regulations, as accepted in *Allgeyer v. Louisiana* (1897); wrote that government had no constitutional power to force Americans to accept paper money as legal tender in *Knox v. Lee* (1871; dissent); opposed loyalty oath requirements for elected offices.

Abe Fortas (1965-1969) As private lawyer, successfully argued *pro bono* case, *Gideon v. Wainwright* (1963), which established right of indigents to counsel in felony cases; interpreted due process clause as broad guarantee of fairness; expanded many due process protections to juvenile offenders in *In re Gault* (1967); recognized students' rights to nondisruptive protests in *Tinker v. Des Moines Independent Community School District* (1969); struck down state prohibition of teaching evolution in *Epperson v. Arkansas* (1968).

Felix Frankfurter (1939-1962) Advocate of judicial self-restraint, with justices carefully balancing complex constitutional principles; denied that all of Bill of Rights applied to states in *Adamson v. California* (1947; concurrence); held that states were not required to follow exclusionary rule in *Wolf v. Colorado* (1949); wanted to allow states to require flag salute rituals, *West Virginia Board of Education v. Barnette* (1943; dissent); strong opponent of racial segregation; demanded strict separation of church and state in *Everson v. Board of Education of Ewing Township* (1947; dissent); highly subjective interpretation of due process in *Rochin v. California* (1952).

Melville W. Fuller (1888-1910*) Strong defender of private property; wrote that Tenth Amendment prohibited federal police powers in *Champion v. Ames* (1903; dissent); accepted racial segregation and wrote that Fourteenth Amendment produced "no revolutionary change"; narrow view of Sherman Act; invalidated income tax in *Pollock v. Farmers' Loan and Trust Co.* (1895).

Ruth Bader Ginsburg (1993-) As a lawyer, argued cases before Court that established intermediate scrutiny for gender-based classifications; consistent supporter of affirmative action, abortion rights, and expansive role for federal government; wrote majority opinion in *United States v. Virginia* (1996), striking down male-only policy of military schools; opposed public funds for special services in religious schools in *Agostini v. Felton* (1997; dissent); dissented in *Bush v. Gore* (2000).

Arthur J. Goldberg (1962-1965) Supporter of legal equality and rights of criminal defendants; recognized defendant's right to remain silent in absence of counsel in *Escobedo v. Illinois* (1964); defended Ninth Amendment rights in *Griswold v. Connecticut* (1965; concurrence); held that association rights could only be infringed by "compelling state interest," *Gilson v. Florida Legislative Investigation Committee* (1963); ruled that foreign travel was protected by Fifth Amendment in *Aptheker v. Secretary of State* (1964).

Horace Gray (1882-1902†) Supporter of expansive view of congressional powers and attempted to limit applications of substantive due process; accepted citizenship of anyone born in United States, regardless of race or national origin, in *United States v. Wong Kim Ark* (1898).

Robert C. Grier (1846-1870) Generally supporter of states' rights view of Tenth Amendment; sanctioned double jeopardy for those who aided runaway slaves in *Moore v. Illinois* (1852).

John Marshall Harlan (1877-1911†) Author of more dissenting opinions that would eventually become law than any other justice; although former slave holder, opposed racial segregation and dissented in *Plessy v. Ferguson* (1896); rejected strict applications of freedom of contract doctrine, as in *Lochner v. New York* (1905; dissent); argued for incorporation of all of first eight amendments into Fourteenth Amendment, as in *Hurtado v. California* (1884; dissent).

John M. Harlan II (1955-1971) Interpreter of due process clause as body of evolving principles rather than shorthand formula for first eight amendments; opinion in *National Association for the Advancement of Colored People v. Alabama* (1958) was first to protect First Amendment freedom of association; interpreted Smith Act so that prosecution of subversive activities was difficult; used substantive due process to protect privacy in *Poe v. Ullman* (1961) and later; opposed Miranda restrictions on police interrogations; interpreted Fourth Amendment as requiring "reasonable expectation of privacy," in *Katz v. United States* (1967; concurrence).

Oliver Wendell Holmes (1902-1932) Perhaps most influential twentieth century justice; argued for judicial restraint when applying substantive due process doctrine and rejected generic right of privacy; formulated libertarian "clear and present danger" test for regulating speech in *Abrams v. United States* (1919; dissent); supported eugenics policies in *Buck v. Bell* (1927); did not believe that wiretaps were forbidden by Fourth Amendment; formulated modern view of takings clause in *Pennsylvania Coal Co. v. Mahon* (1922).

Charles Evans Hughes (1910-1916; 1930-1941*) Moderately progressive Republican who strongly defended free expression rights in *Stromberg v. California* (1931) and *Near v. Minnesota* (1931); insisted on fair procedures in criminal trials, as in *Powell v. Alabama* (1932); author of *West Coast Hotel Co. v. Parrish* (1937), which ended use of substantive due process to overturn economic regulations.

Ward Hunt (1873-1882) Usually supporter of legislation protecting rights of African Americans; in circuit trial, rejected Susan Anthony's claim that Fourteenth Amendment applied to voting rights for women.

James Iredell (1790-1799†) Generally defender of states' rights; dismissed natural law approach to judicial review and argued that Court should overturn statutes only if they contradicted written Constitution in *Calder v. Bull* (1798).

Howell E. Jackson (1893-1895†) Moderate southerner who supported an expansive role for national government; strongly dissented on income tax in *Pollock v. Farmers' Loan & Trust* (1895).

Robert H. Jackson (1941-1954†) Supporter of national power over that of states; wrote classic defense of freedom of expression in *West Virginia Board of Education v. Barnette* (1943); balanced expressive freedom with need for public order in *Terminiello v. Chicago* (1949; dissent); supported vigorous prosecution of Communists in cases such as *Dennis v. United States* (1951); advocated caution when overturning racial segregation; argued for judicial self-restraint in his book *The Struggle for Judicial Supremacy* (1941); criticized for serving as prosecutor in the Nuremburg Trials.

John Jay (1789-1795*) First chief justice; committed nationalist who made substantial contributions to the development of a strong Supreme Court; opposed states' sovereign immunity in *Chisholm v. Georgia* (1793); negotiated unpopular Jay's Treaty while on Court.

Thomas Johnson (1792-1793) Maryland politician who wrote the Court's first published opinion in *Georgia v. Brailsford* (1792), dissenting from the majority's granting of an injunction on a loyalist's claim.

William Johnson (1804-1834†) Independent Jeffersonian southerner who supported broad congressional power to regulate commerce but held that federal judges had no authority to create or enforce common-law crimes in *United States v. Hudson and Goodwin* (1812); a slave owner who denounced the denial of due process to slave rebel Denmark Vessey. Called the "first dissenter."

Anthony M. Kennedy (1988-) Moderate conservative, often casting the swing vote, especially on issues of individual liberty and abortion; approved mandatory drug tests when justified for public safety in *Skinner v. Railway Labor Executives Association* (1989); proposed no-coercion standard for religious establishment cases in *Lee v. Weisman* (1992); joined majority in *Bush v. Gore* (2000); a strong supporter of gay rights, as in *Lawrence v. Texas* (2003); endorsed use of international law.

Joseph Lamar (1911-1916†) Usually supported the majority; expanded delegation to executive branch in *United States v. Grimaud* (1911); ignored free speech claims in *Gompers v. Buck's Stove and Range Co.* (1911); diplomatic mission to Latin America in 1914.

Lucius Q. C. Lamar (1888-1893†) Southerner called the "great pacificator"; usually voted with majority in Fuller Court; supporter of broad legislative discretion to formulate public policy, as in *Chicago, Milwaukee, and St. Paul Railroad Co. v. Minnesota* (1890).

Brockholst Livingston (1807-1823†) Approved state prosecutions of seditious libel while on New York Supreme Court; strong supporter of Chief Justice Marshall; eight opinions on prize ship cases; questions of his judicial ethics in communications about cases.

Horace H. Lurton (1910-1914†) Oldest man ever appointed; conservative judicial values; former Confederate officer who supported states' rights under the Tenth Amendment.

Joseph McKenna (1898-1925) Defender of expansive view of federal police power legislation in cases such as *Hoke v. United States* (1913) and *Adair v. United States* (1908; dissent), but found that due process clause prohibited minimum-wage laws in *Adkins v. Children's Hospital* (1923).

John McKinley (1838-1852†) Kentuckian who supported state sovereignty in *Bank of Augusta v. Earle* (1839) and other cases; frequently absent from Court.

John McLean (1830-1861†) Opponent of slavery who dissented in *Prigg v. Pennsylvania* (1842) and *Dred Scott v. Sandford* (1857) but agreed that Congress had authorized fugitive slave law in *Jones v. Van Zandt* (1847); moderate on states' rights under Tenth Amendment.

James C. McReynolds (1914-1941) One of the "Four Horsemen" with conservative views on civil rights, First Amendment, defendants' rights, and economic regulations; saw no constitutional necessity for appointment of counsel in capital cases in *Powell v. Alabama* (1932; dissent); supported prosecution of young people for displaying red flag in *Stromberg v. California* (1931).

John Marshall (1801-1835*†) Remembered as the "great chief justice"; Federalist who asserted judicial review in *Marbury v. Madison* (1803); advocated broad interpretation of commerce clause, contract clause, and elastic clause, with narrow view of states' rights; ruled that Bill of Rights did not apply to states in *Barron v. Baltimore* (1833); often referred to natural rights in early years; author of Cherokee cases.

Thurgood Marshall (1967-1991) Committed African American liberal who consistently supported affirmative action programs, abortion rights, and strict application of exclusionary rule; defended broad view of free speech in *Police Department of Chicago v. Mosley* (1972); held that individuals have right to own obscene materials in private homes in *Stanley v. Georgia* (1969); argued that death penalty was always unconstitutional in *Gregg v. Georgia* (1976; dissent); proposed "sliding scale" model of judicial scrutiny in *San Antonio Independent School District v. Rodriguez* (1973).

Stanley Matthews (1881-1889†) Held that grand jury indictment was not essential under due process clause of Fourteenth Amendment in *Hurtado v. California* (1884); held that Fourteenth Amendment prohibited legislation with discriminatory results in *Yick Wo v. Hopkins* (1886).

Samuel F. Miller (1862-1890†) Supporter of narrow interpretation of Fourteenth Amendment so that none of Bill of Rights applied to states in *Slaughterhouse Cases* (1873); dismissed doctrine of substantive due process.

Sherman Minton (1949-1956) Advocate of judicial restraint toward legislative and executive branches; accepted restrictions on free speech and association in interest of national security; upheld New York law that prohibited members of subversive organizations from teaching in public schools in *Adler v. Board of Education* (1952).

William H. Moody (1906-1910) Had expansive views of congressional power over interstate commerce; refused to apply to states the privilege against self-incrimination in *Twining v. New Jersey* (1908).

Alfred Moore (1800-1804) His one recorded opinion, *Bas v. Tingy* (1800), held that France was an enemy nation in the undeclared naval war.

Frank Murphy (1940-1949†) Liberal who asserted that the Fourteenth Amendment made all of the first eight amendments plus other fundamental rights binding on states; included peaceful picketing as form of free speech in *Thornhill v. Alabama* (1940); excluded fighting words and obscenity from First Amendment protection in *Chaplinsky v. New Hampshire* (1942); denounced "legalization of racism" in *Korematsu v. United States* (1944; dissent); dissented when Court did not apply Fourth Amendment exclusionary rule to states in *Wolf v. Colorado* (1949).

Samuel Nelson (1845-1872) Supporter of states' rights under the Tenth Amendment; concurred in *Dred Scott v. Sandford* (1857), but did not endorse Taney's views on citizenship and the Missouri Compromise; minority in the Prize Cases (1863); strong proponent of judicial restraint.

Sandra Day O'Connor (1981-2006) Moderate conservative whose subtle distinctions often decided 5-4 votes; upheld right to abortion but defended "unduly burden" regulations in *Planned Parenthood v. Casey* (1992); allowed police to conduct noncoercive requests to search private belongings in *Florida v. Bostick* (1991); evaluated establishment cases with government endorsement of religion test, as in *Lynch v. Donnelly* (1984); required "strict scrutiny" test in affirmative action but upheld preferences in *Grutter v. Bollinger* (2003); joined the majority in *Bush v. Gore* (2000).

William Paterson (1793-1806†) Framer of the Constitution who espoused judicial review and supported supremacy of the federal government over states; participated in most cases of 1790's, including *Ware v. Hylton* (1796); upheld repeal of Judiciary Act of 1801.

Rufus W. Peckham (1896-1909†) Laissez-faire constitutionalist who wrote best-known substantive due process case, *Lochner v. New York* (1905); denied that first eight amendments were binding on states, as in *Maxwell v. Dow* (1900).

Mahlon Pitney (1912-1922) Strong defender of liberty of contract doctrine, as in *Wilson v. New York* (1917; dissent); took narrow view of defendants' rights in cases such as *Frank v. Mangum* (1915); rejected freedom of speech claims against Espionage Act of 1917, as in *Pierce v. United States* (1920).

Lewis F. Powell, Jr. (1972-1987) Moderate "balancer" who often provided swing vote; allowed racial preferences but not quotas in *Regents of the University of California v. Bakke* (1978); limited federal habeas corpus reviews of alleged Fourth Amendment violations in *Stone v. Powell* (1976); established balancing test for determining speedy trial requirement in *Barker v. Wingo* (1972); prohibited disproportionately severe penalties in noncapital cases in *Solem v. Helm* (1983); author of "open fields" exception in Fourth Amendment cases.

Stanley F. Reed (1938-1957) Economic liberal but generally conservative on issues of civil rights and liberties; wrote that the privilege against self-incrimination did not apply to states in *Adamson v. California* (1947); was last justice to join unanimous Court in *Brown v. Board of Education* (1954).

William H. Rehnquist (1972-1986; 1986-2005*†) As law clerk, wrote controversial memorandum defending "separate but equal" doctrine; defended capital punishment and opposed most Warren-era expansions of defendants' rights; rejected right to abortion in *Roe v. Wade* (1973) and later cases; opposed affirmative action; cautious on substantive due process; denied a constitutional right to assisted suicide; created public safety exception to the Miranda rule in *Quarles v. New York* (1984); expanded Fifth Amendment property rights in *Rolan v. City of Tigard* (1994); resurrected states' rights under Tenth and Eleventh Amendments; ordered end of Florida recount in *Bush v. Gore* (2000).

John G. Roberts, Jr. (2005- *) Moderate conservative on the D.C. Circuit Court. Usually joined the conservatives during his first term on issues of criminal justice, property rights, and executive power; recognized federal authority over Oregon's death with dignity law; supported exception for the exclusionary rule in *Hudson v. Michigan* (2006).

Owen J. Roberts (1930-1945) Author of decisions that often appeared to lack consistency; made famous "switch in time" to uphold minimum wage laws in *West Coast Hotel Co. v. Parrish* (1937); applied freedom of petition to states in *Hague v. Congress of Industrial Organizations* (1939); held that First Amendment religious freedom was binding on states in *Cantwell v. Connecticut* (1940); denied that states must provide counsel for indigent defendants in *Betts v. Brady* (1942); opposed Japanese displacement in *Korematsu v. United States* (1944; dissent); voted to uphold white primary in *Smith v. Allwright* (1944; dissent).

John Rutledge (1790-1791) Original member of the Court who served one uneventful year; agreed to return captured Dutch ship in his only opinion, *Talbot v. Janson* (1795).

Wiley B. Rutledge, Jr. (1943-1949†) Staunch liberal who defended preferred position of First Amendment freedoms in cases such as *Thomas v. Collins* (1945); argued that all of first eight amendments plus other rights were binding on states through Fourteenth Amendment; endorsed Japanese resettlement in *Korematsu v. United States* (1944).

Edward T. Sanford (1923-1930†) Moderate who wrote that freedom of speech guarantee of First Amendment was binding on states in landmark case, *Gitlow v. New York* (1925); often voted to uphold federal and state regulations of business.

Antonin Scalia (1986-) Staunch conservative who advocated textualism and original understanding in his book *A Matter of Interpretation* (1997); denied that Constitution protected right to abortions or generic right of privacy in *Cruzan v. Missouri Department of Health* (1990; concurrence); supported broad protections of private property through takings clause, as in *Lucas v. South Carolina Coastal Council* (1992); rejected strict scrutiny test for restrictions on religious liberty in *Employment Division, Department of Human Resources v. Smith* (1990); consistently opposed affirmative action; usually defended freedom of expression, as in flag burning and hate speech cases; ordered end of Florida recount in *Bush v. Gore* (2000); opposed references to international law.

George Shiras, Jr. (1892-1903) Frequent supporter of using substantive due process doctrine to overturn economic regulations; supported liberal view of due process rights of individuals, as in *Wong Wing v. United States* (1896).

David H. Souter (1990-) "Closet liberal" who defended expansive use of substantive due process in right of privacy cases, as in *Planned Parenthood v. Casey* (1992); consistent supporter of affirmative action and gay rights; skeptical of states' rights; narrow view of property rights; expansive view of defendants' rights; voted with the minority in *Bush v. Gore* (2000).

John Paul Stevens (1975-) Increasingly liberal positions on issues of civil liberty, affirmative action, and Fourth Amendment; held that police usually need warrant to enter private home for an arrest in *Payton v. New York* (1980); argued for single standard of review for all equal protection cases; overturned an anti-indecency statute for the Internet in *Reno v. ACLU* (1997); insisted on high wall between church and state in cases such as *Wallace v. Jaffree* (1985); espoused narrow property rights under takings clause; opposed the majority in *Bush v. Gore* (2000).

Potter Stewart (1959-1981) Moderate who often broke tie votes; expanded right to public demonstrations in *Edwards v. South Carolina* (1963); liberalized Fourth Amendment protections in *Katz v. United States* (1967); consistently favored strengthening free speech; opposed substantive due process in 1965, but endorsed doctrine in *Roe v Wade* (1973; concurrence); held that women had no constitutional right to public funding of abortions in *Harris v. McRae* (1980); upheld capital punishment with due process in *Gregg v. Georgia* (1976); opposed racial preferences.

Harlan Fiske Stone (1925-1941; 1941-1946*†) Supporter of presumption of constitutionality when examining governmental regulations of business; wrote seminal "footnote four" (1938), suggesting special judicial scrutiny for minority rights and constitutional prohibitions; wrote many liberal dissents, such as *Minersville School District v. Gobitis* (1940), later accepted by Court's majority.

Joseph Story (1812-1845†) Usually agreed with Chief Justice Marshall in federal powers over states, as in *Martin v. Hunter's Lessee* (1816); tried to harmonize natural justice and positive law in cases such as the one involving the schooner*La Jeune Eugénie* (1822); ardent supporter of private property; author of influential *Commentaries on the Constitution* (1833); often dissented from rulings by the Taney Court.

William Strong (1870-1880) Defender of right of African Americans to serve jury duties in *Strauder v. West Virginia* (1880); supported laws mandating Christian practices and advocated constitutional amendment to recognize "supreme authority" of Christian revelation.

George Sutherland (1922-1938) Intellectual spokesman for substantive due process and property rights, as in *Adkins v. Children's Hospital* (1923); favored selective application of first eight amendments to states; wrote opinions expanding rights of counsel and free expression, as in *Powell v. Alabama* (1932).

Noah H. Swayne (1862-1881) Dissenter in *Slaughterhouse Cases* (1873) and broadly interpreted individual rights under Fourteenth Amendment; defended Lincoln's policies restricting civil liberties; not considered an outstanding justice.

William H. Taft (1921-1930*) Former president who gave a narrow view of congressional power under Tenth Amendment in *Bailey v. Drexel Furniture Co.* (1922); articulated "automobile exception" to Fourth Amendment in *Carroll v. United States* (1925); allowed use of wiretaps without warrant in *Olmstead v. United States* (1928); despite conservatism, recognized legislative prerogatives in *Adkins v. Children's Hospital* (1923).

Roger Brooke Taney (1836-1864*†) Maryland Jacksonian who gave greater support for states' rights and less protection for private property than Marshall Court; applied Fifth Amendment to defend slave holders' rights in *Scott v. Sandford* (1857); condemned President Lincoln's "arbitrary arrests" in *Ex parte Merryman* (1861).

Clarence Thomas (1991-) Conservative African American who voted to restrict affirmative action, defendants' rights, and rights of privacy and abortion; expansive views of takings clause and states' rights under Tenth Amendment; endorsed "neutrality" and "permissible content" tests for aid to religious schools in *Mitchell v. Helms* (2000); open to natural law considerations; joined majority in *Bush v. Gore* (2000).

Smith Thompson (1824-1843†) Defender of states' authority over commerce unless directly conflicting with federal law; disagreed with Marshall in *Ogden v. Saunders* (1827); dissented in *Cherokee Nation v. Georgia* (1831).

Thomas Todd (1807-1826†) Jeffersonian who consistently supported Chief Justice Marshall; often absent because of illness and family affairs; more active on Seventh Circuit.

Robert Trimble (1826-1828†) Usually reliable supporter of Chief Justice Marshall's views on federalism, but dissented in *Ogden v. Saunders* (1827).

Willis Van Devanter (1911-1937) One of conservative "Four Horsemen" who consistently voted to support states' rights and the liberty of contract doctrine; voted to overturn New Deal laws and dissented from the more liberal post-1937 decisions.

Fred M. Vinson (1946-1953*†) Moderate conservative on issues of free speech and national security, as in *Dennis v. United States* (1951); opposed racial segregation in early civil rights cases such as *Sweatt v. Painter* (1950); wrote the *Steel Seizure Case* (1952); consider one of the less successful chief justices.

Morrison R. Waite (1874-1888*†) Supporter of restricting authority of Congress to protect civil rights in *United States v. Cruikshank* (1876); rejected substantive due process as barrier to government regulations of business in *Munn v. Illinois* (1877); held that prohibition on polygamy did not violate First Amendment in *Reynolds v. United States* (1879).

Earl Warren (1953-1969*) Chief justice who presided over unprecedented expansion of individual liberties and civil rights; held that due process clause of Fifth Amendment mandated equal protection and prohibited racial segregation in *Bolling v. Sharpe* (1954); demanded due process principles in congressional investigations in *Watkins v. United States* (1957); ruled that police must inform detained persons of constitutional rights in *Miranda v. Arizona* (1966); ruled antimiscegenation laws violated equal protection and substantive liberty in *Loving v. Virginia* (1967); interpreted Eighth Amendment in terms of "evolving standards of decency" in *Trop v. Dulles* (1958).

Bushrod Washington (1799-1829†) George Washington's favorite nephew who liberally defined privileges and immunities of national citizenship in *Corfield v. Coryell* (1823); enforced Sedition Act of 1798 while riding circuit.

James M. Wayne (1835-1867†) Southern slave holder who concurred in *Scott v. Sandford* (1857), asserting that the Missouri Compromise violated the Fifth Amendment; moderate on Tenth Amendment; stayed on the Court during the Civil War; upheld Lincoln's blockade in the *Prize Cases* (1863), but opposed test oaths after the war.

Byron R. White (1962-1993) Nondoctrinaire pragmatist who supported civil rights; gradually became critic of affirmative action; endorsed many restrictions on obscenity; supported prosecution of flag desecration; rejected idea of newsman's privilege; favored an accommodationist view on public support of religious schools; advocated limitations on exclusionary rule and opposed requirement of Miranda warnings; dissented in *Roe v. Wade* (1973); rejected constitutional rights for homosexual practices in *Bowers v. Hardwick* (1986).

Edward D. White (1894-1910; 1910-1921*†) Holder of erratic positions on governmental powers to regulate economy; held that Fifth Amendment did not apply to Native American courts in *Talton v. Mayes* (1896); endorsed military conscription in *Selective Draft Law Cases* (1918).

Charles E. Whittaker (1957-1962) Nonideological conservative who often provided swing vote in 5-4 decisions; one of first justices to apply equal protection clause to voting rights in *Gomillion v. Lightfoot* (1960; concurrence); wrote *Staub v. Baxley* (1958) overturning requirement of license with excessive discretion.

James Wilson (1789-1798†) Framer of the Constitution who combined ideas of popular sovereignty and strong national government in *Lectures on Law* (1790-1791); asserted doctrine of judicial review in *Hayburn's Case* (1792); opposed states' sovereign immunity in *Chisholm v. Georgia* (1793).

Levi Woodbury (1846-1851†) Defender of slavery who upheld the Fugitive Slave Law of 1793 in *Jones v. Van Zandt* (1847); usually supported the majority in the Taney Court, but dissented on grounds of states' rights in the *Passenger Cases* (1849).

William B. Woods (1881-1887†) Narrowly interpreted the Fourteenth Amendment; overturned the Ku Klux Klan Act of 1871 in *United States v. Harris* (1883) based on the Tenth Amendment; wrote that the Second Amendment was not binding on states in *Presser v. Illinois* (1886).

Justices Ranked by Years of Service (Through 2006)

Justice	*Begin*	*End*	*Years*
William O. Douglas	1939	1975	36
John Marshall	1801	1835	34
Hugo L. Black	1937	1971	34
William J. Brennan, Jr.	1956	1990	34
Stephen J. Field	1863	1897	34
John M. Harlan	1877	1911	34
Joseph Story	1812	1845	33
William H. Rehnquist	1972	2005	33
James M. Wayne	1835	1867	32
John Paul Stevens	1975	*	32
John McLean	1830	1861	31
Byron R. White	1962	1993	31
Oliver W. Holmes, Jr.	1902	1932	30
William Johnson	1804	1834	30
Bushrod Washington	1799	1829	30
John Catron	1837	1865	28
Roger B. Taney	1836	1864	28
Samuel F. Miller	1862	1890	28
Samuel Nelson	1845	1872	27
Joseph McKenna	1898	1925	27
James C. McReynolds	1914	1941	27
Edward D. White	1894	1921	27
Willis Van Devanter	1911	1937	26
Sandra Day O'Connor	1981	2006	25
Gabriel Duvall	1811	1835	24
Robert C. Grier	1846	1870	24
Harry A. Blackmun	1970	1994	24
Thurgood Marshall	1967	1991	24
Louis D. Brandeis	1916	1939	23
Nathan Clifford	1858	1881	23
Felix Frankfurter	1939	1962	23
Potter Stewart	1959	1981	22
Joseph P. Bradley	1870	1892	22
Melville W. Fuller	1888	1910	22
Harlan Fiske Stone	1925	1946	21
Antonin Scalia	1986	*	21

(continued)

Justices Ranked by Years of Service—continued

Justice	*Begin*	*End*	*Years*
David J. Brewer	1890	1910	20
Horace Gray	1882	1902	20
William Cushing	1790	1810	20
Smith Thompson	1824	1843	19
Thomas Todd	1807	1826	19
Stanley Reed	1938	1957	19
William R. Day	1903	1922	19
Noah Swayne	1862	1881	19
Anthony M. Kennedy	1988	*	19
Tom C. Clark	1949	1967	18
Peter V. Daniel	1842	1860	18
Warren E. Burger	1969	1986	17
Charles E. Hughes	1910	1916	17
(*as chief justice*)	1930	1941	
David H. Souter	1900	*	17
Brockholst Livingston	1807	1823	16
John M. Harlan II	1955	1971	16
Pierce Butler	1923	1939	16
Earl Warren	1953	1969	16
George Sutherland	1922	1938	16
Clarence Thomas	1991	*	16
Samuel Chase	1796	1811	15
David Davis	1862	1877	15
Henry B. Brown	1891	1906	15
Owen J. Roberts	1930	1945	15
Lewis F. Powell, Jr.	1972	1987	15
Henry Baldwin	1830	1844	14
Morrison R. Waite	1874	1888	14
Ruth Bader Ginsburg	1993	*	14
William Paterson	1793	1806	13
Rufus W. Peckham	1896	1909	13
Robert H. Jackson	1941	1954	13
Harold H. Burton	1945	1958	13
Stephen G. Breyer	1994	*	13
Samuel Blatchford	1882	1893	11
William Strong	1870	1880	10
Mahlon Pitney	1912	1922	10

*Still serving in early 2007.

Notable Supreme Court Rulings

Cases covered in articles in the main text are marked with asterisks (*).

*Abington School District v. Schempp**
374 U.S. 203 (June 17, 1963)
Reaffirming that the First Amendment mandates a high wall between church and state, an 8-1 majority prohibited public schools from devotional Bible readings and recitation of the Lord's Prayer.

Ableman v. Booth
62 U.S. 506 (Mar. 7, 1859)
Upheld the constitutionality of the 1850 Fugitive Slave Law and strongly affirmed that federal statutes override state laws.

Abrams v. United States
250 U.S. 616 (Nov. 10, 1919)
Upheld the prosecution of anarchists under the Sedition Act, although Justice Holmes dissented with a libertarian version of the clear and present danger standard of free speech. Superseded by *Brandenburg v. Ohio* (1969).

Adair v. United States
208 U.S. 161 (Jan. 27, 1908)
Basing its decision on the freedom of contract doctrine, the Court overturned a federal law that had prohibited yellow dog contracts. Reversed in 1937.

*Adamson v. California**
332 U.S. 46 (June 23, 1947)
Reaffirmed that the Fifth Amendment did not apply to state laws, which would be reversed in 1964, but the case remains significant because it brought forth a debate on the issue of incorporation.

*Adarand Constructors v. Peña**
515 U.S. 200 (June 12, 1995)
Required lower courts to use the "strict scrutiny" standard when examining the constitutionality of federal programs mandating preferences based on race.

Adderley v. Florida
385 U.S. 39 (Nov. 14, 1966)
Upheld a criminal trespass conviction of civil rights demonstrators for refusing to leave a nonpublic driveway on jail premises, finding that the police conduct was not motivated by speech content.

Adkins v. Children's Hospital
261 U.S. 525 (Apr. 9, 1923)
Ruling that a federal minimum-wage law was unconstitutional, the Court vigorously reaffirmed laissez-faire principles and the freedom of contract doctrine. Overturned in *West Coast Hotel Co. v. Parrish* (1937).

Agostini v. Felton
521 U.S. 203 (June 23, 1997)
Overturning a 1985 precedent, a 5-4 majority upheld the constitutionality of the use of tax money to send public school teachers into parochial school for specialized services.

Akron v. Akron Center for Reproductive Health
462 U.S. 416 (June 15, 1983)
Overturned several abortion restrictions in a city ordinance and strongly reaffirmed that women have a fundamental right to have abortions, with Justice Sandra Day O'Connor articulating the "undue burden" standard.

Albemarle Paper Co. v. Moody
422 U.S. 405 (June 25, 1975)
Held that a company's pre-employment tests having discriminatory effects violated the 1964 Civil Rights Act because they were not sufficiently "job related."

Albertson v. Subversive Activities Control Board
382 U.S. 70 (Nov. 15, 1965)
In this final case involving the registration requirements for communists in the 1950 McCarran Act, the Court held that the requirements violated the self-incrimination clause.

Allegheny County v. American Civil Liberties Union Greater Pittsburgh Chapter
492 U.S. 573 (July 3, 1989)
Disallowed government sponsorship of a pious Christmas display, which was found to promote a religious message, while allowing the display of a menorah next to a Christmas tree.

*Allgeyer v. Louisiana**
165 U.S. 578 (1897) (Mar. 1, 1897)
The Court's first application of the freedom of contract doctrine to overturn a state law as unconstitutional. Remained a precedent until 1937.

American Communications Association v. Douds
339 U.S. 382 (May 8, 1950)
Upheld the portion of the Taft-Hartley Act that required labor union leaders to affirm that they were not members of the Communist Party, based on a balancing of the clear and present danger test.

American Library Association, United States v.
539 U.S. 197 (June 23, 2003)
Upheld the constitutionality of the Children's Internet Protection Act, requiring public libraries to install antipornographic filters on computers with Internet access.

Antelope, The
10 Wheat. (23 U.S.) 66 (Mar. 16, 1825)
While declaring that the slave trade was contrary to principles of natural justice, the Court nevertheless held that sovereign nations under international law might allow the practice.

Aptheker v. Secretary of State
378 U.S. 500 (June 22, 1964)
Held that the restrictions on international travel in the 1950 McCarran Act were overly broad in not considering degrees of communist involvement, based on a right to travel in the Fifth Amendment.

Argersinger v. Hamlin
407 U.S. 25 (June 12, 1972)
Having ruled in 1965 that states must provide counsel for poor defendants charged with felonies, the justices unanimously extended the requirement to misdemeanor cases having a threat of imprisonment.

Arizona v. Fulminante
499 U.S. 279 (Mar. 26, 1991)
Applied "harmless error" analysis to criminal trials in which a coerced confession is erroneously admitted, so that such an error would not automatically require that the conviction be overturned.

Arlington Heights v. Metropolitan Housing Development Corp.
429 U.S. 252 (Jan. 11, 1977)
Reaffirmed that the Fourteenth Amendment prohibited intentional racial discrimination, but not simply policies having a disproportionate racial impact.

*Ashcroft v. Free Speech Coalition**
535 U.S. 234 (Apr. 16, 2002)
Held that portions of the 1996 Child Pornography Prevention Act were unconstitutionally broad, especially the ban on computer-generated child pornography that did not exploit any victims.

Ashwander v. Tennessee Valley Authority
297 U.S. 288 (Feb. 17, 1936)
Upheld the constitutionality of the TVA, based on Congress's authority for national defense and interstate commerce. Justice Louis Brandeis's concurrence included the seven "Ashwander guidelines."

Atkins v. Virginia
536 U.S. 304 (June 20, 2002)
Overturning a 1989 decision, the Court prohibited the execution of mentally retarded criminals, noting that most states prohibited the practice, which did not have functions of deterrence or retribution.

Atwater v. Lago Vista
523 U.S. 318 (Apr. 24, 2001)
Declaring that the Fourth Amendment does not prohibit a warrantless arrest for minor misdemeanors, the Court upheld an arrest for a seatbelt violation punishable only by a fine.

Automobile Workers v. Johnson Controls
499 U.S. 187 (Mar. 20, 1991)
Interpreting the Pregnancy Discrimination Act of 1983, the Court struck down a private company's fetal-protection policy that barred women of childbearing capacity from jobs with significant lead exposure.

Bailey v. Drexel Furniture Co.
259 U.S. 20 (May 15, 1922)
Held that a special tax designed to discourage child labor violated states' rights under the Tenth Amendment. Abandoned in *Mulford v. Smith* (1939).

*Baker v. Carr**
369 U.S. 186 (Mar. 26, 1962)
Overruling *Colegrove v. Green* (1946), this landmark decision recognized that the courts may examine allegations of unequal representation resulting from malapportioned legislative districts. Led to *Reynolds v. Sims* (1964) and numerous cases.

Ballard v. United States
329 U.S. 187 (Dec. 9, 1946)
Required that women must be included for jury service in federal trials located in states where women were legally eligible for service, even if they were not actually summoned for state trials.

Ballew v. Georgia
435 U.S. 223 (Mar. 21, 1978)
While upholding *Williams v. Florida* (1970), the Court held that six jurors is the absolute minimum in all criminal cases.

Bank of Augusta v. Earle
38 U.S. 519 (Mar. 9, 1839)
While recognizing that the comity clause gave corporations a conditional right to do business in other states, the Court held that states might limit or even prohibit this right with explicit legislation.

Bank of the United States v. Deveaux
9 U.S. (5 Cranch) 61 (Mar. 15, 1809)
Recognizing that a corporation possessed state citizenship for the purpose of diversity jurisdiction, but that its location of citizenship was that of its shareholders. Modified in 1844.

Barenblatt v. United States
360 U.S. 109 (June 8, 1959)
Upheld a contempt conviction for refusal to testify in a congressional hearing, emphasizing the public's interest in opposing communist infiltration and finding no infringement on First Amendment rights.

Barker v. Wingo
407 U.S. 514 (June 22, 1972)
To decide whether a trial was delayed for an unreasonable period of time, the Court established a balancing test that included the length of delay, the reasons for delay, the harm to the defendant, and whether the defendant requested a speedy trial.

*Barnes v. Glen Theatre**
501 U.S. 560 (June 21, 1991)
While reaffirming that erotic dancing is expressive conduct protected by the First Amendment, the Court upheld a state's ban on complete nudity in public places.

*Barron v. Baltimore**
32 U.S. 243 (Feb. 16, 1833)
Held that the first eight amendments were not binding on the states—a major precedent until a long series of incorporation decisions began in 1897.

Bates v. State Bar of Arizona
433 U.S. 350 (June 27, 1977)
Held that states may not prohibit lawyers from advertising the prices of routine legal services.

*Batson v. Kentucky**
476 U.S. 79 (Apr. 30, 1986)
Overturning an African American's conviction by an all-white jury, the Court found that a racial pattern of excluding potential jurors creates an inference of discrimination.

Belle Terre v. Boraas
616 U.S. 1 (Apr. 1, 1974)
Upheld the constitutionality of a local zoning ordinance that prohibited most unrelated groups from living together in a single-unit dwelling.

Benton v. Maryland
395 U.S. 785 (June 23, 1969)
Incorporated the Fifth Amendment protection against double jeopardy into the Fourteenth Amendment so that it was binding on the states.

Berman v. Parker
348 U.S. 26 (Nov. 22, 1954)
Interpreted the term "public use" to refer to any policy that reasonably promotes the public interest, providing legislatures with great discretion in deciding how to use the eminent domain power.

Betts v. Brady
316 U.S. 455 (June 1, 1942)
Allowed states not to provide counsel for indigent defendants in noncapital-felony trials. Reversed in *Gideon v. Wainwright* (1963).

Bigelow v. Virginia
421 U.S. 809 (June 16, 1975)
Declared that the First Amendment protects commercial advertising to "some degree" and overturned a state statute prohibiting advertisements of abortion services.

BMW of North America v. Gore
517 U.S. 559 (May 20, 1996)
Held that a punitive award of five hundred times the amount of actual damages was "grossly excessive," which violated the due process clause of the Fourteenth Amendment.

Board of Education of Oklahoma City v. Dowell
498 U.S. 237 (Jan. 15, 1991)
Allowed federal district courts to end court-supervised busing plans when the effects of state-encouraged segregation have been removed "as far as practicable" and a local school board has complied with a desegregation order for a "reasonable period of time."

*Boerne v. Flores**
521 U.S. 507 (June 25, 1997)
In striking down the Religious Freedom Restoration Act of 1993, a 6-3 majority asserted that Congress has no authority to override a valid judicial interpretation by statute.

Bogan v. Scott-Harris
523 U.S. 44 (Mar. 3, 1998)
Held that local legislators have the same absolute immunity from prosecution for their legislative activities as federal and state legislators.

*Bolling v. Sharpe**
347 U.S. 479 (May 17, 1954)
A companion to *Brown v. Board of Education,* unanimous ruling that the equal protection clause applies to the federal government via the due process clause of the Fifth Amendment.

Bowers v. Hardwick
478 U.S. 186 (June 30, 1986)
Held that the U.S. Constitution does not protect a right to engage in consensual homosexual conduct. Reversed in 2003.

Bowsher v. Synar
478 U.S. 714 (July 7, 1986)
Disallowed the comptroller general from making budget cuts, because Congress may not invest one of its own officers with powers that properly belong to the executive branch.

*Boy Scouts of America v. Dale**
530 U.S. 640 (June 28, 2000)
Emphasizing that private organizations have rights of free expression and association, the Court held that the Boy Scouts did not have to obey New Jersey's law banning discrimination against gays.

Boyd v. United States
116 U.S. 616 (Feb. 1, 1886)
Anticipated the exclusionary rule and expanded privacy rights relating to unreasonable searches and seizures and compulsory self-incrimination.

*Bradwell v. Illinois**
83 U.S. 130 (Apr. 15, 1873)
Upheld a state law that forbade women from entering the legal profession, based on an acceptance of traditional gender roles.

*Brandenburg v. Ohio**
395 U.S. 444 (Feb. 27, 1969)
Overturned a person's conviction for suggesting a need for violence at a Ku Klux Klan rally, establishing that advocacy may be punished only if it is intended to produce imminent lawless action and likely to do so.

Branzburg v. Hayes
408 U.S. 665 (June 29, 1972)
Ruled that the First Amendment did not provide journalists with a special privilege to protect confidential sources when testifying at criminal trials.

Brecht v. Abrahamson
507 U.S. 619 (Apr. 21, 1993)
The Court held that, when criminal trials are found to have Miranda violations, the convictions must not be overturned unless the error causes "a substantial and injurious effect or influence" on the trial's outcome.

Breedlove v. Suttles
302 U.S. 277 (Dec. 6, 1937)
Rejected plaintiff's argument that a state's poll tax was unconstitutional because of its exemption of the young, the aged, the blind, and women.

Briscoe v. Bank of the Commonwealth of Kentucky
36 U.S. 257 (Feb. 11, 1837)
Allowed state-owned banks to issue notes as legal tender, thereby expanding state control over currency and banking in the period of the Taney Court.

Bronson v. Kinzie
42 U.S. 311 (Feb. 23, 1843)
Basing its decision on the contracts clause, the Court overturned debtor-relief laws that had restricted the rights of creditors to foreclose on mortgages. Overturned in *Home Building and Loan Association v. Blaisdell* (1934).

*Brown v. Board of Education**
347 U.S. 483 (May 17, 1954)
Reversing *Plessy v. Ferguson* (1896), the Court unanimously held that de jure (legally mandated) segregation of the public schools was prohibited by the equal protection clause of the Fourteenth Amendment.

Brown v. Maryland
12 Wheat. (25 U.S.) 419 (Mar. 12, 1827)
Held that a state tax on imported goods that were still in the original packaging and not mixed with other goods violated both the ban on import taxes and the commerce clause. Modified in *Woodruff v. Parham* (1869).

*Brown v. Mississippi**
297 U.S. 278 (Feb. 17, 1936)
Overturned criminal convictions of African Americans because their confessions were obtained by coercive means "revolting to the sense of justice."

Buchanan v. Warley
245 U.S. 60 (Nov. 5, 1917)
Basing its decision on the liberty of contract principle, the Court struck down state laws that mandated racial segregation in the purchase of homes.

*Buck v. Bell**
274 U.S. 200 (May 2, 1927)
Upheld the constitutionality of a eugenics law requiring sterilization of persons deemed to be "feebleminded." Moderated in *Skinner v. Oklahoma* (1942).

Buckley v. Valeo
424 U.S. 1 (Jan. 30, 1976)
Prohibited Congress from limiting the amount of money that political candidates may contribute to their own campaigns, although the Court permitted most other limits on political contributions.

Budd v. New York
143 U.S. 517 (Feb. 29, 1892)
Reaffirmed that state legislatures may regulate rates charged by strategic businesses "affected with a public interest."

Bunting v. Oregon
243 U.S. 426 (June 12, 1917)
Influenced by the Brandeis Brief, a 5-3 majority upheld a state's maximum-hour law, which weakened but did not overturn the freedom of contract doctrine.

Burstyn v. Wilson
343 U.S. 495 (May 26, 1952)
Reversing a 1915 decision, the Court unanimously held that since films were a medium for expressing ideas, they enjoyed a degree of First Amendment protection.

Burton v. Wilmington Parking Authority
365 U.S. 715 (Apr. 17, 1961)
Forbade a state agency from leasing public property to a private restaurant on terms inconsistent with the equal protection principle.

*Bush v. Gore**
531 U.S. 98 (Dec. 12, 2000)
In stopping a court-ordered recount of Florida's presidential election based on the equal protection clause, the Court's 5-4 ruling had the effect of deciding that George W. Bush would be the next president.

Butler, United States v.
297 U.S. 1 (Jan. 6, 1936)
Struck down the regulations in the 1933 Agricultural Adjustment Act (AAA) for violating the Tenth Amendment, while interpreting the general welfare clause as an independent grant of congressional power.

Butz v. Economou
438 U.S. 478 (June 29, 1978)
Held that high officials of the executive branch, with rare exceptions, do not enjoy absolute immunity from civil suits.

*Calder v. Bull**
3 U.S. 368 (Aug. 8, 1798)
While ruling that ex post facto limitation did not apply to civil laws, the justices expressed a variety of different views about judicial review and natural law—the Court's first serious discussion of these issues.

California, United States v.
332 U.S. 19 (June 23, 1947)
Held that the federal government, not the states, had full dominion and mineral rights over the three-mile strip of submerged coastal lands. Partially overridden by the Submerged Lands Act (1953).

California v. Acevedo
500 U.S. 565 (May 30, 1991)
Established "one clear-cut rule" for allowing a warrantless search of either a vehicle or a closed container in a vehicle whenever the police have probable cause.

California v. Cabazon Band of Indians
480 U.S. 202 (Feb. 25, 1987)
Recognizing that tribes retain sovereignty rights, the Court held that Public Law 280 did not authorize states to prohibit activities on Indian land not prohibited elsewhere—implying expansive gaming rights.

Cantwell v. Connecticut
310 U.S. 296 (May 30, 1940)
Held that the religious freedom of the First Amendment applied to the states through the Fourteenth Amendment and recognized a broad freedom to express religious ideas considered offensive.

*Carolene Products Co., United States v.**
304 U.S. 144 (Apr. 25, 1938)
Justice Harlan Stone's seminal Footnote Four suggested that the Court should use "more exacting judicial scrutiny" when examining restrictions

on disadvantaged minorities, explicit constitutional prohibitions, and democratic processes.

Carroll v. United States
267 U.S. 132 (Mar. 2, 1925)
Established the "car search exception," permitting the police to stop and search a vehicle based on probable cause but without a warrant.

Carter v. Carter Coal Co.
298 U.S. 238 (Mar. 18, 1936)
A 5-4 decision based on the Tenth Amendment that struck down a New Deal statute regulating the coal industry. Reversed by 1941.

Champion v. Ames
188 U.S. 321 (Feb. 23, 1903)
The Court upheld a federal statute that prohibited the trafficking of lottery tickets in interstate commerce; its broad definition of commerce established a de facto federal police power.

Chaplinsky v. New Hampshire
315 U.S. 568 (Mar. 9, 1942)
Upheld a conviction for highly offensive name-calling in public, establishing the "fighting words exception" to the First Amendment. Application has been limited by later decisions.

Charles River Bridge v. Warren Bridge
36 U.S. 420 (Feb. 12, 1837)
In holding that only clear and explicit terms of corporate charters were legally binding, the Taney Court departed from the firm defense of property rights under the contacts clause in *Dartmouth College v. Woodward* (1819).

Cherokee Nation v. Georgia
30 U.S. 1 (Mar. 18, 1831)
Declared that the Cherokee Nation was not a sovereign, independent country and defined the Cherokee as a "domestic dependent nation." Modified the next year.

Chevron U.S.A. v. Echazabel
536 U.S. 73 (June 10, 2002)
Interpreting the Americans with Disabilities Act (1990), the Court unanimously upheld the right of employers to refuse to hire a person whose disability makes the job dangerous for that person or others.

*Chicago, Burlington, and Quincy Railroad Co. v. Chicago**
166 U.S. 226 (Mar. 1, 1897)
The first incorporation decision: By requiring a state to pay just compensation when taking private property, the Court made the Fifth Amendment's takings clause binding on the states through the Fourteenth Amendment.

Chicago, Milwaukee, and St. Paul Railway Co. v. Minnesota
134 U.S. 418 (Mar. 24, 1890)
Applied due process principles to establish that rates set by government are subject to judicial review, a fundamental tenet of modern administrative law.

Chicago v. Morales
527 U.S. 41 (June 10, 1999)
Held that an antiloitering ordinance was unconstitutionally vague because it failed to give citizens and the police clear indications of what was illegal.

*Chimel v. California**
395 U.S. 752 (June 23, 1969)
Held that when a valid arrest is made, the Fourth Amendment permits the police to search the arrested person in the area "within his immediate control."

*Chinese Exclusion Cases** (*Chew Heong v. United States*; *United States v. Jung Ah Lung*; and *Lee Joe v. United States*)
112 U.S. 536(Dec. 8, 1884); 124 U.S. 621(Feb. 13, 1888); 149 U.S. 698 (May 15, 1893)
When examining the Chinese exclusion laws between 1884 and 1893, the Court initially gave narrow protection for Chinese reentering the United States, but it eventually succumbed to anti-Chinese prejudices, even upholding a retroactive law that required deportation of any Chinese lacking a residential certificate.

*Chisholm v. Georgia**
2 U.S. 419 (Feb. 18, 1793)
In its first major decision, the Court held that the U.S. Constitution allowed a citizen of one state to sue another state in federal court. Superseded by the Eleventh Amendment.

*Church of Lukumi Babalu Aye v. Hialeah**
508 U.S. 520 (June 11, 1993)
Overturning a local ban on animal sacrifices, the Court established the "strict scrutiny" test in examining any law targeting religious conduct for special restrictions.

*Civil Rights Cases**
109 U.S. 3 (Oct. 15, 1883)
In overturning the public accommodations section of the 1875 Civil Rights Act, an 8-1 majority held that the Fourteenth Amendment applied only to state action and that Congress may not punish private acts of discrimination. Reversed in 1964.

Clark Distilling Co. v. Western Maryland Railway Co.
242 U.S. 311 (Jan. 8, 1917)
Upheld a federal law prohibiting shipments of alcoholic beverages into dry states, thereby enhancing Congress's authority to regulate interstate commerce.

Classic, United States v.
313 U.S. 299 (May 26, 1941)
Partially overturning a 1921 precedent, the Court allowed Congress to regulate primary elections, which prepared the way for striking down white primaries in *Smith v. Allwright* (1944).

*Clinton v. City of New York**
524 U.S. 417 (June 25, 1998)
Ruled the line-item veto was unconstitutional because it allowed the president to amend legislation passed by Congress.

*Clinton v. Jones**
520 U.S. 681 (May 27, 1997)
Unanimously held that a sitting president does not possess immunity from civil lawsuits relating to unofficial conduct.

Cohen v. California
403 U.S. 15 (June 7, 1971)
Overturned the conviction of a man for wearing a jacket displaying indecent language, thereby expanding First Amendment protection for offensive and provocative speech.

Cohen v. Cowles Media Co.
501 U.S. 663 (June 24, 1991)
Held that the First Amendment does not protect newspapers from a breech-of-contract lawsuit for breaking a promise of confidentiality.

Cohens v. Virginia
19 U.S. 264 (Mar. 3, 1821)
Chief Justice John Marshall used a minor dispute over the sale of lottery tickets in Virginia to assert the Court's jurisdiction over state court decisions about federal questions.

Coker v. Georgia
433 U.S. 584 (June 29, 1977)
Held that capital punishment for the crime of rape is an excessive and disproportionate penalty, therefore violating the prohibition against cruel and unusual punishments.

Cole v. Richardson
405 U.S. 676 (Apr. 18, 1972)
Held that states may require public employees to swear or affirm to uphold and defend the Constitution and oppose the illegal overthrow of the government, so long as the oaths are consistent with those required by government officials in Articles II and VI of the Constitution.

Colegrove v. Green
328 U.S. 549 (June 10, 1946)
In holding reapportionment to be a "nonjusticiable political question," the Court blocked judicial efforts to correct malapportioned legislative districts until overruled in *Baker v. Carr* (1962).

Coleman v. Miller
307 U.S. 433 (June 5, 1939)
Decided that most processes for amending the Constitution were political questions entrusted to Congress.

Collector v. Day
78 U.S. 113 (Apr. 3, 1871)
Based on the Tenth Amendment and the doctrine of dual sovereignty, the "Day Doctrine" disallowed the federal government from taxing the income of state employees. Reversed in *Graves v. New York ex rel. O'Keefe* (1939).

Columbus Board of Education v. Penick
443 U.S. 449 (July 2, 1979)
Basing its decision on a finding of state-supported segregation, the Court upheld a lower court's order for massive busing in a large urban district.

Communist Party v. Subversive Activities Control Board
367 U.S. 1 (June 5, 1961)
Upheld the registration provisions of the McCarran Act of 1950, although the Court declined a constitutional ruling until they were actually enforced, which came in *Albertson v. Subversive Activities Control Board* (1965).

Cooley v. Board of Wardens of the Port of Philadelphia
53 U.S. 299 (Mar. 2, 1852)
In upholding a state statute regulating navigation standards, the Court formulated the doctrine of "selective exclusiveness," allowing states to regu-

late aspects of interstate commerce in the absence of federal laws. The doctrine was severely restricted in 1886.

Cooper v. Aaron
358 U.S. 1 (Sept. 12, 1958)
Held that fear of violence did not provide justification for postponing school desegregation and strongly affirmed that the Supreme Court's interpretations are binding on state governments.

Corrigan v. Buckley
271 U.S. 323 (May 24, 1926)
Allowed private citizens to enter into racially restrictive covenants for the sale of property, which were judicially enforceable until 1948.

Counselman v. Hitchcock
142 U.S. 547 (Jan. 11, 1892)
Held that the privilege against self-incrimination extends beyond criminal trials to grand jury proceedings and other investigations. Modified in 1972.

Cox v. Louisiana
379 U.S. 536 (Jan. 18, 1965)
Overturned the conviction of civil rights demonstrators who had blocked traffic, based on evidence that the prosecutions had been motivated by disdain for the demonstrators' political views.

Cox v. New Hampshire
312 U.S. 569 (Mar. 31, 1941)
Upheld the right of local governments to place nondiscriminatory restrictions on religious demonstrations in order to maintain safe and orderly streets.

Coyle v. Smith
221 U.S. 559 (May 29, 1911)
Allowed Oklahoma to choose its own capital despite a congressional stipulation at the time of admission, based on the equal prerogatives of the states.

Craig v. Boren
429 U.S. 190 (Dec. 20, 1976)
Overturning a law that treated males and females differently when they purchased beer, the Court announced that sex-based classifications were subjected to a heightened level of judicial scrutiny.

Craig v. Missouri
29 U.S. 410 (Mar. 12, 1830)
Overturned a statute authorizing state-issued loan certificates to serve as a form of currency. Mostly reversed by the Taney Court in 1837.

Crow Dog, Ex parte
109 U.S. 557 (Dec. 17, 1883)
Acknowledged that federal law may preempt tribal authority, but only when Congress has expressed its clear intent to do so.

*Cruikshank, United States v.**
92 U.S. 542 (Mar. 27, 1876)
By deciding that the Fourteenth Amendment did not authorize federal protection for individuals' civil rights, the Court disallowed enforcement of anti-Ku Klux Klan laws, thereby helping to restore white supremacy. Reversed in the 1960's.

*Cruzan v. Director, Missouri Department of Health**
497 U.S. 261 (June 25, 1990)
Although recognizing a Fourteenth Amendment "liberty interest" to refuse any medical intervention, the Court allowed states to demand "clear and convincing" evidence of a person's desire to suspend life-support services.

Cumming v. Richmond County Board of Education
175 U.S. 528 (Dec. 18, 1899)
Allowing a Georgia school board to close only the high school for African American students, the Court failed to enforce the "equal" part of the "separate but equal" doctrine.

Cummings v. Missouri
71 U.S. 277 (Mar. 20, 1867)
Overturning Reconstruction-age statutes that had required oaths of past loyalty as conditions of employment, the Court found them to be unconstitutional ex post facto laws and bills of attainder.

*Curtiss-Wright Export Corp., United States v.**
299 U.S. 304 (Dec. 21, 1936)
Declared that the federal government possesses sovereign and inherent powers to conduct foreign relations, with the president having nonenumerated prerogatives in the area.

Cutter v. Wilkinson
544 U.S. (May 31, 2005)
Held that a federal law requiring prisons to accommodate the religious needs of inmates does not violate the establishment clause.

Dames and Moore v. Regan
453 U.S. 654 (July 2, 1981)
Upheld actions taken by President Jimmy Carter during the Iran hostage crisis, expanding presidential powers beyond those explicitly mentioned in law.

*Darby Lumber Co., United States v.**
312 U.S. 100 (Feb. 3, 1941)
Using a broad interpretation of the commerce clause, this landmark decision upheld a federal law regulating working conditions for employees producing goods for interstate commerce.

Dartmouth College v. Woodward
17 U.S. 518 (Feb. 2, 1819)
By deciding that state charters of private institutions were protected by the contracts clause, the Court enhanced the protection of vested corporate property from changes by the states.

Davis v. Bandemer
478 U.S. 109 (June 30, 1986)
Held that a gerrymandering scheme that benefits the dominant political party is subject to judicial scrutiny if the minority lacks a fair chance to influence the process.

Davis v. Beason
133 U.S. 333 (Feb. 3, 1890)
Allowed Idaho territory to deny the vote to members of a religious denomination that advocated the illegal practice of polygamy.

*Debs, In re**
158 U.S. 564 (May 27, 1895)
In upholding a federal injunction against a labor union to preserve the orderly flow of interstate commerce, the Court gave a green light to the use of antilabor injunctions in future strikes.

*DeJonge v. Oregon**
299 U.S. 353 (Jan. 4, 1937)
In overturning DeJonge's conviction for holding a protest meeting in violation of the state's criminal syndicalism law, the Court applied the First Amendment right of assembly to the states.

Dennis v. United States
341 U.S. 494 (June 4, 1951)
Affirming the convictions of eleven Communist Party leaders for advocating revolution contrary to the 1940 Smith Act, the Court endorsed the "grave and probable danger test," which limited rights of expression.

DeShaney v. Winnebago County Department of Social Services
489 U.S. 189 (Feb. 22, 1989)
Ruling that the state was not liable for its social workers' failure to remove a child from a dangerous situation, the Court found that the due process clause did not confer any affirmative right to government aid.

Dickerson v. United States
530 U.S. 428 (2000)
Overturning the admissibility of a voluntary confession given without a *Miranda* warning, Chief Justice William Rehnquist wrote that *Miranda* had become "part of our national culture."

Dillon v. Gloss
256 U.S. 368 (May 16, 1921)
Recognized Congress's authority over time limits for ratifying constitutional amendments and upheld a federal conviction for transporting liquors contrary to the Volstead Act.

Dobbins v. Erie County
41 U.S. 435 (Mar. 4, 1842)
Basing its decision on a nineteenth century view of federalism, the Court ruled that a state could not tax income derived from a federal office. Overruled in 1939.

Dodge v. Woolsey
59 U.S. 331 (Feb. 6, 1856)
Recognizing that a state statute specifying taxes on chartered banks constituted a contractual obligation, the Court held that a later tax was unconstitutional. Subsequently rejected.

Doe v. Bolton
410 U.S. 179 (Jan. 22, 1973)
In a companion case to *Roe v. Wade* (1973), the Court struck down Georgia's restrictions on abortions.

Dolan v. City of Tigard
512 U.S. 374 (June 24, 1994)
Held that a city's requirement of donating land for flood control to obtain a building permit was an unconstitutional taking of private property without just compensation.

Dombrowski v. Pfister
380 U.S. 499 (Apr. 26, 1965)
Allowing a federal court to enjoin the enforcement of a vague state statute with bad faith and harassment, the Court departed from the traditional

practice of not intervening in state proceedings until they are finalized. Modified in *Younger v. Harris* (1971).

Drayton, United States v.
536 U.S. 194 (June 17, 2002)
Held that the police, when conducting random bus searches for drugs or weapons, are not required to inform passengers that they have a constitutional right to refuse to be searched.

Duncan v. Kahanamoku
327 U.S. 304 (Feb. 25, 1946)
Overturned convictions of citizens by military tribunals in Hawaii during World War II, because these proceedings had not been authorized by Congress.

*Duncan v. Louisiana**
391 U.S. 145 (May 20, 1968)
Overturning a misdemeanor conviction, the Court made the Sixth Amendment's right to jury trial applicable to the states through the Fourteenth Amendment.

Duplex Printing Co. v. Deering
254 U.S. 443 (Jan. 3, 1921)
Upheld use of antitrust injunctions to stop secondary boycotts, despite labor's antitrust exclusion in the Clayton Act. Overruled by the Norris-LaGuardia Act (1932).

E. C. Knight Co., United States v.
156 U.S. 1 (Jan. 21, 1895)
Narrowly interpreting commerce under the 1890 Sherman Antitrust Act, the Court held that the act was not intended to prohibit monopolies in manufacturing. Rendered invalid in the 1930's.

Edelman v. Jordan
415 U.S. 651 (Mar. 25, 1974)
Held that the Eleventh Amendment prohibited federal lawsuits against a state without its consent, brought by citizens of either that state or another state.

Edmonson v. Leesville Concrete Co.
500 U.S. 614 (June 3, 1991)
Extended the prohibition against the preemptory exclusion of potential jurors on the basis of race to include civil trials.

Edwards v. Aguillard
482 U.S. 578 (June 19, 1987)
Struck down a state law requiring balanced treatment of "evolution science" and "creation science," based on its unconstitutional purpose of advancing a religious viewpoint.

Edwards v. California
314 U.S. 160 (Nov. 24, 1941)
In striking down a law banning indigents from entering California, the Court strengthened the constitutional right to travel, although the justices disagreed about the source of this right.

Edwards v. South Carolina
372 U.S. 229 (Feb. 5, 1963)
Overturning breach of peace convictions of civil rights demonstrators, the Court limited "time, place, and manner" restrictions on expressions of unpopular views in peaceful assemblies.

Eichman, United States v.
496 U.S. 310 (June 11, 1990)
Striking down a federal law that outlawed all forms of mistreatment of the U.S. flag, the Court clarified the theory of free expression in *Texas v. Johnson* (1989).

Eisenstadt v. Baird
405 U.S. 438 (Mar. 22, 1972)
Holding that a law outlawing the sale of contraceptives to unmarried persons violated equal protection, the court reaffirmed the right of privacy in *Griswold v. Connecticut* (1965).

Elfbrandt v. Russell
384 U.S. 11 (Apr. 18, 1966)
Invalidated a loyalty oath statute for public employees because of its failure to distinguish among the different reasons for belonging to organizations with illegal purposes. Clarified in *Cole v. Richardson* (1972).

Elrod v. Burns
427 U.S. 347 (June 28, 1976)
Held that the dismissal of nonpolicy-making public employees for their party membership violated First Amendment rights.

*Employment Division, Department of Human Resources v. Smith**
494 U.S. 872 (Apr. 17, 1990)
Holding that states were not required to make a religious exception for the use of illegal drugs, the Court allowed indirect restraints on religious con-

duct if the law had a secular purpose and was generally applicable to all persons.

*Engel v. Vitale**
370 U.S. 421 (June 25, 1962)
Held that the First Amendment's establishment clause prohibited public schools from conducting or sponsoring prayer ceremonies, even if the prayers were vague and nondenominational.

*Epperson v. Arkansas**
393 U.S. 97 (Nov. 12, 1968)
Ruled that laws banning the teaching of evolution in the public schools were inconsistent with the First Amendment.

Erie Railroad Co. v. Tompkins
304 U.S. 64 (Apr. 25, 1938)
Denying the existence of "federal general common law" in federal lawsuits involving citizens of different states, the Court overturned the precedent of *Swift v. Tyson* (1842).

Escobedo v. Illinois
378 U.S. 478 (June 22, 1964)
Overturned a murder conviction because it was based on a confession that had been obtained after police interrogators refused to honor the suspect's requests to see his lawyer. Superseded by *Miranda v. Arizona* (1966).

Euclid v. Ambler Realty Co.
272 U.S. 365 (Oct. 12, 1926)
Established the constitutionality of zoning ordinances as a legitimate form of police power, thereby laying the foundation for modern land-use regulations.

Evans v. Abney
396 U.S. 435 (Jan. 29, 1970)
Faced with racially discriminatory restrictions on park land donated to a municipality, the Court decided that the land must be returned to the donor's heirs.

*Everson v. Board of Education of Ewing Township**
330 U.S. 1 (Feb. 10, 1947)
Upheld the use of tax money in transporting students to parochial schools, emphasizing that the primary beneficiaries were the families and that the policy maintained religious neutrality.

Ewing v. California
538 U.S. 11 (Mar. 5, 2003)
While upholding California's "three strikes and you're out" law, which treats a third crime as a felony, the Court also upheld a defendant's prison term of fifty years for shoplifting videotapes worth $150.

Fay v. Noia
372 U.S. 391 (Mar. 18, 1963)
Held that in "exceptional circumstances" persons convicted of state offenses may gain habeas corpus relief in federal courts without exhausting the remedies in state courts.

Feiner v. New York
340 U.S. 315 (Jan. 15, 1951)
Upheld the conviction of a radical street oratory for violating a statute that criminalized the use of offensive or abusive language. Superseded by *Brandenburg v. Ohio* (1969).

Feist Publications v. Rural Telephone Service Co.
499 U.S. 340 (Mar. 27, 1991)
Denying a copyright claim for a telephone directory, the Court held that the copyright clause of the Constitution authorizes Congress to protect only original works, not the gathering of information.

*Ferguson v. City of Charleston**
532 U.S. 67 (Mar. 21, 2001)
Held that state hospitals may not test maternity patients for criminal evidence of illegal drug use without their consent or a valid search warrant.

Ferguson v. Skrupa
372 U.S. 726 (Apr. 22, 1963)
In upholding a state regulation of private business, Justice Hugo Black declared that the Court would no longer apply substantive due process analysis to business regulations.

First English Evangelical Lutheran Church of Glendale v. Los Angeles
482 U.S. 304 (June 9, 1987)
Examining an ordinance prohibiting construction in a floodplain, the Court recognized for the first time that a land-use regulation may sometimes amount to a Fifth Amendment taking of property that requires compensation.

First National Bank of Boston v. Bellotti
435 U.S. 765 (Apr. 26, 1978)
Held that a statute banning corporations from spending money to influence the outcome of a referendum violated the First Amendment, a decision that expanded the theory of *Buckley v. Valeo* (1976).

Flast v. Cohen
392 U.S. 83 (June 10, 1968)
In permitting a taxpayer to sue the federal government for expenditures alleged to violate the establishment clause, the Court greatly modified a 1923 precedent on judicial standing.

Fletcher v. Peck
10 U.S. 87 (Mar. 16, 1810)
Broadly constructing the contracts clause to enhance protection against legislative interference of vested rights in private property, the Court for the first time declared that a state law was unconstitutional.

*Florida v. Bostick**
501 U.S. 429 (June 18, 1991)
Allows the police to approach individuals randomly in public places and ask permission to search their belongings, but the request must not appear coercive.

Frank v. Mangum
237 U.S. 309 (Apr. 19, 1915)
Upheld a district court's refusal to accept a habeas corpus petition from Leo Frank—who was sentenced to death—under conditions of mob intimidation, but the Court granted relief in the similar case of *Moore v. Dempsey* (1923).

Frontiero v. Richardson
411 U.S. 677 (May 14, 1973)
Held that a federal law giving a spousal benefit only to males violated the equal protection clause, but only a plurality voted to apply strict scrutiny to classifications based on sex. Modified in *Craig v. Boren* (1976).

Frothingham v. Mellon
262 U.S. 447 (June 4, 1923)
Held that payment of taxes did not establish the standing necessary to challenge in court the constitutionality of congressional spending. Modified in *Flast v. Cohen* (1968).

Fullilove v. Klutznick
448 U.S. 448 (July 2, 1980)
Upheld a federal race-based classification requiring public works projects to reserve a 10 percent quota for minority-controlled businesses, applying the standard of intermediate scrutiny. Modified in *Adarand Constructors v. Peña* (1995).

*Furman v. Georgia**
408 U.S. 238 (June 29, 1972)
Held that capital punishment as practiced throughout the country in 1972 violated the Eighth Amendment, but the Court allowed the penalty with procedural reforms in *Gregg v. Georgia* (1976).

*Garcia v. San Antonio Metropolitan Transit Authority**
469 U.S. 528 (Feb. 19, 1985)
Reversing a 1976 decision, a 5-4 majority held that the commerce clause empowered Congress to require state and local governments to provide minimum wages and overtime pay—a decision that removed almost all federalism. Modified in *Printz v. United States* (1997).

Garrison v. Louisiana
379 U.S. 64 (Nov. 23, 1964)
Overturning a criminal libel conviction for criticisms of elected judges, the Court reaffirmed that any political libel action could be sustained only by proof of "actual malice."

Gault, In re
387 U.S. 1 (May 15, 1967)
Landmark decision that provided juvenile defendants with many (but not all) of the rights of adult defendants under the due process clause of the Fourteenth Amendment.

Geduldig v. Aiello
417 U.S. 484 (June 17, 1974)
Upheld the constitutionality of a California law that withheld disability benefits from pregnant women, an unpopular decision overturned by the 1978 Pregnancy Discrimination Act.

Gelpcke v. Dubuque
68 U.S. 175 (Jan. 11, 1864)
Rejecting an 1862 ruling on state courts, the Court refused to follow the Iowa Supreme Court's latest construction of its state constitution, a decision considered a precursor to substantive due process cases.

Genesee Chief v. Fitzhugh
53 U.S. 443 (Feb. 20, 1852)
By upholding an 1845 federal law that authorized federal jurisdiction over the Great Lakes, the Court substantially expanded the powers of Congress to regulate inland lakes and rivers.

Georgia v. Randolph
Docket No. 04-1067 (Mar. 22, 2006)
Upheld the constitutionality of a police search in which two co-occupants of a home are present, with one consenting and the other refusing.

Gertz v. Robert Welch
418 U.S. 323 (June 25, 1974)
While reaffirming that public figures must prove "actual malice" to recover damages for defamation, a "private individual" need only show negligence to use normal care in reporting.

*Gibbons v. Ogden**
22 U.S. 1 (Mar. 2, 1824)
Held that a federal steamboat license nullified an earlier state-granted monopoly, defined commerce broadly to include all aspects of trade, and recognized that federal power to regulate interstate commerce took precedence over the concurrent power of the states.

*Gideon v. Wainwright**
372 U.S. 335 (Mar. 18, 1963)
A landmark case holding that the states must provide counsel for indigent defendants in felony trials.

*Gitlow v. New York**
268 U.S. 652 (June 8, 1925)
While upholding Gitlow's conviction for writing and distributing a socialist pamphlet, Justice Edward Sanford declared that the First Amendment's guarantee of free speech applies to the states through incorporation into the Fourteenth Amendment.

Globe Newspaper Co. v. Superior
457 U.S. 596 (June 23, 1982)
Overturned a law requiring exclusion of the press from all trials involving testimony of minors for sexual offenses, but recognized that courts may deny access when it serves a compelling state interest.

Gold Clause Cases (*Norman v. Baltimore & Ohio Railroad Co.; Nortz v. United States; Perry v. United States*)
294 U.S. 240; 294 U.S. 317; 294 U.S. 330 (Feb. 18, 1935)
Upholding the 1933 nullification of all contracts that had required payment in gold, the Court recognized that Congress may override private contracts inconsistent with its constitutional authority over the monetary policy.

Goldberg v. Kelly
397 U.S. 254 (Mar. 23, 1970)
Viewing statutory entitlement to welfare as a form of property, the Court held that state agencies must provide welfare recipients with evidentiary hearings before ending their benefits.

Goldfarb v. Virginia State Bar
421 U.S. 773 (June 16, 1975)
Held that the 1890 Sherman Antitrust Act prohibited state bar associations from setting minimum fees for legal services.

Goldwater v. Carter
444 U.S. 996 (Dec. 13, 1979)
Refusing to decide whether President Jimmy Carter had the authority to terminate a treaty without Senate approval, the justices in the majority disagreed about why the issue was nonjusticiable.

Gomillion v. Lightfoot
364 U.S. 339 (Nov. 14, 1960)
Striking down a city boundary for discriminating by race, the decision suggested that the Court might soon hold apportionment cases to be justiciable, which happened in *Baker v. Carr* (1962)

Gompers v. Buck's Stove and Range Co.
221 U.S. 418 (May 15, 1911)
Recognizing broad powers of lower courts to issue injunctions restraining both words and deeds, the Court used a technicality to overturn a criminal contempt citation of labor unions.

Gonzales v. Oregon
Docket No. 04-623 (Jan. 17, 2006)
Held that the Controlled Substances Act did empower the federal government to prosecute physicians prescribing lethal doses of drugs under Oregon's Death with Dignity Act.

*Good News Club v. Milford Central School**
533 U.S. 98 (June 11, 2001)
Held that all public schools must open their doors for afterschool religious activities on the same basis that school policy permits other after-hour activities.

Graham v. Richardson
403 U.S. 365 (June 14, 1971)
In striking down an Arizona law requiring U.S. citizenship for welfare benefits, the Court established that alienage is a suspect classification under the equal protection clause.

*Gratz v. Bollinger/Grutter v. Bollinger**
539 U.S 306; 539 U.S. 244 (June 23, 2003)
Finding that a diverse student body is a compelling government interest, the Court upheld the constitutionality of a narrowly tailored admissions program giving individualized racial preferences.

Graves v. New York ex rel. O'Keefe
306 U.S. 466 (Mar. 27, 1939)
Held that states may tax the salaries of federal employees, a decision that reversed *Collector v. Day* (1871).

Gray v. Sanders
372 U.S. 368 (Mar. 18, 1963)
Struck down Georgia's county-unit system of elections for giving unequal weight to urban voters and also introduced the standard of "one person, one vote."

Green v. Biddle
21 U.S. 1 (Decided Mar. 5, 1821; redecided Feb. 27, 1823)
Overturning Kentucky property laws that benefited actual settlers to the detriment of titleholders, the Court extended the contracts clause to encompass public agreements between states.

Green v. County School Board of New Kent County
391 U.S. 430 (May 27, 1968)
Overturning a "freedom of choice" plan that preserved de facto segregation, the Court declared that equal protection required an actual dismantling of racially segregated schools.

*Gregg v. Georgia**
428 U.S. 153 (July 2, 1976)
Upheld Georgia's revised capital punishment law and announced that capital punishment, with proper procedures and safeguards, is not inherently unconstitutional.

Griffin v. California
380 U.S. 609 (Apr. 28, 1965)
Overruling *Adamson v. California* (1947), the Court held that states violate the Fifth Amendment if they permit prosecutors or judges to comment on a defendant's failure to testify in a criminal proceeding.

Griffin v. County School Board of Prince Edward County
180 U.S. 609 (May 25, 1964)
Struck down a state law allowing counties to close the public schools rather than desegregate and announced that "the time for mere deliberate speed has run out."

*Griggs v. Duke Power Co.**
401 U.S. 424 (Mar. 8, 1971)
Interpreted the 1964 Civil Rights Act to require employers to demonstrate that any job qualifications adversely affecting underrepresented minorities are clearly related to job performance.

*Griswold v. Connecticut**
381 U.S. 479 (June 5, 1965)
Overturned a Connecticut statute prohibiting the sale of contraceptives to married couples, thereby establishing a constitutional right to privacy, the basis for *Roe v. Wade* (1973).

Grosjean v. American Press Co.
297 U.S. 233 (Feb. 10, 1936)
Ruled that a discriminatory state tax applicable only to large newspapers violated the First Amendment's press freedom.

Grove City College v. Bell
465 U.S. 555 (Feb. 28, 1984)
Narrowly interpreting Title IX of the Federal Education Act of 1972, the Court allowed funds to be cut only from the college's specific programs that discriminated against women, but Congress in 1988 clarified the statute to apply to funds for the entire college.

Groves v. Slaughter
40 U.S. 449 (Mar. 10, 1841)
Held that an amendment to Mississippi's state constitution that banned bringing slaves into the state for sale was not binding in the absence of legislation to enforce it.

Grovey v. Townsend
295 U.S. 45 (Apr. 1, 1935)
Having ruled in 1932 that state governments may not engage in race discrimination in primaries, the Court ruled that the ruling did not apply to

political parties, because they were private organizations. Reversed in *Smith v. Allwright* (1944).

Guest, United States v.
383 U.S. 745 (Mar. 28, 1966)
Broadly constructing two Reconstruction-era statutes that criminalized violent interference with constitutional rights, the Court expanded the circumstances in which Congress might punish private individuals for such acts. Decided the same day as *United States v. Price.*

Guinn v. United States
238 U.S. 347 (June 21, 1915)
Struck down grandfather clauses as a violation of the Fifteenth Amendment.

Hague v. Congress of Industrial Organizations
307 U.S. 496 (June 5, 1939)
Introduced the public forum doctrine, requiring that streets, parks, and other public places must be accessible for assemblies and the discussion of public issues.

Hall v. DeCuir
95 U.S. 485 (Jan. 14, 1878)
Overturned a Reconstruction-age state law mandating racial integration on carriers engaged in interstate commerce, which was under the exclusive supervision of Congress.

*Hamdan v. Rumsfeld**
548 U.S.___(June 29, 2006)
Held that the president did not have the authority to establish military commissions to try foreign nationals without congressional authorization. In addition, the Court held that foreign detainees had the rights guaranteed by the Geneva Conventions on Prisoners of War.

*Hammer v. Dagenhart**
247 U.S. 251 (June 3, 1918)
Striking down federal restrictions on child labor, the Court reaffirmed that Congress could regulate only goods and services in interstate commerce, not the manufacturing of goods for commerce. Reversed in *United States v. Darby Lumber Co.* (1941).

Harper v. Virginia State Board of Elections
383 U.S. 663 (Mar. 24, 1966)
Banned the use of poll taxes as a requirement for voting in state elections, which had not been covered in the Twenty-Fourth Amendment.

Harris v. McRae
448 U.S. 297 (June 30, 1980)
Declaring that the Constitution does not confer entitlements to services, the Court upheld the Hyde Amendment (1976), prohibiting federal funding for abortions except in a few special cases.

Harris v. New York
401 U.S. 222 (Feb. 24, 1971)
Held that if confessions are inadmissible because of police failure to give Miranda warnings, they may be used to impeach the credibility of a criminal defendant who takes the stand to testify.

Hawaii Housing Authority v. Midkiff
467 U.S. 229 (May 30, 1984)
Upholding a land reform act that authorized the state to take property for sale to existing tenants, the Court almost entirely abandoned "public use" as a limit on eminent domain actions.

Hayburn's Case
2 U.S. 409 (1792)
In written letters to President George Washington, five justices asserted the doctrine of judicial review in announcing that they would not perform an executive-like task required in a federal statute.

Head Money Cases
112 U.S. 580 (Dec. 48, 1885)
Approving a federal head tax on each immigrant, the Court held that immigration was a form of foreign commerce over which Congress may exercise plenary power.

*Heart of Atlanta Motel v. United States**
379 U.S. 241 (Dec. 14, 1964)
A landmark decision, which upheld the public accommodations section of the 1964 Civil Rights Act, based on Congress's plenary power to regulate interstate commerce.

Helvering v. Davis
301 U.S. 619 (May 24, 1937)
Affirmed the constitutionality of the 1935 Social Security Act, based on Congress's constitutional authority to collect taxes and provide for the general welfare.

Hiibel v. Sixth Judicial District Court of Nevada
542 U.S. 177 (June 21, 2004)
Held that with reasonable suspicion of criminal involvement the police may require a person to identify himself.

Hirabayashi v. United States
320 U.S. 81 (June 21, 1943)
Ruled that the exigencies of World War II justified a military curfew, which was applied almost exclusively to Japanese Americans.

Hodgson v. Minnesota
497 U.S. 417 (June 25, 1990)
In approving an abortion requirement for a minor to notify two parents provided there was a judicial bypass, a 5-4 majority signaled that many restrictions on abortion rights might be acceptable.

Holden v. Hardy
169 U.S. 366 (Feb. 28, 1898)
Approved a statutory eight-hour workday in mines and smelters, recognizing that states had police powers to protect safety and health and that the freedom of contract principle was not absolute.

Holmes v. Jennison
39 U.S. 540 (Mar. 4, 1840)
Memorable because of Chief Justice Roger Taney's vigorous affirmation of the federal government's exclusive powers over foreign relations.

Home Building and Loan Association v. Blaisdell
290 U.S. 398 (June 8, 1934)
By upholding a Depression-era moratorium on the foreclosure of homes and farms, the Court greatly limited the scope of the obligations-of-contracts clause.

Hoyt v. Florida
368 U.S. 57 (Mar. 12, 1961)
Upheld a woman's murder conviction, denying her claim of an unfair trial based on the state's sex discrimination in jury selection. Overruled by *Taylor v. Louisiana* (1975).

Hudson and Goodwin, United States v.
11 U.S. 32 (Feb. 13 or Mar. 14, 1812)
Dismissing indictments for common-law seditious libel, the Court ended a long-standing dispute by disavowing the existence of federal common law of crimes—a decision that remains good law.

*Hudson v. Michigan**
547 U.S.___(June 15, 2006)
A major departure from the Court's earlier rulings on the exclusionary rule, which allowed the use of criminal evidence that is the fruit of searches conducted contrary to the "knock-and-announce" rule.

Hudson v. Palmer
468 U.S. 517 (July 3, 1983)
Held that prison inmates lack the rights to privacy and protection against searches under the Fourth Amendment.

Humphrey's Executor v. United States
295 U.S. 602 (May 27, 1935)
Upheld congressional legislation that prohibited the president from removing members of independent regulatory commissions on policy grounds before their terms ended, thereby limiting *Myers v. United States* (1926).

Hurley v. Irish-American Gay, Lesbian, and Bisexual Group of Boston
515 U.S. 557 (June 19, 1995)
Recognizing the First Amendment right of private organizers of a ethnic parade to refuse participation by gay groups, the Court reasoned that a parade was a speech event not amounting to state action.

Hurtado v. California
110 U.S. 516 (Mar. 3, 1884)
Allowed states to disregard the Fifth Amendment requirement for grand jury indictments, which is not considered a "fundamental principle of liberty and justice"—a decision that remains good law.

*Hustler Magazine v. Falwell**
485 U.S. 46 (Feb. 24, 1988)
Overturning a libel award to a religious leader who had been depicted in an admittedly outrageous parody, the Court applied the "actual malice" standard to public figures experiencing emotional distress.

Hutchinson v. Proxmire
443 U.S. 111 (June 26, 1979)
Held that the speech or debate clause in Article I of the Constitution applies only to statements made on the floor of the House or Senate, thereby allowing libel suits against members of Congress for press releases and newsletters.

Hylton v. United States
3 U.S. 171 (Mar. 8, 1796)
By agreeing to review the constitutionality of a federal tax, the Court appeared to assume that it had the power of judicial review.

Illinois ex rel. McCollum v. Board of Education
333 U.S. 203 (Mar. 8, 1948)
Disallowed release-time in public schools for voluntary religious instruction, arguing that this public support for religion violated the establishment clause. Modified by *Zorach v. Clauson* (1952).

Illinois v. McArthur
531 U.S. 326 (Feb. 20, 2001)
Allowed the use of evidence obtained when the police restrained McArthur from entering his home for two hours, while waiting for a search warrant, to prevent his destroying evidence.

Immigration and Naturalization Service v. Chadha
464 U.S. 919 (June 23, 1983)
Ruling that the legislative veto was unconstitutional, the Court's majority found that it intruded into the executive domain and subverted the legislative process set out in the Constitution.

International Shoe Co. v. Washington
326 U.S. 310 (Dec. 3, 1945)
Held that a state may require payments to its unemployment compensation fund from any out-of-state company that maintains systematic and continuous business activities within the state.

Jackson v. Metropolitan Edison Co.
419 U.S. 345 (Dec. 23, 1974)
In a ruling involving a utility company, the Court set a standard for determining when actions by private entities were public enough to fall under the constitutional limitations applied to the government.

Jacobellis v. Ohio
378 U.S. 528 (June 22, 1964)
Ruling that a French film was not obscene and could not be banned, the justices expressed a variety of theoretical views.

Jacobson v. Massachusetts
197 U.S. 11 (Feb. 20, 1905)
Upheld a state fine for refusals to submit to vaccination, balancing the individual's liberty against the state's police power to protect the public's health.

*Johnson and Graham's Lessee v. McIntosh**
21 U.S. 543 (8 Wheat) (Mar. 10, 1823)
Referring to the joint doctrines of discovery and conquest, the Court recognized that the federal government possesses full authority to decide the property rights of Native Americans.

Johnson v. Louisiana
400 U.S. 356 (Jan. 10, 1972)
Held that convictions based on nonunanimous jury verdicts in state criminal trials do not violate due process standards of the Fourteenth Amendment. Clarified in *Burch v. Louisiana* (1979).

Johnson v. Santa Clara County
480 U.S. 616 (Mar. 25, 1987)
Rejected a "reverse discrimination" claim in which a female employee was promoted over a white male employee who was slightly more qualified.

Johnson v. Zerbst
304 U.S. 458 (May 23, 1938)
Held that in federal criminal proceedings indigent defendants have a Sixth Amendment right to be represented by counsel. Extended to the states in *Gideon v. Wainwright* (1963).

Joint Anti-Fascist Refugee Committee v. McGrath
341 U.S. 123 (Apr. 30, 1951)
Held that the Truman administration had violated constitutional rights by issuing a list of subversive organizations without first providing opportunities for hearings or for appeals.

Jones v. Alfred H. Mayer Co.
392 U.S. 409 (June 17, 1968)
By broadly interpreting the Thirteenth Amendment to encompass the badges and incidents of slavery, the Court issued a landmark decision that established Congress's authority to legislate against private racial discrimination. Expanded in *Runyon v. McCrary* (1976).

Jones v. Van Zandt
46 U.S. 215 (Mar. 5, 1847)
Upheld the civil liability of an abolitionist for disobeying the 1793 Fugitive Slave Act, declaring that the legitimacy of slavery was a political question for the states to decide.

Kagama, United States v.
118 U.S. 375 (May 10, 1886)
Upheld the 1885 Major Crimes Act, thereby recognizing Congress's constitutional power to enforce criminal statutes relating to Native Americans on reservations.

Kansas v. Crane
534 U.S. 407 (Jan. 22, 2002)
Upheld the civil confinement of a sex offender after serving a prison term based on evidence that the offender had difficulty controlling his behavior.

Kansas v. Hendricks
521 U.S. 346 (June 23, 1997)
Upheld a state's violent sexual predator statute, finding that it did not violate standards of substantive due process clause and that the constitutional restrictions on criminal legislation did not apply.

Kastigar v. United States
406 U.S. 441 (May 22, 1972)
Held that a revised federal immunity statute did not violate the Fifth Amendment in compelling witnesses to testify under grants of immunity.

*Katz v. United States**
389 U.S. 347 (Dec. 18, 1967)
Overturning a 1928 precedent, the Court held that the police must obtain a warrant before wiretapping any private conversation and recognized Fourth Amendment protection for places with "a reasonable expectation of privacy."

Katzenbach v. McClung
379 U.S. 294 (Dec. 14, 1964)
Utilized the commerce clause to uphold enforcement of civil rights legislation over a small local restaurant that had only an indirect and almost indiscernible connection to interstate commerce.

Katzenbach v. Morgan
384 U.S. 641 (June 13, 1966)
Upheld a literary provision of the 1965 Voting Rights Act, thereby recognizing Congress's authority to enforce its own interpretation of the Fourteenth Amendment equal protection guarantee.

*Kelo v. City of New London**
545 U.S.___(June 23, 2005)
Upheld the authority of governments under eminent domain to take private property against an owner's will for the purpose of transferring it to private developers to promote econmic development.

Kendall v. United States ex rel. Stokes
37 U.S. (12 Pet.) 524 (Feb. 26-27, 1838)
Held that federal executive officers must act in accordance with laws passed by Congress, rejecting a cabinet member's claim that he was answerable only to the president.

Kent v. Dulles
357 U.S. 116 (June 16, 1958)
Held that the secretary of state may not deny passports because of political activities without an explicit act of Congress, while also recognizing a constitutional right to international travel.

Kentucky v. Dennison
65 U.S. 66 (Mar. 14, 1861)
Ruled that the Court had no power to force a state governor to comply with the constitutional obligation of extraditing an accused person to another state. Overturned in *Puerto Rico v. Branstad* (1987).

Ker v. California
374 U.S. 23 (June 10, 1963)
Held that states are to be held to federal standards in applying the Fourth Amendment exclusionary rule. The Court's endorsement of unannounced entry into a private home was revised in *Payton v. New York* (1980).

Keyes v. Denver School District No. 1
413 U.S. 189 (June 21, 1973)
In its first school desegregation case outside the South, the Court approved a districtwide busing plan even though official policies had encouraged segregation in only part of the district.

Keyishian v. Board of Regents
385 U.S. 589 (Jan. 23, 1967)
Struck down a New York loyalty law requiring public school teachers to certify nonmembership in any organization on a subversive list, finding the required statement to be vague and overly broad.

Keystone Bituminous Coal Association v. DeBenedictis
480 U.S. 470 (Mar. 9, 1987)
Upheld a Pennsylvania law prohibiting underground mining that causes damage to surface structures, finding the law did not violate either the takings clause or the contracts clause.

Kidd v. Pearson
128 U.S. 1 (Oct. 22, 1888)
Erected a distinction between manufacturing and commerce, a distinction often used to limit Congress's powers under the commerce clause, until finally rejected in the New Deal period.

Kilbourn v. Thompson
103 U.S. 168 (1881)
Limited Congress's power to investigating only for the purposes of considering future legislation. No longer binding.

Kirby v. Illinois
406 U.S. 682 (June 7, 1972)
Limiting *United States v. Wade* (1967), the Court held that the right to counsel of suspects placed in a lineup does not take effect until after an indictment or its equivalence.

Kirkpatrick v. Preisler
394 U.S. 526 (Apr. 7, 1969)
Modifying *Wesberry v. Sanders* (1964), the Court required states to make serious efforts to achieve mathematical precision in making U.S. congressional districts equal in population.

Klopfer v. North Carolina
386 U.S. 213 (Mar. 13, 1967)
Applied the Sixth Amendment's promise of a speedy trial to the states through the Fourteenth Amendment under the incorporation doctrine.

*Korematsu v. United States**
323 U.S. 14 (Dec. 18, 1944)
Basing its decision on military necessity, the Court upheld the exclusion of persons of Japanese ancestry from the West Coast, while recognizing that racial distinctions are inherently suspect.

Kunz v. New York
340 U.S. 290 (Jan. 15, 1951)
Holding that an ordinance requiring permits for religious services on public streets was too broad, the Court helped established that limitations on speech must be narrowly drawn.

*Kyllo v. United States**
533 U.S. 363 (June 11, 2001)
Held that police must have search warrants to use thermal imagers to detect patterns of heat coming from private homes.

Lanza, United States v.
260 U.S. 377 (Dec. 11, 1922)
Allowed prosecution of a bootlegger in both state and federal court, thereby limiting the Fifth Amendment protection against double jeopardy.

Lassiter v. Northampton County Board of Elections
360 U.S. 45 (June 8, 1959)
Upheld the states' right to impose literacy tests for voting. Superseded by the Voting Rights Act of 1965.

*Lawrence v. Texas**
539 U.S. 558 (June 26, 2003)
Overturning *Bowers v. Hardwick* (1986), the Court held that the criminalizing of homosexual conduct between consenting adults in private homes violates their "liberty rights" under due process.

*Lee v. Weisman**
505 U.S. 577 (June 24, 1992)
A 5-4 decision that prohibited public schools from conducting prayer services at graduation ceremonies.

Legal Tender Cases (*Hepburn v. Griswold* and *Knox v. Lee*)
75 U.S. 603 (Feb. 7, 1870); 79 U.S. 457 (May 1, 1871)
Overruling the *Hepburn* ruling in *Knox v. Lee*, a 5-4 majority established Congress's authority to compel creditors to accept its paper money in payment of debt, with Chief Justice Salmon Chase, who had defended greenbacks as secretary of the treasury, voting with the minority.

*Lemon v. Kurtzman**
403 U.S. 602 (June 28, 1971)
While vetoing state subsidies for teachers of parochial schools, the Court established a three-part *Lemon* test for evaluating which forms of governmental assistance violate the establishment clause.

Leon, United States v.
468 U.S. 897 (July 5, 1984)
Permitted the use of criminal evidence from a search conducted pursuant to a warrant issued by a neutral magistrate, even if the warrant was ultimately found to be defective.

License Cases
46 U.S. (5 How.) 504 (Jan. 21, 1847)
Upheld the validity of state taxes on the sale of imported liquor, a decision that influenced development of the doctrine of selective exclusiveness.

Local 28 of Sheet Metal Workers International v. EEOC
478 U.S. 421 (July 2, 1986)
Approved a court order requiring a hiring quota to increase the number of minority workers as a remedy for a union's past discrimination.

*Lochner v. New York**
198 U.S. 45 (Apr. 17, 1905)
In the most famous case applying the doctrine of economic substance due process, the Court overturned a state law setting maximum number of hours for bakery workers. Overturned in 1937.

Locke v. Davey
540 U.S. 712 (Feb. 25, 2004)
Held that states do not violate religious freedom if they provide scholarships for college students majoring in secular subjects but exclude ministerial students majoring in theology.

Loewe v. Lawlor
208 U.S. 274 (Feb. 3, 1908)
This so-called Danbury Hatters' case weakened labor unions by holding that the Sherman Antitrust Act did not provide them with exemption from damage suits. Modified by the Clayton Act of 1914.

Lone Wolf v. Hitchcock
187 U.S. 553 (Jan. 5, 1903)
Sometimes called the "Indian's *Dred Scott* case." The Court recognized Congress's plenary authority over Native American affairs, including the power to abrogate treaties unilaterally.

*Lopez, United States v.**
514 U.S. 549 (Apr. 26, 1995)
Striking down a federal law that banned guns from school zones, a 5-4 majority of the Rehnquist Court ruled that Congress had exceeded its powers under the commerce clause—the first ruling of its kind in half a century.

Louisiana ex rel. Francis v. Resweber
329 U.S. 459 (Jan. 13, 1947)
After a mechanical failure prevented the successful electrocution of a convicted murderer, the Court ruled that a second trip to the electric chair would not violate the Eighth Amendment.

Louisville, Cincinnati, and Charleston Railroad Co. v. Letson
43 U.S. 497 (Mar. 7, 1844)
Overturning an 1809 decision, the Court held that a corporation had its home in the state where it was chartered, thereby extending the diversity jurisdiction of the federal courts.

Louisville, New Orleans, and Texas Railway Co. v. Mississippi
133 U.S. 587 (Mar. 3, 1890)
Upheld a Mississippi law mandating separate but equal accommodations on all railroad cars, even though earlier decisions had disallowed state regulations of interstate commerce.

Lovell v. City of Griffin
303 U.S. 444 (Mar. 28, 1938)
Held that a city ordinance prohibiting the distribution of pamphlets without a permit violated the First Amendment's freedom of speech provisions, ignoring the religious aspect of the case.

Lovett, United States v.
238 U.S. 303 (June 3, 1946)
Held that the portion of a federal statute naming three federal employees as ineligible for compensation was an unconstitutional bill of attainder.

*Loving v. Virginia**
388 U.S. 1 (June 12, 1967)
Struck down sixteen southern state statutes that outlawed interracial marriages, based on the equal protection clause.

Lucas v. South Carolina Coastal Council
505 U.S. 647 (June 29, 1992)
Granted property owners the right to compensation under the takings clause if environmental regulations totally eliminate the value of the land, unless the regulations are necessary to prevent a public harm.

Luther v. Borden
7 How. (48 U.S.) 1 (Jan. 3, 1849)
Refusing to decide a dispute in Rhode Island between two rival governments, the Court held that the meaning of "Republican form of government" is a political question left to Congress's judgment.

Lynch v. Donnelly
465 U.S. 668 (Mar. 5, 1984)
Upheld the constitutionality of a city-sponsored Christmas display in which a nativity scene was accompanied by nonreligious images, with Justice Sandra O'Connor introducing the endorsement of religion test.

McCardle, Ex parte
74 U.S. 506 (Apr. 12, 1869)
Dismissed the case after Congress's withdrawal of the Court's appellate jurisdiction under the Habeas Corpus Act, a decision that probably does not affect the Court's authority to rule on the constitutionality of federal laws.

*McCleskey v. Kemp**
481 U.S. 279 (Apr. 22, 1987)
Refused to rule that capital punishment is unconstitutional because of statistical racial disparities in the rendering of death sentences, based on a lack of evidence of discriminatory intent.

McCleskey v. Zant
499 U.S. 467 (Apr. 16, 1991)
Held that federal courts may not accept second habeas corpus petitions in cases of death sentences except in extraordinary circumstances.

*McConnell v. Federal Election Commission**
540 U.S. 93 (Dec. 10, 2003)
Reviewing the 2002 McCain-Feingold Act, the Court held that the ban on unlimited contributions to political parties (called soft money) does not violate rights of free speech.

McCray v. United States
195 U.S. 27 (May 31, 1904)
Established that Congress's taxing power may be used to regulate commerce, thereby providing an additional basis for federal police power.

*McCulloch v. Maryland**
17 U.S. 316 (Mar. 6, 1819)
Broadly interpreting the elastic clause, the Marshall Court upheld the constitutionality of the Bank of the United States, thereby establishing a foundation for expansive federal involvement in the economy.

McKeiver v. Pennsylvania
403 U.S. 528 (June 21, 1971)
Narrowly interpreting *In re Winship* (1970), the Court held that the right to a jury trial did not apply to juvenile proceedings and evaluated due process by the standard of "fundamental fairness."

McLaurin v. Oklahoma State Regents for Higher Education
339 U.S. 637 (June 5, 1950)
Overruled a state statute requiring the racial segregation of facilities in a state university that admitted African Americans to graduate programs, a ruling that anticipated *Brown v. Board of Education.*

Mahan v. Howell
410 U.S. 315 (Feb. 15, 1973)
Relaxed mathematical equality standards for redistricting state legislative districts, requiring a good-faith effort to achieve districts as nearly equal as practicable. Did not apply to congressional districts.

Mallory v. United States
354 U.S. 449 (June 24, 1957)
Affirmed the Court's "supervisory power" to establish rules of evidence in federal criminal cases that go beyond due process requirements, subject to limitations by Congress.

Malloy v. Hogan
378 U.S. 1 (June 15, 1964)
Established that the Fifth Amendment's privilege against compulsory self-incrimination is binding on the states via incorporation into the Fourteenth Amendment.

*Mapp v. Ohio**
367 U.S. 643 (June 19, 1961)
A landmark decision that made both the Fourth Amendment and its exclusionary rule applicable to the states via incorporation.

*Marbury v. Madison**
5 U.S. 137 (Feb. 24, 1803)
The first case in which the Court held a congressional statute to be unconstitutional and therefore invalid—establishing the Court's power of judicial review.

Marshall v. Barlow's
436 U.S. 307 (May 23, 1978)
Found that warrantless inspections or "searches" by Occupational Safety and Hazards Act (OSHA) inspectors violated the Fourth Amendment.

Martin v. Hunter's Lessee
14 U.S. 304 (Mar. 20, 1816)
Justice Joseph Story's landmark opinion asserting the Court's appellate jurisdiction to review state supreme courts' judgments relating to federal questions.

Martin v. Mott
25 U.S. 19 (Feb. 2, 1827)
Upholding President James Madison's authority to interpret federal law in taking control of state militias, the Court recognized that a president has extensive prerogatives as commander in chief.

Martin v. Wilks
490 U.S. 755 (June 12, 1989)
Held that white firefighters had a constitutional right to challenge preferential treatment for African Americans according to a consent decree. Modified by the Civil Rights Act of 1991.

Maryland v. Buie
494 U.S. 325 (Feb. 8, 1990)
Authorized the police, when making an arrest in a home, to undertake a "protective sweep" of areas they reasonably believe may harbor a dangerous person.

Maryland v. Craig
497 U.S. 836 (June 27, 1990)
Upholding a conviction in which young children had testified over closed-circuit television, the Court held that defendants in child abuse cases have no constitutional right to confront young accusers.

Massachusetts v. Mellon
262 U.S. 447 (June 4, 1923)
Refused to rule on Congress's authority to use subsidies to encourage states to participate in federal programs, finding that the question was nonjusticiable—a decision that advanced federal powers.

Massiah v. United States
377 U.S. 201 (May 18, 1964)
Expanded the rights of criminal defendants by holding that the prosecution may not use evidence deliberately elicited from an indicted defendant outside the presence of counsel.

Masson v. New Yorker Magazine
501 U.S. 496 (Jan. 14, 1991)
Held that the First Amendment does not prevent public persons from winning libel suits against journalists who deliberately distort the meaning of their statements.

Maxwell v. Dow
176 U.S. 581 (Feb. 26, 1900)
Upholding a criminal conviction, eight justices reaffirmed that the Bill of Rights did not apply to the states, although Justice John Harlan anticipated many of the later incorporation decisions.

Memoirs v. Massachusetts
383 U.S. 413 (Mar. 31, 1966)
Ruling that John Cleland's novel *Fanny Hill* (1748) was not obscene, the Court endorsed libertarian obscenity standards that included "utterly without redeeming social value." Modified in *Miller v. California* (1973).

Meritor Savings Bank v. Vinson
477 U.S. 57 (June 19, 1986)
Recognized that sexual harassment constitutes a form of gender discrimination, thereby allowing employees to bring sexual harassment lawsuits against employers under Title VII of the 1964 Civil Rights Act.

Metro Broadcasting v. Federal Communications Commission
497 U.S. 547 (June 27, 1990)
Endorsed an affirmative action program to the broadcasting industry requiring only an important government interest, although this was changed to strict scrutiny by *Adarand v. Peña* (1995).

*Meyer v. Nebraska**
262 U.S. 390 (June 4, 1923)
Stuck down a law that forbade teaching children non-English languages, the Court's first use of substantive due process to defend a noneconomic liberty.

Miami Herald Publishing Co. v. Tornillo
418 U.S. 241 (June 25, 1974)
Struck down a state law requiring newspapers to print the reply of any political candidate, recognizing that the First Amendment protects journalistic discretion.

Michael M. v. Superior Court of Sonoma County
450 U.S. 464 (Mar. 23, 1981)
Applied intermediate scrutiny in upholding a state law that punished males but not females for statutory rape.

*Michigan Department of State Police v. Sitz**
496 U.S. 444 (Feb. 27, 1990)
Recognizing the states' substantial and legitimate interest in curbing drunken driving, the Court upheld the constitutionality of enforcing sobriety checkpoints in strategic locations.

Michigan v. Long
463 U.S. 1062 (July 6, 1983)
In addition to allowing the police to search for weapons in passenger compartments of vehicles, the Court announced its presumption that state courts' decisions are based on federal law absent clear assertion of "independent and adequate state grounds."

Milkovich v. Lorain Journal Co.
497 U.S. 1 (June 21, 1990)
In lawsuits for libel based on accusations of falsehood, the Court held that a statement in the form of an opinion may be judged libelous if it implies a defamatory assertion.

Miller v. California; Paris Adult Theatre v. Slaton
413 U.S. 15; 413 U.S. 49 (June 21, 1973)
Reaffirming that obscenity had no First Amendment protection, the Court's three-pronged test for determining obscenity included considerations for community standards and serious cultural values.

*Milligan, Ex parte**
71 U.S. 2 (Apr. 3, 1866; opinions released Dec. 17, 1866)
Held that military courts may not exercise jurisdiction over civilians when civil courts are operating, a landmark ruling that has sometimes not been applied to foreign nationals in time of war.

Milliken v. Bradley
418 U.S. 717 (July 25, 1974)
Held that a court-ordered busing plan for Detroit could not require the busing of students across school district lines when there was no evidence that the neighboring districts were responsible for the segregation.

Minersville School District v. Gobitis
310 U.S. 586 (June 3, 1940)
Upheld a compulsory flag salute ceremony in public schools, but the ruling was soon overturned in *West Virginia State Board of Education v. Barnette* (1943).

Minnesota v. Carter
525 U.S. 83 (Dec. 1, 1998)
Held that visitors in a private home who are there for a short time to conduct a business transaction have no reasonable expectation of privacy for purposes of a Fourth Amendment search and seizure.

Minor v. Happersett
88 U.S. 162 (Mar. 9, 1875)
Ruled that the equal protection clause did not guarantee the right of women to vote and that voting qualifications were left up to the states. Modified by *Reynolds v. Sims* (1964).

Miranda v. Arizona
384 U.S. 436 (June 13, 1966)
A landmark ruling to ensure that confessions are voluntary, requiring the police before interrogations to notify suspects of their constitutional rights to remain silent, to know that statements may be used in court, and to have assistance of counsel.

Mississippi University for Women v. Hogan
458 U.S. 718 (July 1, 1982)
Held that the Fourteenth Amendment required a traditionally all-women's nursing school to admit male students, even though the state provided comparable training for men in state schools.

Mississippi v. Johnson
71 U.S. 475 (Apr. 15, 1867)
Held that courts had no power to stop the president from enforcing an allegedly unconstitutional statute, noting that the president's actions may later be challenged in the courts.

Missouri ex rel. Gaines v. Canada
305 U.S. 337 (Dec. 12, 1938)
Chipping away at the separate but equal doctrine, the Court ruled that states must provide equal opportunities for legal education within the borders of the state.

Missouri v. Holland
252 U.S. 416 (Apr. 19, 1920)
Reasserting the supremacy of federal treaties over state authority, the Court held that the Tenth Amendment did not put any limits on federal government's powers to make and enforce treaties.

Missouri v. Jenkins
515 U.S. 70 (June 12 1995)
In the Court's second examination of a lower court's ambitious interdistrict plan for integrating an entire metropolitan region, a 5-4 majority overturned the plan because of a lack of evidence that outlying districts had engaged in unconstitutional segregation.

Mistretta v. United States
488 U.S. 361 (Jan. 18, 1989)
Held that the Criminal Sentencing Commission, despite its combination of functions and personnel of the three branches, did not violate the separation of powers principle, because Congress's direction was sufficiently specific and detailed.

Mitchell v. Helms
530 U.S. 793 (June 28, 2000)
Upheld the use of federal funds to lend computers and other instructional material to religious and other schools, weakening further the restrictions of *Lemon v. Kurtzman* (1971).

Mobile v. Bolden
446 U.S. 55 (Apr. 22, 1980)
Reaffirming that the Fourteenth and Fifteenth Amendments prohibit only "purposeful discrimination," the Court upheld an at-large voting system in which no African American had ever been elected. Partially overturned in the 1982 Voting Rights Act.

Monell v. Department of Social Services
436 U.S. 658 (June 6, 1978)
Overturning a 1961 ruling, the Court held that civil rights plaintiffs may seek monetary recovery from municipalities in federal court for official policies that violate constitutional rights.

*Moore v. City of East Cleveland**
431 U.S. 494 (May 31, 1977)
Applied the doctrine of substantive due process to strike down a local zoning ordinance that prohibited a grandmother from living with her grandsons in a single-unit residence.

Moore v. Dempsey
261 U.S. 86 (Feb. 19, 1923)
In ordering a federal district court to review a trial when the jury was intimated by an angry mob, this landmark decision marked the beginning of the Court's increased scrutiny of state criminal trials and a liberalized use of habeas corpus petitions to counter state violations of constitutional rights.

Moose Lodge v. Irvis
497 U.S. 163 (June 12, 1972)
Applying the doctrine of state action, the Court held that a state agency did not violate the equal protection clause when it issued a liquor license to a private club that practiced racial discrimination. Superseded in some states by public accommodations laws.

Morehead v. New York ex rel. Tipaldo
298 U.S. 587 (June 1, 1936)
A highly unpopular decision that used the freedom of contract doctrine to strike down a New York minimum-wage law for women. Reversed in *West Coast Hotel Co. v. Parrish* (1937).

Morgan v. Virginia
328 U.S. 373 (June 3, 1946)
Struck down segregation in interstate public transportation because of the need for a uniform policy of interstate commerce, a ruling that did not apply to state laws governing intrastate commerce.

Morrison, United States v.
529 U.S. 598 (May 15, 2000)
Viewing violence against women as an issue for the states' police powers, a 5-4 majority held that Congress had no authority to enforce the 1994 Violence Against Women Act under the commerce clause.

Morrison v. Olson
487 U.S. 654 (June 29, 1988)
Upheld the constitutionality of the 1978 independent counsel statute, providing for almost unlimited investigations of senior executive officers. The law expired in 1999.

Mugler v. Kansas
123 U.S. 623 (Dec. 5, 1887)
Approving a state's prohibition of alcoholic beverages while warning that there were limits to a state's police power, this transitional decision encouraged the later triumph of substantive due process.

Mulford v. Smith
307 U.S. 38 (Apr. 17, 1939)
Relying on a broad interpretation of the commerce clause while ignoring the Tenth Amendment, the Court upheld the constitutionality of the 1938 Agricultural Adjustment Act.

Muller v. Oregon
208 U.S. 412 (Feb. 24, 1908)
Although continuing to endorse the freedom of contract doctrine, the Court accepted the Brandeis Brief's thesis that women had special needs justifying a limitation on the number of hours worked.

*Munn v. Illinois**
94 U.S. 113 (Mar. 1, 1877)
A historic ruling recognizing that states might exercise their police powers to regulate rates of grain warehouses and other strategic businesses that are "affected with a public interest." Modified in *Nebbia v. New York* (1934).

Murdock v. Memphis
87 U.S. 590 (Jan. 11, 1875)
Affirmed that state courts continue to have final authority over questions of state constitutions and laws, because Congress had not expressed a clear intent to change this basic principle of federalism.

Murdock v. Pennsylvania
319 U.S. 105 (May 3, 1943)
Striking down a city ordinance requiring religious proselytizers to pay a fee, the Court declared that First Amendment freedoms occupy a "preferred position" in constitutional law.

Murphy v. Waterfront Commission of New York
378 U.S. 52 (June 15, 1964)
Held that government-compelled incriminating testimony obtained under immunity statutes obtained by one government (federal or state) may not be used as evidence in another jurisdiction.

Murray's Lessee v. Hoboken Land and Improvement Co.
59 U.S. (18 How.) 272 (Feb. 19, 1856)
Defining "due process" broadly as settled English legal traditions that have been modified by U.S. conditions, the Court upheld the use of Treasury Department administrative warrants to recover embezzled funds.

Muskrat v. United States
219 U.S. 346 (Jan. 23, 1911)
Dismissing a "friendly lawsuit" without clashing interests, the Court affirmed that its constitutional authority extended only to deciding "cases and controversies"—not to giving advisory opinions.

Myers v. United States
272 U.S. 52 (Oct. 25, 1926)
Recognizing the president's inherent power over the executive branch, the Court struck down a statute requiring the Senate's approval for dismissal of executive officers. Modified by *Humphrey's Executor v. United States* (1935).

*National Association for the Advancement of Colored People v. Alabama**
357 U.S. 357 (June 30, 1958)
Established that a "freedom of association" was implicit in First Amendment guarantees of free expression and assembly, and also part of the substantive liberty guaranteed by the Fourteenth Amendment.

National Association for the Advancement of Colored People v. Button
371 U.S. 415 (Jan. 14, 1963)
Striking down a law limiting civil rights suits, the Court recognized the constitutional right of an organization to use the courts to promote their missions—litigation being a form of political speech.

National Endowment for the Arts v. Finley
524 U.S. 569 (June 25, 1998)
Upholding a 1990 statute directing the National Endowment for the Arts to consider standards of decency and respect for diverse beliefs in making awards, the Court interpreted the direction to be an exhortation rather than a restriction on expression.

National Labor Relations Board v. Jones and Laughlin Steel Corp.
301 U.S. 1 (Apr. 12, 1937)
In upholding a law to protect collective bargaining, this landmark ruling overturned most restrictions derived from the freedom of contract doctrine and from narrow interpretations of the commerce clause.

National League of Cities v. Usery
426 U.S. 833 (Mar. 2, 1976)
Basing its decision on a broad view of status' rights under the Tenth Amendment, the Court in a 5-4 majority forbade Congress from requiring state and local governments to pay the minimum wage. Reversed in *Garcia v. San Antonio Metropolitan Transit Authority* (1985).

*National Treasury Employees Union v. Von Raab**
489 U.S. 656 (Mar. 21, 1989)
Upholding a drug-testing program for employees in law enforcement, the Court applied a balancing test to conclude that public safety concerns outweighed the privacy expectations of the employees.

Neagle, In re
135 U.S. 1 (Apr. 14, 1890)
Applying a statute that prohibited states from prosecuting individuals for actions in pursuance of federal law, the Court interpreted "law" broadly to include executive orders, while also affirming the inherent powers of the president.

*Near v. Minnesota**
283 U.S. 697 (Jan. 30, 1931)
Reversing a state law that authorized judges to stop publications deemed lewd or scandalous without trials, this incorporation decision applied the First Amendment's freedom of press to the states.

Nebbia v. New York
291 U.S. 502 (Mar. 5, 1934)
Abandoning the "affected with a public interest" doctrine that had restricted the kinds of businesses to be regulated, the Court upheld a state law that authorized a board to fix the retail price of milk.

Nebraska Press Association v. Stuart
427 U.S. 539 (June 30, 1976)
Rejected gag orders on the press to protect the rights of criminal defendants to a fair trial; employed a version of the clear and present danger test to evaluate judges' restrictions on the First Amendment.

Nevada Department of Human Resources v. Hibbs
538 U.S. 721 (May 27, 2003)
Allowing a state employee to sue the state for violating the 1993 Family and Medical Leave Act, the Court recognized Congress's power to abrogate the state's immunity when opposing discrimination.

New State Ice Co. v. Liebmann
285 U.S. 262 (Mar. 21, 1932)
By overturning a state law that conferred a monopoly on existing businesses, the Court affirmed a strong commitment to free market competition. Modified during the New Deal period.

New York State Club Association v. City of New York
487 U.S. 1 (June 20, 1988)
Upholding a city law that prohibited racial, religious, or sex discrimination in almost all private clubs, the Court emphasized that the law did not restrict any First Amendment rights of expression.

*New York Times Co. v. Sullivan**
376 U.S. 254 (Mar. 9, 1964)
A monumental landmark decision that enlarged freedom of the press by requiring, in libel suits, that public officials must prove that the press used "actual malice," meaning a reckless disregard for the truth.

*New York Times Co. v. United States**
403 U.S. 713 (June 30, 1971)
In this famous Pentagon Papers case, the Court held that governmental may not engage in the "prior restraint" of the news media, except to stop immediate, inevitable, and direct harm to American forces.

New York v. Belton
483 U.S. 454 (July 1, 1984)
Expanded the range of warrantless automobile searches to include a search pursuant to a custodial arrest of a person in the automobile.

*New York v. Ferber**
458 U.S. 747 (July 2, 1982)
Upheld a state ban on all forms of child pornography, recognizing government's compelling interest in fighting the sexual exploitation of children.

New York v. Miln
36 U.S. 102 (Feb. 16, 1837)
Held that states under police powers could control persons on boats traveling in inland waterways, avoiding the issue of federal powers over commerce. Superseded by *Edwards v. California* (1941).

Nguyen v. Immigration and Naturalization Service
533 U.S. 53 (June 1, 2001)
Upholding a federal law with different citizenship requirements depending on whether the citizen parent is the father or the mother, a 5-4 majority found justification in an important government objective.

Nixon, United States v.
418 U.S. 683 (July 24, 1974)
Ruled that "executive privilege" was secondary to the demands of due process in criminal trials, thereby requiring President Richard Nixon to obey a subpoena to turn over his recorded conversations.

Nixon v. Administrator of General Services
433 U.S. 425 (Apr. 28, 1977)
Upheld a 1974 statute that authorized the General Services administration to take control of former president Richard Nixon's nonprivate presidential papers and to make them available to the public.

Nixon v. Condon
286 U.S. 73 (May 2, 1932)
Overturned a Texas statute designed to disenfranchise African Americans by authorizing executive committees of political parties to set voting qualifications for primary elections.

Nixon v. Herndon
272 U.S. 536 (Mar. 7, 1927)
In the first of a series of white primary cases, the Court overturned a Texas statute that explicitly prohibited African Americans from voting in Democratic Party primaries.

Nollan v. California Coastal Commission
483 U.S. 825 (June 26, 1987)
Reviewing a requirement that owners of beachfront property donate land for a public pathway to obtain a building permit, the Court held that the requirement was a taking that required just compensation.

Norfolk & Western Railroad v. Ayers
538 U.S. 135 (Mar. 10, 2003)
Upheld the right of workers to sue an employer based on their reasonable fear of future cancer developing out of the asbestosis acquired from on-the-job exposure.

Norris v. Alabama
294 U.S. 587 (Apr. 1, 1935)
The second Scottsboro case, ruling that the defendants had been denied a fair trial because African Americans had been systematically excluded from juries.

Northern Securities Co. v. United States
193 U.S. 197 (Mar. 14, 1904)
Broadly interpreting the Sherman Antitrust Act, the Court ordered the dissolving of a large holding company, finding that it was an unlawful combination restraining interstate trade.

Noto v. United States
367 U.S. 290 (June 5, 1961)
Unlike its companion case, *Scales v. United States,* a 5-4 majority overturned Noto's convictions under the Smith Act, based on insufficient evidence of his advocating the illegal goals of the Communist Party.

O'Brien, United States v.
391 U.S. 367 (May 27, 1968)
Upholding O'Brien's conviction for burning his draft card, the Court's test for symbolic speech cases included a valid government interest and one unrelated to the suppression of expression.

Ogden v. Saunders
25 U.S. (12 Wheat) 213 (Feb. 19, 1827)
Accepting the concurrent power of states to pass insolvency statutes, the Court upheld a New York law that allowed debtors to be discharged from obligations incurred after passage of the law, in contrast to *Sturges v. Crowninshield* (1817), which had overturned a retroactive insolvency law.

O'Gorman and Young v. Hartford Fire Insurance Co.
282 U.S. 251 (Jan. 5, 1931)
Upholding a state law that regulated the fees that insurance companies paid to local agents, this 5-4 decision greatly restricted protection for the liberty of contract doctrine by way of substantive due process.

Ohio v. Akron Center for Reproductive Health
497 U.S. 502 (June 25, 1990)
Upheld a statute requiring notification of one parent of an unmarried minor before having an abortion, although with provision for a judicial bypass.

Olmstead v. United States
277 U.S. 438 (June 4, 1928)
Allowed prosecutors to use evidence obtained by wiretaps placed outside homes without a warrant, holding that these conversations were not protected by the Fourth Amendment. Reversed in *Katz v. United States* (1967).

Oregon v. Mitchell
400 U.S. 112 (Dec. 21, 1970)
Held that Congress had the authority to lower the voting age in federal elections, but not in state elections. Made irrelevant by the Twenty-sixth Amendment.

Oregon Waste Systems v. Department of Environmental Quality
510 U.S. 93 (Apr. 4, 1994)
Struck down Oregon's policy of taxing out-of-state solid wastes three times higher than the wastes originating in the state, finding that the policy unduly affected interstate commerce.

Orr v. Orr
440 U.S. 268 (Mar. 5, 1979)
Applying the heightened scrutiny standard, the Court held that Alabama's law making husbands, but not wives, liable for alimony payments was a violation of the equal protection clause.

Osborn v. Bank of the United States
22 U.S. 738 (Mar. 19, 1824)
Reaffirming a 1819 decision, the Court overturned a state tax on the Bank of the United States, with Chief Justice Marshall proclaiming federal jurisdiction over any case involving the bank.

Osborne v. Ohio
495 U.S. 103 (Apr. 18, 1990)
Upheld statutes that criminalize the mere possession of child pornography, based on the expectation that such laws will help reduce the exploitation of children.

Pacific Mutual Life Insurance Co. v. Haslip
499 U.S. 1 (Mar. 4, 1991)
Upheld sizable punitive awards made by juries, although the Court acknowledged that an extremely irrational award might violate due process standards—anticipating *BMW of North America v. Gore* (1996).

Pacific States Telephone and Telegraph Co. v. Oregon
223 U.S. 118 (Feb. 19, 1912)
Held that the use of initiatives and referendums to make laws was compatible with the Constitution's requirement of a republican form of government.

*Palko v. Connecticut**
302 U.S. 319 (Nov. 12, 1937)
Declined to make the Fifth Amendment's prohibition against double jeopardy binding on the states, with Justice Benjamin Cardozo's classic de-

fense of the selective incorporation doctrine. Reversed in *Benton v. Maryland* (1969).

Palmer v. Thompson
403 U.S. 217 (June 14, 1971)
Upheld Memphis's decision to close public swimming pools rather than operating them on an integrated basis, accepting the city's plausible nondiscriminatory explanation at face value.

Panama Refining Co. v. Ryan
293 U.S. 388 (Jan. 7, 1935)
In a companion to *Schechter Poultry Corp. v. United States,* the Court held that a broad delegation of authority to the executive branch was unconstitutional because of a lack of clear standards for enforcement.

Pasadena Board of Education v. Spangler
427 U.S. 424 (June 28, 1976)
A busing case in the Court held that a school board was not required to make annual adjustments to maintain racial proportions in particular schools, once de jure segregation had ended.

Passenger Cases
48 U.S. (7 How.) 283 (Feb. 7, 1849)
Banned state-levied taxes on incoming passengers, holding that such taxes directly regulated interstate commerce, with Chief Justice Taney emphasizing the right of travel.

Patterson v. McLean Credit Union
491 U.S. 164 (June 15, 1989)
Although reaffirming *Runyon v. McCrary* (1976), which applied the 1866 Civil Rights Act to private contacts, a 5-4 majority held that the law prohibited only discrimination in hiring and did not apply to on-the-job discrimination. The 1991 Civil Rights Act broadened the law to forbid discrimination in all phases of employment.

Paul v. Virginia
75 U.S. (8 Wall.) 168 (Nov. 1, 1869)
Allowed states to charge special taxes on out-of-state insurance companies, ruling that corporations were not citizens for purposes of the comity clause. Superseded by decisions of 1886 and 1944.

*Payne v. Tennessee**
501 U.S. 808 (June 27, 1991)
Reversing 1987 and 1989 rulings, the Court held that the Eighth Amendment does not forbid juries from considering victim impact statements during the sentencing phase of capital trials.

Payton v. New York
501 U.S. 808 (Apr. 15, 1980)
Held that police officers need an arrest warrant before making a nonconsensual entry into a suspect's home, unless there are "exigent circumstances."

Penn Central Transportation Co. v. City of New York
438 U.S. 104 (June 26, 1978)
Held that restrictions on the expansion of a building designated a historic landmark do not constitute a taking, because they protect important public interests without impeding existing uses.

Pennoyer v. Neff
95 U.S. 714 (Jan. 21, 1878)
Ruled that the Tenth Amendment prohibited a state from exercising direct authority and jurisdiction over persons and property outside its territory. Modified in *International Shoe Co. v. Washington* (1945).

Pennsylvania Coal Co. v. Mahon
260 U.S. 393 (Dec. 11, 1922)
Held that a land-use regulation became a taking that required compensation if it went "too far," a subjective standard. Significantly modified in later years.

Pennsylvania v. Nelson
350 U.S. 497 (Apr. 2, 1956)
Held that states may not prosecute cases of anticommunist subversion, because of the federal government's dominant interest and the pervasiveness of federal antisubversive legislation.

Pennsylvania v. Wheeling and Belmont Bridge Co.
54 U.S. 518 (Feb. 6, 1852)
Examining a bridge over the Ohio River alleged to interfere with interstate commerce, the Court affirmed federal authority whenever state and federal law conflict.

Penry v. Lynaugh
492 U.S. 302 (June 26, 1989)
Upheld the constitutionality of capital punishment sentences for mentally retarded criminals. Overturned by *Atkins v. Virginia* (2002).

Personnel Administrator of Massachusetts v. Feeney
442 U.S. 256 (June 5, 1979)
Upheld veterans' hiring preferences in public employment, finding that the intent of the policy was neutral—therefore not discriminatory toward women under the Fourteenth Amendment.

*Pierce v. Society of Sisters**
268 U.S. 510 (Mar. 17, 1925)
Applying substantive due process to noneconomic liberties, the Court held that parents have a constitutional right to send their children to private schools. Anticipated *Griswold v. Connecticut* (1965).

*Planned Parenthood of Southeastern Pennsylvania v. Casey**
505 U.S. 833 (June 29, 1992)
While reaffirming a woman's constitutional right to an abortion before the fetus attains viability, the Court recognized that states may enact restrictions not putting an "undue burden" on that right.

*Plessy v. Ferguson**
163 U.S. (May 18, 1896)
Held that the equal protection clause did not prohibit government-mandated segregation as long as accommodations were equal for both races. Reversed in *Brown v. Board of Education* (1954).

Plyler v. Doe
457 U.S. 202 (June 15, 1982)
Used heightened scrutiny in holding that the denial of educational benefits to the children of illegal aliens violates the equal protection clause.

Pointer v. Texas
380 U.S. 400 (Apr. 5, 1965)
Overturning a conviction based on a transcribed testimony, the Court applied the Sixth Amendment right of confrontation to the states with the same limitations as those of the federal government.

Pollock v. Farmers' Loan and Trust Co.
157 U.S. 429 (Decided Apr. 8, 1895; redecided May 20, 1895)
A 5-4 majority held that a federal income tax was an unconstitutional direct tax. Overturned by the Sixteenth Amendment.

Pottawatomie County v. Earls
536 U.S. 822 (June 27, 2002)
Recognizing students' diminished expectation of privacy, the Court upheld a school policy of requiring drug tests for all students participating in any extracurricular activities.

Powell v. Alabama
287 U.S. 45 (Nov. 7, 1932)
In this first of the Scottsboro cases, the Court required states to provide indigent defendants with counsel whenever necessary for a fair trial. Expanded in *Gideon v. Wainwright* (1963).

Powell v. McCormick
395 U.S. 486 (June 16, 1969)
Held that Congress may not exclude an elected member for reasons other than those cited in the Constitution; also, that a vote for expulsion for misbehavior must be clearly understood as such.

Powers v. Ohio
499 U.S. 400 (Apr. 1, 1991)
Held that the equal protection principle forbade preemptory challenges aimed at excluding African Americans from juries in criminal trials of white defendants.

Presser v. Illinois
116 U.S. 252 (Jan. 4, 1886)
Upheld an Illinois law that banned parades with guns by any groups other than the organized militia, emphasizing that the Second Amendment was not binding on the states.

Price, United States v.
383 U.S. 767 (Mar. 28, 1966)
Broadly interpreted Reconstruction-era statutes to allow federal prosecution of private citizens who had acted in concert with Mississippi police to murder three civil rights workers in Mississippi.

Prigg v. Pennsylvania
41 U.S. 539 (Jan., 1842)
Upheld the 1793 Fugitive Slave Act and recognized the constitutional right of slave owners to capture escaped slaves, but also held that state officials were not required to assist. The decision contributed to passage of the Fugitive Slave Act of 1850.

*Printz v. United States**
521 U.S. 98 (June 27, 1997)
Basing its decision on the Tenth Amendment, the Court in a 5-4 majority overturned a federal statute requiring local law enforcement officers to conduct background checks on prospective handgun purchasers.

Prize Cases
67 U.S. 635 (Mar. 10, 1863)
Upholding President Abraham Lincoln's blockade of Confederate ports without Congress's authorization, a 5-4 majority recognized broad presidential powers to suppress an insurrection according to the rules of war.

Providence Bank v. Billings
29 U.S. 514 (Mar. 22, 1830)
Rejecting a bank's claim of exception from state taxes, the Marshall Court established that the contracts clause protects only those privileges that are explicitly declared in the corporate charter.

Prudential Insurance Co. v. Benjamin
328 U.S. 408 (June 3, 1946)
Held that a state, with Congress's consent, may enact a law regulating some aspect of interstate commerce, which would be unconstitutional without this consent.

Puerto Rico v. Branstad
483 U.S. 219 (June 23, 1987)
Overturning a principle of federalism that had been recognized in *Kentucky v. Dennison* (1861), the Court ruled that the federal courts may force a state governor to extradite a fugitive.

*Quirin, Ex parte**
317 U.S. 1 (July 31, 1942)
Rejecting a habeas corpus petition during World War II, the Court authorized the execution of seven German saboteurs who had been convicted by a military court in the United States.

R.A.V. v. City of St. Paul
505 U.S. 377 (June 22, 1992)
Held that a city's hate speech ordinance violated the First Amendment because it discriminated on the basis of the content of the speech.

*Raich v. Gonzales**
545 U.S.___(June 6, 2005)
Upheld enforcement of federal statutes criminalizing the use of marijuana for all purposes, even in those states that have legalized the substance for medical purposes.

Rasul v. Bush
534 U.S. 466 (June 28, 2004)
Ruled that foreign citizens kept in detention by the U.S. military in Guantanamo Bay, Cuba, had the right to petition for habeas corpus relief in U.S. courts.

Red Lion Broadcasting Co. v. Federal Communications Commission
393 U.S. 367 (June 9, 1969)
Upheld the fairness doctrine that required television and radio broadcasters to provide reply time for those criticized on air.

*Reed v. Reed**
404 U.S. 71 (Nov. 22, 1971)
A landmark case, the first in which the equal protection clause was applied to strike down a statute for gender discrimination. The rationality test was extended to heightened scrutiny in *Craig v. Boren* (1976).

Reese, United States v.
92 U.S. 214 (Mar. 27, 1876)
Asserting that the Fifteenth Amendment did not guarantee a right to vote, the Court invalidated parts of the 1870 Enforcement Act for exceeding the scope of the amendment, thereby allowing southern states to disenfranchise African Americans.

*Regents of the University of California v. Bakke**
438 U.S. 265 (June 28, 1978)
Struck down the use of rigid quotas in admissions policies in higher education, but approved the use of limited preferences to increase the numbers of underrepresented minorities.

Reitman v. Mulkey
387 U.S. 369 (May 29, 1967)
Held that a provision in the California state constitution that allowed discrimination in housing violated the Fourteenth Amendment.

Reno v. American Civil Liberties Union
521 U.S. 844 (June 26, 1997)
Struck down a 1996 federal statute that had made it a crime knowingly to send indecent materials to a minor over the Internet, based on the act's vagueness and its limits on the rights of adults.

Republican Party of Minnesota v. White
536 U.S. 765 (June 27, 2002)
Struck down a state law that prohibited candidates in judicial elections from expressing their viewpoints on disputed legal or political issues.

*Reynolds v. Sims**
377 U.S. 533 (June 15, 1964)
One of the *Reapportionment Cases* that held the apportionments of legislative districts in six states deprived citizens of equal protection; the Court declared that "one person, one vote" is the rule for all state legislative bodies, including upper houses.

*Reynolds v. United States**
98 U.S. 145 (May 5, 1879)
Upheld a federal statute prohibiting polygamy, explaining that the First Amendment protects all religious beliefs but not religiously motivated practices that are harmful to the public interest.

Richardson, United States v.
418 U.S. 166 (June 25, 1974)
Held that citizens do not have standing to sue the federal government unless they can show a direct personal injury, with a narrow reading of the exceptions under *Flast v. Cohen* (1968).

Richmond Newspapers v. Virginia
448 U.S. 555 (July 2, 1980)
Ruled that the First Amendment guarantees the right of the public and the press to attend criminal trials. A harm exception was recognized in *Globe Newspaper Co. v. Superior Court* (1982).

Richmond v. J. A. Croson Co.
488 U.S. 469 (Jan. 23, 1989)
Held that state and local governments must justify racial preferences by the strict scrutiny standard, thus making it more likely that affirmative action programs will be found unconstitutional.

Ring v. Arizona
536 U.S. 584 (June 25, 2002)
Held that a judge, without a sitting jury, cannot determine the aggravating circumstances necessary to imposing the death penalty—a decision that applied to at least 150 sentences in six states.

Robel, United States v.
389 U.S. 258 (Dec. 11, 1967)
Struck down a 1950 federal law disallowing Communist Party members from working in a defense facility, holding that the law was overly broad and violated the right of association.

Roberts v. United States Jaycees
468 U.S. 609 (July 3, 1984)
Upheld the application of a state statute banning sex discrimination to a large private club, emphasizing that the addition of women would not require changes in the announced purposes of the organization.

Robinson v. California
370 U.S. 660 (June 25, 1962)
In overturning a statute that punished the status of being a drug addict without evidence of illegal conduct, the Court established that the Eighth

Amendment's restriction on punishment is binding on the states via incorporation.

*Rochin v. California**
342 U.S. 165 (Jan. 2, 1952)
Without making the Fifth Amendment or the exclusionary rule binding on the states, the Court held that evidence obtained in a shocking and grossly unfair manner may not be used in a criminal trial.

*Roe v. Wade**
410 U.S. 113 (Jan. 22, 1973)
The famous landmark case that recognized the constitutional right of women to abortions before fetal viability; also ruled a fetus is not a person under the Fifth and Fourteenth Amendments.

Romer v. Evans
517 U.S. 620 (May 20, 1996)
Basing its decision on the Fourteenth Amendment, the Court struck down Amendment 2 of the Colorado constitution, which had prohibited local governments from passing ordinances designed to protect individuals from discrimination based on sexual orientation.

*Rompilla v. Beard**
545 U.S.___(June 20, 2005)
Recognizing a Sixth Amendment right to "effective counsel," the Court overturned a criminal conviction in which the defense lawyer had failed to look for mitigating evidence at the sentencing phase.

*Roper v. Simmons**
543 U.S. 551 (Mar. 1, 2005)
Overturning a 1989 opinion, a 5-4 majority prohibited the executions of persons who were minors at the time of the crime; the Court referred to a national consensus and international opinion.

Rosenberg v. United States
346 U.S. 273 (June 19, 1953)
Following four unsuccessful appeals, Justice William O. Douglas granted a stay based on questions of applicable law, but the next day a 6-3 majority vacated the stay, allowing the execution to proceed that evening.

Ross, United States v.
456 U.S. 798 (June 1, 1982)
Overturning a 1981 decision, the Court extended the "automobile exception" to allow the police, when conducting a warrantless search of a car based on probable cause, also to search containers in the car.

Rostker v. Goldberg
453 U.S. 57 (June 25, 1981)
Held that a statute prohibiting women from military combat provided sufficient justification to exclude them from mandatory draft registration.

*Roth v. United States/ Alberts v. California**
354 U.S. 476 (June 24, 1957)
These companion cases reaffirmed that obscenity is not protected by the First Amendment and required a test: an average person's judgment that the work "as a whole" appeals to the "prurient interest." This test subsequently was modified.

Rummel v. Estelle
445 U.S. 263 (Mar. 18, 1980)
Upholding Texas's recidivist statute, the Court found that a mandatory sentence of life imprisonment for three offenses, involving a total of $229, did not constitute a cruel and unusual punishment.

Rumsfeld v. Forum for Academic and Institutional Rights
Docket No. 04-1151 (Mar. 6, 2006)
Upholding a federal law that withholds funds from universities restricting access of military recruiters, the Court reasoned that allowing access did not indicate endorsement of military policies.

Runyon v. McCrary
427 U.S. 160 (June 25, 1976)
Reaffirming the constitutionality of the 1866 Civil Rights Act under the Thirteenth Amendment, the Court applied the act's antidiscrimination provision in contracts to a private nonsectarian school.

Rust v. Sullivan
500 U.S. 173 (May 23, 1991)
Upheld the constitutionality of a "gag rule" that imposed restrictions on abortion counseling in federally funded birth control clinics.

Rutan v. Republican Party of Illinois
497 U.S. 62 (Jan. 16, 1990)
Held that the First Amendment prohibits discriminatory treatment of non-policy-making governmental employees because of their political beliefs or associations.

*San Antonio Independent School District v. Rodriguez**
411 U.S. 1 (Mar. 21, 1973)
Affirming that socioeconomic status is not a suspect classification, the Court applied the minimal scrutiny test to hold that the unequal funding of school districts does not violate the equal protection clause.

Santa Clara County v. Southern Pacific Railroad Co.
118 U.S. 394 (May 10, 1886)
Announced without dissent that corporations are to be classified as "legal persons" under the Fourteenth Amendment, with all the rights of natural persons.

Santa Clara Pueblo v. Martinez
436 U.S. 49 (May 15, 1978)
Authorized tribal courts to decide almost all cases related to the 1968 Indian Bill of Rights, thereby strengthening tribal self-government and restricting an individual Native American's opportunity for federal relief.

Scales v. United States
367 U.S. 203 (June 5, 1961)
Unlike its companion case, *Noto v. United States*, this case, in a 5-4 majority, upheld Junius Scales's conviction under the Smith Act, based on his active participation in the illegal advocacy of the Communist Party. Superseded by *Brandenburg v. Ohio* (1969).

*Schechter Poultry Corp. v. United States**
295 U.S. 495 (May 27, 1935)
The famous "sick chicken case," in which the Court unanimously held that the New Deal's National Industrial Recovery Act unconstitutionally delegated legislative power to the president.

*Schenck v. United States**
249 U.S. 47 (Mar. 3, 1919)
In upholding a World War I conviction of Charles Schenck for encouraging opposition to military conscription, Justice Holmes's application of the clear and present danger test protected free speech less than in *Abrams v. United States* (1919).

*Scott v. Sandford**
60 U.S. 393 (Mar. 6-7, 1857)
Held that Congress lacked constitutional power to exclude slavery from the territories and that persons of African ancestry could not be citizens of the United States. Superseded by amendments.

Selective Draft Law Cases
245 U.S. 366 (Jan. 7, 1918)
Unanimously held that the 1917 Selective Service Act did not violate the prohibition against involuntary servitude in the Thirteenth Amendment.

Sell v. United States
539 U.S. 166 (June 18, 2003)
Held that the government may not force a criminal defendant to take antipsychotic drugs in order to become fit to stand trial except when the drugs are medically beneficial to the defendant.

Seminole Tribe v. Florida
517 U.S. 44 (Mar. 27, 1997)
Recognizing the doctrine of sovereign immunity, a 5-4 majority held that the Eleventh Amendment prevents Congress from authorizing Native American lawsuits against states to enforce federal legislation.

Shapiro v. Thompson
394 U.S. 618 (Apr. 21, 1969)
Overturned states' one-year residency requirements as a condition for receiving welfare benefits, based on both the right to travel and the equal protection clause.

Shaw v. Hunt
517 U.S. 899 (June 13, 1996)
Held that the equal protection clause prohibits the drawing of irregularly shaped congressional districts designed to produce electoral majorities of racial and ethnic minorities.

*Shelley v. Kraemer**
344 U.S. 1 (May 3, 1948)
Although allowing private individuals to enter into racially restrictive housing contracts, the Court prohibited their enforcement in courts of law, based on the state action doctrine.

Sheppard v. Maxwell
384 U.S. 333 (June 6, 1966)
Struck down a murder conviction based on the unfairness of excessive publicity before and during the trial, a decision that encouraged trial judges to fashion a variety of remedies.

*Sherbert v. Verner**
374 U.S. 398 (June 17, 1963)
Applied the "compelling state interest" test to decide the constitutionality of indirect burdens on religious freedom. Modified by *Employment Division of Human Resources v. Smith* (1990).

*Shipp, United States v.**
214 U.S. 386 (May 24, 1909)
This, the only criminal trial ever conducted by the Supreme Court, demonstrated the Court's authority and raised the question of whether the Sixth Amendment applied to the states.

Shreveport Rate Cases
234 U.S. 342 (June 8, 1914)
Upholding the broad authority of the Interstate Commerce Commission to regulate railroads, the Court condemned intrastate rates that were lower than interstate rates.

Siebold, Ex parte
100 U.S. 371 (Mar. 8, 1880)
Upheld a requirement in the Enforcement Acts making it a federal crime for a state official to disobey either federal or state laws in a federal election, thus limiting the doctrine of dual sovereignty.

Skinner v. Oklahoma
316 U.S. 535 (June 1, 1942)
Ruled that states could not require sterilization because of criminality or moral turpitude, recognizing that "liberty of procreation" is a basic civil right.

Skinner v. Railway Labor Executives Association
489 U.S. 602 (Mar. 21, 1989)
Upheld the Federal Railroad Administration's requirement for warrantless drug testing of railroad employees suspected of involvement in a train accident.

*Slaughterhouse Cases**
83 U.S. 36 (Apr. 14, 1873)
Rejecting a challenge to a state-created monopoly, the Court held that the Fourteenth Amendment's "privileges or immunities" did not include rights of national citizenship, with the result that the amendments constituting the Bill of Rights were not binding on the states.

Slochower v. Board of Education of New York City
350 U.S. 551 (Apr. 9, 1956)
Held that the Fourteenth Amendment prohibited the summary dismissal of a public college teacher for invoking his privilege against self-incrimination at a congressional hearing. Subsequently modified.

*Smith v. Allwright**
321 U.S. 649 (Apr. 3, 1944)
Held that political parties may not exclude African Americans from primaries, based on the Fourteenth and Fifteenth Amendments.

Smith v. City of Jackson
544 U.S. (Mar. 30, 2005)
Interpreting the 1967 Age Discrimination in Employment Act, the Court held that plaintiffs do not have to prove intentional discrimination, but only a negative effect on older employees.

Smyth v. Ames
169 U.S. 466 (Mar. 7, 1898)
Held that the Fourteenth Amendment protected the right of a regulated business to a fair return on its current value and prescribed a complex method for determining reasonable rates.

Solem v. Helm
463 U.S. 277 (June 28, 1983)
Held that the Eighth Amendment's proscription of cruel and unusual punishment prohibited disproportionately severe penalties in noncapital cases.

South Carolina v. Katzenbach
383 U.S. 301 (Mar. 17, 1966)
Upheld the constitutionality of the entire 1965 Voting Rights Act, recognizing Congress's broad discretion under section 2 of the Fifteenth Amendment.

South Dakota v. Dole
483 U.S. 203 (June 23, 1987)
Upheld a federal requirement that each state impose a minimum drinking age of twenty-one in order to receive its entire allotment of federal highway funds.

South-Eastern Underwriters Association, United States v.
322 U.S. 533 (June 5, 1944)
Reversing numerous precedents, the Court held that insurance companies doing business across state lines were subject to the Sherman Antitrust Act. Overturned by the 1945 McCarran Act.

Spallone v. United States
493 U.S. 265 (Jan. 10, 1990)
Severely limited the discretion of district judges to fine a local legislator for voting against compliance with a legitimate court order. Expanded to absolute immunity in *Bogan v. Scott-Harris* (1998).

Springer v. United States
102 U.S. 586 (Jan. 24, 1881)
Upheld the constitutionality of the 1862 income tax enacted to finance the Civil War, finding that only land taxes and poll taxes were direct taxes.

Standard Oil Co. v. United States
221 U.S. 1 (May 15, 1911)
When upholding a lower court's decree dissolving the Standard Oil Company under the Sherman Antitrust Act, the Court ruled that the act applies only to "unreasonable" restraints of trade, thereby limiting the act's application.

Stanford v. Kentucky
492 U.S. 391 (June 26, 1989)
Upheld the execution of juveniles over the age of sixteen, but was overturned in *Roper v. Simmons* (2005).

Stanley v. Georgia
394 U.S. 557 (Apr. 7, 1969)
Declared that adults have a right to possess legally obscene materials in the privacy of their own homes. Limited by *Osborne v. Ohio* (1990).

Stanton v. Stanton
421 U.S. 7 (Apr. 15, 1975)
Basing its decision on the equal protection clause, the Court voided a child-support statute specifying a majority age for males that was different from the age for females.

Stenberg v. Carhart
530 U.S. 214 (June 28, 2000)
Held that Nebraska's ban on "partial birth abortions" was unconstitutional for placing an undue burden on the woman's decision and for not including an exception for health.

Steward Machine Co. v. Davis
301 U.S. 548 (May 24, 1937)
Upheld, by a 5-4 vote, the portion of the 1935 Social Security Act that established unemployment compensation, based on Congress's power of taxation for the general welfare.

Stone v. Mississippi
101 U.S. 814 (May 10, 1880)
Allowed Mississippi to use its police power to end the sale of lottery tickets despite the terms of a corporate charter, thereby limiting restraints on state governments from the contracts clause.

Stone v. Powell
428 U.S. 465 (July 6, 1976)
Established the "Stone Exception" in Fourth Amendment cases, holding that state prisoners may not obtain habeas corpus relief in a federal court when the state has provided a fair hearing on the issue.

Strauder v. West Virginia
100 U.S. 303 (Mar. 1, 1880)
Ruled that a West Virginia statute reserving jury service to "white male persons" violated the equal protection clause. Extended to exclusion without legislation in *Ex parte Virginia* (1880).

Strawbridge v. Curtiss
7 U.S. 267 (Feb. 13, 1806)
Established the rule of "complete diversity" in federal courts, requiring that in lawsuits with multiple parties, each dispute must involve residents from different states.

Stromberg v. California
283 U.S. 359 (May 18, 1931)
Overturning California's ban on the display of red flags, this landmark case was the Court's first application of the Fourteenth Amendment to protect "symbolic speech."

Stuart v. Laird
5 U.S. 299 (Mar. 2, 1803)
Upholding the repeal of the 1801 Judiciary Act on narrow and technical grounds, the Marshall Court avoided a major conflict with the Jefferson administration and the Republican-controlled Congress.

Sturges v. Crowninshield
17 U.S. 122 (Feb. 17, 1819)
Basing its decision on the contracts clause, the Court struck down a state insolvency law that enabled persons to be discharged from preexisting debts. An alternative statute was upheld in *Ogden v. Saunders* (1827).

*Swann v. Charlotte-Mecklenburg Board of Education**
402 U.S. 1 (Apr. 20, 1971)
Allowed federal district courts great discretion to order extensive busing plans to desegregate schools whenever governmental action was found to have contributed to racially segregated schools.

Sweatt v. Painter
339 U.S. 629 (June 5, 1950)
By enforcing the "equality" requirement of *Plessy v. Ferguson* (1896), the Court made it impossible for states to continue segregated law schools—helping prepare for *Brown v. Board of Education* (1954).

Swift and Co. v. United States
196 U.S. 375 (Jan. 30, 1905)
Adopting the stream of commerce doctrine, the Court held that antitrust laws could be constitutionally applied to stockyard transactions. Helped prepare for pro-New Deal decisions.

Swift v. Tyson
41 U.S. 1 (Jan. 25, 1842)
In suits under diversity jurisdiction, the Court allowed federal courts to exercise independent judgment on commercial law rather than follow the state courts. Overruled in *Erie Railroad Co. v. Tompkins* (1938).

Talton v. Mayes
163 U.S. 376 (May 18, 1896)
Approved a murder conviction by a five-member jury in a Cherokee court; reaffirmed by the modifications allowed in the 1968 Indian Bill of Rights.

Taylor v. Louisiana
419 U.S. 522 (Jan. 21, 1975)
Striking down a method of jury selection that tended to exclude women, the Court recognized the fundamental right of all defendants to a jury drawn from a representative cross section of the community.

*Tennessee v. Garner**
471 U.S. 1 (Mar. 27, 1985)
Striking down Tennessee's policy concerning fleeing suspects, the Court limited the use of deadly force to situations when the police have probable cause to fear death or great physical harm.

Tennessee v. Lane
541 U.S. 509 (May 17, 2004)
Upheld the right of a private citizen to sue a state for violation of the Americans with Disabilities Act by not making courthouses accessible to disabled persons.

Terminiello v. Chicago
337 U.S. 1 (May 16, 1949)
Overturning the conviction of a speaker for creating a disturbance with anti-Semitic remarks, a 5-4 majority limited application of the "fighting words" doctrine with the clear and present danger standard.

Terry v. Adams
345 U.S. 461 (May 4, 1953)
In this last of Texas's white primary cases, the Court forbade the use of unofficial primaries by a private club purposely organized to disenfranchise black citizens contrary to the Fifteenth Amendment.

*Terry v. Ohio**
392 U.S. 1 (June 10, 1968)
Authorized the practice called "stop and frisk," allowing police to question suspicious persons based on reasonable suspicion rather than probable cause and to pat them down for purposes of safety.

Texas v. Hopwood
518 U.S. 1033-1034 (July 1, 1996)
Denied review of a circuit court decision prohibiting most affirmative action programs. Superseded by *Grutter v. Bollinger* (2003).

*Texas v. Johnson**
491 U.S. 397 (June 21, 1989)
Held that laws punishing flag desecration violate the First Amendment. Strengthened in *United States v. Eichman* (1990).

Texas v. White
74 U.S. 700 (Apr. 12, 1869)
Recognized that the United States is "an indestructible union," that Confederate acts were void, and that Congress had authority over Reconstruction under both the guarantee clause and the political question doctrine.

Thornburgh v. American College of Obstetricians and Gynecologists
476 U.S. 747 (June 11, 1986)
Struck down a Pennsylvania law that placed significant restrictions on abortion rights. The 5-4 split increased speculation that a future appointment by President Ronald Reagan might result in the reversal of *Roe v. Wade* (1973).

Thornhill v. Alabama
310 U.S. 88 (Apr. 22, 1940)
Basing its decision on First Amendment rights of free speech and peaceful assembly, the Court overturned a statute that prohibited picketing by labor unions, but recognized that states may regulate which kinds of picketing are allowed.

Time, Inc. v. Hill
385 U.S. 374 (Jan. 9, 1967)
Held that the "actual malice" rule applied to "private persons" when they sued news media for nondefamatory inaccuracies in the process of reporting an incident of public interest.

*Tinker v. Des Moines Independent Community School District**
393 U.S. 503 (Feb. 24, 1969)
Held that public schools may not punish a student for wearing a symbol to express a viewpoint in a nondisruptive way, thereby strengthening First Amendment rights for students.

Trop v. Dulles
356 U.S. 86 (Mar. 31, 1958)
Held that depriving a person of citizenship violates the Eighth Amendment, which draws its meaning from "the evolving standards of decency" of a maturing society.

Truax v. Corrigan
257 U.S. 312 (Dec. 19, 1921)
Basing its decision on business owners' rights to due process and equal protection, the Court struck down a state law prohibiting the use of injunctions against strikers. Reversed in *Senn v. Tile Layers Union* (1937).

Twining v. New Jersey
211 U.S. 78 (Nov. 9, 1908)
Reflecting a consensus of the period, an 8-1 majority held that the Fifth Amendment privilege against self-incrimination did not apply to the states. Overturned in *Malloy v. Hogan* (1964).

Tyson v. Banton
273 U.S. 418 (Feb. 28, 1927)
Reaffirming that the states could regulate only "business affected with a public interest," the Court struck down a law restricting ticket scalping. Overturned in *Nebbia v. New York* (1934).

Ullman v. United States
350 U.S. 42 (Mar. 26, 1956)
Approving a requirement for persons to testify in grand juries with immunity, the Court held that the privilege against self-incrimination protects only against criminal punishment, not effects like loss of a job.

United Jewish Organizations of Williamsburgh v. Carey
430 U.S. 144 (Mar. 1, 1997)
Upheld a state reapportionment plan that was based on a numerical racial quota, finding that it did not abridge the right to vote on account of race.

United Mine Workers, United States v.
330 U.S. 258 (Mar. 6, 1947)
Approved of injunctions to stop strikes in coal mines operated by the federal government under the Smith-Connally Act and held that the Norris-LaGuardia Act did not apply to government operations.

United Public Workers v. Mitchell
330 U.S. 75 (Feb. 10, 1947)
Held that the 1940 Hatch Act did not violate the First Amendment, even though the act significantly restricted the political speech of federal employees.

United States District Court, United States v.
407 U.S. 297 (Feb. 24, 1972)
Forbade the use of criminal evidence of subversive activities obtained by the Justice Department via the electronic surveillance of American citizens without search warrants approved by neutral magistrates.

United States Term Limits v. Thornton
514 U.S. 779 (May 22, 1995)
Striking down the limits on years of congressional service adopted by twenty-three states, a 5-4 majority held that the states may not add to the qualifications found in Article I of the Constitution.

United Steelworkers of America v. Weber
443 U.S. 193 (June 27, 1979)
Allowed private employers to establish voluntary affirmative action programs, including some quotas, to eliminate manifest racial imbalance, even without evidence of past discrimination.

Ursery, United States v.
518 U.S. 267 (June 24, 1996)
Held that the civil forfeiture of property does not normally constitute criminal punishment for purposes of the double jeopardy clause.

Van Orden v. Perry; McCreary County v. American Civil Liberties Union
545 U.S.___(June 27, 2005)
In companion cases dealing with the establishment clause, the Court allowed a forty-year-old monument of the Ten Commandments to stand but held that a recent display was an unconstitutional promotion of religion.

Veazie Bank v. Fenno
75 U.S. 533 (Dec. 13, 1869)
Upheld the constitutionality of a federal tax on banknotes issued by a state-chartered bank.

*Virginia, United States v.**
516 U.S. 2264 (June 26, 1996)
Applying the "intermediate scrutiny" test, the Court held that the policy of not admitting female cadets to a state-supported military academy violated the equal protection clause.

*Virginia v. Black**
538 U.S. 343 (Sept. 11, 2002)
Defending the right to express unpopular ideas, the Court overturned a criminal conviction for a cross burning where there was no evidence of intent to threaten or intimidate.

Virginia v. Tennessee
148 U.S. 503 (Apr. 3, 1893)
Recognizing the boundary between two states that both had recognized in an 1803 compact, the Court held that Congress need approve only those compacts that affect federal powers.

Virginia v. West Virginia
206 U.S. 290 (May 27, 1907)
In this first of nine cases concerning West Virginia's responsibility for Virginia's pre-Civil War debt, the Court appointed a fact-finding master to settle the issue. The controversy continued until 1919.

Wabash, St. Louis, and Pacific Railway Co. v. Illinois
118 U.S. 557 (Oct. 25, 1886)
Overruling *Peik v. Chicago* (1877), the Court held that states may not regulate the rates of railroad shipments in interstate commerce. The decision prompted Congress to create the Interstate Commerce Commission (1887).

Wade, United States v.
388 U.S. 218 (June 12, 1967)
Held that putting criminal suspects in a lineup does not violate the self-incrimination clause, but that such suspects have a right to counsel during lineups. Modified in *Kirby v. Illinois* (1972).

*Wallace v. Jaffree**
472 U.S. 38 (June 4, 1985)
Struck down a state law that authorized schools to devote a minute of silence for "meditation or voluntary prayer," with the justices expressing a diversity of interpretations of the establishment clause.

Walz v. Tax Commission
397 U.S. 664 (May 4, 1970)
Upholding New York's tax exemptions for property used exclusively for religious purposes, the Court noted that the exemptions also applied to property used for charitable and educational purposes.

Wards Cove Packing Co. v. Atonio
490 U.S. 642 (June 5, 1989)
Rejecting an accusation of discrimination based on the disparate impact of employment qualifications, the Court held that plaintiffs had the burden of proving discrimination. Overruled by the 1991 Civil Rights Act.

Ware v. Hylton
3 U.S. 199 (Mar. 7, 1796)
Overturned a Virginia law for being incompatible with the 1783 treaty with Britain, based on the supremacy clause.

Washington v. Commercial Passenger Fishing Vessel Association
433 U.S. 658 (July 2, 1979)
Interpreting a treaty's "right of taking fish" to imply a "50-50" harvest share between Indians and non-Indians, the Court established precedent for later decisions in Wisconsin and Minnesota.

Washington v. Davis
426 U.S. 229 (June 7, 1976)
Ruled that plaintiffs must show a discriminatory intent, not merely a disparate impact, to prevail under the equal protection requirements of the Fifth and Fourteenth Amendments. Not applicable to statutory cases.

*Washington v. Glucksberg**
521 U.S. 702 (June 26, 1997)
Held that persons have no right to have assistance in committing suicide, while reaffirming *Cruzan v. Director, Missouri Department of Health* (1990).

Watkins v. United States
354 U.S. 178 (June 17, 1957)
Establishing due process guidelines for congressional investigations, the Court held that committees must clearly explain their purposes and that witnesses may refuse to answer irrelevant questions.

*Webster v. Reproductive Health Services**
492 U.S. 490 (July 3, 1989)
Upheld a state's abortion law that recognized the interests of "unborn children," regulated pre-abortion counseling, and required viability tests of fetuses after twenty weeks.

Weeks v. United States
232 U.S. 383 (Feb. 24, 1914)
Mandated use of the exclusionary rule in federal criminal trials, which was extended to the states in *Mapp v. Ohio* (1961).

Weems v. United States
217 U.S. 349 (May 2, 1910)
The first time the Court overturned a criminal sentence as "cruel and unusual," declaring that the meaning of the term should be determined by current sensibilities—an idea influential in later decisions.

Weinberger v. Wiesenfeld
420 U.S. 636 (Mar. 19, 1975)
Held that a benefit of the Social Security Act that disfavored men was "irrational" and therefore contrary to the equal protection principle of the Fifth Amendment.

Wesberry v. Sanders
376 U.S. 1 (Feb. 17, 1964)
Required that U.S. congressional districts within a given state be as nearly equal in population as possible. The Court required mathematical precision in *Kirkpatrick v. Preisler* (1969).

*West Coast Hotel Co. v. Parrish**
300 U.S. 379 (Mar. 29, 1937)
Abandoning the freedom of contract theory that had been reaffirmed in *Morehead v. New York ex rel. Tipaldo* (1936), a 5-4 majority authorized governmental discretion to regulate working conditions and employee rights.

West River Bridge Co. v. Dix
47 U.S. 507 (Jan. 31, 1848)
Moderating protection for private property under the contracts clause, the Taney Court expanded states' powers of eminent domain to prevail over franchise contracts; recognized that the police power cannot be contracted away.

West Virginia State Board of Education v. Barnette
319 U.S. 624 (June 14, 1943)
Landmark decision recognizing that the First Amendment prohibits states from requiring public school students to participate in ceremonies saluting the flag and declaring the pledge of allegiance. Reversed *Minersville School District v. Gobitis* (1940).

Weston v. Charleston
27 U.S. 624 (Mar. 18, 1829)
Struck down a state tax on income derived from federal debt certificates, reaffirming the theory of federalism in *McCulloch v. Maryland* (1819).

Whitney v. California
274 U.S. 357 (May 26, 1927)
Unanimously upheld Whitney's conviction for membership in radical organizations, but Justice Brandeis's concurrence anticipated the libertarian standards of *Brandenburg v. Ohio* (1969).

*Whren v. United States**
517 U.S. 806 (June 10, 1996)
Held that the subjective motivations of police officers were irrelevant when stopping cars based on probable cause of traffic violations, however minor.

Wickard v. Filburn
317 U.S. 111 (Nov. 9, 1942)
In upholding the wheat quota of a New Deal program, the Court expanded the definition of "commerce" to include products not marketed because of their effect on prices.

Wiener v. United States
357 U.S. 349 (June 30, 1958)
Strengthening *Humphrey's Executor v. United States* (1935), the Court held that the president must obey federal legislation forbidding the dismissal of quasi-judicial officials "except for cause."

Williams v. Florida
399 U.S. 78 (June 22, 1970)
Approved a state statute that mandated six-person juries in all noncapital felony trials. Extended to civil trials in *Colegrove v. Battin* (1973).

Williams v. Mississippi
170 U.S. 213 (Apr. 25, 1898)
The Court ignored its 1886 ruling and upheld the murder conviction of an African American in a trial in which no African Americans served on the jury.

Willson v. Blackbird Creek Marsh Co.
27 U.S. 245 (Mar. 20, 1829)
Allowing states to exercise a concurrent power to regulate interstate commerce when federal action was "dormant," the Marshall Court anticipated *Cooley v. Board of Wardens of the Port of Philadelphia.*

Winship, In re
397 U.S. 358 (Mar. 31, 1970)
Building on *In re Gault* (1967), the Court ruled that any judicial proceeding involving a possible loss of liberty must use the standard of guilt beyond a reasonable doubt.

*Wisconsin v. Mitchell**
509 U.S. 476 (June 11, 1993)
Upholding a state's "hate crime" statute, the Court found no First Amendment violation in enhanced punishment for criminals who selected victims on the basis of racial, ethnic, or sexual bias.

*Wisconsin v. Yoder**
406 U.S. 205 (May 15, 1972)
Using the compelling interest standard, the Court held that states violate religious freedom if they require the children of Amish and similar religious sects to attend high school.

Wolf v. Colorado
338 U.S. 25 (June 27, 1949)
Held that the Fourth Amendment's freedom from unreasonable searches was binding on the states but not the exclusionary rule. Overruled in *Mapp v. Ohio* (1961).

Wolff Packing Co. v. Court of Industrial Relations
262 U.S. 522 (June 11, 1923)
Overturning a state law mandating arbitration of labor disputes, the Court defined the businesses that could be regulated under the "affected with a public interest" doctrine. Reversed in *Nebbia v. New York* (1934).

Wong Kim Ark, United States v.
169 U.S. 649 (Mar. 28, 1898)
Basing its decision on the Fourteenth Amendment, the Court held that a person born in the United States of alien parents is a U.S. citizen—an important decision for persons of Asian ancestry.

Woodruff v. Parham
75 U.S. 123 (Nov. 8, 1869)
Prohibited states from charging discriminatory sales taxes on goods from other states, but modifying *Brown v. Maryland* (1827), the Court allowed the taxes that did not benefit in-state products.

Woodson v. North Carolina
428 U.S. 280 (July 2, 1976)
Held that a statute requiring the death penalty for first-degree murder violated the Eighth Amendment, primarily for lack of opportunity for "particularized consideration."

*Worcester v. Georgia**
31 U.S. 515 (Feb. 20, 1832)
Overturning a state regulation of Indian territory, the Court held that the federal government has exclusive jurisdiction in the matter and that the tribes retained "substantial elements of sovereignty."

Yakus v. United States
321 U.S. 414 (Mar. 27, 1944)
Upheld the 1942 Price Control Act, which included a statutory requirement that any constitutional challenge under the act would first be reviewed by a special tribunal before being review by the Supreme Court.

Yarbrough, Ex parte
110 U.S. 651 (Mar. 3, 1884)
Upheld the conviction of a Ku Klux Klansman for obstructing a citizen's right to vote, although the Court reverted to the state action doctrine in the similar case of *James v. Bowman* (1903).

Yarborough v. Alvarado
541 U.S. 652 (June 1, 2004)
In allowing use of a juvenile's confession obtained in a two-hour police interview, the Court held that the police were not required to consider a person's age in deciding issues of Miranda rights.

Yates v. United States
354 U.S. 298 (June 17, 1957)
In reversing the convictions of some Communist Party leaders under the 1940 Smith Act, the Court signaled a change in the direction of its treatment of unpopular organizations.

Yick Wo v. Hopkins
118 U.S. 356 (May 10, 1886)
Clearly expanded the reach of the Fourteenth Amendment, but the Court's decision in this case was ignored until the mid-twentieth century.

Young, Ex parte
209 U.S. 123 (Mar. 23, 1908)
Held that the Eleventh Amendment does not prohibit a federal court from hearing a lawsuit against a state official for violating a federal law.

Young v. American Mini Theatres
427 U.S. 50 (June 24, 1976)
Held that the First Amendment permits communities to use zoning ordinances that significantly restrict the location of theaters and bookstores dealing in sexually explicit materials.

Younger v. Harris
401 U.S. 37 (Feb. 23, 1971)
Reinforced the doctrine of abstention, prohibiting federal judges from intervening in most state court proceedings before they have been finalized.

*Youngstown Sheet and Tube Co. v. Sawyer**
343 U.S. 579 (June 2, 1952)
Overturning President Harry S. Truman's seizure of steel plants during a wartime emergency, the Court refused to recognize presidential authority to seize and operate private businesses without prior congressional approval.

*Zelman v. Simmons-Harris**
536 U.S. 639 (June 27, 2002)
Continuing the trend of limiting the wall-of-separation tradition, the Court upheld Cleveland's program of using public funds for tuition vouchers to attend private religious schools.

Zorach v. Clauson
343 U.S. 306 (Apr. 28, 1952)
Upheld a voluntary release-time program for students to receive religious instruction outside school property, without the expenditure of any public funds.

Zurcher v. The Stanford Daily
436 U.S. 547 (May 31, 1978)
Upholding the search and seizure of a newspaper office for photographs of a violent demonstration, the Court held that the Fourth Amendment does not provide special search provision for press offices. The resulting uproar led to the Privacy Protection Act of 1980, which limited search warrants in newsrooms to instances in which members of the press are suspected of wrongdoing.

Thomas Tandy Lewis

The Constitution of the United States of America

We the People of the United States, in Order to form a more perfect Union, establish Justice, insure domestic Tranquility, provide for the common defence, promote the general Welfare, and secure the Blessings of Liberty to ourselves and our Posterity, do ordain and establish this Constitution for the United States of America.

ARTICLE I.

SECTION 1. All legislative Powers herein granted shall be vested in a Congress of the United States, which shall consist of a Senate and House of Representatives.

SECTION 2. The House of Representatives shall be composed of Members chosen every second Year by the People of the several States, and the Electors in each State shall have the Qualifications requisite for Electors of the most numerous Branch of the State Legislature.

No Person shall be a Representative who shall not have attained to the Age of twenty five Years, and been seven Years a Citizen of the United States, and who shall not, when elected, be an Inhabitant of that State in which he shall be chosen.

Representatives and direct Taxes shall be apportioned among the several States which may be included within this Union, according to their respective Numbers, which shall be determined by adding to the whole Number of free Persons, including those bound to Service for a Term of Years, and excluding Indians not taxed, three fifths of all other Persons. The actual Enumeration shall be made within three Years after the first Meeting of the Congress of the United States, and within every subsequent Term of ten Years, insuch Manner as they shall by Law direct. The number of Representatives shall not exceed one for every thirty Thousand, but each State shall have at Least one Representative; and until such enumeration shall be made, the State of New Hampshire shall be entitled to chuse three, Massachusetts eight, Rhode Island and Providence Plantations one, Connecticut five, New York six, New Jersey four, Pennsylvania eight, Delaware one, Maryland six, Virginia ten, North Carolina five, South Carolina five, and Georgia three.

When vacancies happen in the Representation from any State, the Executive Authority thereof shall issue Writs of Election to fill such Vacancies.

The House of Representatives shall chuse their Speaker and other Officers; and shall have the sole Power of Impeachment.

SECTION 3. The Senate of the United States shall be composed of two Senators from each State, chosen by the Legislature thereof, for six Years; and each Senator shall have one Vote.

Immediately after they shall be assembled in Consequence of the first Election, they shall be divided as equally as may be into three Classes. The Seats of the Senators of the first Class shall be vacated at the Expiration of the second Year, of the second Class at the Expiration of the fourth Year, and of the third Class at the Expiration of the sixth Year, so that one third may be chosen every second Year; and if Vacancies happen by Resignation, or otherwise, during the Recess of the Legislature of any State, the Executive thereof may make temporary Appointments until the next Meeting of the Legislature, which shall then fill such Vacancies.

No Person shall be a Senator who shall not have attained to the Age of thirty Years, and been nine Years a Citizen of the United States, and who shall not, when elected, be an Inhabitant of that State for which he shall be chosen.

The Vice President of the United States shall be President of the Senate, but shall have no Vote, unless they be equally divided.

The Senate shall chuse their other Officers, and also a President pro tempore, in the Absence of the Vice President, or when he shall exercise the Office of President of the United States.

The Senate shall have the sole Power to try all Impeachments. When sitting for that Purpose, they shall be on Oath or Affirmation. When the President of the United States is tried, the Chief Justice shall preside: And no Person shall be convicted without the Concurrence of two thirds of the Members present.

Judgment in Cases of Impeachment shall not extend further than to removal from Office, and disqualification to hold and enjoy any Office of honor, Trust or Profit under the United States: but the Party convicted shall nevertheless be liable and subject to Indictment, Trial, Judgment and Punishment, according to Law.

SECTION 4. The Times, Places and Manner of holding Elections for Senators and Representatives, shall be prescribed in each State by the Legislature thereof; but the Congress may at any time by Law make or alter such Regulations, except as to the Places of chusing Senators.

The Congress shall assemble at least once in every Year, and such Meeting shall be on the first Monday in December, unless they shall by Law appoint a different Day.

SECTION 5. Each House shall be the Judge of the Elections, Returns and Qualifications of its own Members, and a Majority of each shall constitute a Quorum to do Business; but a smaller Number may adjourn from day to day, and may be authorized to compel the Attendance of absent Members, in such Manner, and under such Penalties as each House may provide.

Each House may determine the Rules of its Proceedings, punish its Members for disorderly Behaviour, and, with the Concurrence of two thirds, expel a Member.

Each House shall keep a Journal of its Proceedings, and from time to time publish the same, excepting such Parts as may in their Judgment require Secrecy; and the Yeas and Nays of the Members of either House on any question shall, at the Desire of one fifth of those Present, be entered on the Journal.

Neither House, during the Session of Congress, shall, without the Consent of the other, adjourn for more than three days, nor to any other Place than that in which the two Houses shall be sitting.

SECTION 6. The Senators and Representatives shall receive a Compensation for their Services, to be ascertained by Law, and paid out of the Treasury of the United States. They shall in all Cases, except Treason, Felony and Breach of the Peace, be privileged from Arrest during their Attendance at the Session of their respective Houses, and in going to and returning from the same; and for any Speech or Debate in either House, they shall not be questioned in any other Place.

No Senator or Representative shall, during the Time for which he was elected, be appointed to any civil Office under the Authority of the United States, which shall have been created, or the Emoluments whereof shall have been encreased during such time; and no Person holding any Office under the United States, shall be a Member of either House during his Continuance in Office.

SECTION 7. All Bills for raising Revenue shall originate in the House of Representatives; but the Senate may propose or concur with Amendments as on other Bills.

Every Bill which shall have passed the House of Representatives and the Senate, shall, before it becomes a Law, be presented to the President of the United States; If he approve he shall sign it, but if not he shall return it, with his Objections to that House in which it shall have originated, who shall enter the Objections at large on their Journal, and proceed to reconsider it. If after such Reconsideration two thirds of that House shall agree to pass the Bill, it shall be sent, together with the Objections, to the other House, by which it shall likewise be reconsidered, and if approved by two thirds of that House, it shall become a Law. But in all such Cases the Votes of both Houses shall be determined by yeas and Nays, and the Names of the Persons voting for and against the Bill shall be entered on the Journal of each House respectively. If any Bill shall not be returned by the President within ten Days (Sundays excepted) after it shall have been presented to him, the Same shall be a Law, in like Manner as if he had signed it, unless the Congress by their Adjournment prevent its Return, in which Case it shall not be a Law.

Every Order, Resolution, or Vote to which the Concurrence of the Senate and House of Representatives may be necessary (except on a question of Adjournment) shall be presented to the President of the United States; and before the Same shall take Effect, shall be approved by him, or being disapproved by him, shall be repassed by two thirds of the Senate and House of Representatives, according to the Rules and Limitations prescribed in the Case of a Bill.

SECTION 8. The Congress shall have Power To lay and collect Taxes, Duties, Imposts and Excises, to pay the Debts and provide for the common Defence and general Welfare of the United States; but all Duties, Imposts and Excises shall be uniform throughout the United States;

To borrow Money on the credit of the United States;

To regulate Commerce with foreign Nations, and among the several States, and with the Indian Tribes;

To establish an uniform Rule of Naturalization, and uniform Laws on the subject of Bankruptcies throughout the United States;

To coin Money, regulate the Value thereof, and of foreign Coin, and fix the Standard of Weights and Measures;

To provide for the Punishment of counterfeiting the Securities and current Coin of the United States;

To establish Post Offices and post Roads;

To promote the Progress of Science and useful Arts, by securing for limited Times to Authors and Inventors the exclusive Right to their respective Writings and Discoveries;

To constitute Tribunals inferior to the supreme Court;

To define and punish Piracies and Felonies committed on the high Seas, and Offenses against the Law of Nations;

To declare War, grant Letters of Marque and Reprisal, and make Rules concerning Captures on Land and Water;

To raise and support Armies, but no Appropriation of Money to that Use shall be for a longer Term than two Years;

To provide and maintain a Navy;

To make Rules for the Government and Regulation of the land and naval Forces;

To provide for calling forth the Militia to execute the Laws of the Union, suppress Insurrections and repel Invasions;

To provide for organizing, arming, and disciplining the Militia, and for governing such Part of them as may be employed in the Service of the United States, reserving to the States respectively, the Appointment of the Officers, and the Authority of training the Militia according to the discipline prescribed by Congress;

To exercise exclusive Legislation in all Cases whatsoever, over such District (not exceeding ten Miles square) as may, by Cession of particular States, and the Acceptance of Congress, become the Seat of the Government of the United States, and to exercise like Authority over all Places purchased by the Consent of the Legislature of the State in which the Same shall be, for the Erection of Forts, Magazines, Arsenals, dock-Yards and other needful Buildings;—And

To make all Laws which shall be necessary and proper for carrying into Execution the foregoing Powers, and all other Powers vested by this Constitution in the Government of the United States, or in any Department or Officer thereof.

SECTION 9. The Migration or Importation of such Persons as any of the States now existing shall think proper to admit, shall not be prohibited by the Congress prior to the Year one thousand eight hundred and eight, but a Tax or duty may be imposed on such Importation, not exceeding ten dollars for each Person.

The Privilege of the Writ of Habeas Corpus shall not be suspended, unless when in Cases of Rebellion or Invasion the public Safety may require it.

No Bill of Attainder or ex post facto Law shall be passed.

No Capitation, or other direct, Tax shall be laid, unless in Proportion to the Census or Enumeration herein before directed to be taken.

No Tax or Duty shall be laid on Articles exported from any State.

No Preference shall be given by any Regulation of Commerce or Revenue to the Ports of one State over those of another: nor shall Vessels bound to, or from, one State be obliged to enter, clear, or pay Duties in another.

No Money shall be drawn from the Treasury, but in Consequence of Appropriations made by Law; and a regular Statement and Account of the Receipts and Expenditures of all public Money shall be published from time to time.

No Title of Nobility shall be granted by the United States: And no Person holding any Office of Profit or Trust under them, shall, without the Consent of the Congress, accept of any present, Emolument, Office, or Title, of any kind whatever, from any King, Prince, or foreign State.

SECTION 10. No State shall enter into any Treaty, Alliance, or Confederation; grant Letters of Marque and Reprisal; coin Money; emit Bills of Credit; make any Thing but gold and silver Coin a Tender in Payment of Debts; pass any Bill of Attainder, ex post facto Law, or Law impairing the Obligation of Contracts, or grant any Title of Nobility.

No State shall, without the Consent of the Congress, lay any Imposts or Duties on Imports or Exports, except what may be absolutely necessary for executing its inspection Laws: and the net Produce of all Duties and Imposts, laid by any State on Imports or Exports, shall be for the Use of the Treasury of the United States; and all such Laws shall be subject to the Revision and Control of the Congress.

No State shall, without the Consent of Congress, lay any Duty of Tonnage, keep Troops, or Ships of War in time of Peace, enter into any Agreement or Compact with another State, or with a foreign Power, or engage in War, unless actually invaded, or in such imminent Danger as will not admit of delay.

ARTICLE II.

SECTION 1. The executive Power shall be vested in a President of the United States of America. He shall hold his Office during the Term of four Years, and, together with the Vice President, chosen for the same Term, be elected, as follows

Each State shall appoint, in such Manner as the Legislature thereof may direct, a Number of Electors, equal to the whole Number of Senators and Representatives to which the State may be entitled in the Congress: but no Senator or Representative, or Person holding an Office of Trust or Profit under the United States, shall be appointed an Elector.

The Electors shall meet in their respective States, and vote by Ballot for two Persons, of whom one at least shall not be an Inhabitant of the same State with themselves. And they shall make a List of all the Persons voted for, and of the Number of Votes for each; which List they shall sign and certify, and transmit sealed to the Seat of the Government of the United States, directed to the President of the Senate. The President of the Senate shall, in the Presence of the Senate and House of Representatives, open all the Certificates, and the Votes shall then be counted. The Person having the greatest Number of Votes shall be the President, if such Number be a Majority of the whole Number of Electors appointed; and if there be more than one who have such Majority, and have an equal Number of Votes, then the House of Representatives shall immediately chuse by Ballot one of them for President; and if no Person have a Majority, then from the five highest on the List the said House shall in like manner chuse the President. But in chusing the President, the Votes shall be taken by States, the Representation from each State having one Vote; A quorum for this Purpose shall consist of a Member or Members from two thirds of the States, and a Majority of all the States shall be necessary to a Choice. In every Case, after the Choice of the President, the Person having the greatest Number of Votes of the Electors shall be the Vice President. But if there should remain two or more who have equal Votes, the Senate shall chuse from them by Ballot the Vice President.

The Congress may determine the Time of chusing the Electors, and the Day on which they shall give their Votes; which Day shall be the same throughout the United States.

No Person except a natural born Citizen, or a Citizen of the United States, at the time of the Adoption of this Constitution, shall be eligible to the Office of the President; neither shall any person be eligible to that Office who shall not have attained to the Age of thirty five Years, and been fourteen Years a Resident within the United States.

In Case of the Removal of the President from Office, or of his Death, Resignation, or Inability to discharge the Powers and Duties of the said Office, the Same shall devolve on the Vice President, and the Congress may by Law provide for the Case of Removal, Death, Resignation or Inability, both of the President and Vice President, declaring what Officer shall then act as President, and such Officer shall act accordingly, until the Disability be removed, or a President shall be elected.

The President shall, at stated Times, receive for his Services, a Compensation, which shall neither be increased nor diminished during the Period for which he shall have been elected, and he shall not receive within that Period any other Emolument from the United States, or any of them.

Before he enter the Execution of his Office, he shall take the following Oath or Affirmation:—"I do solemnly swear (or affirm) that I will faithfully execute the Office of President of the United States, and will to the best of my Ability, preserve, protect and defend the Constitution of the United States."

SECTION 2. The President shall be Commander in Chief of the Army and Navy of the United States, and of the Militia of the several States, when called into the actual Service of the United States; he may require the Opinion, in writing, of the principal Officer in each of the executive Departments, upon any Subject relating to the Duties of their respective Offices, and he shall have Power to grant Reprieves and Pardons for Offenses against the United States, except in Cases of Impeachment.

He shall have Power, by and with the Advice and Consent of the Senate, to make Treaties, provided two thirds of the Senators present concur; and he shall nominate, and by and with the Advice and Consent of the Senate, shall appoint Ambassadors, other public Ministers and Consuls, Judges of the supreme Court, and all other Officers of the United States, whose Appointments are not herein otherwise provided for, and which shall be established by Law: but the Congress may by Law vest the Appointment of such inferior Officers, as they think proper, in the President alone, in the Courts of Law, or in the Heads of Departments.

The President shall have Power to fill up all Vacancies that may happen during the Recess of the Senate, by granting Commissions which shall expire at the End of their next Session.

SECTION 3. He shall from time to time give to the Congress Information of the State of the Union, and recommend to their Consideration such Measures as he shall judge necessary and expedient; he may, on extraordinary Occasions, convene both Houses, or either of them, and in Case of Disagreement between them, with Respect to the Time of Adjournment, he may adjourn them to such Time as he shall think proper; he shall receive Ambassadors and other public Ministers; he shall take Care that the Laws be faithfully executed, and shall Commission all the Officers of the United States.

SECTION 4. The President, Vice President and all civil Officers of the United States, shall be removed from Office on Impeachment for, and Conviction of, Treason, Bribery, or other high Crimes and Misdemeanors.

ARTICLE III.

SECTION 1. The judicial Power of the United States, shall be vested in one supreme Court, and in such inferior Courts as the Congress may from time to time ordain and establish. The Judges, both of the supreme and inferior Courts, shall hold their Offices during good Behaviour, and shall, at stated Times, receive for their Services, a Compensation, which shall not be diminished during their Continuance in Office.

SECTION 2. The judicial Power shall extend to all Cases, in Law and Equity, arising under this Constitution, the Laws of the United States, and Treaties made, or which shall be made, under their Authority;—to all Cases affecting Ambassadors, other public Ministers and Consuls;—to all Cases of admiralty and maritime Jurisdiction;—to Controversies to which the United States shall be a Party;—to Controversies between two or more States; between a State and Citizens of another State; between Citizens of different States,—between Citizens of the same State claiming Lands under Grants of different States, and between a State, or the Citizens thereof, and foreign States, Citizens or Subjects.

In all Cases affecting Ambassadors, other public Ministers and Consuls, and those in which a State shall be Party, the supreme Court shall have original Jurisdiction. In all the other Cases before mentioned, the supreme Court shall have appellate Jurisdiction, both as to Law and Fact, with such Exceptions, and under such Regulations as the Congress shall make.

The Trial of all Crimes, except in Cases of Impeachment, shall be by Jury; and such Trial shall be held in the State where the said Crimes shall have been committed; but when not committed within any State, the Trial shall be at such Place or Places as the Congress may by Law have directed.

SECTION 3. Treason against the United States, shall consist only in levying War against them, or in adhering to their Enemies, giving them Aid and Comfort. No Person shall be convicted of Treason unless on the Testimony of two Witnesses to the same overt Act, or on Confession in open Court.

The Congress shall have Power to declare the Punishment of Treason, but no Attainder of Treason shall work Corruption of Blood, or Forfeiture except during the Life of the Person attainted.

ARTICLE IV.

SECTION 1. Full Faith and Credit shall be given in each State to the public Acts, Records, and judicial Proceedings of every other State; And the Congress may by general Laws prescribe the Manner in which such Acts, Records and Proceedings shall be proved, and the Effect thereof.

SECTION 2. The Citizens of each State shall be entitled to all Privileges and Immunities of Citizens in the several States.

A Person charged in any State with Treason, Felony, or other Crime, who shall flee from Justice, and be found in another State, shall on Demand of the executive Authority of the State from which he fled, be delivered up, to be removed to the State having Jurisdiction of the Crime.

No person held to Service or Labour in one State, under the Laws thereof, escaping into another, shall, in Consequence of any Law or Regulation therein, be discharged from such Service or Labour, but shall be delivered up on Claim of the Party to whom such Service or Labour may be due.

SECTION 3. New States may be admitted by the Congress into this Union; but no new State shall be formed or erected within the Jurisdiction of any other State; nor any State be formed by the Junction of two or more States, or Parts of States, without the Consent of the Legislatures of the States concerned as well as of the Congress.

The Congress shall have Power to dispose of and make all needful Rules and Regulations respecting the Territory or other Property belonging to the United States; and nothing in this Constitution shall be so construed as to Prejudice any Claims of the United States, or of any particular State.

SECTION 4. The United States shall guarantee to every State in this Union a Republican Form of Government, and shall protect each of them against Invasion; and on Application of the Legislature, or of the Executive (when the Legislature cannot be convened) against domestic Violence.

ARTICLE V.

The Congress, whenever two thirds of both Houses shall deem it necessary, shall propose Amendments to this Constitution, or, on the Application of the Legislatures of two thirds of the several States, shall call a Convention for proposing Amendments, which, in either Case, shall be valid to all Intents and Purposes, as Part of this Constitution, when ratified by the Legislatures of three fourths of the several States, or by Conventions in three fourths thereof, as the one or the other Mode of Ratification may be proposed by the Congress; Provided that no Amendment which may be made prior to the year one thousand eight hundred and eight shall in any Manner affect the first and fourth Clauses in the Ninth Section of the first Article; and that no State, without its Consent, shall be deprived of its equal Suffrage in the Senate.

ARTICLE VI.

All Debts contracted and Engagements entered into, before the Adoption of this Constitution, shall be as valid against the United States under this Constitution, as under the Confederation.

This Constitution, and the Laws of the United States which shall be made in Pursuance thereof; and all Treaties made, or which shall be made, under the Authority of the United States, shall be the supreme Law of the Land; and the Judges in every State shall be bound thereby, any Thing in the Constitution or Laws of any State to the Contrary notwithstanding.

The Senators and Representatives before mentioned, and the Members of the several State Legislatures, and all executive and judicial Officers, both of the United States and of the several States, shall be bound by Oath or Affirmation, to support this Constitution; but no religious Test shall ever be required as a Qualification to any Office or public Trust under the United States.

ARTICLE VII.

The Ratification of the Conventions of nine States, shall be sufficient for the Establishment of this Constitution between the States so ratifying the Same.

Done in Convention by the Unanimous Consent of the States present the Seventeenth Day of September in the Year of our Lord one thousand seven hundred and eighty seven and of the Independence of the United States of America the Twelfth. In Witness whereof We have hereunto subscribed our Names,

Amendments to the U.S. Constitution

AMENDMENT I.

Congress shall make no law respecting an establishment of religion, or prohibiting the free exercise thereof; or abridging the freedom of speech, or of the press, or the right of the people peaceably to assemble, and to petition the Government for a redress of grievances.

[ratified December, 1791]

AMENDMENT II.

A well regulated Militia, being necessary to the security of a free State, the right of the people to keep and bear Arms, shall not be infringed.

[ratified December, 1791]

AMENDMENT III.

No Soldier shall, in time of peace be quartered in any house, without the consent of the Owner, nor in time of war, but in a manner to be prescribed by law.

[ratified December, 1791]

AMENDMENT IV.

The right of the people to be secure in their persons, houses, papers, and effects, against unreasonable searches and seizures, shall not be violated, and no Warrants shall issue, but upon probable cause, supported by Oath or affirmation, and particularly describing the place to be searched, and the persons or things to be seized.

[ratified December, 1791]

AMENDMENT V.

No person shall be held to answer for a capital, or otherwise infamous crime, unless on a presentment or indictment of a Grand Jury, except in cases arising in the land or naval forces, or in the Militia, when in actual service in time of War or public danger; nor shall any person be subject for the same offence to be twice put in jeopardy of life or limb, nor shall be compelled in any criminal case to be a witness against himself, nor be deprived of life, liberty, or property, without due process of law; nor shall private property be taken for public use without just compensation.

[ratified December, 1791]

AMENDMENT VI.

In all criminal prosecutions, the accused shall enjoy the right to a speedy and public trial, by an impartial jury of the State and district wherein the crime shall have been committed; which district shall have been previously ascertained by law, and to be informed of the nature and cause of the accusation; to be confronted with the witnesses against him; to have compulsory process for obtaining witnesses in his favor, and to have the assistance of counsel for his defence.

[ratified December, 1791]

AMENDMENT VII.

In Suits at common law, where the value in controversy shall exceed twenty dollars, the right of trial by jury shall be preserved, and no fact tried by a jury shall be otherwise re-examined in any Court of the United States, than according to the rules of the common law.

[ratified December, 1791]

AMENDMENT VIII.

Excessive bail shall not be required, nor excessive fines imposed, nor cruel and unusual punishments inflicted.

[ratified December, 1791]

AMENDMENT IX.

The enumeration in the Constitution, of certain rights, shall not be construed to deny or disparage others retained by the people.

[ratified December, 1791]

AMENDMENT X.

The powers not delegated to the United States by the Constitution, nor prohibited by it to the States, are reserved to the States respectively, or to the people.

[ratified December, 1791]

AMENDMENT XI.

The Judicial power of the United States shall not be construed to extend to any suit in law or equity, commenced or prosecuted against one of the United States by Citizens of another State, or by Citizens or Subjects of any Foreign State.

[ratified February, 1795]

AMENDMENT XII.

The Electors shall meet in their respective states, and vote by ballot for President and Vice-President, one of whom, at least, shall not be an inhabitant of the same state with themselves; they shall name in their ballots the person voted for as President, and in distinct ballots the person voted for as Vice-President, and they shall make distinct lists of all persons voted for as President, and of all persons voted for as Vice-President, and of the number of votes for each, which lists they shall sign and certify, and transmit sealed to the seat of the government of the United States, directed to the President of the Senate;—The President of the Senate shall, in the presence of the Senate and House of Representatives, open all the certificates and the votes shall then be counted;—The person having the greatest number of votes for President, shall be the President, if such number be a majority of the whole number of Electors appointed; and if no person have such majority, then from the persons having the highest numbers not exceeding three on the list of those voted for as President, the House of Representatives shall choose immediately, by ballot, the President. But in choosing the President, the votes shall be taken by states, the representation from each state having one vote; a quorum for this purpose shall consist of a member or members from two-thirds of the states, and a majority of all the states shall be necessary to a choice. And if the House of Representatives shall not choose a President whenever the right of choice shall devolve upon them, before the fourth day of March next following, then the Vice-President shall act as President, as in the case of the death or other constitutional disability of the President.—The person having the greatest number of votes as Vice-President, shall be the Vice-President, if such number be a majority of the whole number of Electors appointed, and if no person have a majority, then from the two highest numbers on the list, the Senate shall choose the Vice-President; a quorum for the purpose shall consist of two-thirds of the whole number of Senators, and a majority of the whole number shall be necessary to a choice. But no person constitutionally ineligible to the office of President shall be eligible to that of Vice-President of the United States.

[ratified June, 1804]

AMENDMENT XIII.

SECTION 1. Neither slavery nor involuntary servitude, except as a punishment for crime whereof the party shall have been duly convicted, shall exist within the United States, or any place subject to their jurisdiction.

SECTION 2. Congress shall have power to enforce this article by appropriate legislation.

[ratified December, 1865]

AMENDMENT XIV.

SECTION 1. All persons born or naturalized in the United States and subject to the jurisdiction thereof, are citizens of the United States and of the State wherein they reside. No State shall make or enforce any law which shall abridge the privileges or immunities of citizens of the United States; nor shall any State deprive any person of life, liberty, or property, without due process of law; nor deny to any person within its jurisdiction the equal protection of the laws.

SECTION 2. Representatives shall be apportioned among the several States according to their respective numbers, counting the whole number of persons in each State, excluding Indians not taxed. But when the right to vote at any election for the choice of electors for President and Vice President of the United States, Representatives in Congress, the Executive and Judicial officers of a State, or the members of the Legislature thereof, is denied to any of the male inhabitants of such State, being twenty-one years of age, and citizens of the United States, or in any way abridged, except for participation in rebellion, or other crime, the basis of representation therein shall be reduced in the proportion which the number of such male citizens shall bear to the whole number of male citizens twenty-one years of age in such State.

SECTION 3. No person shall be a Senator or Representative in Congress, or elector of President and Vice President, or hold any office, civil or military, under the United States, or under any State, who, having previously taken an oath, as a member of Congress, or as an officer of the United States, or as a member of any State legislature, or as an executive or judicial officer of any State, to support the Constitution of the United States, shall have engaged in insurrection or rebellion against the same, or given aid or comfort to the enemies thereof. But Congress may by a vote of two-thirds of each House, remove such disability.

SECTION 4. The validity of the public debt of the United States, authorized by law, including debts incurred for payment of pensions and bounties for services in suppressing insurrection or rebellion, shall not be questioned. But neither the United States nor any State shall assume or pay any debt or obligation incurred in aid of insurrection or rebellion against the United States, or any claim for the loss or emancipation of any slave; but all such debts, obligations and claims shall be held illegal and void.

SECTION 5. The Congress shall have power to enforce, by appropriate legislation, the provisions of this article.

[ratified July, 1868]

AMENDMENT XV.

SECTION 1. The right of citizens of the United States to vote shall not be denied or abridged by the United States or by any State on account of race, color, or previous condition of servitude.

SECTION 2. The Congress shall have power to enforce this article by appropriate legislation.

[ratified February, 1870]

AMENDMENT XVI.

The Congress shall have power to lay and collect taxes on incomes, from whatever source derived, without apportionment among the several States, and without regard to any census or enumeration.

[ratified February, 1913]

AMENDMENT XVII.

The Senate of the United States shall be composed of two Senators from each State, elected by the people thereof, for six years; and each Senator shall have one vote. The electors in each State shall have the qualifications requisite for electors of the most numerous branch of the State legislatures.

When vacancies happen in the representation of any State in the Senate, the executive authority of such State shall issue writs of election to fill such vacancies: *Provided*, That the legislature of any State may empower the executive thereof to make temporary appointments until the people fill the vacancies by election as the legislature may direct.

This amendment shall not be so construed as to affect the election or term of any Senator chosen before it becomes valid as part of the Constitution.

[ratified April, 1913]

AMENDMENT XVIII.

SECTION 1. After one year from the ratification of this article the manufacture, sale, or transportation of intoxicating liquors within, the importation thereof into, or the exportation thereof from the United States and all territory subject to the jurisdiction thereof for beverage purposes is hereby prohibited.

SECTION 2. The Congress and the several States shall have concurrent power to enforce this article by appropriate legislation.

SECTION 3. This article shall be inoperative unless it shall have been ratified as an amendment to the Constitution by the legislatures of the several States, as provided in the Constitution, within seven years from the date of the submission hereof to the States by the Congress.

[ratified January, 1919; repealed December, 1933]

AMENDMENT XIX.

The right of citizens of the United States to vote shall not be denied or abridged by the United States or by any State on account of sex.

Congress shall have power to enforce this article by appropriate legislation.

[ratified August, 1920]

AMENDMENT XX.

SECTION 1. The terms of the President and Vice President shall end at noon on the 20th day of January, and the terms of Senators and Representatives at noon on the 3d day of January, of the years in which such terms would have ended if this article had not been ratified; and the terms of their successors shall then begin.

SECTION 2. The Congress shall assemble at least once in every year, and such meeting shall begin at noon on the 3d day of January, unless they shall by law appoint a different day.

SECTION 3. If, at the time fixed for the beginning of the term of the President, the President elect shall have died, the Vice President elect shall become President. If a President shall not have been chosen before the time fixed for the beginning of his term, or if the President elect shall have failed to qualify, then the Vice President elect shall act as President until a President shall have qualified; and the Congress may by law provide for the case wherein neither a President elect nor a Vice President elect shall have qualified, declaring who shall then act as President, or the manner in which one who is to act shall be selected, and such person shall act accordingly until a President or Vice President shall have qualified.

SECTION 4. The Congress may by law provide for the case of the death of any of the persons from whom the House of Representatives may choose a President whenever the right of choice shall have devolved upon them, and for the case of the death of any of the persons from whom the Senate may choose a Vice President whenever the right of choice shall have devolved upon them.

SECTION 5. Sections 1 and 2 shall take effect on the 15th day of October following the ratification of this article.

SECTION 6. This article shall be inoperative unless it shall have been ratified as an amendment to the Constitution by the legislatures of three-fourths of the several States within seven years from the date of its submission.

[ratified January, 1933]

AMENDMENT XXI.

SECTION 1. The eighteenth article of amendment to the Constitution of the United States is hereby repealed.

SECTION 2. The transportation or importation into any State, Territory, or possession of the United States for delivery or use therein of intoxicating liquors, in violation of the laws thereof, is hereby prohibited.

SECTION 3. This article shall be inoperative unless it shall have been ratified as an amendment to the Constitution by conventions in the several States, as provided in the Constitution, within seven years from the date of the submission hereof to the States by the Congress.

[ratified December, 1933]

AMENDMENT XXII.

SECTION 1. No person shall be elected to the office of the President more than twice, and no person who has held the office of President, or acted as President, for more than two years of a term to which some other person was elected President shall be elected to the office of the President more than once. But this Article shall not apply to any person holding the office of President when this Article was proposed by the Congress, and shall not prevent any person who may be holding the office of President, or acting as President, during the term within which this Article becomes operative from holding the office of President or acting as President during the remainder of such term.

SECTION 2. This article shall be inoperative unless it shall have been ratified as an amendment to the Constitution by the legislatures of three-fourths of the several States within seven years from the date of its submission to the States by the Congress.

[ratified February, 1951]

AMENDMENT XXIII.

SECTION 1. The District constituting the seat of Government of the United States shall appoint in such manner as the Congress may direct:

A number of electors of President and Vice President equal to the whole number of Senators and Representatives in Congress to which the District would be entitled if it were a State, but in no event more than the least populous State; they shall be in addition to those appointed by the States, but they shall be considered, for the purposes of the election of President and Vice President, to be electors appointed by a State; and they shall meet in the District and perform such duties as provided by the twelfth article of amendment.

SECTION 2. The Congress shall have power to enforce this article by appropriate legislation.

[ratified March, 1961]

AMENDMENT XXIV.

SECTION 1. The right of citizens of the United States to vote in any primary or other election for President or Vice President, for electors for President or Vice President, or for Senator or Representative in Congress, shall not be denied or abridged by the United States or any State by reason of failure to pay any poll tax or other tax.

SECTION 2. The Congress shall have power to enforce this article by appropriate legislation.

[ratified January, 1964]

AMENDMENT XXV.

SECTION 1. In case of the removal of the President from office or of his death or resignation, the Vice President shall become President.

SECTION 2. Whenever there is a vacancy in the office of the Vice President, the President shall nominate a Vice President who shall take office upon confirmation by a majority vote of both Houses of Congress.

SECTION 3. Whenever the President transmits to the President pro tempore of the Senate and the Speaker of the House of Representatives his written declaration that he is unable to discharge the powers and duties of his office, and until he transmits to them a written declaration to the contrary, such powers and duties shall be discharged by the Vice President as Acting President.

SECTION 4. Whenever the Vice President and a majority of either the principal officers of the executive departments or of such other body as Congress may by law provide, transmit to the President pro tempore of the Senate and the Speaker of the House of Representatives their written declaration that the President is unable to discharge the powers and duties of his office, the Vice President shall immediately assume the powers and duties of the office as Acting President.

Thereafter, when the President transmits to the President pro tempore of the Senate and the Speaker of the House of Representatives his written declaration that no inability exists, he shall resume the powers and duties of his office unless the Vice President and a majority of either the principal officers of the executive department or of such other body as Congress may by law provide, transmit within four days to the President pro tempore of the Senate and the Speaker of the House of Representatives their written declaration that the President is unable to discharge the powers and duties of his office. Thereupon Congress shall decide the issue, assembling within forty-eight hours for that purpose if not in session. If the Congress, within twenty-one days after receipt of the latter written declaration, or, if Congress is not in session, within twenty-one days after Congress is required to assemble, determines by two-thirds vote of both Houses that the President is unable to discharge the powers and duties of his office, the Vice President shall continue to discharge the same as Acting President; otherwise, the President shall resume the powers and duties of his office.

[ratified February, 1967]

AMENDMENT XXVI.

SECTION 1. The right of citizens of the United States, who are eighteen years of age or older, to vote shall not be denied or abridged by the United States or by any State on account of age.

SECTION 2. The Congress shall have power to enforce this article by appropriate legislation.

[ratified July, 1971]

AMENDMENT XXVII.

No law, varying the compensation for the services of the Senators and Representatives, shall take effect, until an election of Representatives shall have intervened.

[ratified May 7, 1992]

Categorized List of Entries

CITIZENSHIP, IMMIGRATION, AND NATURALIZATION

CIVIL RIGHTS

COMMERCE AND CONTRACTS

CONSTITUTION, U.S.

COURT ADMINISTRATION, STRUCTURE, AND PROCEDURES

Certiorari, writ of
Chief justice
Circuit riding
Conference of the justices
Constitutional interpretation
Delegation of powers
Dissents
Diversity jurisdiction
Due process, procedural
Due process, substantive
Executive privilege
Full faith and credit
Habeas corpus
Judicial activism
Judicial review
Judicial scrutiny
Judicial self-restraint
Opinions, writing of
Oral argument
Public forum doctrine
Reporting of opinions
Resignation and retirement
Review, process of
Rule of reason
Rules of the Court
Salaries of justices
Seriatim opinions
Solicitor general
Standing
Statutory interpretation
Workload

DEFENDANT RIGHTS
Automobile searches
Batson v. Kentucky
Bill of attainder
Brown v. Mississippi
Chimel v. California
Counsel, right to
Double jeopardy
Due process, procedural
Eighth Amendment
Exclusionary rule
Fifth Amendment
Florida v. Bostick
Fourth Amendment
Gideon v. Wainwright
Jury, trial by
Katz v. United States
Mapp v. Ohio
Michigan Department of State Police v. Sitz
Miranda rights
Palko v. Connecticut
Privacy, right to
Rochin v. California
Search warrant requirement
Self-incrimination, immunity against
Sixth Amendment
Tennessee v. Garner
Terry v. Ohio
Witnesses, confrontation of

EMPLOYMENT DISCRIMINATION
Affirmative action
Age discrimination
Allgeyer v. Louisiana
Americans with Disabilities Act
Contract, freedom of
Employment discrimination
Equal protection clause
Gender issues
Griggs v. Duke Power Co.
Race and discrimination

FAMILY AND MARRIAGE
Abortion
Birth control and contraception
Buck v. Bell
Fundamental rights
Gay and lesbian rights
Gender issues
Griswold v. Connecticut
Illegitimacy

Loving v. Virginia
Moore v. City of East Cleveland
Pierce v. Society of Sisters
Planned Parenthood of Southeastern Pennsylvania v. Casey
Privacy, right to
Reynolds v. United States
Roe v. Wade
Webster v. Reproductive Health Services

FEDERALISM AND STATES' RIGHTS
Chisholm v. Georgia
Comity clause
Commerce, regulation of
Darby Lumber Co., United States v.
Elastic clause
Federalism
Full faith and credit
Garcia v. San Antonio Metropolitan Transit Authority
Gibbons v. Ogden
Lopez, United States v.
McCulloch v. Maryland
Police powers
Printz v. United States
Separation of powers
States' rights and state sovereignty
Tenth Amendment

FREEDOM OF ASSEMBLY AND ASSOCIATION
Assembly and association, freedom of
Brandenburg v. Ohio
DeJonge v. Oregon
First Amendment
National Association for the Advancement of Colored People v. Alabama
Public forum doctrine
Time, place, and manner regulations

FREEDOM OF SPEECH AND PRESS
Bad tendency test
Barnes v. Glen Theatre
Brandenburg v. Ohio
Censorship
Cold War
Epperson v. Arkansas
Espionage acts
First Amendment
Flag desecration
Gitlow v. New York
Near v. Minnesota
New York Times Co. v. Sullivan
New York Times Co. v. United States
Obscenity and pornography
Public forum doctrine
Sedition Act of 1798
Seditious libel
Smith Act
Speech and press, freedom of
Symbolic speech
Time, place, and manner regulations
Vietnam War
War and civil liberties

GENDER ISSUES
Abortion
Birth control and contraception
Bradwell v. Illinois
Buck v. Bell
Employment discrimination
Ferguson v. City of Charleston
Ginsburg, Ruth Bader
Illegitimacy
Privacy, right to
Reed v. Reed
Roe v. Wade
Virginia, United States v.

HISTORICAL SUBJECTS
Civil Rights movement
Civil War

HOUSING DISCRIMINATION

INCORPORATION DOCTRINE

ISSUES BEFORE THE COURT

JUDICIAL ACTIVISM AND SELF-RESTRAINT

JUDICIAL REVIEW

JURIES

JUSTICES

Clark, Tom C.
Clarke, John H.
Clifford, Nathan
Curtis, Benjamin R.
Cushing, William
Daniel, Peter V.
Davis, David
Day, William R.
Douglas, William O.
Duvall, Gabriel
Ellsworth, Oliver
Field, Stephen J.
Fortas, Abe
Frankfurter, Felix
Fuller, Melville W.
Ginsburg, Ruth Bader
Goldberg, Arthur J.
Gray, Horace
Grier, Robert C.
Harlan, John M., II
Harlan, John Marshall
Holmes, Oliver Wendell
Hughes, Charles Evans
Hunt, Ward
Iredell, James
Jackson, Howell E.
Jackson, Robert H.
Jay, John
Johnson, Thomas
Johnson, William
Kennedy, Anthony M.
Lamar, Joseph R.
Lamar, Lucius Q. C.
Livingston, Brockholst
Lurton, Horace H.
McKenna, Joseph
McKinley, John
McLean, John
McReynolds, James C.
Marshall, John
Marshall, Thurgood
Matthews, Stanley
Miller, Samuel F.
Minton, Sherman
Moody, William H.
Moore, Alfred
Murphy, Frank
Nelson, Samuel
O'Connor, Sandra Day
Paterson, William
Peckham, Rufus W.
Pitney, Mahlon
Powell, Lewis F., Jr.
Reed, Stanley F.
Rehnquist, William H.
Roberts, John
Roberts, Owen J.
Rutledge, John
Rutledge, Wiley B., Jr.
Sanford, Edward T.
Scalia, Antonin
Shiras, George, Jr.
Souter, David H.
Stevens, John Paul
Stewart, Potter
Stone, Harlan Fiske
Story, Joseph
Strong, William
Sutherland, George
Swayne, Noah H.
Taft, William H.
Taney, Roger Brooke
Thomas, Clarence
Thompson, Smith
Todd, Thomas
Trimble, Robert
Van Devanter, Willis
Vinson, Fred M.
Waite, Morrison R.
Warren, Earl
Washington, Bushrod
Wayne, James M.
White, Byron R.
White, Edward D.
Whittaker, Charles E.
Wilson, James

Woodbury, Levi
Woods, William B.

LEGAL TERMS AND PROCEDURES

Advisory opinions
Appellate jurisdiction
Briefs
Certiorari, writ of
Dissents
Diversity jurisdiction
Due process, procedural
Due process, substantive
Full faith and credit
Habeas corpus
Judicial activism
Judicial review
Judicial scrutiny
Judicial self-restraint
Opinions, writing of
Oral argument
Reporting of opinions
Review, process of
Rule of reason
Seriatim opinions
Standing
Statutory interpretation

LAWS AND LEGISLATION

Antitrust law
Bankruptcy law
Bill of attainder
Bill of Rights
Civil law
Comity clause
Common law
Common law, federal
Constitutional law
Contracts clause
Eighth Amendment
Elastic clause
Eleventh Amendment
Environmental law
Equal protection clause
Espionage acts
Fifteenth Amendment
Fifth Amendment
First Amendment
Fourteenth Amendment
Fourth Amendment
General welfare clause
Grandfather clauses
Guarantee clause
Immigration law
Judiciary Act of 1789
Natural law
Ninth Amendment
Poll taxes
Second Amendment
Sedition Act of 1798
Sixth Amendment
Smith Act
Sunday closing laws
Takings clause
Tenth Amendment
Thirteenth Amendment

PRIVACY RIGHTS

Abortion
Bill of Rights
Birth control and contraception
Censorship
Due process, substantive
Fourth Amendment
Fundamental rights
Gay and lesbian rights
Griswold v. Connecticut
Lawrence v. Texas
Moore v. City of East Cleveland
Ninth Amendment
Obscenity and pornography
Privacy, right to
Roe v. Wade

RACE DISCRIMINATION

Affirmative action

Bolling v. Sharpe
Brown v. Board of Education
Capital punishment
Civil Rights Cases
Civil Rights movement
Cruikshank, United States v.
Employment discrimination
Grandfather clauses
Griggs v. Duke Power Co.
Heart of Atlanta Motel v. United States
Housing discrimination
Japanese American relocation
Korematsu v. United States
Loving v. Virginia
McCleskey v. Kemp
Peonage
Plessy v. Ferguson
Race and discrimination
Regents of the University of California v. Bakke
Restrictive covenants
School integration and busing
Scott v. Sandford
Segregation, de facto
Segregation, de jure
Smith v. Allwright
State action
Swann v. Charlotte-Mecklenburg Board of Education
Thirteenth Amendment

RELIGIOUS ISSUES

Abington School District v. Schempp
Bill of Rights
Boerne v. Flores
Church of Lukumi Babalu Aye v. Hialeah
Employment Division, Department of Human Resources v. Smith
Engel v. Vitale
Epperson v. Arkansas
Everson v. Board of Education of Ewing Township
Evolution and creationism
First Amendment
Good News Club v. Milford Central School
Lee v. Weisman
Lemon v. Kurtzman
Loyalty oaths
Religion, establishment of
Religion, freedom of
Reynolds v. United States
Sherbert v. Verner
Sunday closing laws
Wallace v. Jaffree
Wisconsin v. Yoder
Zelman v. Simmons-Harris

SEARCH AND SEIZURE

Automobile searches
Chimel v. California
Exclusionary rule
Ferguson v. City of Charleston
Florida v. Bostick
Fourth Amendment
Hudson v. Michigan
Incorporation doctrine
Katz v. United States
Kyllo v. United States
Mapp v. Ohio
Michigan Department of State Police v. Sitz
National Treasury Employees Union v. Von Raab
Privacy, right to
Rochin v. California
Search warrant requirement
Terry v. Ohio
Whren v. United States

SEPARATION OF POWERS

Advisory opinions
Bill of attainder
Boerne v. Flores
Clinton v. City of New York

INDEXES

Court Case Index

Photo Index

Subject Index